Alfred Douglas

A Poet's Life and His Finest Work

Lord Alfred Douglas, 1894

Caspar Wintermans

Alfred Douglas

A Poet's Life and His Finest Work

Peter Owen
London and Chester Springs, PA, USA

PETER OWEN PUBLISHERS
73 Kenway Road, London SW5 0RE

Peter Owen books are distributed in the USA by Dufour Editions Inc.,
Chester Springs, PA 19425-0007

First published in Great Britain 2007
Original title: *Alfred Douglas: De boezemvriend van Oscar Wilde*
(De Arbeiderspers, Amsterdam, 1999)

Enlarged translation of the text made by the author.
© Caspar Wintermans 2007

This publication was made possible by a grant from the Foundation for the Production and
Translation of Dutch Literature.

ISBN: 0 7206 1270 5
ISBN-13: 978 0 7206 1270 7
A catalogue record for this book is available from the British Library.

Printed and bound in Great Britain by Cambrian Printers Ltd, Aberystwyth

To
Alexander van Abswoude

Dedication

What shall I say, what word, what cry recall,
What god invoke, what star, what amulet,
To make a sonnet pay a hopeless debt,
Or bind a winged heart with a madrigal?
Weak words are vainer than no words at all,
The barrier of flesh divides us yet;
Your spirit, like a bird caught in a net,
Beats ever an impenetrable wall.

This is my book, and there as in a glass,
Darkly beheld, the shadow of my mind
Wavers and flickers like a flame of fire.
So through your eyes, it may be, it will pass,
And I shall hold my wild shy bird confined
In the gold cage of shadowless desire.

A.D.

Acknowledgements

This book would not have materialized without the help of numerous people to whom I wish to render profuse thanks: the late Sheila Colman, curatrix of the Lord Alfred Douglas Literary Estate; her successors, John Rubinstein and John D. Stratford; my literary agent, Jeffrey Simmons; Lord Gawain Douglas; Évanghélia Stead; John Cooper; the editorial and production team at Peter Owen Publishers; Joan Navarre; Julia D. Smith; Ian Anstruther; Neil McKenna; Robert Kirkpatrick; Brendan G. Carroll; David Rose; Roger Custance, Archivist of Winchester College; Patricia Aske, Assistant Librarian at Corpus Christi College, Cambridge; Robin Darwall-Smith, Archivist of Magdalen College, Oxford; Caroline Dalton, Archivist of New College, Oxford; John Kaye, Keeper of the Archives, Queen's College, Oxford; Richard Childs, County Archivist, West Sussex County Record Office, Chichester; Nicole Boyer of the *Mercure de France*, Paris; the staffs of the British Library, London; the Bodleian Library, Oxford; the Brotherton Library, University of Leeds; the Library of the University of Reading; the Bibliothèque Doucet and the Bibliothèque Nationale, Paris; David J. Brown, Vice-President of the Havergal Brian Society; Wiljan van den Akker; G. Krishnamurti and Steven Halliwell, respectively the Honorary Founder and Honorary Secretary/Treasurer of the Eighteen Nineties Society; Margaret M. Maison, Alan Clodd, Rohinten Mazda and the late Brocard Sewell, *O. Carm.*, members of the aforesaid association.

I am deeply grateful to the late Mary, Viscountess Eccles (formerly Mary Hyde) for allowing me access to her unrivalled private collection of Douglas manuscripts. My thanks also go to her Librarian, Gabriel Austin; Stephen R. Tabor, formerly Librarian of the William Andrews Clark Memorial Library, University of California, Los Angeles; Philip Milito, Technical Assistant to the New York Public Library; Margaret M. Sherry, Reference Librarian/Archivist, Rare Books and Special Collections, Princeton University, New Jersey; Elizabeth E. Fuller, Librarian of the Rosenbach Museum, Philadelphia; the staffs of the Rare Book and Manuscript Library of the Columbia University, New York; and the Harry Ransom Humanities Research Center, University of Texas at Austin.

A special tribute should be paid to the staff of the Royal Library in The Hague, notably to Marieke van Delft, Ina Dijkstra, Dennis Schouten, Annemarie Snelderwaard, Reinder Storm and the ever-cheerful Margreet Vos.

For criticizing my chapters or providing me with indispensable encouragement I am indebted to Antoine Bodar; Gerard van Emmerik; Gerlof Janzen; Esther Nanlohy; Marjolijn van Riemsdijk; Bart Visman; Michael and Sylvia Cameron; Fokas Holthuis; Ton Leenhouts; Remco Meijer; Paul Snijders; Menno Voskuil; Jan Keijser; Anneke Mooi; Johan Polak (I salute his memory); the incomparable Martin Ros; Adrian Cooper; Danielle Guérin; my darling friend, Oleg Dumanskiy; my dear parents, my sister and brothers.

Wouter van der Helm has rendered important technical assistance.

Finally, as far as Oscar Wilde's grandson, Merlin Holland, Alan Marshall and the Meuters-Dikkers family are concerned, my vocabulary is insufficient to thank them as they would like and as they deserve.

C.W.
The Hague, September 1990–August 2005

Contents

Acknowledgements   7
List of Illustrations   13

Alfred Douglas: A Poet's Life

Introduction   17
1. A Privileged Youth   21
2. A Notorious Friendship   31
3. A Resounding Scandal   47
4. A Decadent's Downfall   59
5. Loyalty, Machinations and Some Misunderstandings   71
6. Reunion in Naples and Death in Paris   83
7. A Runaway Match   99
8. Never Rude, Except on Purpose   115
9. A Fiery Furnace of Affliction   129
10. Liberation Through Incarceration   149
11. A Testament of Beauty   169
List of Abbreviations   173
Notes to the Text   175

The Poems

Autumn Days   207
A Winter Sunset   208
Prince Charming   209
Two Loves   210
De Profundis   212
In Sarum Close   212
In Winter   213
To Shakespeare   214
Apologia   214
Hymn to Physical Beauty   215
Night Coming into a Garden   218

Night Going out of a Garden   219
In an Ægean Port   220
The Sphinx   220
In Praise of Shame   221
A Prayer   222
Lust and Hypocrisy   222
Impression de Nuit   223
A Ballad of Hate   224
The Image of Death   224
Rondeau   225
To Sleep   226
In Memoriam: Francis Archibald Douglas . . .   227
Væ Victis!   227
Sonnet, Dedicated to Those French Men of Letters . . .   229
The Garden of Death   230
Rejected   231
St Martin's Summer   233
Plainte Éternelle   233
Ode to My Soul   234
The Travelling Companion   235
Ode to Autumn   236
Spring   237
The Poet and the Moon   238
Wine of Summer   239
Sonnet on the Sonnet   242
The City of the Soul   242
A Triad of the Moon   244
Ennui   246
The Legend of Spinello of Arezzo   247
Palmistry   248
The Dead Poet   249
The Traitor   249
Dies Amara Valde   250
Forgetfulness   250
Premonition   251
To a Silent Poet   251
Rewards   252
The Green River   253
To Olive   253

Silence	256
A Christmas Carol	257
Beauty and the Hunter	257
The Poet	258
Proem	259
A Christmas Sonnet	259
Behold, Your House Is Left Unto You Desolate	260
Stones for Bread	260
Before a Crucifix	261
The Unspeakable Englishman	261
Lighten Our Darkness	262
On a Showing of the Nativity	262
House of Bread	263
To a Certain Judge	263
In Excelsis (I–IX, Epilogue)	264
To — with an Ivory Hand Mirror	269
Oxford Revisited	269
Winston Churchill	270
The Wastes of Time	271

Translations from the French of Charles Baudelaire

Harmonie du soir	272
Le Balcon	274
Recueillement	276
La Beauté	278
Notes to the Poems	281
Index of First Lines	319
Bibliography	323
General Index	371

Illustrations

Cover: Lord Alfred Douglas in 1892 (Lord Alfred Douglas, *Oscar Wilde et quelques autres*, translated from the English by Arnold van Gennep, Paris: Librairie Gallimard, 1930)

Facing title page: Lord Alfred Douglas, 1894 (*The Autobiography of Lord Alfred Douglas*, London: Martin Secker, London, 1929)

Between pages 186 and 187

Bosie aged eight; a watercolour by Henry Richard Graves (*The Autobiography of Lord Alfred Douglas*, London: Martin Secker, 1929)

The editorial staff of *The Pentagram*, 1888: Edward Lidderdale, Lord Alfred Douglas, Edmund B. Phipps (courtesy of the Rare Book and Manuscript Library, Columbia University, New York)

Oscar Wilde, portrayed by Phil May in 1893 (*The Letters of Oscar Wilde*, edited by Rupert Hart-Davis, London: Rupert Hart-Davis, 1962)

The real picture of Dorian Gray! The Charterhouse Press's 1904 unauthorized reprint of Oscar's novel reproduced as its frontispiece a photogravure of a portrait signed 'Basil Hallward', which, according to an intriguing note prefixed to the text, was the painting that had given Oscar the idea for his book.

'A Dream of Decadence on the Cherwell': Oscar and Bosie at Oxford, immortalized in May 1893 by a contributor to a university magazine, *The New Rattle* (Vol. I, No. 3, 20 May 1893; Per. G.A. Oxon 4° 285, courtesy of the Bodleian Library, Oxford)

Oscar and Bosie, *c.* 1893 (Ekkehard Böhm, *Kultur-Tagebuch, 1900 bis heute*, Braunschweig: Westermann, 1984)

A portrait of Bosie by Walter Spindler, reproduced in *Poems* (Paris:

Mercure de France, 1896)

Oscar and Bosie in Naples, autumn 1897 (courtesy of the William Andrews Clark Memorial Library, University of California, Los Angeles)

Olive Custance, 1902 (*The Autobiography of Lord Alfred Douglas*, London: Martin Secker, 1929)

Bosie *c*. 1903. Photograph by George Charles Beresford (courtesy of the National Portrait Gallery, London)

Frontispiece to *The Collected Poems of Lord Alfred Douglas* (London: Martin Secker, 1919)

A photograph of Bosie in front of the Old Bailey, taken during the trial of *Allan* versus *Pemberton-Billing*, reproduced on the front page of the *Daily Mirror*, 5 June 1918 (courtesy of the British Library, Newspaper Library, London)

Bosie *c*. 1928 (*The Autobiography of Lord Alfred Douglas*, London: Martin Secker, 1929)

Bosie in the company of Sheila Colman, Easter 1944 (H. Montgomery Hyde, *Lord Alfred Douglas: A Biography*, London: Methuen, 1982)

Lord Gawain Douglas, Bosie's great-nephew, holding the English Heritage Blue Plaque unveiled at 1 St Ann's Court, Hove, on the 134th birthday of the poet, 22 October 2004. Photograph by Adrian Cooper, the project's initiator

The Archangel Michael chasing Lucifer and his adherents from Heaven, depicted by Spinello of Arezzo (*c*. 1346–1410) in the S. Agnolo chapel in the Basilica di S. Francesco, Arezzo (photograph © Scala, Florence). It was this fresco which inspired Douglas to write a poem on the painter in 1898

Between pages 58 and 59

The arrest of Oscar Wilde; woodcut from the *Illustrated Police Budget* (Jonathan Goodman, *The Oscar Wilde File*, London: Allison and Busby, 1988)

Between pages 62 and 63

Wilde in the dock; the cover of the sensational *Illustrated Police News*, 4 May 1895 (Jonathan Goodman, *The Oscar Wilde File*, London: Allison and Busby, 1988)

Between pages 66 and 67

A woodcut from the *Illustrated Police News* depicting the fight between Queensberry and his son, Percy, on 21 May 1895 (Jonathan Goodman, *The Oscar Wilde File*, London: Allison and Busby, 1988)

Introduction

An article called 'Lesser Lights', which appeared in the *English Review* in 1905, invited its readers to spare a thought for those sprigs of nobility who inherited a resplendent title without the cash to live up to it – the younger sons light-heartedly 'flung off' by barons, dukes and earls. Theirs was a hard fate. 'Poor Lord Henry, Lord Thomas, Lord Arthur, and Lord Charles!' the writer exclaimed. 'In how many cases would it not have been better for you if a gentle millstone had been tied round your aristocratic neck, and you had been respectfully but firmly lowered into the depths of some glassy stream or frowning tarn, or ornamental sheet of water in the precincts of your father's finely-timbered park. For if it is a privilege to *have* younger sons it is very much the reverse to *be* one.'[1]

This sigh was heaved by the impecunious Lord Alfred Douglas, third child of the Marquess of Queensberry, who, typically, never got paid for the article.[2] His name, whenever it is mentioned, often evokes fierce and hostile reactions. Indeed, judging by the language his critics employ, it would seem that some of them would not have minded if, at a tender age, Lord Alfred had been pushed into a pond or otherwise dispatched. He has been dubbed 'an utterly spoiled brawler',[3] a 'selfish profiteer'[4] 'an unscrupulous hedonist',[5] 'a parasite',[6] a 'twerp'[7] and a 'swine'.[8] These flowers of speech are fairly recent, but in essence they hardly differ from those applied to him a century ago. Few persons, in fact, have received quite such a bad press.

Why? The case for the prosecution has been lyrically put by an overseas member of the English Society bearing the name of the man Lord Alfred is supposed to have wronged.

Ode to Oscar Wilde

The wild Oscar Wilde loved very much Alfred Douglas
But Alfred didn't love Wilde like he wanted.
Usual it goes that way between two people.
Like in that case the one mend it more than the other.
Love is always so fragile like you have chosen.
Alas, Douglas had the bad character.
He played with Oscar's love like with a glass,
It fell and broke, not only Oscars's love,
But also the great Wilde.
Who died in the Parisian hotel d'Alsace.
Now he is buried alone en lonesome at the graveyard Père Lachaise,
Where I yet came several times.

These lines were indited by Danny Cannoot. He comes from Kortrijk, Belgium.[9] His poem, for all its linguistic peculiarities, testifies to a genuine and touching admiration for its dedicatee. Oscar Wilde inspires strong feelings, not least among homosexuals, many of whom look upon him as a gay martyr led to his doom by his boyfriend, 'Bosie' Douglas. The latter is perceived as the pleasure-loving aristocrat who wished to humiliate his father and who, to achieve this, encouraged Oscar to sue the Marquess for criminal libel – only to drop Oscar like a hot brick when the tables were turned and Oscar himself, not Queensberry, was convicted (to two years' hard labour). After his release Bosie supposedly sponged off the playwright for a couple of months in Naples, until Oscar's money ran out and Bosie once again abandoned him. To top it all, the young man, having come into a modest fortune when his father died, is believed to have refused to support Oscar financially.

Bosie owes his reputation as a Judas and rake, first, to a number of Oscar's letters, including *De Profundis*, which was written in prison – letters that are not particularly truthful, as will be shown – and, second, to an extremely unreliable biography by Frank Harris, *Oscar Wilde: His Life and Confessions* (1916). The lies it contains about Bosie have been rehashed by more authors than one, which is the more amazing considering that Harris himself came to admit he had traduced him.[10]

Harris was at pains to point out that his depiction of Bosie had been partly the result of discussions and correspondence with Oscar's literary executor, Robert Ross, who had 'misled' him 'time and again'.[11] Ross at that juncture – that is to say, in 1925 – had been in his grave for seven years, his death at the early age of forty-nine having been hastened by his legal battles with Bosie. Their feud undoubtedly constitutes the darkest chapter in the career of his Lordship; no honest biographer should shirk from admitting this. But the adherents of Ross, some of whom are as thin-skinned as those of Oscar, should also face the fact that their hero, who behaved impeccably towards Oscar and the likes of Wilfred Owen, behaved despicably towards the one who had supplanted him in Oscar's affections. No quarter was given by either opponent; but Ross managed to appear the more respectable of the two. He could be quite ruthless without seeming to be so. His own solicitor conceded this when he described his deceased client as 'a very subtle propagandist in his own favour [who had] biassed opinion most unfairly against Douglas'.[12]

Many accusations that continue to be brought against Bosie can be easily refuted since they are factually incorrect. For instance, in order to counter the claim, put forward by a journalist, that Bosie omitted to slip money into Oscar's hand when he (Bosie) had received a legacy ('It did not occur to him to remember Wilde'),[13] it suffices to point to Bosie's chequebook which happily establishes the contrary.[14]

A man may also be blackened, however, by telling the truth, but not the *whole* truth, about him. By not elucidating how someone came to take certain decisions – by *chronicling* his behaviour without *explaining* it – an incomplete and therefore wrong impression may emerge. Thus Bosie has been blamed (and with good reason) for publishing, in 1914, *Oscar Wilde and Myself*. This book not only slates Oscar's character and his works, it also states that Bosie had been unaware of his friend's sexual tastes. *Oscar Wilde and Myself* had been ghostwritten for the greater part by T.W.H. Crosland, 'a circumstance', according to Martin Koomen, 'which doesn't palliate its hypocrisy and mendacity, and which aggravates, perhaps, its shamelessness'.[15] Quite so. But Mr Koomen says nothing whatever about the book's genesis, the terrible provocations Bosie had had to endure, nor does he mention the fact that Bosie subsequently repudiated the book and set forth a true account of his relations with Oscar in his *Autobiography* (1929), in *Without Apology* (1938) and in *Oscar Wilde: A Summing-Up* (1940).

Incidentally, it is not least because of the polemical style of these works that Bosie is often considered to have been, primarily, a grumbler. True, he could be rather touchy at times (his niece, Violet, a trained nurse, maintained he had an over-active thyroid),[16] but he could also be most charming and kind, capable of discussing his past with friends without getting angry. Yet when he took up his pen his sense of humour forsook him, and he appeared unable to describe his life with calm and detachment.

The story of that life is a gripping one, a Greek tragedy with elements of soap. It features neither angels nor devils – 'There is good and bad in every one of us,' as a blackmailer once remarked to Oscar[17] – presenting us instead with a wonderful cast of interesting, talented, attractive, exasperating, at times impossible actors, men and women of flesh and blood, swayed by passions and instincts which slumber or stir, as the case may be, in you and in me. The shadow of Wilde broods over it all, and proof of Bosie's devotion to him, while not making the artist's downfall any less catastrophic, certainly serves to make it less squalid and far more romantic. Moreover, the young man 'like a narcissus, so white and gold', whom Oscar 'worshipped',[18] was himself capable of inspiring unswerving loyalty in others. One of the most moving documents I was privileged to read in the course of my research is a letter in a boyish hand, dated 25 June 1895 – that is to say, exactly a month after Oscar's conviction, when Bosie had been forced to travel to the Continent, his reputation in tatters. The letter was sent by Charles Hickey, aged twenty-two or thereabouts, to More Adey, a friend of Oscar, Ross and Bosie. Wrote Hickey: 'If Bosie cares to go to Havre, Dieppe or some place like that, I would willingly join him, but my mother must not know it; she has told me that if ever I see him again, she will cut me off without a penny.'[19] Whatever became of 'Charley' (as he signed himself)? We know that he emigrated to America before the end of the century and that Oscar presented him with an inscribed copy of *The Importance of Being Earnest*; that is all. The evidence of his courageous support for Bosie survives, however, and its production may contribute, I hope, towards the rehabilitation of a much-maligned man, a first-rate poet whose literary accomplishments have unfortunately been obscured by his involvement in the most sensational society scandal of the *fin de siècle*: the trials of Oscar Wilde.

1

A Privileged Youth

Alfred Bruce Douglas, born at Ham House near Worcester on 22 October 1870, sprang from an old Scottish line. The motto of this famous clan was *Forward*, and medieval roughs with sobriquets like 'Douglas the Grim' and 'the Black Douglas' had taken it to heart: they had stopped at nothing where their ambitions were at stake. Most of the poet's forebears had been notorious for their eccentricity, their libido and their belligerence, and although Lord Alfred no longer unsheathed a sword to fight out *his* differences, we need not look far for the origin of his pugnacity.

His father, John Sholto Douglas, the ninth Marquess of Queensberry[1] – 'Q' to his friends – had impulsively married Sybil Montgomery in 1866. She was a gracious young lady of bewildering beauty who, when driving in Hyde Park, attracted attention to such an extent that people clambered on chairs to catch a glimpse of her.

Five children, idolized by their mother, came of this union: Francis, Percy, Alfred, Sholto and Edith.

The Marchioness was less lucky with her bewhiskered husband. Their characters diverged: Sybil, mild and civilized, was artistically disposed and gave her offspring a taste for music, painting, literature – subjects that failed to captivate 'Q'. He had received a rather elementary education and had hardly read a book since becoming a midshipman on the *Britannia* when he was twelve. Sport was his passion; an accomplished horseman, a good shot and a powerful pugilist, he had, with one of his cronies, formulated the Queensberry Rules which are still supposed to be obeyed by boxers.

The family resided at Kinmount House, an imposing neo-Georgian mansion near Annan in the county of Dumfries. As his affection for

Sybil cooled, Queensberry tended to put in fewer and fewer appearances there. He was in London most of the time, amusing himself with prostitutes – or 'clergyman's daughters', as they used to be called in those days – describing his escapades in explicit letters to his wife when he felt in the mood to annoy her. The Marquess may have been a nobleman; a gentleman he was not.

Apart from his extramarital relationships and his pamphlets on 'free love', he caused outrage by publicly airing his atheistic views. In a theatre where an unsympathetic agnostic was put on stage he once created a row by hurling a bouquet of vegetables at the actors, whereupon he was unceremoniously removed from the auditorium. He refused to swear the parliamentarians' oath of allegiance to the Sovereign, which he labelled 'Christian tomfoolery', thereby forfeiting his seat as Representative Peer in the House of Lords. Queensberry had neither tact nor patience. He inspired terror instead of respect; events would show it was dangerous to oppose him.

The upbringing of his children did not concern him over-much (Alfred would later chronicle the fact that his father had taught him absolutely *nothing*),[2] but he was quite lavish as far as pocket-money was concerned. He nevertheless always apologized for 'giving so little'; he was just a poor beggar, he said. He used to commiserate with friends whom he described as being 'ruined', but who in reality, as Alfred discovered, were very well off. No one told him how to handle money, and this gap in his education explains the financial nonchalance he displayed in his youth. Oscar, not exactly a paragon of thrift himself, once jocularly referred to a book he should write in collaboration with him: *How to Live Above One's Income: For the Use of the Sons of the Rich*.[3] Alas, it never materialized.

Alfred was his mother's favourite; there can be no doubt about that. She coddled him, she cuddled him, she read to him from Shakespeare's works before he went to sleep, and called him 'Boysie', which the infant pronounced 'Bosie'. This nickname, in its slightly corrupted form, would stick to him for the rest of his life.

In his earliest years Bosie was looked after by a number of nannies, including a Scotswoman who, if necessity arose, had recourse to a hairbrush to lend force to her arguments; he subsequently passed through a couple of exclusive preparatory schools, going to Winchester College when he was fourteen. His first months there were difficult. Like most newcomers he had to endure the pranks of the bullies, but what shocked him was their utter contempt for anything religious. This lack of respect was not confined to their conversation. One of the prefects, for example, habitually hurled pieces of bread at the figure of the Messiah on a reproduction of Da Vinci's *Last Supper* that adorned the dining-room. Bosie's indignation at these practices was of short duration, however. Lady Queensberry had paid slight attention to her children's religious instruction; it was therefore hardly surprising that in his new surroundings her son, while retaining 'a sneaking fancy' for Christ,[4] came to fling aside his faith in due course.

He quickly lost his innocence at Winchester, too. His initiation in what was euphemistically called 'the public-school nonsense' formed a subject he did not discuss in his letters to his mother and which he would only touch upon gingerly in his reminiscences – unlike Trelawney Backhouse who had known Bosie and who, in his (as yet) unpublished memoirs, summed up his own days at Winchester as 'a carnival of unbridled lust'.[5] But then Backhouse had a weakness for exaggeration.

Bosie, having once conformed to the mores of an upper-class college, felt quite happy there; 'life was simply one long dream of joy and fun'.[6] He was certainly not a model student, although he took care to avoid getting behind with his work. His modest performances as a cricketer and footballer were balanced by his record as a long-distance runner. He was sent to the Headmaster more than once to get a licking; but as this worthy gentleman could not believe that a boy with such an angelic countenance was capable of committing the smallest transgression, he escaped again and again – until one of the teachers went to see the Headmaster in person and convinced him of the necessity of applying the birch . . .

It was during his final year at Winchester that Bosie made his first literary forays. With two friends he founded *The Pentagram*, a weekly in which some of his nonsense rhymes appeared and which proved so successful that even some Old Wykehamists subscribed to it. A photograph survives that shows the editors dressed in tweed, their collars starched. Like most Victorians who posed for the camera, they look self-assured and a bit serious.

Queensberry meanwhile had sold most of the family's estates. The Marchioness moved to London, which did not mean that she saw more of her husband than before. He 'kept house' with his current mistress near by, and when Sybil one day complained about this, he came up with an ingenious suggestion. Why shouldn't they form a *ménage à trois?* That would content both parties, he assured her: the Marchioness would once again live under the same roof with her spouse, and he would not have to do without his girlfriend's company.

For Sybil, this was the limit. So far she had refused to heed the advice of her father, who had urged her to divorce, but now she saw no other way out. The marriage was dissolved in 1887; the formalities lasted a mere fifteen minutes, since the reputation of Queensberry's concubine was well known. The Marquess, bound to pay alimony on a regular basis, sometimes tried to shirk his obligations, which forced Sybil to have recourse to her solicitors to make him cough up.

This behaviour was not without its consequences. Bosie, when a small boy, had greatly admired his ever-absent father, but he was old enough now to comprehend how shockingly his mother had been treated. He began to detest 'Q', who in turn formed the impression that Sybil and her children sided against him. He even felt wronged.

Oxford! Oxford, 'City of weathered cloister and worn court, / Gray city of strong towers and clustering spires',[7] still a place of breathtaking magnificence, albeit less calm, less idyllic perhaps, than it was in 1889 when Bosie arrived there.

He found the university's 'Hellenic' (that is to say, homosexual) atmosphere entirely to his taste. A contemporary remembered later with barely concealed nostalgia how 'cultured' undergraduates in those days used to hang reproductions of homoerotic drawings by Simeon Solomon on their walls, 'little notes of illicit sentiment' bearing titles such as *Antinoüs* or *Love Dying from the Breath of Lust* that would be wisely replaced by more conventional pictures when Uncle Peter or Aunt Jane came up for Gaudies and Commemoration.[8]

Bosie's name had been entered at Magdalen College, and he made quite an impression there, as witnessed by the caricatures of him that appeared in various undergraduate magazines. His friends thought him amusing and brilliant – 'an erratic and most attractive person, defiant of public opinion, generous, irresponsible and extravagant'.[9] The dons, however, were amazed at his insolence without being able to do much about it, as he seemingly managed to remain within the bounds of politeness. He had cards printed which read:

> Lord Alfred Douglas presents his compliments to . . . . . . and
> regrets that he will be unable to . . . . . . in consequence of . . . . .

Instead of the paper they were expecting, the dons would sometimes find a filled-in card in their pigeon-hole:

> Lord Alfred Douglas presents his compliments to *Professor Smith* and regrets that he will be unable to *show up an essay on the Evolution of the Moral Idea* in consequence of *not having prepared one.*[10]

Bosie preferred revelling in fine music to attending boring lectures. He was to be found at Magdalen Chapel almost every evening where hymns were sung for the greater glory of God. A pianist of some merit, he studied harmony and counterpoint and, interestingly, composed at least one madrigal, 'Country Singers, Leave Not Mute',[11] a setting of a lyric by one of his closest friends in Oxford, the amiable, hyper-correct Lionel Johnson, a student with a formidable memory, an addiction to liquor and a baby face. This last feature he had in common with Bosie; they also shared a poetical talent as remarkable as their utter lack of insight into the most elementary mathematics. They may have been lovers; they certainly discussed poetry in the small hours, as Johnson used to shine at his brightest at night. Shakespeare was their hero, but they cared for modern literature as well. Lionel lent Bosie *The Picture of Dorian Gray*, a recently published novel which produced 'a terrific effect' on the lad; he read it about fourteen times running[12] Johnson, as it happened, was acquainted with its author – an Irishman – and wondered whether Douglas would care to meet him. The answer came pat. Why, yes, of course! An appointment was duly made, and on a fateful day in July 1891 the two got into a cab and drove to 16 Tite Street, Chelsea, the address of Oscar Fingal O'Flahertie Wills Wilde.

Oscar Wilde was thirty-six when he shook Bosie's hand for the first time. His star was rising. After a successful tour through the United States where he had lectured on art in general and on that of the Pre-Raphaelites in particular, he had married, in 1884, Constance Lloyd, who had borne him two children, Cyril and Vyvyan. From 1887 to 1889 he had been the editor of the *Woman's World*, a fashionable magazine in which contributions from such notables as the Countess of Portsmouth and the Queen of Rumania had appeared. Oscar had even ventured to approach Queen Victoria – perhaps Her Majesty had written some poems in her youth that might be suitable for inclusion in the *Woman's World*? This proved not to be the case.

> Really what will not people say and invent [the monarch commented]. Never cd the Queen in her whole life write *one line* of *poetry* serious or comic or make *a Rhyme* even. This is therefore all *invention & a myth*.[13]

In 1889 Oscar had published 'The Portrait of Mr W.H.', an essay in which he argued against the prevailing opinion that Shakespeare's sonnets had been dedicated for the greater part to a noble Maecenas. Oscar maintained they were addressed to Shakespeare's 'Lord of my love',[14] William Hughes, a young actor who had taken the roles of Rosalind and Juliet at a time when women were debarred from appearing on the stage. The theory that Shakespeare had succumbed to the charms of an adolescent had raised a good deal of dust, but a veritable storm of protest had arisen after the publication, in July 1890, of *The Picture of Dorian Gray* in *Lippincott's Monthly Magazine*. Critics had decried it as decadent and immoral; according to the *Scot's Observer*, for instance, Oscar had penned a novel for catamites and their customers,[15] while the *St James's Gazette* had wondered whether the author should be prosecuted or not.[16]

The Picture of Dorian Gray tells of a young man who only becomes conscious of his beauty when he looks at his portrait. Fascinated by the philosophy of Lord Henry Wotton – a cynical charmer who preaches sensuality and who points out to him the brevity of youth – Dorian Gray expresses the wish that the years will not leave their mark on his face but on his portrait. This is exactly what happens. Little by little the figure on the canvas grows old: wrinkles appear in its forehead, the eyes dim, the golden hair loses its gloss. But Dorian Gray himself remains young. His moral deterioration, also, is shown on the picture. With every crime he commits, the portrait's glance grows more evil. Every heart he breaks causes the painted mouth to grin more sardonically. The portrait, hidden in a locked-up room, thus functions as a reflection of a corrupted soul.

Eternal youth, infinite passion, pleasures subtle and secret, wild joys and wilder sins – he was to have all these things. The portrait was to bear the burden of his shame. That was all.[17]

In 1891 a revised and enlarged version of *The Picture of Dorian Gray* had appeared as a book; a signed copy was the first present Bosie received from Wilde.

To Oscar, who cheerfully confessed he 'could resist everything except temptation', Bosie proved an irresistible temptation indeed. He was a budding poet; his blood was blue; he had great charm, and was moreover gifted with quite extraordinary beauty. Nature, he once said with his tongue in his cheek, had stamped him with the sign of her approval.[18] A French journalist subsequently rhapsodized in print over Bosie's 'noble, carefully drawn features, bright, kind eyes, wistful smile, high forehead, thin, blond hair and delicate hands': 'tout le désignait à la sympathie d'un poète'.[19]

This panegyric dates from 1904. Bosie's appearance at that time, however, hardly differed from how he looked when as a student of twenty he had entered Oscar's study in the summer of 1891, for he continued to resemble a schoolboy until well in his thirties – a circumstance which gave rise to misapprehensions. He was twenty-one when a lady invited him to a children's party.[20] He was twenty-six when he was denied admittance into a casino, and five years afterwards a baroness queried whether he was still at school![21]

Need we labour the point that Oscar felt he had encountered Dorian Gray himself? After Bosie's first visit it seemed to him as if he had drunk tea with 'the visible incarnation of that unseen ideal whose memory haunts artists like an exquisite dream' – to quote a relevant passage from his novel.[22] Oscar was wildly, passionately, devotedly, but not hopelessly, in love.

For his feelings were reciprocated.

It was not the exterior of the plumpish Wilde that impressed Bosie; it was the quality of his conversation that enthralled him. Oscar was a peerless raconteur, a wizard with words who, seemingly without effort, managed to gild what was drab and what was trite. No one felt bored in his presence; with his melodious voice he could draw from his hearers' eyes tears of emotion and tears of laughter at will. A friend who once had a cold, which was so bad that he could not go to the dentist to be treated for the toothache that plagued him, perceived to his astonishment that after an unexpected visit from Oscar he had been cured of *both* ailments – so much had he roared with laughter at the stories that Oscar had told him.

The writer liked to pull the legs of serious and respectable people, of whom, then as now, there were a great many around. 'Football is all very well for rough girls,' he once said with a smooth face to a pompous schoolmaster, 'but it is hardly suitable for delicate boys.'[23] Such remarks always caused Bosie to split his sides, which was much frowned upon by the aforementioned serious and respectable people. Oscar's intimates all agreed that his wit is only palely reflected in his works. One day in Oscar's company, Bosie recalled, was more amusing than a complete volume of *Punch*. Humour played an important part in their relationship; and it was not Oscar who made all the quips, as has been supposed. 'The disadvantage of being Oscar's great friend,' sighs Bosie in an early play dealing with the couple's love affair, 'is that all one's best remarks are believed to be his. I have a little wit of my own, I hope.'[24] He certainly had.

Oscar was not just a figure of fun, of course; he was a great scholar, a generous man who possessed the art of consolation. Bosie adored him. 'There is nothing I would not do for him,' he assured his mother, 'and if he dies before I do I shall not care to live any longer. The thought of such a thing makes everything black before my eyes. Surely there is nothing but what is fine and beautiful in such a love as that of two people for one another, the love of the disciple and the philosopher.'[25]

By degrees the philosopher and his disciple became inseparable.

Those who frequented Oscar's circle were sure to meet the artists who flourished during the final, intriguing decade of the nineteenth century, and Bosie made the acquaintance of the likes of Walter Pater, Oscar's timid tutor who, in *The Renaissance*, had urged his readers to live life to the full; John Gray, a dandy 'with a promising career behind him',[26] whose poetical début, *Silverpoints*, is among the most sumptuous books of an era noted for its sumptuous books; the portraitist William Rothenstein; the essayist and caricaturist Max Beerbohm; the tragic poet Ernest Dowson; the writer Ada Leverson, alias 'the Sphinx'; the illustrator Aubrey Beardsley; the French poet and novelist Pierre Louÿs, author of the apocryphal *Chansons de Bilitis*; and Paul Verlaine, with whom the friends drank absinthe in a Parisian bar – absinthe, the Decadents' favourite drink, which Bosie could not stomach.[27]

The Decadents set the tone at the time. Most of them scarcely bothered about ethical and social issues; they concentrated on luxuriating in and producing art which, like Schopenhauer, they looked upon as the only escape from humdrum routine. Withdrawn in their ivory towers, these aesthetes had neither the hope nor even the wish to appeal to the masses or to influence them; their poems appeared in proportionally small editions (Oscar's ideal issue was limited to five hundred signed copies for particular friends, six for the general public and one for the American market).[28] They were enthralled by the unconscious and the supernatural; their bible was *À Rebours*, a novel by Joris-Karl Huysmans, published in 1884, in which the last scion of a degenerated, noble family turns away from the world to enjoy the pleasures of art at his country seat. A poisonous book, according to a delighted Oscar; a revelation to Bosie.

Bosie, as we have said, was to be found at Oscar's side most of the time during the years that preceded the latter's downfall – a fact deeply deplored in *De Profundis* afterwards. Oscar alleged in this screed that Bosie had continually distracted him; the young man would not have realized that seclusion is required to get on with one's work; as long as Bosie had been in his company, Oscar had never been able to write a single line.[29]

This accusation is categorically untrue. As Bosie pointed out, Oscar 'was too keen an artist to allow anything or anybody to come between him and what he would call a realisable mood'.[30] While writing *A Woman of No Importance*, Oscar was staying with Bosie at Babbacombe, near Torquay. The two were together in London and Goring when *An Ideal Husband* took shape. Oscar commenced *A Florentine Tragedy* during a holiday with Bosie in Italy, and they stayed at Worthing when *The Importance of Being Earnest* flew from Oscar's pen. Bosie's presence did not impede him from writing his plays at all. On the contrary.

Whereas in *De Profundis* the incarcerated Wilde lamented that his creativity had been undermined by his association with Bosie, he rightly described, in a petition to the Home Secretary, the years before his arrest as the most brilliant and productive phase of his career: a period in which four of his plays had been successfully produced and in which he had published numerous books that had caused quite a stir at home and abroad.[31]

Oscar had been able to be that prolific not in spite of but partly as a result of his friendship with Bosie; for it should be borne in mind that in Oscar's life Bosie occupied the same place as does the eponymous hero of *The Picture of Dorian Gray* in that of the painter Basil Hallward, who concedes he cannot be happy if he does not see his bosom friend every day, in the presence of whom he is able to produce his greatest masterpieces.[32] Likewise, Lord Alfred Douglas was – in Shakespeare's phrase – Oscar Wilde's 'tenth Muse',[33] his chief source of inspiration.[34] We have his own word for it. 'What wisdom is to the philosopher, what God is to his saint,' he wrote to Bosie a few days before he was sentenced to two years' imprisonment, 'you are to me.'[35]

Holy ground.

2

A Notorious Friendship

On 22 February 1892 the triumphant première took place in London of *Lady Windermere's Fan*, 'a new and original play, in four acts, by Oscar Wilde'. Afterwards the author, holding a lighted cigarette between his fingers, appeared before the limelight to congratulate the audience on its *intelligent appreciation* of his melodrama. The critics were outraged; the theatregoers were delighted; and Oscar made quite a lot of money out of the play's run. The days of plenty had begun.

It was during the summer of that year that the artist, having been invited to lunch at Lady Battersea's, informed his hostess that if he had to work for a living he would like to be a shepherd.

'I think you would find looking after a lot of sheep rather tiring,' she said.

'Oh,' rejoined Oscar, 'I would not like to have more than one sheep.'

'Well, you've got one lamb already with a golden fleece,' said Lady Battersea, referring to Bosie, who – beaming with pleasure – was also seated at table.

Bosie, recounting this story in a letter dispatched in the late 1930s, assured his correspondent that her Ladyship's remark had been wholly 'innocent'.[1] It may have been; but already the air was filled with rumours concerning the two. The friendship between the famous man of letters and the young aristocrat was nothing if not conspicuous, for in the music halls and fashionable restaurants where they presented themselves they made no bones about their mutual admiration. Robert Harborough Sherard met them at the Café Royal one early afternoon after lunch. To him they looked like men 'who thoroughly enjoyed each other's company and who were truly happy to be together'. He was enchanted with Bosie's 'perfect manners, his entire absence of "side" [and] the ready wit with which he "came back" to each of

Oscar's sallies'.[2] On that occasion the couple were clearly on their best behaviour. There were other occasions as well. A bookseller who claimed to have provided Oscar with spicy novels once spotted them seated in the Empire Theatre, Oscar having his arm round the neck of Bosie, 'who was pressed against him in a gesture which would have been considered improper even in a less strait-laced milieu'.[3] Across the Channel eyebrows were raised, too. A member of the staff of the Mercure de France, sipping tea and thereafter some wine with them at the Hôtel de l'Athénée in Paris, felt bound to leave them hurriedly when Oscar, slightly drunk, ventured to slip his arm round Bosie's waist.[4] The exploits of high-class courtesans like Liane de Pougy and Émilienne d'Alençon, who counted princes and bankers, and women as well, among their bedfellows, were tolerated and even admired at the turn of the century; but gentlemen who preferred their own sex were despised or, at best, laughed out of court by most people.

Robert Baldwin Ross did not object in principle to men kissing men. Perish the thought. He kissed a great many during his life. But he felt uncomfortable at the thought of Oscar kissing 'the red rose-leaf lips'[5] of Bosie, in whom he recognized a redoubtable rival.

Ross had been born in Canada but brought to London in 1871 by his widowed mother when two years old. Criticizing the Cambridge University authorities had cost him dear: fellow-students had ducked him in the fountain of King's College, and he had indignantly left the place, never to return. This had happened in 1889, about three years after he had become Oscar's lover – Oscar's first ever lover, as he is alleged to have claimed.[6] Back in the capital he began to move in literary circles, contributing articles to the *Saturday Review*. Estimates of his character varied greatly. 'Ross is here,' Lionel Johnson wrote in an undated letter to a minor poet. 'What be his morals, I know not: himself is delightful.'[7] The Rev. Biscoe Wortham, who *did* know his morals (two of his sons having been seduced by 'Robbie' or 'Bobbie', as he was called), thought him a 'scoundrel'.[8] Oscar praised his protégé's cleverness, charm and excellent taste[9] and would dedicate *The Importance of Being Earnest* to him, no mean compliment. Bosie, in his memoirs, granted that Ross had been a man of brains and ability, besides being a good talker.[10] The number of admirers he acquired in his maturity is impressive, but did they *really* know him? Reginald Turner, that other loyal friend of Oscar's, the one who would nurse the author during his last illness, thought they did not. Writing to Sherard in 1933, he remarked:

> We all know what great qualities [Ross] had and they have been fully and properly acknowledged. But only his intimates whose acquaintance with him extended over *early and late* times knew him as he was . . . When he was criticised or opposed he lost his heart and his head. My own criticism of him cost me his friendship – that is to say, it became of an entirely different quality. He was, of course, intensely vain and jealous and stopped at nothing to get his ends . . . To his later friends he was a hero, but to his older friends, who knew him, he was not . . . Well, he got what he liked, recognition.[11]

The jealousy that Ross had for Bosie did not manifest itself immediately. In fact, his feelings for the dazzling playboy who dedicated one of his ballads[12] to him were highly ambivalent. Bosie has put it on record that 'in the early days' he used to be 'very fond' of Ross. The letters he sent him, frankly relating his sexual adventures, show the degree of intimacy that existed between them, and Ross's letters to Bosie, according to the latter, contained declarations of Ross's devotion to him 'in as extravagant terms as those used by Wilde'.[13] Perhaps the vendetta that would ultimately wreck their lives had its roots in a web of emotions even more complicated than either of them would have dared to admit. Be that as it may, as Oscar tended to spend more and more of his time with Bosie, Ross must have mentally cursed Johnson for bringing the two men together.

The relationship began to trouble Bosie's parents as well. Queensberry, who had given ear to twaddle and gossip, instructed his son to put a stop to it; but Bosie – who failed to see why he should heed a father who had never heeded him – begged him to mind his own business. Whereat 'Q' called him a fool and a baby, using less complimentary terms to designate Wilde.

Then, on an autumn day in 1892, an extraordinary thing happened. Queensberry entered the Café Royal, sat down and, looking round, noticed Oscar and Bosie who were lunching together. Now or never! the undergraduate thought. Ignoring his father's frowns, Bosie went up to him and invited him to meet Oscar Wilde . At first the Marquess refused, but Bosie insisted, and so the arch-enemies to be shook hands.

Oscar, fully aware of Queensberry's antipathy to him, managed to twist him round his little finger. He engaged him in an amusing conversation, and Bosie, who tactfully left them after a while, was greatly pleased when his father wrote to him afterwards, withdrawing everything he had said against Oscar. He called him 'a wonderful man', adding that he fully understood now why Bosie so gushed about him.

But Lady Queensberry remained to be reassured. She sent a letter to the President of Magdalen College, Sir Herbert Warren: did *he* look upon Mr Wilde as a suitable companion for her son? Warren answered her that Lord Alfred should count himself lucky to be an intimate of an artist as prominent as the author of *The Picture of Dorian Gray*.

As it happened, the friendship between Oscar and Bosie was even more intimate than the Marchioness could conjecture, for the two had become lovers in January 1892 or thereabouts, their familiarities extending over a period of less than three years. Bosie did not really relish sex with Oscar, and he was not really Oscar's 'type'. Where sensual passions were concerned, Oscar preferred less refined boys – riff-raff in fact. In the pursuit of his pleasures he was extremely indiscreet, thereby incurring enormous risks. In 1886 an Act had come into force outlawing *all* sexual contacts between males, irrespective of whether they took place in public or in private. This was grist to the mill of the underworld, of course; the Act (which was abolished as late as 1967) lived up to its nickname, 'the Blackmailer's Charter'.

Bosie was quite indiscreet in his affairs with boys and young men, too. Even one with whom he was on sleeping terms warned him that he was indulging in gay sex 'to a reckless and highly dangerous degree'.[14] Indeed, Bosie was 'rented' in the spring of 1892 and turned to Oscar for help, who put the matter into the hands of the solicitor, Sir George Lewis, who came to an agreement with the extortioner.[15] Such mishaps occurred frequently in Oscar's circle: Robert Ross and Reginald Turner (alias the boy-snatcher of Clements Inn) found themselves in the same quandary more than once.

In *De Profundis* Bosie would be taken to task because of his carelessness with revealing letters Oscar had sent him, letters that fell into the hands of Queensberry's henchmen and were used as evidence against the sender.[16] Bosie may be justly blamed for this nonchalance, but Oscar himself was tarred with the same brush. One gets the impression that the two not just put up with the dangers inextricably linked with their promiscuity (their 'eternal quest for beauty',[17] as Bosie called it) but that they perceived a humorous side to these as well. Thus Oscar made Bosie a present of a little valise marked 'CL' – 'Compromising Letters'.[18] Both men behaved in a breathtakingly irresponsible way.

'Feasting with panthers' was Oscar's phrase to describe his pranks with male prostitutes; 'the danger was half the excitement'.[19] Inevitably he would get into serious trouble sooner rather than later.

On a beautiful spring day, while people were still flocking to see *Lady Windermere's Fan*, the doorbell was rung at 16 Tite Street, Chelsea. Two students from Oxford presented themselves, begging for an interview with the master of the house. Would he be so kind as to receive them?

They were ushered into his study where Oscar lay stretched on a sofa. What, he queried, gave him the pleasure of their visit?

With some trepidation they told him about their scheme to launch a magazine, *The Spirit Lamp*; and they hoped that he . . . might he, perhaps . . . would he be willing to contribute something, say, a sonnet?

Oscar, who had been listening attentively, shook his head. No, regrettably he had nothing to offer them. Then one of his guests – hiding his disappointment as best he could – asked whether he had any suggestion regarding the colour of the cover. Oh yes, he had.

'Green,' said Oscar dreamily, 'a beautiful, subtle green . . .'

And then he showed them out, remarking casually that he thought orange a dreadful colour.

The first number of *The Spirit Lamp* was issued on 6 May 1892; its cover was orange.[20]

Magazines mushroomed in Oxford, but few of them lasted. *The Spirit Lamp*'s life-span, too, was short (fourteen numbers were published in all), but its contents were of a remarkably high standard. This was mainly due to the industry of the student to whom the editorial torch was handed after a few months and who, as he did not take his examinations *that* seriously, was able to devote much time to the venture: Lord Alfred Douglas, whose 'pleasant, comfortable rooms, well lined with books'[21] were situated in the High Street, next door to the premises of the printer, James Thornton.

Bosie had caught the attention with a clever article on the difference between undergraduates and the Dons: 'The real reason why Dons are so uninteresting is that they stand out against a background of such intense interest and beauty that they appear darker and duller than they really are.'[22] In the six numbers he edited, short stories, essays and poems of his appeared. These revealed undeniable literary talent; but not all he wrote met with unqualified appreciation. His parody on Plato's dialogues, the university authorities thought, ridiculed the Deity, and it caused his disappearance from Oxford for some time.[23]

The magazine's contributors included Lionel Johnson, Max Beerbohm, Count Erik Stenbock, the art historian John Addington Symonds, Robbie Ross and, inevitably, Oscar Wilde. Even Queensberry collaborated, submitting a lyric consisting of four rhymed stanzas. 'When I am dead, cremate me,' it opened.[24] As a rule, the poems that appeared in *The Spirit Lamp* were less down to earth.

The review bore an 'aesthetic' signature: verses on Hylas, Ganymede and Hyacinthus alternated with articles on Verlaine and Wilde. 'The "washings out" of a decadent academy,' *The Ephemeral* jeered, in an effort to tempt Bosie to a controversy.[25] He duly obliged. 'Dear Sir,' he wrote in a letter that was published in *The Ephemeral* on 20 May 1893,

> Next to the praise of the cultivated and the admiration of the brilliant, there is nothing so gratifying to the feelings of the editor of a magazine like *The Spirit Lamp* as the abuse of the Philistine and the scorn of the vulgar. Praise and admiration from the brilliant and the cultivated have been freely given to *The Spirit Lamp*, but up to the present time, the abuse and scorn of the Philistine have been too infrequent and too sparingly expressed to give me very great cause for pride and self-congratulation. I am deeply grateful to you.[26]

The circulation of *The Spirit Lamp* was quite respectable, but its financial situation was precarious and did not improve when Bosie decided to cut all advertisements. The magazine, highly sought after by collectors nowadays, went down, albeit with the flag nailed to the mast: in 1912 the *Morning Post* deemed it 'the best of Oxford's many momentary periodicals'.[27]

The extinguishing of *The Spirit Lamp* coincided with the end of Bosie's university career, for he left Magdalen College in June without a degree. His mother was disappointed; his father was furious (which was odd, inasmuch as he believed academic laurels to be utterly useless);[28] his lover, lastly, pointed out to him with a grin that he was treading in the footsteps of Shelley and Swinburne, who likewise had failed to get a degree and had remained under-graduates all their lives; and he honoured him with a special commission. The summer of that year was taken up by a play written in French by an Irishman, which was to be translated into English by a Scot.[29]

The play in question, finished by Oscar in 1891, was *Salomé*, the history of the princess who succeeds in obtaining the head of St John the Baptist on a silver charger, enabling her to kiss the lips of the ascetic who had rejected her.

The London première of *Salomé*, starring the famous Sarah Bernhardt in the principal role, had been torpedoed in 1892 by the censor. One Mr Pigott saw fit to cancel the performance of the play because it contained biblical characters, thereby contravening a sixteenth-century law enacted as part of a wholesale suppression of popish sentiments. Oscar, who always lost his sense of reality when his sense of humour forsook him, had declared himself in a newspaper interview to be so incensed by these developments that he contem-plated emigrating to France. He had not gone, after all, contenting himself – in expectation of a Parisian production of *Salomé* – with the publication of the text in February 1893. The book had been acclaimed by Bosie in *The Spirit Lamp*, and Oscar, who wished to bring out an English version of his tragedy in one act, now begged him to undertake the translation.

Bosie set to work with enthusiasm. On 30 August he proudly informed the publisher, John Lane, that the job was done; but Oscar was not pleased with the result and made so many changes that Bosie preferred to distance himself from the project. 'I have decided to relinquish the affair altogether,' he wrote to Lane after lengthy dis-cussions with Oscar. 'You and Oscar can arrange between you as to who the translator is to be. My private opinion is that unless Oscar translates it himself, he will not be satisfied.'[30]

A sensible comment. Another translation, provided by Aubrey Beardsley (who illustrated the play),[31] was even less to Oscar's liking. Tempers had risen – the number of telegrams exchanged was 'simply scandalous',[32] Beardsley told Ross – when finally a compromise was reached: Oscar returned to Bosie's text and corrected it at will;

Bosie's name would only be mentioned in the dedication.[33] 'Let me assure you,' the young man wrote to Lane on 16 November,

> that nothing would have induced me to sanction the publication of *Salomé* without my name on the title-page (and the matter was left entirely in my hands by Mr Wilde), if I had not been persuaded that the dedication which is to be made to me is of infinitely greater artistic and literary value than the appearance of my name on the title-page. It was only a few days ago that I fully realized that the difference between the dedication of *Salomé* to me by the author and the appearance of my name on the title-page is the difference between a tribute of admiration from an artist and a receipt from a tradesman.[34]

Lane had more problems. Some of Beardsley's drawings were indecent, he thought, and had to be replaced with plates that were not. As a result the book only came off the press in February 1894, two months later than had been planned. Not that the critics would have looked upon it as a suitable Christmas present: one of them had described the French version as being 'morbid, *bizarre*, repulsive'.[35]

Oscar and Bosie squabbled a lot about the merits of the latter's *Salomé* translation, but whether Oscar was really told that Bosie was 'under no intellectual obligation of any kind to [him]'[36] – as alleged in *De Profundis* – may be strongly doubted. The letters which Bosie addressed to his mother that winter from Cairo contain an ardent defence of his friend who, he said, '[had] taught [him] everything that [he] knew that is worth knowing'. 'You cannot do anything against the power of my affection for Oscar Wilde and of his for me,' he continued. 'I am passionately fond of him, and he of me. "There never was a better bargain driven."'[37]

Bosie amused himself very much in Egypt, where, he wrote to Ross, the beautiful boys were 'numerous and very accessible'.[38] For a few months he was the guest of the British Consul-General, Lord Cromer, who liked him[39] and whose wife was a friend of Sybil; and Sybil had been urging her son to go away on a holiday which, she thought, he badly needed.

In Luxor he made the acquaintance of Robert Hichens, a journalist with literary ambitions. He found Bosie 'very amusing, capital company',[40] greatly admired his sparkling conversation, and thoroughly drew him out on his relations with Wilde.

After a week-long stay in Athens – the Acropolis impressed him far more than the pyramids – Bosie travelled to Paris in March, from whence he sent a cable to Oscar, begging him to meet him there. Oscar, who did not hesitate for a moment and who crossed the Channel immediately, gave a completely imaginary account of their reunion later on in *De Profundis:* Bosie would have swamped him with hysterical telegrams, some of which ran to ten or eleven pages; he had threatened to commit suicide if Oscar refused to see him in Paris; at dinner at Voisin's, at supper at Paillard's he had 'again and again' shed 'tears like rain', holding Oscar's hand as though he were 'a penitent child', etc.[41] Few passages in *De Profundis* filled Bosie with more astonishment.

Back home, he redeemed a promise by introducing Hichens to Oscar. The reporter now knew both men who in London had become the talk of the town and carried out a plan that summer which he had devised while at Luxor: he portrayed them in a satirical novel that was published on 15 September 1894, *The Green Carnation.*[42]

Oscar figures as the eloquent and much-discussed aesthete Esmé Amarinth, author of that decadent masterpiece *The Soul of Bertie Brown*. Bishops look upon him as a monster, and monsters would like him to become a bishop.[43] Bosie appears as Lord Reginald Hastings. He resembles 'some angel in a church window designed by Burne-Jones',[44] and worships beauty – which explains why his mantelpiece bears only photographs of himself.

> It is so interesting to be young, with pale gilt hair and blue eyes, and a face in which the shadows of fleeting expressions come and go, and a mouth like the mouth of Narcissus. It is so interesting to oneself. Surely one's beauty, one's attractiveness, should be one's own greatest delight.[45]

Esmé Amarinth and Lord Reginald Hastings amply discuss sin and the complicated technique of sinning. They consider themselves to be proficient sinners, but their favourite sin is not disclosed by the author.

His identity, by the way, caused much speculation. *The Green Carnation* had been issued anonymously, which all the more tickled the public's curiosity. Some reviewers wondered if Oscar himself had written the book. The truth came speedily to light; and so it happened that Hichens received two telegrams on the same day, one from Oscar, one from Bosie. They told him that 'all was discovered' and that he had better 'go into hiding' to escape their 'revenge'.[46]

The two did not mind, then, being poked fun at (rather they felt flattered), but Queensberry was less charmed with the novel. In it, he was depicted as a philistine at odds with his impertinent son, 'sniffing ostentatiously'[47] whenever he meets him. Very funny, Bosie thought. And factually correct, as the *entente* between himself and Queensberry had been of short duration; but before going further into this matter we must point out that the Marquess was at variance with his other children, too. The Douglas brothers, who were wont to call each other 'darling', referred to 'that brute' when talking about their father. He had only himself to thank for it, really.

Take the case of his heir, Francis Archibald, Viscount Drumlanrig. He was a sensitive chap who in 1889 had caused a sensation when, as a Lieutenant in the Coldstream Guards, he had subscribed to the Dockers' Fund (the London dockers having gone on strike to enforce a number of perfectly reasonable demands). 'Francy' was summoned forthwith to a subalterns' court martial, although it seems his popularity was such that he was not actually punished.[48] In 1892 he had become the private secretary of the Foreign Secretary, Lord Rosebery, who was so pleased with his subordinate that he wanted to appoint him Lord-in-Waiting to the Queen. One had to occupy a seat in the House of Lords as a preliminary, and to Francis *that* was a delicate point. For his father, it will be remembered, had forfeited his place there on account of his refractory behaviour and still felt much aggrieved by this. It was therefore not inconceivable that he would resent the honour intended for his son. However, on being approached 'Q' did not in the slightest object to Rosebery's plan. Francis asked if he might have this consent in black and white. The Marquess wrote to Rosebery and to the Prime Minister, expressing his approval.

But Francis had hardly been installed as member of the House of Lords when his father changed his mind. The same politicians and the Queen received furious letters from him, and when in June 1893 Rosebery went to the German resort of Homburg, Queensberry was at his heels, intending to horse-whip him. The Minister fled to his hotel room, locking the door, and was finally saved by the Prince of Wales who somehow managed to calm down the Marquess, prevailing on him to return to England. Needless to say, Francis felt acutely embarrassed.

His brother, Percy, also had good reason to complain about their father's deportment. In 1893 he had married a clergyman's daughter (in the original sense of the term: her father was the vicar of Boyton near Launceston). At the wedding Queensberry had been conspicuous by his absence, as he considered the bride to be 'low-born'. He refused to see her and, later, her children; but he did send her letters which greatly upset her.

When, a month after the publication of *The Green Carnation*, the family assembled for a most melancholy reason – Francis was being buried – 'Q' was in the news again. On 24 October he divorced his second wife, a seventeen-year-old whom he had induced to marry him in spite of her family's protests and whom he deserted on the day following the wedding. It was this man who, during the Wilde trials, would be hailed as the respectable paterfamilias.

His relations with Bosie had not improved either, as we have said. The Marquess had been angry at his failure to get a degree; he was displeased because his diplomatic career, which Sybil had mapped out, had come to nothing;[49] and, most of all, Bosie's friendship with Oscar vexed him. True, he had at the time described the author as 'a wonderful man', permitting his son to associate with him – but once again he had changed like a leaf on a tree. Bosie had been ordered to drop Oscar and, on refusing to comply, had lost the allowance that Queensberry paid him, a sanction which did not have the desired effect as Bosie received money from his mother and his grandfather regularly.

The conflict with 'Q' was pushed to extremes after Bosie's return from Egypt. Michel van der Plas calls the young man's animosity to Queensberry 'perverse',[50] while Martin Koomen raises his hands in horror at Bosie's 'tremendous hatred for his begetter'.[51] Yet surely one has to admit that the Marquess made it well-nigh impossible for him to obey the fourth commandment, not least because he continually affirmed he had *not* begotten him – and the easiest way to get a rise out of Bosie was to traduce his mother, which was what Queensberry did. 'You reptile,' he wrote to him on 24 August 1894 in a letter in which he advised him to become a road-sweeper, 'you are no son of mine and I never thought you were.'[52] 'You miserable creature,' another epistle opened,

If you are my son, it is only confirming proof to me, if I needed any, how right I was to face every horror and misery I have done rather than run the risk of bringing more creatures into the world like yourself . . . When quite a baby, I cried over you the bitterest tears a man ever shed, that I had brought such a creature into the world, and unwittingly had committed such a crime. If you are not my son, and in this Christian country with these hypocrites 'tis a wise father who knows his own child and no wonder on the principles they intermarrry on, but to be forewarned is to be forearmed. No wonder you have fallen a prey to this horrible brute . . . You must be demented.[53]

Bosie later wondered whether Queensberry's eccentricity had not been partly caused by his numerous 'terrible falls'.[54] A reckless jockey, the Marquess had been unhorsed repeatedly, breaking all his limbs at least once in the process (and his collarbone two or three times); moreover, as a boxer he had taken many blows that may well have inflicted permanent brain damage.

Anyhow, Bosie was not prepared to dance to his father's piping. WHAT A FUNNY LITTLE MAN YOU ARE, he cabled to him after receiving one of his more outrageous letters. But when Queensberry threatened to thrash him when he found him in the company of Oscar, and when he started verbally abusing the waiters who served the two friends, Bosie became more careful. He let it be known that he carried a revolver with which he would defend himself if attacked. This weapon went off by accident during a stay at the Berkeley Hotel. No one got hurt; the damage was limited to a hole in the ceiling. Queensberry, however, to whom the incident was reported, was sufficiently taken aback to keep quiet for a few months.

When John Francis Bloxam, a student of Exeter College, Oxford, decided to start a magazine, he resolved it would be very special indeed. Each year three issues would appear in an edition limited to a hundred copies, beautifully printed on hand-made paper with broad margins. Something for the connoisseur. Bloxam named his periodical *The Chameleon*, 'A Bazaar of Dangerous and Smiling Chances'.

Two years previously the founders of *The Spirit Lamp* had begged Oscar to contribute something that would add lustre to their first number; Bloxam, a friend of Bosie's, did the same and proved more lucky than his colleagues had been. Oscar liked him a lot – 'an undergraduate of strange beauty',[55] he called him; he gave him advice[56] and handed him his 'Phrases and Philosophies for the Use of the Young', a set of aphorisms including

In examinations the foolish ask questions that the wise cannot answer

and

To love oneself is the beginning of a life-long romance[57]

that was given a prominent place in the first *Chameleon*, which was published on 1 December 1894. Its cover was green.

Its contents were blue. 'Two Loves', which is among the best-known lyrics of Bosie's; 'The Shadow of the End', a prose-poem written by a schoolmaster who, in the opinion of some, would be well advised to take up another profession;[58] 'Love in Oxford', 'At Dawn' and 'Les Décadents', a song wherein 'old sins' are toasted – all these contributions were unblushingly gay.

Robert Sherard, who was not, later described Bloxam in one of his books as 'an inadequately birched schoolboy'[59] thereby expressing the opinion of most of his contemporaries. The instinctive hatred towards homosexuals was indeed so ferocious that one cannot but be amazed at the pluck Bloxam showed in coming up with such a magazine at such a time.

Oscar and Bosie were only too willing to assist in the venture, for they were in the forefront of a group of writers who hoped to bring about a change in the public attitude towards Greek Love. It was, as Bosie subsequently admitted, a constant topic of their conversation.[60] George Ives, that most closeted of the pioneers of gay lib, noted approvingly in his diary that 'the Cause' was 'sacred' to Bosie,[61] and Bosie effusively praised Oscar for all he had done for 'the new culture' by financially and morally supporting those gays who had run into trouble with blackmailers or the police.[62] A few unfortunates' names crop up in Bosie's correspondence, such as those of Charles Alan Fyffe, Fellow and Estates Bursar of University College, Oxford, and Major W.H. Parkinson, both of whom chose to commit suicide rather than appear before the man in red who reads the law.[63] Parkinson cut his throat with a piece of broken glass, and Bosie, to show his sympathy, sported a single eyeglass for a while. The fate of these men upset him and deprived him of sleep.

The Chameleon also contained a whimsical essay by Lionel Johnson, 'On the Appreciation of Trifles', which among other things extolled the fragrance of soap and the graceful uniforms of telegraph boys and which ended: 'It would be very sad if there were no one left to shock.'[64]

To-Day's reviewer *was* shocked. His fulminations against the paper forced Bloxam to suppress it at once.

It was principally 'The Priest and the Acolyte' that had given offence. The hero of this anonymous story is a young chaplain who, sitting in the confessional, wonders why his parishioners cannot be a little more original in their vices and who proceeds to fall in love with his fourteen-year-old server. The fellow visits him night after night, procuring him 'the intoxicating delight' of 'beautiful boyish lips raining kisses on his own'; when their liaison comes to light, the priest says a mass 'for the repose of [their] souls', poisons the consecrated wine and empties the chalice with his beloved.[65]

This piece of blasphemous camp, written by Bloxam (a future vicar, incidentally), would be fully discussed shortly afterwards in the course of Oscar's cross-examination by Queensberry's counsel. Oscar was accused of corrupting the young; his association with a periodical such as *The Chameleon* seriously weakened his case. That he professed not to have seen the story before its appearance in print, that he called it 'bad and indecent', that he pretended to have urged the editor to withdraw the magazine from circulation directly on reading it is quite understandable.[66] After all he was, figuratively, fighting for his life. Of course he concealed in court the fact that he had heartily enjoyed Bloxam's story and had encouraged him to publish it when a cautious friend had advised against it;[67] it is logical that he did not divulge having asked Ada Leverson to contribute something to the second number.[68] But to blame Bosie in *De Profundis* for all that had happened was childish.

> One day you come to me and ask me, as a personal favour to you, to write something for an Oxford undergraduate magazine, about to be started by some friend of yours, whom I had never heard of in all my life, and knew nothing about. To please you – what did I not always do to please you? – I sent him a page of paradoxes

destined originally for the *Saturday Review*. A few months later
I find myself standing in the dock of the Old Bailey on account
of the character of the magazine.[69]

Oscar probably did not pay much attention to the commotion
surrounding *The Chameleon* as he was engrossed by the rehearsals
of his new play, *An Ideal Husband*, which was first performed at the
Haymarket on 3 January 1895, a sumptuous show that proved highly
successful. 'Oscar Wilde is the fashion,' a critic remarked.[70]

The artist was now at the height of his fame. He was enjoying
himself immensely and seemed unaware of the dramatic turn his life
was soon to take. But the cautious friend just referred to, George Ives,
had entrusted his forebodings to his journal on New Year's Day. 'After
going among that set,' he wrote, alluding to Oscar and Bosie, 'it is
hard to mix in ordinary society, for they have a charm which is rare
and wonderful. I wish they were less extravagant and more real; so
gifted and so nice, yet . . . I see the storm of battle coming.'[71]

After a holiday of some weeks with Bosie in Algiers, Oscar
returned to London where his 'Trivial Comedy for Serious People',
The Importance of Being Earnest, went into rehearsals. The city was
placarded with posters announcing its première.

Queensberry was one of those who had bought a ticket. He had a
bunch of vegetables, too. He intended to hurl it at Oscar when he
appeared before the curtain after the last act to deliver one of his
speeches. The plot was revealed, however, and when on the evening
of 14 February the Marquess tried to gain admittance to the St James's
Theatre he was prevented from doing so by policemen guarding all
the entrances. For the space of three hours, while a blizzard was raging
and while the great and the good were delighting in Oscar's finest
stage-work, 'Q' vainly endeavoured to crash the gates. Then he beat
a retreat, seething with anger, devising new schemes – determined
to wreck the career of *that man*, Wilde!

It was on the twenty-eighth of the month that the porter of the
Albemarle Club handed the dramatist a visiting-card which had been
left there for him by Queensberry a few days before. Oscar reeled as
he read its inscription: 'For Oscar Wilde posing somdomite'. What
these words meant, the slip of the pen notwithstanding, was perfectly
clear. They were a challenge; and Oscar made the mistake of
accepting it. He sued his tormentor for criminal libel.

3

A Resounding Scandal

Few prisoners are likely to have been longing for the arrival of the police so fervently as the Marquess of Queensberry, who was arrested on 2 March. He had at last attained his end: Oscar had walked into the trap.

Unquestionably Oscar should never have taken legal steps against the nobleman. In *De Profundis* he made Bosie, and Bosie alone, responsible for this fateful decision: his instigations had induced him to disregard the advice of his other friends, and take up the gauntlet that Queensberry had thrown down. The image, formulated in this long and bitter letter, of Bosie as Oscar's 'evil genius', has subsequently been adopted by numerous biographers and journalists, but none of them has condemned Bosie as venomously and with quite as much gusto as Michel van der Plas. Bosie, he tells us, was 'inclined to destruction, like a blood-sucker, a parasite', a 'young profligate' who may be blamed for Oscar's downfall because he harboured 'the unnatural desire to deal a deadly blow to his father by means of a trial in which Oscar should act as the accuser, while he, the beautiful, young friend, could safely sit on the sideline'. Bosie 'used his venerated master, Oscar Wilde' to fight out a quarrel with his father, which resulted in the doom of the writer 'to whom he owed everything except his good looks'.[1]

This cuts no ice. Mr van der Plas remarks that what Bosie describes as 'our case' was really his personal feud with his father[2] and thereby ignores the fact that it was Queensberry's ceaseless harassment *of Wilde* that ultimately drove the latter to resort to the law. The Marquess had insulted him in numerous letters to Bosie and others. He had made scenes in bars and restaurants the two used to frequent. In June 1894 he had even paid an unexpected visit to Tite Street (accompanied by a heavyweight boxer, it is alleged) to accuse the artist of lewdness. Oscar's correspondence shows just how much he was exasperated by all this. 'It is intolerable to be dogged by a maniac,' he wrote to Bosie,[3] and when he had received Queensberry's card with its inscription, he informed Ross: 'I don't see anything now but a criminal prosecution. My whole life seems ruined by this man. The tower of ivory is assailed by the foul thing.'[4]

This does not mean, of course, that Bosie was not involved in the fight between his friend and his father; far from it. It is a pity, however, that neither he nor Oscar could fathom the whole gamut of motives that prompted Queensberry. What is more, the Marquess himself will not have realized that it was partly *jealousy* which underlay his hounding of Oscar.

Queensberry's situation uncannily resembles the predicament of the surly merchant Simone, a character in Oscar's *Florentine Tragedy* (1894) who has no eyes for his wife's beauty until she starts an affair with Prince Guido, a fine specimen of gilded youth who puts his nose out of joint. Likewise, Queensberry's latent love for his son (whom he believed he hated wholeheartedly) was typically only awakened when an outsider had stepped on to the stage: Oscar Wilde, the famous artist in whose company Bosie preferred to be, Oscar Wilde, whose charm had beguiled the Marquess in the Café Royal. His admiration for him had afterwards changed, as we have seen, into an almost pathological aversion. Whence this somersault? It would seem that Queensberry – on second thoughts, as it were – regarded Oscar as a *rival*; and he treated him accordingly. You love to hate the one who loves the one you hate to love but love.

The merchant in the above-mentioned play finally throttles the prince with his bare hands. Queensberry's method was slightly more subtle: by provoking his antagonist to drag him into the courtroom, the Marquess induced Oscar to put his own neck in the noose.

It was the London correspondent of a Dutch newspaper who explained to his readers just how abominably clever Queensberry's tactics had been. The Marquess had handed his infamous card *openly* to the porter of the Albemarle Club, who had read it and then put it into an envelope. Oscar, in other words, had been *publicly* libelled; and according to the reporter there was an unwritten club rule compelling a member whose honour had been thus impugned on the club's premises to resort to the law to clear his reputation. Anyone disobeying this rule would tacitly admit that he was not a gentleman and automatically lose his membership of all the clubs to which he belonged.[5]

Oscar was left without much of a choice; and, anyhow, there would always have come another insult, and another, and yet another, for his enemy was nothing if not pertinacious.

Bosie never denied that he had encouraged Oscar to bring an action against 'Q', but there is no doubt that even without his incitement Oscar was determined to do so. It is a little-known fact – in *De Profundis* it is passed over in silence – that after the first night of *The Importance of Being Earnest* Oscar had tried to prosecute Queensberry because of his efforts to disturb the performance. Bosie was not involved in this. He did not even know what was going on, for he was still in Algeria ('held fast by the lassoo of desire to a sugar-lipped lad' named Ali)[6] and only returned, post-haste, when his brother informed him of their father's machinations. 'I had not wished you to know,' Oscar had written in a letter that Bosie found on arriving in Paris. 'Percy wired you without telling me. I am greatly touched by your rushing over Europe. For my own part I had determined you should know nothing. I feel now that, without your name being mentioned, all will go well.'[7]

Oscar believed that he would succeed in spiking Queensberry's guns; but the solicitors he consulted later concluded that it would be unwise to venture upon a prosecution, since the theatrical manager and his staff, whose testimony would be indispensable to Oscar, absolutely refused to cooperate.[8] What Oscar needed was *tangible evidence* of Queensberry's smear campaign. He got it soon enough.

Oscar, according to Bosie, did not inform him of Queensberry's next move (the visiting-card with inscription) and his reaction (another visit, with Bobbie Ross, to the office of Humphreys, Son and Kershaw, solicitors) until after a warrant had been obtained for Queensberry's arrest.[9] Bosie fully endorsed Oscar's decision; he only expressed surprise that he had turned to Humphreys, Son and Kershaw. Why, Bosie asked, had Oscar not called on his old friend, Sir George Lewis, of the firm of Lewis and Lewis? That was a pertinent question; we shall return to it later.

Queensberry meanwhile claimed he had libelled Oscar 'for the public benefit'. To win his trial, he had to prove that Oscar 'posed as a somdomite'. A written statement of his allegations, a plea of justification, was drawn up and, according to rule, handed to the other side.

In the course of the magistrates' court proceedings in Great Marlborough Street on 9 March, Queensberry's evidence appeared scanty. He possessed a letter from Oscar to Bosie which had been passed to him by professional blackmailers; in addition, he intended to have Oscar cross-examined about the supposed immorality of his works.

The trial was fixed for 3 April. Oscar and Bosie were looking forward to it with confidence. 'I saw Humphreys today,' Bosie wrote excitedly to his brother Percy. 'He says everything is splendid and we are going to walk over.'[10] The businessman Ernest Leverson had advanced £500 to pay the costs, Oscar himself had raised £800, and Bosie had managed to scrape together £360. This money was now partly spent, foolishly, on a short holiday in Monte Carlo.

While the two were amusing themselves abroad, Queensberry, released on bail, did not remain idle. He hired a number of private detectives, former policemen, who diligently began to look for supplementary evidence. Before long they had tracked down a group of male prostitutes who were made to understand that they themselves would end up in gaol if they refused to testify against Oscar. Incidentally, Queensberry's assistants did not scruple to disregard the law. Thus the premises of Alfred Taylor, a procurer whose compromising correspondence was seized, were invaded without a search warrant.

When Oscar and Bosie returned to London they found at the office of Humphreys, Son and Kershaw their opponent's revised plea of justification. It enumerated the names of no fewer than ten young men whom Oscar 'had debauched with unnatural vice',[11] which ought to have convinced him that he had no earthly chance of emerging victorious from the contest. His friends did their utmost to impress this upon him. Frank Harris, for instance, the former editor of the *Fortnightly Review*, urged him to leave the country. But Oscar was like those who, having ears, hear not.

Bosie was equally deaf to his friends' pleas. His optimism was founded on his conviction that he would be able to take the wind out of the defence sails by laying bare Queensberry's past in the witness box. He intended to explain two things to the jury: that a sybarite such as the Marquess was the last person who had a right to accuse somebody else of being immoral; and that Queensberry should not be seen as a tender father who only meant well by him (Bosie) but, on the contrary, as a practising misanthrope whose aim was to humiliate his son and blast the career of his son's friend. These disclosures, Bosie believed, would ensure Oscar's victory, and he gave a 'proof' (a written statement) of his proposed evidence to Humphreys.[12] The youngster was itching to be called as a witness; Michel van der Plas's observation that Bosie expected 'he could safely sit on the side-line' is therefore peculiarly inept, as is his remark that 'he knew, really, that Wilde would lose his case'.[13] Bosie had not the slightest idea of jurisprudence. He was but twenty-four, 'absolutely fearless, sceptical of danger at all times', in Ross's words,[14] and incapable of adequately judging the situation.

From the forty-year-old Oscar, on the other hand, more common sense might have been expected. He had been in court when the celebrated Parnell case was being heard[15] and should therefore have known that a trial was no child's play. Why, then, did he obstinately refuse to drop his action against Queensberry?

To answer this question one has to analyse Oscar's character, as Hesketh Pearson pointed out;[16] and such an analysis shows that his attitude towards the trial was ambiguous. He was convinced he would win it; and he was convinced he would lose it. The paradox is that *both* viewpoints induced him not to back off.

Success had gone to Oscar's head, and he consequently under-estimated the risks he was taking. He was a famous man ('the fashion', a reviewer had recently written), a wit whose comedies drew packed houses; the Prince of Wales and the Prime Minister attended his first nights and deigned to compliment him afterwards – or, more precisely, he deigned to receive their compliments afterwards. The smart set's darling, he fancied himself invulnerable, unassailable; why should he fear Queensberry? Should Oscar Wilde, the Lord of Language, really bother about an individual who was incapable even of correctly spelling his insults? To think he would be unable to hold his own against such a buffoon was ridiculous, really.

At the same time Oscar was fully aware that he was marching to his downfall. He was not only a playwright but also, and chiefly, an *actor*. He saw himself as a symbolic figure,[17] as the protagonist of an exciting drama – a drama that would be incomplete without catastrophe. *De Profundis* reveals his fascination with Christ; he considered Him to be an artist,[18] himself to be a second Messiah. The ovations of those who had queued to see his plays had been his hosannahs. Now the time for his Golgotha had come.[19]

If 'the fatality of the friendship' between Oscar and Bosie really lay in the fact 'that one of [these] two was bent on destruction',[20] it was not, as Michel van der Plas maintains, Bosie who wished to destroy Oscar (why on earth should he?); Oscar himself was resolved to jump headlong into the sea. It was in his nature. 'Sometimes I think that the artistic life is a long and lovely suicide,' he had written to an admirer once, 'and am not sorry that it is so.'[21]

Such a state of mind explains why Oscar turned to Humphreys, Son and Kershaw and not to his friend Sir George Lewis. Lewis, he said, 'knows all about us – and forgives us all'.[22] Lewis would have pointed out to him that bringing an action against Queensberry would be madness; he would have thrown the visiting-card in the fire, as he told Oscar when the latter came to see him afterwards, when it was too late. Oscar knew this and so went to Humphreys, who was wholly ignorant of his private life. Sir Edward Clarke, the advocate whom Humphreys begged to represent Oscar, declared he would only do so if Mr Wilde would assure him on his word of honour that the accusations against him were completely untrue. Oscar stood up and solemnly swore he was innocent.

It is not inconceivable that in consultation he referred to the case of *Gatty v. Farquharson*. There was, he may have told Clarke, an exact parallel with his own case against 'Q'. And Clarke, who had defended Farquharson, may well have believed him.

Charles Tindall Gatty, born in 1851, was a friend of Oscar and Bosie – he was one of Bosie's 'many admirers',[23] as Oscar put it – who in 1892 had tried to become a Liberal member of the House of Commons. The voters of West Dorset had not elected him, and Gatty accused his rival, Henry R. Farquharson (Conservative), of having resorted to a dirty-tricks campaign to win the election, the MP having claimed on the hustings that Gatty had been expelled from Charterhouse School for 'abominable' (that is, gay) practices and that in later years he had had immoral relations with printers' boys at Yeovil. Gatty had brought an action for libel and slander in 1893, and the jury had found for him, awarding him £5,000 damages, which, Clarke had protested, was an 'excessive' amount.[24]

Was Gatty, a life-long bachelor, a homosexual? Had there been any truth in Farquharson's stories? We do not know. But his successful litigation is likely to have influenced Oscar.

In the days preceding the trial Oscar endeavoured to cheer up his wife and friends by telling them that he and Bosie had consulted Mrs Robinson. A few months previously this soothsayer had foretold that he would make 'a long voyage'[25] with Bosie in January. This prediction had come true; but the 'Sybil of Mortimer Street', as Oscar styled her, was wide of the mark when on 25 March she promised him 'a complete triumph'. It was a prophecy that only strengthened the superstitious Oscar's resolution *not* to abscond. He let events take their course; the die had been cast.

The public gallery of the Old Bailey, where the case of *Regina v. Queensberry* opened on 3 April, was packed with curious spectators when the principal actors made their appearance. Women were denied admittance; they were supposed to be too highly strung to attend such a trial.

The prosecutor and the defendant formed a curious contrast. Oscar was exceptionally well groomed. The Marquess was dressed like a stableman[26] and never stopped sucking the brim of his hat, a habit that would increasingly get on Oscar's nerves. In *De Profundis* he spoke of Queensberry's 'bestial grin' and 'apelike face';[27] Queensberry on his side perceived a striking resemblance between Oscar and an iguanodon, a prehistoric amphibious herbivore of colossal dimensions, a picture of which had recently been reproduced in the *Illustrated London News*.[28]

After the indictment had been read, the Marquess was formally asked if he pleaded guilty or not guilty to the charge brought against him – criminal libel.

'Not guilty,' Queensberry answered, casting a contemptuous glance at Oscar.

It was for Clarke to speak now. Truth to tell, his personal appearance was not very attractive. He was below middle height, and of sturdy figure; his face had a strong, almost harsh expression, which might have been mellowed by his brown eyes had they not been half closed under his heavy brows. His whiskers were of the Henrik Ibsen variety (and did not greatly appeal to Bosie). A Freemason and a pious man, Clarke ruminated much on the hereafter; when he was cremated in 1931 his ashes were placed in an urn designed for the occasion which had stood on a bookcase in his dining-room for the last thirty years of his life.[29] With hindsight he was not the ideal advocate for Oscar, with whom he can have felt but slight affinity. Moreover, Merlin Holland's recent research has shown that Sir Edward was not particularly well briefed, and that he even unwittingly provided 'Q' and his legal advisers with additional ammunition by divulging in court information previously unknown to them.[30]

The tone of his opening speech was moderate – much too moderate, thought Bosie, who had expected a violent onslaught on his father. Clarke first sketched the background of the affair. The insult hurled at Mr Wilde – Mr Wilde was alleged to wish to be thought a sodomite – was so gross, he said, that his client could not possibly ignore it. The defendant's plea of justification went a step further: it stated that the prosecutor had been really guilty of unnatural sex offences. Well, it was up to those who had drawn up this document to establish the truth of these accusations.

In an effort to strike a pre-emptive blow at the defence, Clarke then read out a letter from Oscar to Bosie. Its tone was rather high-flown (the recipient was compared with Hyacinthus); but, said Clarke, the sender is a poet, his choice of words poetical. *Honi soit qui mal y pense.*

Finally Sir Edward expressed his amazement at the imputation that *The Picture of Dorian Gray* featured characters whose lifestyle resembled that of the citizens of Sodom and Gomorrah. On the contrary, Clarke argued, the novel was a moral tale in which the hero (the anti-hero, really) ultimately has to pay for his wicked ways.

After his speech Clarke examined first the porter of the Albemarle Club (who had received Queensberry's card) and then his client. Oscar categorically denied ever having transgressed Section 11 of the Criminal Law Amendment Act (the paragraph proscribing all sexual contacts between males).

Then it was the turn of Queensberry's counsel, Edward Carson. A contemporary commented on his 'queer Dublin brogue', his self-possession and 'absence of all pretence at either culture or breeding'. His hair was smooth and black, his profile of almost perfect, if creepy, handsomeness. He looked like a hangman.[31] Oscar knew him; they had been at Trinity College together. 'No doubt he will perform his task with all the added bitterness of an old friend,' he had quipped at being told with whom he had to cross swords.[32]

Carson proved to be a formidable opponent. His very first question undermined Oscar's credibility. The latter had told Clarke that his age was thirty-nine, but Carson knew better. The prosecutor was forty, wasn't he? And the lawyer held up a copy of his birth certificate. A surprised Oscar had to grant that Mr Carson was right.

The jurors frowned. Oscar seemed not to realize that his fate lay in their hands, and that he should not antagonize them. He assumed the air of a great artist, slighting 'illiterate persons' – a blunder, for the middle-class men who made up the jury might feel he was referring to them.

Carson made much of *The Chameleon*, Bloxam's periodical in which Oscar's 'Phrases and Philosophies for the Use of the Young' had appeared, and of *The Picture of Dorian Gray*. Was that last-named work not a classic example of a sodomitical novel? Oscar shrugged his shoulders. He was concerned only with his own views on art, he said; he didn't care tuppence that some bigots thought *Dorian Gray* improper.

Carson quoted a passage wherein the painter Basil Hallward admitted he adored Dorian 'madly, extravagantly, absurdly'. Surely that was a description of unnatural passion? Did Mr Wilde ever have such feelings for a young man? 'I have never given adoration to anybody except myself,' Oscar answered.[33] But one of his letters to Bosie that Carson produced – 'You are the divine thing I want, the thing of grace and genius'[34] – seemed to tell a different story. Wasn't that a sinister epistle? Not at all, Oscar said. Only in the eyes of philistines, perhaps, who lacked the culture to appreciate his poetical style. But it transpired that he had once paid about £20 to a blackmailer to regain the original of another letter to Bosie (of which several copies had been made).[35]

Initially, Oscar put up a fairly good show during Carson's cross-examination. At any rate, he was extremely quick-witted.

'Iced champagne is a favourite drink of mine, strongly against my doctor's orders,' he remarked when tackled about his dinner parties with a couple of gitons.

'Never mind your doctor's orders, sir!' an irritated Carson barked.

'I never do,' said Oscar, suavely, amid hearty laughter.[36]

He only realized the importance of being earnest when it was too late. On the second day of the trial Carson wondered if he had ever kissed a servant called Grainger.

'Oh, dear no!' Oscar blurted out. 'He was a peculiarly plain boy. I pitied him for it.'

Got you! Carson must have thought. 'Was that,' he immediately asked, 'the reason why you did not kiss him?'

'Oh! Mr Carson, you are pertinently insolent.'[37]

But the advocate did not desist from repeating the question, kept repeating the question. Oscar, upset, mumbled inaudible and incoherent answers. From the gallery, no doubt, the traditional buzzing was heard. Bosie must have cringed.

The jurors, who during the initial stages of the trial had got the impression that the prosecutor felt immensely superior to them, were astonished when it now dawned upon them that he liked the company of grooms and valets out of employment – loafers whom they, as respectable bourgeois, tended to despise. Oscar Wilde, it appeared, had treated such vermin to caviare and champagne; he had given them money, had presented them with inscribed silver cigarette cases. What services had they returned? None whatever, Oscar said. Had these boys not been introduced to him by Alfred Taylor? Indeed. And what kind of person was Taylor? Counsel for the defence described him as an individual who, after squandering an inherited fortune of £45,000, had settled in Little College Street, a rough neighbourhood. Taylor had been under police surveillance for quite some time, for in his house (a veritable *lupanar*, gentlemen!) activities took place that could not bear the light of day. The curtains there were always drawn. Meetings were arranged at this place between youths and elderly men who were prepared to spend large sums of money to satisfy their unnatural lusts. And this Taylor, who burned perfumes in his rooms, who kept *a lady's costume* in his wardrobe, this Taylor, who drove his landlady mad, belonged to the intimates of Oscar Wilde! *You can tell a man by the company he keeps!*

Carson's rhetoric did not fail to impress the jury. He announced he had another surprise in store: there were some boys waiting in an adjacent room whom he would call as witnesses and who would explain to what they *really* owed their silver cigarette cases.

In court the tension was almost palpable. When at the end of the afternoon the case was adjourned, Sir Edward knew that his client was lost and that there remained but one thing to be done: the prosecution of Queensberry had to be abandoned at once.

Oscar, on being told this next morning, agreed with his counsel. One of Clarke's juniors, however, wished to fight on, drawing attention to the fact that the defence witnesses were criminals and blackmailers whose testimony might well be discredited. But Clarke knew better, and his opinion prevailed. Besides, it seems that during secret negotiations he had been assured that if the case was dropped nothing more would be heard of the matter.[38]

Carson meanwhile had resumed his opening speech. He was speaking of the prosecutor's dressing up a newsvendor like a respectable, upper-class lad ('Has there ever been confessed in a Court of Justice a more audacious story?')[39] when Sir Edward came in and pulled his colleague's gown. In a low voice the two exchanged a few words, whereupon Carson sat down, and Clarke made a momentous declaration. Mr Wilde, he said, gave up his prosecution of Lord Queensberry, admitting to 'having posed as a sodomite' as far as his letters to Lord Alfred, the publication of *The Picture of Dorian Gray* and his contribution to *The Chameleon* were concerned.

The jurors thereupon deliberated without leaving the box. Their conclusion came as no surprise: the defendant was found *not guilty*, a verdict that was frantically cheered by most of the onlookers.

In the meantime Oscar and Bosie had left the Old Bailey by a side door. The latter greatly blamed Sir Edward for not having called him as a witness; he was convinced – and would remain so to his dying day – that he would have been able to turn the tide by telling the court what sort of man his father was. In this he was wrong. Revelations about Queensberry were quite irrelevant and would not have affected the evidence against Oscar in the slightest. But the fact remains that Bosie and his brother Percy were the only ones who were willing publicly to stand in the breach for Oscar; friends such as Frank Harris (who had been asked to testify to the morality of *Dorian Gray*) had collectively cried off.

It was clear that Oscar could be apprehended at any moment. During lunch at the Holburn Viaduct Restaurant (their appetite must have been small) and afterwards in rooms at the Cadogan which Bosie had booked, Bosie, Reginald Turner and Robbie urged the writer to leave the country while there yet remained an opportunity to do so. Constance, too, hoped that her husband would flee to France. But he was not susceptible to reason, drank one glass after the other and gazed apathetically at the flames in the hearth, muttering that the boat-train had already left. And time went by.

Bosie could bear this tension no longer and went to Westminster Palace shortly before five o'clock to ask one of his cousins, who was an MP, if Oscar would really be charged. The cousin, who had spoken to the Director of Public Prosecutions, told him that this was indeed the case; that a warrant for Oscar's arrest had been issued, and that . . .

'Sloane Street!' Bosie shouted while jumping in the cab which had been waiting for him, and as quickly as possible the coachman drove back to the hotel. But when Bosie tore up the stairs and breathlessly entered his rooms, he found nobody there. His *amicissimus* had been taken in by Scotland Yard.

The arrest of Oscar Wilde

4

A Decadent's Downfall

IT is no exaggeration to compare the reaction of the press and the public to the arrest of Oscar Wilde with the frenzy that overtakes sharks that smell blood. 'Kill the bugger!' ran a telegram which Queensberry was proud to receive,[1] and that was the tenor of the leading articles in most of the evening papers. Oscar could not expect much sympathy from journalists; the disdain with which he had spoken about their profession had made him many enemies who now took the opportunity to curse him – and to curse him with glee. *Schadenfreude* masquerading as moral outrage was rife. The *National Observer*, for instance, admitted preferring a coroner's inquest to another trial,[2] while another paper published an imaginary description of Oscar's first night behind bars – how the prisoner, a prey to insomnia, never stopped pacing up and down in his tiny cell.[3] Oscar, in one of his essays, had called the press the modern equivalent of the medieval rack;[4] the truth of this comparison was conclusively shown in the days following the collapse of his action against 'Q'.

Bosie meanwhile hurried to Bow Street Police Station where Oscar was held[5] and was told there that several sureties were needed before his friend's release on bail could even be contemplated. He therefore turned to the managers in whose theatres Oscar's comedies were being performed. Although the plays had proved extremely lucrative, these gentlemen felt disinclined to support the disgraced author financially; they did not wish to compromise themselves. What was it Mrs Cheveley had said in *An Ideal Husband*? 'Scandals used to lend charm, or at least interest, to a man. Now they crush him. And yours is a very nasty scandal.'[6]

It was, and Bosie was involved in it up to his neck. His name was mentioned in the same breath with Oscar's, his reputation lambasted by pressmen – the English were as kindly disposed towards him as the *tricoteuses* had been to members of the Bourbon family. Rumours circulated that his arrest was impending,[7] and he was urged on all sides to follow the example set by Ross and other homosexual friends of Oscar and to depart. Lady Queensberry begged her son once and for all to break with 'that man' against whom she had warned him over and over again; she adjured him to be 'sensible', to mind his future and to pack his trunks. But the 'miserable youth', the 'lily-livered, lily-fingered sensualist' (as a reporter described him),[8] refused to hurry from the sinking ship like a rat. 'He is quite insane on the subject,' a cousin sighed.[9]

This was Bosie's finest hour. Pending his trial, Oscar was transferred to Holloway Prison, and in the weeks that followed only one person, apart from his solicitor, came to see him every day: Alfred Bruce Douglas. The couple were allowed only fifteen minutes each twenty-four hours to speak to each other – in so far as they managed to make themselves understood, that is. Visits in Holloway were mass meetings; the buzzing of inmates and their friends or relatives, separated by a corridor about a yard in width, swelled into a cacophony which rendered a normal conversation impossible, especially for Oscar, who was hard of hearing. These visits from Bosie nevertheless kept him going during this period, as is revealed in his letters to Ada Leverson and others. Thus he wrote on 9 April: 'Not that I am really alone. A slim thing, gold-haired like an angel, stands always at my side. His presence overshadows me. He moves in the gloom like a white flower.' On 15 April: 'Sometimes there is sunlight in my cell, and every day someone whose name is Love comes to see me, and weeps so much through prison-bars that it is I who have to comfort him.' And on 23 April: 'I feel caught in a terrible net. I don't know where to turn. I care less when I think that [Bosie] is thinking of me. I think of nothing else.'[10]

Sir Edward's thoughts were concentrated on his client's trial. Although Oscar had lied to his counsel when assuring him that he was innocent, Clarke had generously offered to continue to represent him, although he knew that the artist, whose effects had been auctioned by order of his creditors, was unable to pay his fee. Clarke, however, made one condition: Lord Alfred had to leave the country. Oscar had considerable difficulty in persuading his friend to do so. After a heart-rending farewell, Bosie, coerced and under protest, embarked for France on 27 April.[11]

On the previous day the second act had begun of what would turn out to be a legal drama in three acts. Oscar, who looked tired, appeared in the dock along with Alfred Taylor. The latter had nobly refused to avail himself of the opportunity of saving his own skin by giving evidence against Oscar.

Their opponent was Charles Gill. Until recently this lawyer had defended rapists who were active in the parks of London; but when it became increasingly difficult for him to 'get them off', owing to the improved illumination of their hunting-grounds, he had moved to the Treasury.[12]

The witnesses he called did not mince their words when describing what had occurred at the Savoy Hotel and in Oscar's rooms at St James's Place. 'In England,' a Dutch journalist commented, 'literature, the stage and life in general are squeamish to a degree beyond our comprehension. But as soon as one finds oneself in the Courtroom, things change drastically; there everything, literally *everything* is openly said; even the smallest detail of whatever scandal may be aired.'[13]

One of the witnesses the prosecution had drilled (his name was Sidney Mavor) did not, however, live up to expectations. Previously he had made a statement incriminating Oscar, but to Gill's considerable surprise he now denied all accusations of immorality. True, he said, Mr Wilde had dined with him; Mr Wilde, indeed, had pulled his ear and had chucked him under the chin – that was all.

Exit Sidney Mavor! His change of front was owing to Bosie, who had argued with him shortly after Oscar's arrest; a former public-school boy such as Mavor would surely not sink to the level of scum like – and – (two professional blackmailers) by giving evidence against Oscar, just like them? Why not deny in court what he had told the police? Mavor, grabbing Bosie's hand, had promised to do this. And he kept his word.[14]

Clarke succeeded in disposing of yet another witness by exposing him as a perjurer. But Gill had more strings to his bow. A hotel manager explained that his decision to refuse Oscar as a guest had been connected with the unsavoury character of the young men the defendant used to receive in his rooms, and chambermaids blushingly described the state of Oscar's sheets: peculiarly stained. Things were looking pretty bad for him.

On the fourth day of the trial Oscar was cross-examined yet again on *The Chameleon*. Disregarding Clarke's protests, the prosecutor discussed at great length Bosie's lyrics which had appeared in this magazine. Although thematically resembling poems of writers such as Theocritus, Virgil and Catullus (not to mention Elizabethan sonneteers such as Richard Barnfield), they were labelled by Gill as 'literary poison'. Perhaps Mr Wilde could understand that a piece like 'In Praise of Shame' could not pass muster with healthy-minded persons? A question of taste, Oscar thought. Whereupon Gill, with unmistakable sarcasm, read out the closing lines of 'Two Loves'.

> 'Sweet youth,
> Tell me why, sad and sighing, thou dost rove
> These pleasant realms? I pray thee speak me sooth
> What is thy name?' He said, 'My name is Love.'
> Then straight the first did turn himself to me
> And cried, 'He lieth, for his name is Shame,
> But I am Love, and I was wont to be
> Alone in this fair garden, till he came
> Unasked by night; I am true Love, I fill
> The hearts of boy and girl with mutual flame.'
> Then sighing said the other, 'Have thy will,
> I am the Love that dare not speak its name.'

Gill begged Oscar to elucidate this fragment. Were we dealing here with the glorification of some sexual aberration? What exactly was meant by 'the Love that dare not speak its name'? It was a question Oscar had foreseen. He answered:

'The Love that dare not speak its name' in this century is such a great affection of an elder for a younger man as there was between David and Jonathan, such as Plato made the very basis of his philosophy, and such as you find in the sonnets of Michelangelo and Shakespeare. It is that deep, spiritual affection that is as pure as it is perfect. It dictates and pervades great works of art like those of Shakespeare and Michelangelo, and those two letters of mine [to Lord Alfred], such as they are. It is in this century misunderstood, so much misunderstood that it may be described as 'the Love that dare not speak its name', and on account of it I am placed where I am now. It is beautiful, it is fine, it is the noblest form of affection. There is nothing unnatural about it. It is intellectual, and it repeatedly

Wilde in the dock; the cover of the sensational *Illustrated Police News*, 4 May 1895

exists between an elder and a younger man, when the elder has intellect, and the younger man has all the joy, hope and glamour of life before him. That it should be so, the world does not understand. The world mocks at it, and sometimes puts one in the pillory for it.[15]

Now this was an eloquent description of Oscar's friendship with Bosie – a friendship which had developed into a platonic relation. But Oscar was not on trial for his intimacy with Bosie, as he maintained, and he was not condemned because he had written passionate letters to him, as he would claim in *De Profundis*;[16] what was laid to his charge were more prosaic liaisons. He got two years' hard labour – to quote Bernard Shaw – on account of his 'wretched debaucheries with gutter-snipes',[17] affairs that could not be termed 'intellectual'.

None the less his words made a tremendous impression. The public gallery gave him an outright ovation. 'Here was this man,' Max Beerbohm reported to a friend, 'who had been for a month in prison and loaded with insults and crushed and buffeted, perfectly self-possessed, dominating the Old Bailey with his fine presence and musical voice. He has never had so great a triumph, I am sure.'[18]

The case dragged on. Taylor was cross-examined; Clarke made his final speech, followed by that of Taylor's counsel. Charles Gill incited the jury to find the defendants guilty; finally the judge summed up, and the jurors retired to discuss their verdict behind closed doors.

One hundred and sixty-five minutes crept by.

Then the twelve took their places again. The foreman addressed the judge and declared that it had been impossible for them to arrive at an agreement. This irresolution, to which Oscar's moving words had undoubtedly contributed, made a new trial necessary. In the meantime, Sir Edward contended, Oscar had to be set at liberty forthwith. But bureaucracy's mills grind slowly, and a whole week elapsed before he could leave Holloway on 7 May. Bail was fixed at £5,000; this vast sum was jointly raised by Oscar himself, by Percy Douglas and by the Reverend Stewart Headlam. The last named was almost stoned by an angry mob who disapproved of his charitable act.

Queensberry's cronies made it impossible for Oscar to put up at a hotel. They disclosed his identity to the managers, who promptly turned him out. Eventually he found shelter in the house of his mother, but her company and that of his elder brother, Willie, did not improve his peace of mind. Lady Wilde, reduced to a bibulous wreck, pointed out to her son that to jump bail would be to blot the family's scutcheon; Willie, not exactly a teetotaller himself, defended Oscar by proclaiming he had 'a good character': 'You can trust him with a woman anywhere,' he said. Then there was the journalist, Robert Harborough Sherard, who, calling on his friend, heartened him by predicting he would get two years' hard labour and who explained to him how to make prussic acid in case he wished to commit suicide.

Oscar's deplorable situation – '[He] is all day steeping himself in liquor and moaning for Boasy!'[19] the editor of the *National Observer* wrote sadistically to a colleague – reached the ears of Ada and Ernest Leverson. They invited Oscar to come to stay with them, an invitation he gratefully accepted. Under the care of this Jewish couple the author visibly recuperated; at dinner his conversation sparkled as of old. But there was one subject he refused to discuss: the possibility of taking refuge abroad. That, he said, was incompatible with his sense of honour. Besides, his flight would result in confiscation of bail, and he did not want to fail the parson and Percy Douglas. The latter, however, had promised to cover Headlam's expenses; and although the loss of £2,500 would almost ruin him he urged Oscar to clear out 'for God's sake'. But Oscar did not avail himself of this chance, to the despair of Bosie, who had expected shortly to be reunited with him in Paris.

While the preparations for the third trial were in full swing, the Solicitor General, Sir Frank Lockwood, who was due to lead the prosecution, received a visit from Edward Carson. Carson, who during the first round had pressed Oscar exceedingly hard, now begged Lockwood to spare the artist. His career was at an end, his effects had been flogged; wasn't that enough? Lockwood answered that a new trial was 'unavoidable'.

Was the Treasury put under pressure to obtain a conviction of Oscar at all costs? There was, in the words of Sir Edward Hamilton, 'a wide-felt impression that the Judge and Jury were on the last occasion *got at*, in order to shield others of a higher status in life',[20] which impression the government may have wanted to remove by acting towards Oscar with the utmost rigour. It is surmised, also, that Queensberry had threatened, if Oscar was allowed to escape incarceration, to reveal the ins and outs of the death of his eldest son, Francis. He was supposed to have died during a hunting party by the accidental explosion of his gun; in fact, he had killed himself, and it was rumoured that his act of desperation was linked to his intimate – all too intimate – relation with

Lord Rosebery, the then Foreign Secretary, a homosexual who had made him his private factotum.[21]

We may be brief as regards the third trial. Oscar and Taylor were tried separately; Taylor was found guilty on 21 May. Queensberry, greatly rejoicing, dispatched a telegram to his daughter-in-law, Percy's wife, congratulating her on the verdict and, in passing, comparing her husband's complexion with that of a dug-up corpse. He habitually sent her such messages; they were received with mixed feelings.

It so happened that Percy came across his father when the latter was leaving the post office. He politely begged him to cease upsetting his wife, whereupon the Marquess blew a raspberry. To the onlookers' amazement, father and son then began to exchange blows. Some people mistook Percy for Bosie and encouraged 'Q' to teach him a lesson. A bobby succeeded in separating them; they were charged with disorderly behaviour and bound over. Percy, according to the *Illustrated Police News* which published a lurid woodcut of the scuffle, 'had suffered the discoloration of one eye', while his father's silk hat 'showed signs of rather rough usage'.[22]

In the interim Oscar's trial had commenced. Lockwood inquired after Lord Alfred's whereabouts and wanted to know if the defendant was still in touch with him.

'Certainly,' Oscar answered. 'These charges are founded on sand. Our friendship is founded on a rock. There has been no need to cancel the acquaintance.'[23]

One of the jurors wondered 'why Lord Alfred Douglas had not been arrested'. He had received letters from Mr Wilde, hadn't he? Now then!

The curtain came down on 25 May. The jury was satisfied that Oscar was guilty on all counts save one; Taylor joined him in the dock to hear what the judge had in store for them. Sir Alfred Wills (that was his name) first delivered himself of a sermon. He called the case 'the worst [he] had ever tried'. The defendants were 'dead to all sense of shame'. The maximum sentence he could pass, and would pass, he deemed 'totally inadequate'. Both men got the penalty of two years' hard labour.

Taylor took it with British phlegm. Oscar turned pale and staggered. 'And I?' he stammered. 'May I say nothing, my Lord?'[24]

But Wills motioned to the warders, and under a murmur of approval emanating from the majority of those present the prisoners were escorted out of the courtroom.

Hypocrisy had pervaded these proceedings. It can be detected, first, in Queensberry, who had purposely provoked the litigation. He called himself a 'freethinker' and a champion of 'free love', but his notions of freethinking and free love were apparently *conditional*. It was noted before that his 'solicitude for his son' (highly praised by the newspapers) was really a cloak. The peer wished to get even with Bosie and Oscar and hit his son by disgracing his son's friend. He thus managed to kill two birds with one stone.

The judges and prosecutors were hypocritical, too. They pretended to view gay sex as a crime hardly less serious than murder; but they had all been at public school and Oxbridge – institutions where Greek Love may be said to have formed part of the curriculum.[25]

Nor can Oscar himself be altogether absolved from hypocrisy. A martyr he was not. A martyr, after all, proclaims his beliefs. Oscar held gay relations to be 'more noble' than straight ones;[26] but he sued Queensberry for insinuating that he was 'a sodomite' and strenuously denied all accusations brought against him, calling them 'filthy suggestions'.

Oscar fell victim to a stupid, draconian law, and for this he deserves our compassion. He had not corrupted any cherubs; his partners had been 'accomplices', criminals for the greater part, whose countenance, to quote a journalist, 'rendered an interrogation superfluous'.[27]

Bosie, when nearing the end of his life, reflected on the punishment meted out to his friend and remarked that the authorities should have remembered the words Christ had spoken to the Pharisees, who had asked him if a woman who had been caught in the act of adultery should be stoned to death in accordance with Moses' law. 'Let him who is without sin cast the first stone,' said Jesus. And the Pharisees slunk off.

'How,' Bosie wondered, 'can it ever be justifiable for a judge and a jury to send a man to the torture and horror of two years' hard labour for an offence against morals? If they were all sinless saints they *wouldn't* do it, and if they were (as they would be) ordinary human beings and sinners they *couldn't* do it without staining their own consciences.'[28]

Oscar, in a famous passage in *De Profundis*, predicted how the three protagonists in the drama that had landed him behind bars would be classified in the future. Queensberry, he said, would pass for one of those pure-minded fathers who figure in Sunday-School tracts. Bosie would be compared with the Infant Samuel. He himself would

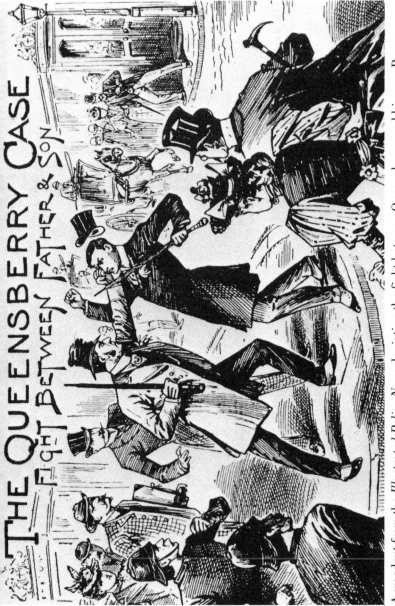

A woodcut from the *Illustrated Police News* depicting the fight between Queensberry and his son, Percy

be placed in Hell, somewhere between Gilles de Retz (a fifteenth-century satanist not exactly noted for his sympathetic treatment of boys) and the Marquis de Sade.[29]

This prediction would be but partially fulfilled. Queensberry did indeed win the applause of the votaries of virtue, but it did not last long. They realized that their hero was deficient in many points; his atheism and his promiscuity were neither forgotten nor forgiven, and soon he was shunned as before. All in all, his crusade against Oscar gave him a hangover which he vainly tried to drown in alcohol. He was profoundly unhappy.

Bosie, by his involvement in the scandal of the century, remained stigmatized for the rest of his life. The reaction, many years afterwards, of Mrs Quiller-Couch to her husband's suggestion to invite Bosie for the weekend is typical. 'My dearr Arrthurr,' she cried, aghast (speaking in her Cornish accent), 'we can't have that man here with small children in the house!'[30]

Oscar's comments in *De Profundis* on his own reputation were far more accurate. His name had become, quite literally, taboo: English boys would not be christened 'Oscar' for quite some time. Decent folk were supposed to hate Mr Wilde and all his works.

This was brought home at the turn of the century to a student, Montague Summers. He was having tea with a friend in the drawing-room one day when suddenly the door was flung open, and the master of the house rushed in, furious and purple-faced.

'Is this filthy thing yours?' he yelled, hurling a copy of Oscar's *Ballad of Reading Gaol* on the table.

Montague picked up the book, carefully, almost reverently closing it. 'Yeth, Father,' he answered mellifluously, lisping as always when he wanted to vex Summers Senior, 'yeth, Father. I have all the workth of the Mathter.'

Whereat he was given the choice to clear out the works of the master or to clear out himself (the works were temporarily sheltered by the friend).[31]

In England the Wilde affair had far-reaching consequences. For not only the homosexual but also the artist had been crucified. Wilde had hymned beauty; Wilde was 'a somdomite'; therefore art should be suspected. 'Beauty' had become a byword, a contemporary observed.[32] Art was something for degenerate weaklings and carpet knights, not something for healthy, muscular fellows (many asthenics seem to have hurriedly joined the local cricket club). Even wit and humour were distrusted. Pray remain as inconspicuous as you possibly can: that appeared to be the motto. Oscar's downfall, in a sense, marked the triumph of mediocrity.

Oscar himself said that his 'record of perversities of passion and distorted romances' might 'fill many scarlet volumes',[33] and some scribblers did not hesitate to introduce him in their pornographic effusions. Thus he was given an active, or a passive, role in the apocryphal confessions of the poet Jacques d'Adelswärd-Fersen, *Les Mémoires du baron Jacques. Lubricités infernales de la noblesse décadente*, ('Priapeville, An IV du XXe siècle foutatif', Paris, 1904), a novel that was sold under the counter.[34]

But there was another side to the Wilde affair as well. In the traumatic days that followed his arrest the author kept up a regular correspondence with Bosie. Bosie's letters were destroyed after Oscar's death by Robert Ross. Oscar's were cherished for many years by Bosie; they prevented them, he said, from putting an end to his life; he 'kissed them and prayed over them day and night';[35] on rare occasions he would show them others, including persons who despised Oscar, and none of them was able to read them without shedding tears. 'I do not believe,' Bosie wrote in his autobiography, 'that my father himself could have read them without a feeling that here was something which he did not understand and which could not be spat upon without terrible risk to the spitter. I defy anyone who retains the least spark of honour to spit upon the real, essential love of one human being for another. And when I say love, I mean love, and not physical passion or desire or anything else.'[36]

These priceless documents, as we have said, were cherished by Bosie – until in 1912, under circumstances that will be explained in due course, he came to read the complete text of *De Profundis*, wherein his affection for, and loyalty to, the incarcerated Oscar were played down.[37] Bosie was then overcome with bitterness; he kindled the fire and burned some 150 letters from Oscar, and act which later made him 'feel almost suicidal'.[38]

However, of these letters, three have risen from the ashes, phoenix-like.

In August 1895 Bosie wrote an article on the Wilde case for the *Mercure de France*, in the course of which he quoted letters that Oscar had sent him shortly before his conviction. The piece was translated into French but in the end remained unpublished. By a most happy coincidence the manuscript of the French translation has survived (unlike Bosie's holograph); and although Oscar's letters have suffered by their translation into French and their retranslation into English, their purport is quite clear, offering conclusive evidence that the virulence of *De Profundis* was the – understandable – outcome of the physical and, especially, mental torments Oscar had had to endure in prison. A quotation:

> Every great love has its tragedy, and now ours has too, but to have known and loved you with such profound devotion, to have had you for a part of my life, the only part I now consider beautiful, is enough for me. My passion is at a loss for words, but you can understand me, you alone. Our souls were made for one another, and by knowing yours through love, mine has transcended many evils, understood perfection, and entered into the divine essence of things.
>
> Pain, if it comes, cannot last for ever; surely one day you and I will meet again, and though my face be a mask of grief and my body worn out by solitude, you and you alone will recognise the soul which is more beautiful for having met yours, the soul of the artist who found his ideal in you, of the lover of beauty to whom you appeared as a being flawless and perfect. Now I think of you as a golden-haired boy with Christ's own heart in you. I know now how much greater love is than everything else. You have taught me the divine secret of the world.[39]

5

Loyalty, Machinations and Some Misunderstandings

Several weeks had gone by since Oscar's conviction. Bosie was lunching on his own in a well-known Paris restaurant when the door was opened and a group of some fourteen gentlemen came in. They were ceremoniously received by the manager, as Edward Saxe-Coburg-Gotha, heir to the British throne, was among them. He was known to Bosie, and to Oscar, whom earlier that year he had congratulated on the success of *An Ideal Husband*. So much had happened in the interim! Bosie hesitated as to what to do; the Prince and his companions were led to their places, passing his table. The young man got up and bowed. Edward looked straight into his eyes – and cut him dead. Bosie blushed with shame. Once again it was brought home to him that he was an outcast.[1]

Disgraced aristocrats usually kept quiet; after a few years they then stood a chance of being readmitted into polite society. Bosie did *not* keep quiet. He could not acquiesce in the punishment inflicted on his friend. Whereas other English and French authors refused to sign a plea in favour of their unfortunate colleague, Bosie broke a lance for him by addressing a petition to Queen Victoria (which was intercepted by Her Majesty's servants) and by protesting in letters to newspaper editors against the treatment of homosexuals in general and of Oscar in particular. On 9 June 1895 he wrote from Paris to Henry Labouchère, founder of *Truth* and originator of the amendment that had proved fatal to Oscar:

> I maintain that these tastes are perfectly natural congenital tendencies in certain people (a very large minority), and that the law has no right to interfere with these people provided they do not harm other people; that is to say, when there is neither

seduction of minors nor brutalization, and where there is no public outrage on morals. Mr Oscar Wilde's case comes under that head, and, as you must know, in France he could not even have been proceeded against. If you *don't* know this, I refer you to the *Code Napoléon* of which an admirable translation has just been issued in England. In Italy all penal laws were abolished by Act of Parliament, some three or four years ago, and in Germany they have been greatly modified. England alone has refused to take any cognizance of the known and admitted facts of modern medical science, and still continues to punish with barbarous cruelty people who have no more right to be regarded as criminals than vegetarians or any other people whose tastes diverge from those of the normal or average man . . .

I confess I have not many hopes for the present age, but *ultimate* liberation from conventional slavery and tyranny is as inevitable as death. I hope I have not bored you, I write what I really mean and feel.

>Your obedient servant
>Alfred Douglas[2]

This was strong stuff in the 1890s. Writing (and signing) such letters required a lot of courage; to overestimate the damage they did to Bosie's reputation is hardly possible. Their recipient's reaction was predictable. Labouchère referred in his columns to Bosie as 'an exceptional young scoundrel', expressing his regret that the exile was not afforded an opportunity to reflect on his unorthodox standpoints in the seclusion of Pentonville.[3] That was very much the general view.

Bosie had foreseen that the likes of Labouchère would not be pleased with his campaign; that Oscar himself strongly disapproved of it surprised him no end.

Oscar had spent the first four weeks of his term in solitary confinement. These four weeks had completely crushed him. And that was just the beginning. There were another 104 in store for him, 702 days, twenty-three hours of every twenty-four to be dragged out in a badly lit, poorly ventilated, bare cell. The monotony and misery of prison life – oakum picking, the sewing of mailbags; a plank bed causing insomnia, food causing diarrhoea; insufficient medical and sanitary provisions; the want of coffee, alcohol and cigarettes; and, above all, the absence of his little sons, whom he adored – had reduced the epicure to a living corpse in a short space of time. Two newspapers stated in June 1895 that he had become insane.[4] This was not true; but it was near the mark.

The imprisoned Oscar had to take three blows of fate: he was declared a bankrupt, his mother died, and his children were entrusted to the care of a guardian. Prey to black thoughts, filled with self-pity and impotent rage, not capable of accepting a verdict which to him was as absurd as it was unjust, Oscar began looking for a scapegoat. He found one in the youth he had loved more than anyone else in the world. The disciple who had not run away when his master had been seized, who had not disowned him but who, on the contrary, had begged to be allowed to testify in his favour in the Sanhedrin; the disciple whom Oscar had regarded as his St John was now made responsible by him for all his troubles. Bosie as Judas!

While Bosie expressed his anguish for Oscar in poems such as 'Vae victis!' and 'Rondeau' ('If he were here!'), Oscar, in the presence of his first visitors, cursed the one whom, shortly before, he had called 'my sweet rose, my delicate flower, my lily of lilies' and 'the dearest of created things'.[5] Whatever he undertook, Oscar would find fault with him.

When the news of Oscar's conviction had reached him in Rouen, Bosie had expressed his intention of immediately returning to England, as may be gathered from an unpublished letter marked 'private' which Ross had sent in great haste to Percy Douglas, urging his Lordship to point out and, if necessary, to exaggerate to Bosie the risk he ran of being arrested should he dare to go back.[6] This sensible advice had prevailed, and Bosie had moved to Le Havre, where his sailing trips in the company of local youths had given rise to spiteful comments in the local papers. Anonymous notes warning him that he was being watched by the police, and a 'mysterious old man' stalking him, got on his nerves,[7] so he travelled to Paris on his way to Sorrento. His maternal grandmother fully approved of this journey, or so it would seem; for although she had died in 1893 she apparently continued to show a tender solicitude in Bosie's welfare; when Lady Queensberry and other female members of the family were having 'a very good séance', the medium's arm was suddenly 'violently agitated'. She asked for pencil and paper, and a message was written in a large hand signed 'Fanny Montgomery', saying that Alfred was in danger and had to be told to go away as far as he could as he was surrounded by 'powerful enemies', although he *did* have 'very good friends in the spirit world'.[8]

On 12 August, after reading Hugues Rebell's comments on the Wilde affair in the *Mercure de France*, Bosie contacted the magazine's editor, Alfred Vallette, asking him if he would be willing to publish an article of his on the same subject. It would, of course, he said, be a defence and justification of Oscar Wilde, an attempt to show how 'inexpressibly moving' his case was, an effort to raise the public's sympathy for him to the highest degree possible. To achieve this, Bosie went on, he would include extracts from certain letters Oscar had addressed to him, which 'on account of their perfect expression of love altogether divine and absolutely pure though passionate, rank among the most magnificent love-letters the world has ever seen'.[9] Vallette agreed to the proposal, and in his little villa commanding a fine view of the Tyrrhenian Sea Bosie composed his apology for Oscar Wilde.

> Those who know not what love is, will write, I know, if fate is against us, that I have had a bad influence upon your life. If they do that, you shall write, you shall say in turn, that it is not so. Our love was always beautiful and noble, and if I have been the butt of a terrible tragedy, it is because the nature of that love has not been understood.[10]

To Bosie's mind these words of his friend constituted a request, nay, an assignment, to plead his cause; and he was convinced that the best way to achieve his friend's rehabilitation was to allow his friend to speak for himself. He quoted Oscar's letters, not because he was a thoughtless narcissist, as his detractors have claimed, but because as a poet he thought that the publication of poetical love letters written by a poet might bring about some change, however small, in the public perception of his friend who was treading the mill in one of Her Majesty's gaols. And because he was an angry young man who had not been given the chance to enter the witness box, he attacked his father's hypocrisy and castigated the Solicitor-General who had called Oscar's sexual instincts 'something lower than the beasts'. And because he loved life he went for the non-conformist killjoys who did their utmost to spoil it, pouring scorn on the 'human apes who have found God's image shameful',[11] the prudes who would not allow a boy to bathe naked in the river on a hot August afternoon because they thought it 'indecent'.[12] And because he was a loyal young man he associated himself with his disgraced lover, saying precisely those things his anxious relations and the world at large did not want him to say, speaking out for the Love that dare not speak its name, declaring himself to be 'proud' of what he was – that is, proud to be gay – 'proud to have been so much loved by a great man, and proud to have suffered for him'.[13] Describing Oscar's incarceration as 'an outrage on civilization', pleading for his release before his body and soul were destroyed by the barbarities of the English penal system, Bosie, paying a fine, final tribute to Oscar's artistic qualities, implored those who had howled for his blood 'not [to] break him on the wheel, but leave him, rather, to his conscience and his God'.[14] It was a remarkable piece.[15]

The article was sent to Paris; it was translated into French and set up in type. Yet published it was not.

This was owing to the intervention of Robert Harborough Sherard. When rumours reached him that the *Mercure de France* would come up with 'an article on [Wilde's] aberration which was to be an apology for, and a glorification of, "the Greek Movement"',[16] he informed Oscar that in it Bosie had ventured to quote some letters Oscar had written him after his arrest. Did Oscar agree to this?

Wilde was furious. No, he did *not* agree. He instructed Sherard, an acquaintance of the journalist who had made the translation, to prevent its appearance. Sherard pulled a few strings, and the article was withdrawn at once. Bosie, dumbfounded, vented his feelings in a letter to More Adey, a mutual friend who was living in London.

I hear you are going to see Oscar soon. Of course I *know every-thing* and I know from what I have heard from Bobbie that my instinct was right and that Oscar has changed about me. I am writing to you now, dear More, unknown to Bobbie, to beg you to do what you can for me with Oscar. If only you could make him understand that though he is in prison he is still the court the jury the judge of my life and that I am waiting for some sign that I am to go on living. There is nobody to play my cards in England, nobody to say anything for me, and Oscar depends entirely on what is said to him, and they all seem my enemies . . .

I am not in prison but I think I suffer as much as Oscar in fact more, just as I am sure that he would have suffered more if he had been free and I in prison. Please tell him that . . . It is such a joy for me to suffer anything for him. Tell him I know I have ruined his life, that everything is my fault, if that pleases him. I don't care. Doesn't he think my life is just as much ruined as his and so much sooner?[17]

Queensberry meanwhile wanted to deliver the finishing stroke to Oscar by applying to him for the legal costs he (Queensberry) had incurred. Oscar could not possibly raise this sum, as his plays had been taken from the boards and the sale of his books had been stopped. His friends being unable to find the money, he was adjudicated bankrupt.

Oscar's complaint, voiced in *De Profundis*, that the Queensberry family had let him down by not footing the bill is only partially founded. Shortly before the calamitous action against his father, Bosie had handed £360 to Oscar; he now had to get along with a modest allowance his mother paid him and was incapable of contributing a substantial amount. Percy Douglas was also unable to come to Oscar's assistance, although there is documentary evidence that he tried to do so.[18] But as a speculator he struggled with serious financial difficulties, borrowing money at exorbitant rates of interest. He was, as Ernest Leverson came to assure Oscar, 'more to be pitied than blamed'.[19] The only member of the Queensberry clan who might have come to Oscar's rescue was Sybil. She despised him, however, and preferred to keep aloof.

When on 24 September Oscar was led to the Bankruptcy Court, a noisy crowd jostled in the corridor, keen on sensation. Among these people was Robbie Ross, who had been able to return to England. Oscar subsequently remembered with gratitude how Ross, on spotting the handcuffed prisoner, raised his hat – a sign of respect which silenced the rabble.[20] It was, indeed, a beautiful gesture.

Less admirable were Ross's efforts to set on Oscar against Bosie. His motive was sheer jealousy; he had been – understandably – hurt that Bosie had supplanted him; now he saw his chance to drive a wedge between the two. Oscar's reaction to Robbie's account of Lord Alfred's 'luxurious life' on Capri, in Naples and Paris, may be conceived.[21] Bosie himself was deluded by Ross into the belief that Oscar did not wish to receive a visit or letter from him (Bosie), a statement that pained him deeply.[22] In *De Profundis* Oscar – understandably – complained about the fact that letters from Bosie had not been forthcoming. His silence was 'horrible'. Why hadn't he written? Oscar asked. Was it cowardice? Was it callousness?[23] It was neither of these; Ross's machinations were alone to blame.

Ross went a step further by blackening Bosie in the eyes of others as well – in those of Constance Wilde and the Leversons, for instance. Bosie learned that the Leversons were alleging that he had prevented Oscar from leaving England when there had still been an opportunity for doing so. 'I wrote a very nice letter to Leverson,' he told Adey, 'asking for a denial or some explanation, but I have had no reply at all. Can you do anything to elucidate the mystery? I am *very fond* of the Leversons, very fond of both and am much distressed at their quite inexplicable conduct.'[24]

Bosie made this enquiry in Paris, where some months earlier he had caused a stir by publishing an article on the Wilde case that had appeared on 1 June 1896 in the *Revue Blanche*.[25] It was an indiscreet piece – no restraint could be expected from Bosie – which had led to fierce personal attacks in the French press.[26]

But there were some who treated him kindly: Ernest La Jeunesse, for example, a journalist who gloried in being the ugliest man in France[27] and whose conversation almost equalled Oscar's; André Gide, who supplied Bosie with 'naughty' photographs of boys;[28] Edmond Jaloux, who presented him with a copy of one of his books;[29] Octave Mirbeau, who sent him a ticket for the first night of one of his plays;[30] Paul Adam, who dedicated a short story to him;[31] the actress Fanny Zaessinger; and the Vallettes. Monsieur Vallette was the *gérant* of the *Mercure de France*. Madame Vallette, using the pseudonym 'Rachilde', published spicy novels such as *Les Hors-nature* (featuring two incestuous brothers) and *La Tour d'amour* (featuring a necrophiliac lighthouse-keeper). She did not mind receiving the stormy petrel in her salon where arty people met on a weekly basis.

Rachilde was struck by Bosie's youthful looks and told him once that he reminded her of the hero of Oscar's decadent masterpiece. 'I am not a Dorian Gray who has a portrait on which the traces of a corrupted soul may be observed,' he answered. 'If, at twenty-six, I resemble an eighteen-year-old, it's simply because my soul is serene and beautiful, albeit a bit tired and ill-treated.'[32]

Alfred Vallette wanted to issue Bosie's poems, a plan that delighted the artist, as earlier attempts to find a publisher in England had failed. 'You will no doubt remark,' he had written on 11 October 1894 to William Heinemann (whose firm had just scored a hit with Hichens's *Green Carnation*), 'that a few of the poems are inspired by a certain "Hellenic" sentiment which might conceivably provoke unintelligent criticism; but I am confident that you will agree with me that there is nothing objectionable in them, and that I have nowhere allowed myself to break through the *reticence* which should belong to a true artist.'[33] Heinemann, however, had deemed the publication of lyrics such as 'In an Ægean Port' and 'In Praise of Shame' to be unwise, and the suicide of Bosie's brother Francis, which occurred later that month, had for the time being thwarted the project.

Vallette now introduced Bosie to Eugène Tardieu, a talented and sympathetic man who provided the French prose translation that was going to be printed on the page facing the English text. To Bosie it seemed fitting to dedicate the volume to Oscar. He begged Ross to bring up the subject when he would visit the prisoner, asking for his permission. This was a commission Ross was only too happy to carry out; unlike Bosie,[34] *he* could predict Oscar's reaction.

Oscar went beserk. Bosie's proposal, he informed Ross on the day after his visit, was 'revolting and grotesque'. All letters he (Oscar) had written to Bosie and all presents he had given him were to be handed to Ross without delay. Ross was instructed to quote Oscar's words in a letter to Bosie, so that the addressee would have 'no loophole of escape'. 'He has ruined my life,' Oscar went on, 'that should content him.'[35] Highly pleased, Ross duly informed his rival.

Bosie's jaw dropped. But he refused to comply with Oscar's wishes, as he told Adey:

> The last time I saw [Oscar] he kissed the end of my finger through an iron grating at Newgate, and he begged me to let nothing in the world alter my attitude and conduct towards him. He wrote me in the same strain many many times and he warned me that all sorts of influences would be brought to bear upon me to make me change, but I have not changed, from first to last I have been absolutely consistent, and absolutely the same. I shall not change now. I decline to listen to anything he says while he is in prison. If he really means what he says and if he is really not mad, he is not the same person that I knew and he is not Oscar, the Oscar to whom I shall always be faithful, and who belongs to me quite absolutely. When lovers quarrel, they return to each other their letters and presents. I and Oscar were lovers, but we have not quarrelled, and as I have not asked for a return of my letters and presents he cannot ask for his.[36]

Bosie's début, simply titled *Poems*, appeared – without dedication to Oscar – on 30 October 1896. Besides the ordinary issue of 1,000 copies at 3 fr. 50 there was a signed *édition de luxe* of twenty – and a signed *édition de grand luxe* of five copies at 10 and 25 fr. respectively.[37] The duodecimo was embellished with a photogravure of Walter Spindler's silverpoint drawing of the author. 'Quand on est titulaire d'un aussi attrayant physique, tel celui révélé par [ce] frontispice,' a reviewer joked, 'on est fondé de porter de féministes jugements sur la mâle beauté.'[38]

The book sold well and was praised by the French critics,[39] but the compliment that pleased Bosie more than any other came from Stéphane Mallarmé, no less. 'One of the rare occasions I congratulated myself on speaking English,' he wrote, 'was when your poems reached me.'[40]

While Mallarmé addressed these lines to the poet, another author was busily penning a much longer, considerably less friendly epistle. In Reading Gaol Oscar Wilde had embarked upon *De Profundis*.

Since the appointment in July 1896 of Major James Osmond Nelson as its governor, things in the prison at Reading had changed for the better. Nelson was genuinely concerned about the welfare of the inmates entrusted to his care; his policy contrasted sharply with his predecessor's rigorous regime, and it was with feelings of gratitude that Oscar came to send him an inscribed copy of *The Ballad of Reading Gaol*.

Physically Oscar felt much better during the final months of his term: he was properly fed and exempted from strenuous labour. Mentally he was in a bad state. His future was uncertain, and he had not as yet come to terms with his past. He was looking for a safety-valve to get rid of his pent-up frustrations and found one in writing the extraordinary document Ross would later call *De Profundis*. Herein he would set down, for the benefit of posterity,[41] the story of his stirring career, and a veritable twilight of the gods it was going to be. Starring: Oscar Fingal O'Flahertie Wills Wilde, the greatest artist of the age; Lord Alfred Bruce Douglas ('Bosie'), his evil genius; and John Sholto Douglas, Marquess of Queensberry, father of the last-named. Had vowed to bring down the greatest artist of the age; would never have achieved this if the artist had not come under the baleful influence of the evil genius.

In none of his other works does Oscar's histrionic nature come more to the fore. He was a past-master at melodrama, witness the following flowers of speech: 'Don't spoil your beautiful young life on my account! . . . You don't know what it is to fall into the pit, to be despised, mocked, abandoned, sneered at – to be an outcast!' 'Child of my shame, be still the child of my shame!' 'Don't come near me. Don't touch me. I feel as if you had soiled me for ever. Oh! what a mask you have been wearing all these years! A horrible painted mask! You sold yourself for money. Oh!' These quotations have been successively chosen from *Lady Windermere's Fan*, *A Woman of No Importance* and *An Ideal Husband*;[42] the same pathos, the same predilection for hyperbole and exclamation may be found in *De Profundis*. Oscar's account of his sufferings behind bars therefore rings rather hollow, as opposed to the letters on prison reform he wrote to the *Daily Chronicle* after his release.[43] Those letters are wholly lacking – not in sentiment but in *false* sentiment. They are as sincere as they are moving.

How insincere, how bitchy, on the other hand, are certain passages in *De Profundis*! What, for instance, is one to make of the observation that Bosie had ceased to be a seraph when he met Oscar? 'The morning dawn of boyhood with its delicate bloom, its clear pure light, its joy of innocence and expectation you had left far behind.'[44] This is a bit rich, flowing from the pen of the man who had once told André Gide he hoped 'thoroughly to have demoralized' Algiers![45] 'It was of you I was thinking when I wrote [that],'[46] Oscar claims, referring to an aphorism ('It is the feet of clay that makes the gold of the image precious') in the book edition of *The Picture of Dorian Gray*, published in April 1891 – three months before his introduction to Bosie. It was childish retrospectively to lecture his friend on his undistinguished university career,[47] if one remembers that at the time he had delightedly pointed out that Shelley and Swinburne, also, had failed to get a degree. It was childish to dwell upon the 'schoolboy's faults' in Bosie's translation of *Salomé*,[48] given the fact that Oscar's French text of the play had bristled with grammatical and orthographical blunders which had been corrected by Pierre Louÿs, André Gide, Adolphe Retté and Stuart Merrill.[49] Oscar's account of the episode of *The Chameleon* has been examined already; and is one seriously to believe that Alfred Taylor, the Little College Street pimp who kept a lady's costume in his wardrobe, and who put it on when, in the privacy of his home, he 'got married' to a catamite, Charles Mason – is one seriously to believe that *Alfred Taylor* had 'more than once'[50] warned Oscar about his relationship with Bosie?

Oscar's expatiations on humility, which are preceded by a truly megalomaniac description of his brilliant talents,[51] ring equally false. 'Perhaps a Cardinal Archbishop, when he kneels to wash the feet of the beggars' – to quote from Max Beerbohm's review of the partial publication of *De Profundis* in 1905 – 'is filled with humility and revels in the experience. Such was Oscar Wilde's humility: the luxurious complement of pride.'[52]

His pride mattered a great deal to Oscar. As a result of his disastrous action against Queensberry he had been pushed from his pedestal; it was essential for his peace of mind that he regain it. The man whose self-esteem had been so shaken that in a petition to the Home Secretary he could describe his sexuality as 'the most horrible form of erotomania', 'a monstrous sexual perversion', calling himself a 'helpless prey of the most revolting passions',[53] regained his pedestal by exaggerating in *De Profundis* his position as a man of letters and by imputing the loss of that position to Bosie. This stab-in-the-back legend Oscar firmly believed in while writing his monumental letter to Bosie and some weeks afterwards. But not much longer.

The lines from *The Ballad of Reading Gaol*:

> Each man kills the thing he loves,
> By each let this be heard . . .[54]

might serve as a proper motto for *De Profundis*, a harangue teeming with hysterical outbursts against Bosie, depicting him as an ungrateful, jaded, selfish, *irritating* little brat who writes doggerel verse.

When at liberty, Oscar quickly changed his tune. Not just as regards Bosie, whom in a letter written before their reunion he described to an acquaintance as a 'most delicate and refined poet . . . a personality of singular charm . . . We love each other deeply,'[55] but also as far as his other friends were concerned. For Bosie had not been the exclusive target of Oscar's wrath: Robert Ross, More Adey and Ernest Leverson, who had looked after his affairs, had been called 'heartless', 'dishonest', 'outrageous', 'fraudulent', 'foolish' and 'utterly incompetent' in his letters.[56] Ross had even been assured that, 'as a friend of mine', he would have 'shown up very well beside [that unfortunate young man]',[57] meaning Bosie.

No profound psychological insight is required to relate these outbursts, highly uncharacteristic of Oscar, to what penologists term gaol fever; and just as a return to his familiar surroundings will speedily cure a person afflicted with homesickness, so did the end of Oscar's imprisonment mark the end of his gaol fever. 'You must not mind the foolish unkind letters,' he wrote on 19 May 1897 – the day of his release – to Robert Ross, who was in Dieppe. 'More has been such a good friend to me and I am so grateful to you all that I cannot find words to express my feelings.'[59]

Having posted this letter, Oscar boarded ship to join Ross and Reginald Turner. Might he have foreseen he was never to return to 'perfidious Albion'? There were less than four years ahead of him. The curtain went up for the final act.

6

Reunion in Naples and Death in Paris

In the heyday of his prosperity and fame Oscar Wilde was gratified to receive numerous invitations from the 'upper ten', and it was during a lunch at the residence of Gladys, Countess de Grey (to whom *A Woman of No Importance* was dedicated) that the conversation touched upon table speeches.

'There is no subject on which I cannot speak at a moment's notice,' the author boasted.

Lord Ribblesdale, eager to test him, raised his glass. 'The Queen,' he proposed.

'She is not a subject,' Oscar parried.[1]

It was seldom that he could not be tempted to discourse upon Victoria, for he adored her and used to tell the most fantastic stories about her, as Bosie remembered.[2] His affection for the monarch in whose name he had been sentenced to two years' hard labour remained intact even when he had finished his term; he did not fail, therefore, to celebrate her Diamond Jubilee on 22 June 1897. Fifteen children from Berneval-sur-Mer, the tiny village on the Channel coast where Bobbie Ross had installed him, were treated by him to strawberries and cream, lemonade and cake; they sang the British and French national anthems, returning home exclaiming (in French) 'Long live the Queen of England! Long live Monsieur Melmoth!' The latter name had been adopted by Oscar – a reference to the hero of a powerful, albeit poorly structured, Gothic novel, *Melmoth the Wanderer*, published in 1820 by his grand-uncle, Charles Robert Maturin. Oscar had chosen 'Sebastian' as his first name, having a special veneration for the youthful martyr whose charms, as depicted by painters such as Reni and Sodoma, tended to stir feelings in him that may not have been altogether religious.

The party in the Queen's honour he described the day after in a letter to Bosie,[3] who was staying in Paris and most eager to see him again. It soon emerged that this would prove problematical, for on all sides people were trying to prevent their reunion: there was Constance Wilde, who saw Bosie as the 'BEAST'[4] that had ruined her husband; Lady Queensberry, who saw Oscar as the corrupter of her son; Robert Ross, who saw Bosie as his rival; while Queensberry, finally, was taken neither with Bosie nor Oscar and had threatened to shoot both of them in case of their resuming contact. He had hired a detective to spy on Oscar, which had induced the latter to cancel at the eleventh hour a rendezvous with Bosie earlier that month. 'I think of you always, and love you always,' he had written to him, 'but chasms of moonless nights divide us.'[5] The tone of this letter, it will be seen, contrasted sharply with that of *De Profundis*.

What, incidentally, had been Bosie's reaction on reading this 'encyclical',[6] as Oscar had humorously dubbed it? Bosie had not reacted at all, for the simple reason that it had never been sent to him.

It had been Oscar's original intention to forward the manuscript from prison via Robbie to Bosie, but dispatching such a huge missive (twenty folio sheets of four pages each) contravened regulations, so on his arrival in Dieppe Oscar had handed it in a sealed envelope to Ross. Could he but have foreseen the havoc *De Profundis* would wreak after his death, could he but have sensed the terrible feud between his two best friends it would give rise to, he would surely have destroyed the document, especially as it had fully served its therapeutic effect on him. But apart from the diatribes against Bosie the work contained purple passages of metaphysical import that might, perhaps, be of some use in the future . . . Oscar had been aware of the letter's dichotomy all along, for on 1 April he had asked Ross to send copies of these fragments, 'good and nice in intention', to a couple of female friends. Moreover, two typewritten copies of the whole thing (one for Ross and one for himself) had to be made, after which the original, as we have said, should be sent to 'A.D.' Perhaps the letter was a little unjust to him; but then 'A.D.' 'thoroughly [deserved] injustice'. Thus wrote the prisoner.[7]

Later on, cured of his gaol fever and settled in his chalet at Berneval, he must have felt extremely relieved he had been unable to send *De Profundis* from his cell to Bosie. Oscar was not a vindictive man. And now, when it dawned on him that his friend, far from forgetting him, had again and again taken up the cudgels on his behalf – in petitions, in newspapers, in the *Revue Blanche* – he felt that, indeed, he had been a little unjust to him. Why then should he saddle him with his 'encyclical' at this stage? Forget it! Least said, soonest mended.

Nevertheless Robert Ross maintained, years afterwards, when war had broken out between him and Bosie, that Oscar had given him oral instructions in Berneval to send Bosie not the manuscript but one of the typed copies of *De Profundis*; which instructions he had duly carried out; adding that Bosie, after reading the first few lines, had destroyed the papers in a rage.[8] Bosie always denied having received this typescript at the time. That, one might say, is a question of Ross's word against Bosie's. But it seems highly unlikely that Oscar wanted Bosie to find on his door-mat a screed in which the sender called him 'my enemy: such an enemy as no man ever had',[9] the destroyer of his art, while simultaneously assuring him in writing that '[their] love [was] the sacrament of [their] lives'[10] and that his (Oscar's) 'only hope of again doing beautiful work in art [was] being with [him]'.[11] It is equally unlikely that, after perusing this indictment or just glancing at its first paragraphs, Bosie would simply pass to the order of the day, without mentioning the work in conversation or in his correspondence, without blaming Oscar in the slightest. That would testify to a degree of meekness and forgiveness on his part which his critics have never granted him. Finally, Vyvyan Holland's[12] hypothesis (echoed by others), that Bosie burned the typescript, 'thinking, in one of the fits of naïvety which sometimes assailed him, that it was the only copy in existence and that his act would put an end to an awkward situation',[13] is plainly absurd. To believe in such naïvety is naïve; Bosie knew quite well that typewriters were not put at the disposal of English prisoners.

Robbie lied when he stated that a copy of *De Profundis* had been sent to Bosie, and he did so to refute Bosie's valid accusation that the literary executor of Oscar Wilde – Ross – had published, in 1905, portions of a letter from Oscar to Bosie without the permission of the recipient who had never received it in the first place. But Ross did *not* lie when he asserted that in the summer of 1897 he had sent Bosie a typescript and that his Lordship had destroyed a document in a fit of anger. Bosie, writing his memoirs thirty years afterwards, admitted he *had* destroyed something; that he had forgotten precisely what it was; but that it had *not* been a copy of *De Profundis*.[14] And in this he was right. The mystery may be elucidated once and for all by looking at letters from Bobbie to Bosie and from Bosie to More Adey which, written shortly after Oscar's release, ended up in the priceless collection of Mary Hyde, Viscountess Eccles.

The typescript Bosie received, courtesy of Robert Ross, was a solicitor's statement setting out the conditions under which Oscar was entitled to get a modest income to be paid by his wife. Bosie read this typescript in its entirety.

The document he destroyed after reading the first few lines was a handwritten letter of some fourteen pages from Ross in which he (Bosie) was violently abused.[15]

Tensions, indeed, were running high. 'You still seem to cling to the idea that Oscar does not want to see me,' Bosie told Bobbie.

> The wish is the father to the thought. You probably overlook the fact that I am passionately devoted to him, and that my longing to see him simply eats my heart away day and night. You must, in the course of your numerous adventures, have had occasions when you were forcibly separated from somebody you were in love with, by the intervention of kindly friends and relations, and I suppose you suffered then. That is my case, only multiplied by ten, in view of all the tragic circumstances. Then you make no allowance for jealousy, the most terrible of all sufferings. You have seen Oscar yourself, and you can see him again as often as you like, and that is all you care.[16]

Oscar and Bosie met at long last at the end of August, in Rouen. It was a scene worthy of the cinema. Bosie was waiting on the station's platform when Oscar's train arrived, and Oscar – who had visibly aged – burst into tears while embracing his friend. 'We walked all day arm in arm, or hand in hand,' Bosie recorded in his autobiography, 'and were perfectly happy.'[17]

Oscar returned to Berneval on the following day but had agreed with Bosie to join him in Naples shortly. For months he had been expecting a visit from his wife; she had not come but had sent him letters the tone of which had not facilitated their rapprochement. Besides, she had informed him that in any case she was determined to leave their sons in England. His shattered nerves as well as the appalling weather had pushed Oscar to the brink of suicide. Small wonder, then, that he yielded to the temptation of travelling with Bosie to sunnier climes. In Italy he hoped to finish *The Ballad of Reading Gaol*, a moving poem which was going to be issued by a London publisher, Leonard Smithers, whom Oscar had come across in Berneval. ('He loves first editions,' Oscar remarked, 'especially of women; little girls are his passion.')[18]

In October the couple moved into the Villa Giudice. This house, romantically situated by the sea, with marble stairs leading down to the beach, turned out to be infested with rats which made Bosie sit up in bed awake for two nights, 'frozen with terror'.[19] The creatures were removed thanks to the combined efforts of a professional rat-catcher and the local witch. The witch burned odours and mumbled incantations; she also told the friends' fortunes. These were far from bright.

The news of their ménage in Naples led to pandemonium. Ross was furious – and surprised, for Oscar, who from tactical considerations had criticized Bosie rather strongly in his letters to Bobbie, had not announced his plans to head for the South. Constance was understandably shocked. Bosie's people, too, were dismayed. Lady Queensberry's hope that, little by little, her son was forgetting Mr Wilde (Bosie, it seems, had deliberately refrained from mentioning him) vanished into thin air. She feared that this time he had irretrievably ruined himself in the eyes of his fellow aristocrats; for 'people like us' did not, as a rule, associate with bankrupt homosexual ex-convicts. The extent to which the establishment was annoyed may be gauged from the fact that the British Ambassador delegated a subordinate to visit the villa, who in private conversation urged Lord Alfred to leave Oscar Wilde. This Lord Alfred refused to do. His immovability not only tarnished his reputation; he could now whistle for the considerable allowance his father had promised to pay him if he but consented to drop Oscar. It is therefore as unjust as it is foolish to state – as a journalist did – that in Naples Oscar 'was keeping house with an unscrupulous hedonist'.[20]

Oscar was angered by the tone of Ross's letters and at first did not even care to answer them. 'It is to a poet I am going back,' he wrote to Reginald Turner, who had wondered if he had taken a wise decision, 'so when people say how dreadful of me to return to Bosie, do say *no* – say that I love him, that he is a poet, and that, after all, whatever my life may have been ethically, it has always been *romantic*, and Bosie is my romance . . . So stick up for us, Reggie, and be nice.'[21]

Visitors to the villa noted how well the two got on. An Oxford acquaintance recalled that Bosie 'was quite infatuated with Oscar',[22] and when the explorer Harry de Windt found himself alone with Oscar the latter was quite effusive in his praise for his young friend, who, he said, 'had supported him through thick and thin'.[23]

They were not idle. Oscar completed *The Ballad of Reading Gaol*, and Bosie wrote some sonnets of outstanding beauty. Next they started collaborating on an opera libretto, but unfortunately the rest they required was denied them.

Constance had undertaken to pay Oscar £3 a week, provided he did not consort with 'evil or disreputable persons'. In her opinion Lord Alfred Douglas belonged to that category, for which reason she ceased her payments about the middle of November. Oscar was amazed that the lawyer who was supposed to attend to his interests had approved of this measure – wrongly, according to Oscar, as there had never been any accusation whatever brought against Bosie. But his fury knew no bounds when he discovered that Ross and More Adey had declared that Constance had the right to act as she did and that Oscar had forfeited his right to an allowance by living together with Bosie. Oscar dipped his pen in gall. How did Ross and Adey get it into their head, he wrote to the latter, to describe Bosie as a 'disreputable person'? They happened to share his sexual preferences, and Oscar reminded Adey that Constance had protested vigorously when she had heard that he had visited him in Reading Gaol. 'If Robbie had lived with me, would you have taken the same course?'[24] Bosie entered the fray as well, but it was all to no avail: Oscar was deprived of his income. His feet were unshackled, but his hands were tied.

When shortly afterwards Lady Queensberry threatened to cut off Bosie's weekly allowance of £8, too, the poets realized that capitulation was inevitable. In consultation with Bosie, Oscar therefore suggested a compromise. It was, he said, absurd to stipulate that he was to shun Bosie, that he was neither to speak nor to write to him. He (Oscar) had endured solitude and silence for two years; to condemn him anew to that now was barbarous. But if he would promise never to live in the same house with him again . . . would Constance then be prepared to resume her payments to her husband?[25] A reaction was not forthcoming.

Bosie meanwhile entered into negotiations with his mother. He declared himself willing to leave Oscar, but on two conditions: first, the Marchioness was to pay the rent of the villa in advance, enabling

Oscar to stay in Naples for at least another three months; second, she had to place a considerable sum at the author's disposal.

Sybil immediately agreed to this, insisting, however, on a written pledge from Oscar stating he would never again live under the same roof with Bosie. Oscar complied with this request[26] and received via More Adey the amount of £200 in two instalments.

Everything had been lost, except honour. Realizing this, Bosie was able to say goodbye to Oscar with a clear conscience; he set off for France in December. From Rome he wrote to his mother, making a noteworthy confession.

I am glad, o so glad! to have got away, to have escaped. I am so afraid that you will not believe me, and I am so afraid of appearing to pose as anything but what I am. But I am not a hypocrite and you must believe me. I wanted to go back to him, I longed for it and for him, because I love him and admire him and think him great, and almost good, but when I had done it and when I got back, I hated it. I was miserable, I wanted to go away. But I couldn't. I was tied by honour.

If he had wanted me to stay I would never have left him, but when I found that he didn't want me to stay and that I might leave him without a breach of loyalty, then I was glad to go. Even then I hid it from myself, I struggled not to let my inward thought get the better of me, and it is only since I have been here two days that I have completely realized and admitted how glad I am to be away. Even when I got here I persuaded myself that I was miserable and that I wanted to go back and I wrote to you in that sense. But now I know what a relief it is to have escaped *honourably* from a sort of prison. I still think it was right to go to him when he asked and at that time I longed to go to him. I felt I must clear up the matter. And as long as I was there, I was bound to fight in his interests and I did it even to the last bitter point. The knowledge that I didn't really want to stay with him only made me more determined not to show the least disloyalty. I was prepared to carry it to the very end. If he had proposed joint suicide I would have accepted . . .

Don't think that I have changed about him or that I think him bad or that I have changed my views about morals . . . I give up nothing and admit no point against him or myself separately or jointly. Do not think either he has been unkind to me or shown himself to me in an unfavourable light. On the contrary, he has been sweet and gentle and will always remain to me as the type of what a gentleman and a friend should be. Only this, I am tired of the struggle and tired of being ill-treated by the World, and I had lost that supreme desire for his society which I had before, and which made a sort of aching void when he was not with me. That has gone and I think and hope for ever.

Up to this, however, I had no excuse to leave him. I simply couldn't do it. If he had been disagreeable to me or if he had turned out different from what I thought, if he had ever behaved in any way differently from how a man of honour and humanity should behave I would have seized the chance. But he didn't. He has always behaved *perfectly* to me. The only thing that happened was that I felt and saw that he really didn't wish me to stay and that it would really be a relief to him if I went away. So at last I was able to get away with a clear conscience.

And it is no use wishing I hadn't ever gone with him to Naples. It was the most lucky thing that ever happened. If I hadn't rejoined him and lived with him for two months, I should *never* have got over the longing for him. It was spoiling my life and spoiling my art and spoiling everything. Now I am free.[27]

Oscar, who in February 1898 settled in Paris, continued to be criticized by his friends for his 'escapade' with Bosie. He thought that was 'very unfair'[28] but failed to understand why his wife's cheques were not forthcoming now that – as he repeatedly assured Ross – Bosie and he had parted company for ever. Did Constance doubt his sincerity? Perhaps he had not made himself sufficiently clear? Right, right, he would write a letter which would be *abundantly* clear.

The facts of Naples, he informed Ross early in March, were very bald and brief. Bosie, for four months, by endless letters, had offered him a 'home'. When Oscar had finally accepted and joined him, he found that Bosie had forgotten all his promises, and was relying on him to raise the necessary funds. He did so, and on this Bosie lived, quite happy. But when it came to contribute his own share, he turned terrible, mean and penurious (except where his own pleasures were concerned), and he simply absconded the moment Oscar's allowance ceased. This was the most bitter experience of a bitter life, Oscar concluded; a blow quite awful and paralysing. He *never* wanted to see Bosie again. 'He fills me with horror. Ever yours, O.W.'[29]

This letter – which Sybil Queensberry would later describe as 'wicked and abominable'[30] – produced the desired effect. Robert Ross, who knew full well that its contents were not in accordance with truth, showed it to Constance. She finally agreed to resume her payments to Oscar. The letter found a place in Robbie's archive. Bosie was blithely unaware of its existence; but the day lay ahead on which, under highly dramatic circumstances, he would come to read it, along with the complete text of *De Profundis*.

Oscar Wilde's swan-song, *The Ballad of Reading Gaol*, was published on 13 February 1898. The work, issued under the pseudonym C.3.3. – Oscar's prison number – achieved a tremendous success. The first edition was quickly exhausted, reprint followed reprint, Oscar's name appearing on the title-page of the seventh edition.

Constance received a copy and thought the ballad 'exquisite'.[31] She did not want to see the poet again, but he saw her one more time, on 7 April, when she appeared to him in a terrible dream. He subsequently learned that she had died that very night, aged forty-one.[32] 'If we had met only once, and kissed each other,' he wrote to a friend. 'It is too late. How awful life is.'[33]

Bosie shortly afterwards moved in a flat in the Avenue Kléber in Paris and was advised by Oscar as regards the choice of furniture. Since their stay in Naples their relationship had settled into a more placid groove. Bosie assured his mother that he still loved and admired the writer, that he was looking forward to his artistic rehabilitation, that he associated himself with him in everything;[34] but Oscar had ceased to be the pivot on which his life hinged. Much to the satisfaction of Ross, incidentally.

Bosie felt homesick for England, and when those in the know had told him he could return there without being collared by Scotland Yard he travelled to London in November, where he got into touch with two publishers: Edward Arnold who, before the end of the year, brought out a collection of nonsense rhymes Bosie had written in his under-graduate days, *Tails With a Twist* 'by a Belgian Hare'; and Grant Richards, to whom he entrusted *The City of the Soul*. It contained his most recent lyrics along with those which had previously appeared in

Poems, with the exception of those in which he 'played with Greek fire',[35] such as 'Two Loves' and 'Prince Charming.'

The City of the Soul was published anonymously in an edition of 500 copies in May 1899. The little volume was received with a storm of applause. 'This is verse of the proud kind that scorns vulgar appreciation, and looks for approbation of connoisseurs,' the *Scotsman* wrote.[36] The *St James's Gazette* hailed the book as 'a treasure-house of gems'.[37] 'A great unknown,' the *Outlook* gushed, 'among crowds of clever versifiers here comes a poet. Need we say more?'[38] The latter review was by Lionel Johnson, the man who had introduced Bosie to Oscar. Johnson, who to his credit had not, like so many others, distanced himself from Bosie after Oscar's downfall,[39] was at this stage ruining his health by consuming large quantities of whisky. A recluse who could not come to terms with his homosexuality, he would be dead in three years' time.

The first edition of *The City of the Soul* sold out in a few months, and a second, again of 500 copies, went to press. Bosie wanted his name to be printed on the title-page, as had previously been agreed with Richards. But the publisher, on second thoughts, demurred; he feared that readers would be put off by the poet's name. Bosie, considering his book to be his vindication, a dignified answer to all the jeers he had received, insisted that Richards keep his promise. In the end the latter's misgivings came true; when in December the second edition appeared, disclosing the author's identity, the public showed no more interest, while the critics (who felt 'duped') kept silence. A third edition would not materialize till 1911, under the aegis of John Lane.

It was Leonard Smithers who, in December 1899, shortly before going bankrupt, published yet another work of Bosie's, *The Duke of Berwick* 'by the Belgian Hare', a comic poem that was illustrated by Anthony Ludovici, the future secretary of Rodin. At the age of eighty he set down his reminiscences of Lord Alfred.

He was invited to discuss the get-up of the volume at Lady Queensberry's house, 18 Cadogan Place, where Bosie and Smithers were waiting for him. A butler served tea, and Smithers asked what price Ludovici thought he should receive for the twelve plates he was going to make. Bashfully, the young man suggested what his father had advised him to propose: two guineas for each drawing. Before Smithers had time to react, he was urged by Bosie to accept these terms, which he did. Bosie then, 'in his melodious, light baritone voice', recited his poem. Ludovici, who thought it was a skit on the Marquess of Queensberry, was carried away.

During the weeks that followed he regularly called at Smithers's office to show his illustrations to publisher and author. His meetings with Bosie 'made this brief period in [his] life one of the happiest [he] could remember'; one afternoon in particular remained with him. Bosie took him aside, gave him 'a playful dig in the ribs' and asked him in a whisper 'what on earth' had induced him to caricature Smithers's secretary as Mademoiselle de la Ponghèra, one of the poem's characters. It was only then that Ludovici perceived the likeness which, he swore, was purely accidental. He offered to change the illustration, but Bosie would not hear of it; he just warned him to keep out of the lady's way in the future . . .

Ludovici was sorry when the time had come to hand in the last drawing.

> Although in those early days I had not yet formed any settled philosophical views about the nature of Man and the relation of Body and Soul, I have since reached many strong convictions on these matters, and among these I hold none more firmly than that, contrary to Socratic belief, Bodily form and appearance are intimately and inseparably related with character and disposition, and that therefore no one who possessed Lord Alfred Douglas's compelling comeliness and charm could possibly be capable of the infamies which his enemies have ascribed to him.[40]

Queensberry – who was not, by the way, poked fun at in *The Duke of Berwick*; that fictitious nobleman was modelled after a Puritan out of *The Picture of Dorian Gray* – died on 31 January 1900, aged fifty-six. Efforts to reconcile him with Bosie had previously come to nothing, or next to nothing. True, thanks to the mediation of a cousin they had met in the smoking-room of the London hotel where Queensberry was staying; and the Marquess, tearfully embracing his 'darling boy', had actually promised to give him back his allowance; but within a week he had sent him a furious letter, telling his darling boy he would not get a farthing until he had explained what his relations with 'that beast Wilde' exactly amounted to. Bosie lay ill in bed when this query reached him. His temperature soared, and he dispatched a most undiplomatic answer. The Marquess, who never realized the extent to which he hurt others but who himself was easily huffed, felt deeply offended. He did not want to see his son again, but his son saw him one more time, months later, from a cab window. And he was shocked, for Queensberry looked dreadful. He was paranoid, believing that 'the Oscar Wilders' were after him. Bosie wrote him another letter, apologizing for the previous one, assuring his father that he only had good feelings towards him. 'Q' did not respond; but his son-in-law told Bosie that the message had been well received.

On his death-bed the peer assured his ex-wife that she had been the only woman he had truly loved. He spat his heir, Percy, in the face; and confessed his sins to his brother Archibald, a Catholic priest. Queensberry renounced his atheism, professed his faith in Jesus Christ and was given conditional absolution. At this, his Reverence observed, a tremendous load seemed to be lifted from him, and he breathed his last peacefully and happily.[41] Writing to *The Times*, Mr Richard Edgcumbe, of Edgbarrow, Crowthorne, Berkshire, paid a warm tribute to the Marquess, speaking of his 'plethora of conscience' and the fearlessness with which he had performed 'a public duty', 'because no one else could be found to risk the odium', by standing up against 'a notorious sybarite'. 'His conduct in the matter was simply heroic.'[42]

Bosie inherited £15,000, an amount which would have enabled him to live on its interest. Instead, he bought some racehorses that he kept at Chantilly, a village north of Paris where he was to be found most of the time during the next eighteen months.

Oscar, like most exponents of the Æsthetic Movement, advocated a sedentary lifestyle, and Bosie, under his influence, had given up sport almost completely since the beginning of their friendship. Now the young Lord, who in *The Spirit Lamp* had laughed at early risers,[43] went in for long rides through the verdant surroundings at break of day, improving his health and spirits in the process. His horsemanship was marvelled at by the hearties, while the pheasants, partridges and grouse populating the grounds of his rich English friends were soon to discover that he tended less and less to suppress his hunting instincts. Indeed, he became a fairly good shot.

Oscar had no enthusiasm for Bosie's 'ridiculous horses' but was keenly interested in the money that had come his way. Judging by Oscar's letters from this period, Bosie failed to support him, being preoccupied with his own pleasures. 'He is really a miser,' Oscar complained to Ross on 29 June 1900, 'but his method of hoarding is spending: a new type.'[44] That was wittily put. It was also totally false. Bosie was no miser. A reliable witness, Reginald Turner, afterwards put on record that his payments to Oscar had been 'lavish'; there was, in fact, no one who supported him as much;[45] he often wined and dined him in Paris, slipping banknotes into his hands; he also sent him cheques from Chantilly, ranging from £10 to £125. Oscar, however – one reluctantly faces the fact – in his final years was not over-scrupulous in financial matters. By virtue of his wife's testament he received a monthly allowance. In addition he got sums from Leonard Smithers, Frank Harris, Bosie and others. There was therefore no reason to bemoan (as he did) the 'meanness' and 'the lack of imagination' of those whose generosity he ought to have praised. He furthermore did not hesitate to sell 'the exclusive rights' of a comedy-in-progress to half a dozen people . . . who were surprised to discover that the transaction had not been as 'exclusive' as all that! The play remained unwritten, for after his 'evil genius' had been forced to leave him at Naples Oscar did not add a single line to his *œuvre*.

His conversational powers, on the other hand, were undiminished, and he kept his hearers spellbound night after night. It was this aspect of Oscar's personality that would inspire Bosie to write one of his most moving sonnets, 'The Dead Poet', 'a song of remembrance in which, as in a looking-glass, against a background of mixed colours from the present and the past, emerges that mysterious man, this Lord of Language who was crowned with the bays of Eloquence'.[46]

In August Bosie travelled to England and dined with Oscar at the Grand Café on the eve of his departure. Oscar's wit scintillated throughout the evening, but he was seized with melancholy when they were sipping their liquors. His end, he sighed, was nigh. Nonsense, Bosie said. And off he went.[47]

But Oscar's presentiment was right. He fell ill in October, and when Bosie learned this he sent him a 'very nice letter'[48] accompanied by a small cheque. Oscar was touched and wept a little. It was the last contact between them.

Initially Ross did not realize the seriousness of the situation, but when some weeks later Oscar's condition began to deteriorate Turner, who was looking after the patient, asked Ross to warn Bosie. The latter was in Scotland and could be located with difficulty. 'If he gets well enough,' he wrote to Ross, 'please tell him that my whole heart and soul is with him, and give him my dearest love.'[49] He then hurried to

Paris, but when he arrived there all was over; his friend had died on 30 November, aged forty-six, in his hotel in the Rue des Beaux-Arts.

'I have made a wonderful discovery,' Oscar had remarked once. 'I find that alcohol taken persistently and in sufficiently large quantities produces all the effects of intoxication.'[50] His consumption of alcohol had certainly contributed to the destruction of his bodily health; meningitis proved fatal to him; but, as a French palmist had previously concluded with utter amazement after studying Oscar's palm, he had been dead already for some time – ever since the doors of his prison cell had closed upon him, in fact.[51]

Bosie, hardly able to grasp what had happened and upset because the coffin was already nailed up, was given an account of Oscar's final days by Robbie Ross. They agreed that Bosie would pay for the funeral; Ross then said he had looked at the deceased's papers, without finding anything of importance. What should be done with these? Should he (Ross) take care of them? Bosie's head was in a whirl. He answered that Ross could do what he thought best. As a result, Ross had been appointed *de facto* Oscar's literary executor, having at his disposal not only the manuscript of *De Profundis* but also a sheaf of letters from Bosie to Oscar, of which we will hear more later.

Oscar had become a Catholic on his death-bed. As a student he had flirted – that is the word – with the Mother Church; all through his life he had felt attracted to the beauty of the Roman ritual, just like the hero of *The Picture of Dorian Gray*.

> The daily sacrifice, more awful really than all the sacrifices of the antique world, stirred him as much by its superb rejection of the evidence of the senses as by the primitive simplicity of its elements and the eternal pathos of the human tragedy that it sought to symbolise . . . The fuming censers, that the grave boys, in their lace and scarlet, tossed into the air like great gilt flowers, had their subtle fascination for him.[52]

The English priest whom Ross had fetched satisfied himself that the dying man was conscious. Oscar received Baptism and Extreme Unction, but the Viaticum could not be administered.

On 3 December the artist was buried in a makeshift grave just outside Paris. Fifty-six people attended the service; Bosie acted as chief mourner. It seemed to him 'as if the sun had gone down'.[53] 'I am miserable and wretched about darling Oscar,' he wrote to Adey. 'My dear More, what is to be done with one's life? I simply don't know. I am utterly sick of the whole business.'[54]

What is to be done with one's life? That question would be answered sooner than Bosie expected. For while the orchestra, so to speak, was playing the funeral march for his late friend, the *prima donna* was waiting behind the scenes for her cue to enter the stage. Olive Custance was her name, and she was cast as the wife of Lord Alfred.

7

A Runaway Match

In 'The Adventure of the Noble Bachelor', a Sherlock Holmes story from 1892, Dr Watson reads from a newspaper to the famous detective. 'There will soon be a call for protection in the marriage market,' the article in question opens, 'for the free-trade principle appears to tell heavily against our home product. One by one the management of the noble houses of Great Britain is passing into the hands of our fair cousins from across the Atlantic.'[1]

At the turn of the century numerous British peers did, indeed, prefer American girls. Their reasons more often than not were practical rather than romantic: there were lots of millionaires' daughters all agog to marry a European aristocrat. The bride got a title, the groom was assured of a royal income. *Probatum est.*

Bosie's contemporaries were therefore hardly surprised that he conceived the plan to look for a wife in the New World. Until recently he had slept with boys and young men, as Oscar's letters show; but he ceased to frequent them. His gay past did not as yet fill him with remorse; he looked upon it as a closed chapter of his life. He had acquired a taste for female beauty, and the prospect of solving his financial problems by uniting himself to a sprightly American lady – he had almost completely squandered his inheritance – provided him with an additional impetus to go a-courting. In his autobiography Bosie declared feeling less compunction to mention this sordid scheme as it was bound to remain a scheme only.[2] For he came across Olive Eleanor Custance, an attractive 26-year-old who had belonged to the regular contributors of the *Yellow Book*, the magazine known as 'the oriflamme of the Decadents'.

Olive wrote poems and fancied poets. Of both sexes: she had had a crush on John Gray, and at the moment she makes her appearance in our story she was flirting with Natalie Clifford-Barney, whose sonnets she greatly admired. On the invitation of this wealthy American lesbian she went to Paris in the spring of 1901 to found with her a 'Sapphic colony'. Much to the chagrin of Pauline Tarn, alias Renée Vivien, Natalie's bosom friend, who thought Miss Custance 'trite, like all English girls' and who went into hysterics when she discovered that Natalie and Olive had spent a night together. The latter ran the risk of being shot, for Renée had a revolver, but fortunately no *crime passionnel* was committed in the end.[3] Besides, the liaison was of short duration. In Venice, a place Olive and Natalie visited shortly afterwards, Olive hung a photograph of a statue of Antinoüs in her hotel room, saying to Natalie that the favourite of the Emperor Hadrian, who had proclaimed him a god after his untimely death, reminded her of Alfred Douglas. On him she had bestowed her heart.[4]

In June she sent him a first letter, expressing her enthusiasm for his poetry. Such a token of sympathy was much appreciated, for since returning to England Bosie had found that many avoided him on account of his involvement in the Wilde scandal. Wherever he appeared, brows were knit, insinuating remarks made; some friends refused to shake his hand. 'I mentally assigned them to the Devil,' Bosie recalled, 'who, by the way, appears to have taken me at my word in a good many cases.'[5] Inevitably, this treatment eroded the spontaneity and cordiality which up till then had characterized the young man. He started to cultivate a certain detachment and tended not to take notice of strangers unless they spoke to him first.

Olive's fan mail was speedily answered. An assignation in a museum came to nothing, as Bosie had gone to the wrong hall, but he had hardly regained his haunt in Duke Street, Portland Square, when the door-bell rang. It was Olive. And it was love at first sight.

In the course of the ensuing weeks the two went in for a hectic mutual courtship. Olive presented Bosie with a copy of her volume of poems, *Opals*; Bosie sent her his portrait and a locket with a lock of his hair. They went out to dine, they went to the theatre, to Paris. Bosie received letters in flowing script and flowery language. A specimen:

> My own boy . . . What a joy to get that last little letter from you
> . . . but now . . . but now at last I *feel* you have really gone and I

am miserable without you . . . Last night I dreamed of you and woke to find my pillow wet with tears . . . and I stretched out my empty arms to you and called you, my Prince, very softly . . . but you were too far away to hear . . . Oh how I miss you . . . your sweet golden head . . . your small red mouth . . . always, it seems, a little shy of my kisses . . . and above all your great blue eyes . . . the most beautiful eyes a boy ever had . . . How my lips love them . . . if only I might kiss them tonight . . . But if I were to write forever I should not be able to tell you how much I love you . . . and don't disdain my love, Sweet . . . many men and women have wanted it . . .

I seem to be scribbling dreadfully . . . but I forget even to write well when I write to you . . . I forget everything except that I love you . . . See! What a child I am! But you will understand because you are a child too, my Darling . . . my own Bosie whom God made for me, I think . . .

Your loving Olive . . .[6]

Some people thought Olive slightly affected.[7]

The letter quoted above dates from 4 October 1901 or thereabouts and was sent to America, whither Bosie had gone in search of a wife. That sounds ludicrous, but the two poets were convinced they could not possibly marry, however much they wanted to; for Olive's father, Colonel Frederic Hambleton Custance[8] – a friend of King Edward, and a man of Victorian principles – would, they knew, never give his permission, first, because Bosie was short of cash (a circumstance which had forced him to sell his race-horses) and, second, because he had been the friend of the unspeakable Wilde. That was why Olive had carefully hidden her passion for Bosie from her swashbuckling parent, just back from the South African war. The fact that their love affair was 'hopeless' and disapproved of by 'the world' in no way impaired its intensity. Far from it! It made it all the more *romantic*, and there were famous precedents: Tristan and Isolde, Romeo and Juliet, Werther and Charlotte . . . These names were undoubtedly mentioned during their clandestine meetings, when Bosie felt bound to point out to his sweetheart that he could no longer postpone his trip to America; which she could understand.

But while leaning on the rails of the liner that brought him to

Portland, Maine, Bosie realized that his quest was doomed to failure. For how, he wrote to Olive, could he ever propose to a plutocrat's daughter when he could only think of his beloved?[9]

The sea was quite rough during the crossing, a foretaste of the stormy scenes in store for Lord Alfred. In Buffalo people avoided him. In Washington he stayed for a few days at the Raleigh, where, according to a reporter,

> he attracted the attention of the clerks and guests . . . by reason of his small stature and the fact that he was much better dressed than most of the men who frequent the lobby. His clothing was of the most correct form, and always proper to the hour of the day . . . The nobleman has very light hair and blue eyes and talks like a typical Englishman. While staying at the hotel he was out every day until very late.[10]

The journalist briefly referred to Bosie's past association with Oscar Wilde. All in all, the article was sympathetic, but some of its readers showed themselves to be less well disposed towards its subject. When on the day of its appearance, 17 December, Bosie entered the bar of the Metropolitan Club, of which he had become an honorary member thanks to a cousin who was Second Secretary of the British Embassy, one gentleman, raising his voice, made a remark traducing Oscar and his kind. It was a shameless provocation. Bosie could hardly control himself; he finished his drink and walked out. His cousin, to whom he turned for consolation, told him that the club's committee had written him a hoity-toity letter, demanding an explanation of why he had introduced such a 'disreputable' person. The Embassy staff stood by the poet, but he felt aggrieved and left for New York, where the *Herald* splashed the story:

CLUB TURNS OUT A BRITISH LORD.
ENTREE TO THE METROPOLITAN CLUB IN WASHINGTON WITHDRAWN FROM ALFRED DOUGLAS.

'For a few days he thoroughly enjoyed himself [in the capital],' the newspaper wrote. 'But then rumors began to creep around about his doings in London and of his friendship for objectionable persons.

Altogether, the affair created a sensation, the echoes of which are still being heard.'[11]

Bosie countered with a letter that was published on Christmas Eve. It ended:

> Apparently the objection of the Metropolitan Club and the American press generally to me is the frequently stated fact that, having been a friend of Oscar Wilde before his downfall, I continued to be so after his release from prison, and that almost alone of all his countless former friends I attended his funeral. I have never attempted to deny these facts, and I have yet to learn that they constitute a serious indictment against my character, either as a gentleman or a Christian.

It would be wrong, however, to say that Bosie's stay in the United States was merely a series of embarrassing scenes. He did meet some nice people, as is testified to by his correspondence with Natalie Barney (of whom he saw a great deal). Its tone is quite frivolous. 'I will bring Frank completely clothed to lunch,' he informed her on 14 January 1902, 'and if necessary he can be completely unclothed afterwards.'[12] As for heiresses, he had met 'quantities'[13] of them, but he had kept them at bay. With a sigh of relief he returned to England. There he was told that Olive was engaged to George Charles Montagu.

In itself this was no surprising development. Colonel Custance had been urging his eldest daughter to marry for a long time. She knew she could not suggest Bosie as the groom, and Bosie knew that, too. But he found it hard to accept that she had selected Montagu, of all people. George had been a childhood friend of his, to whom, in shining contrast with many others, the Wilde scandal had made no difference; Bosie, after his exile, had been received by him with open arms; the two had been almost inseparable for quite a while – until the moment came for George to seek election to Parliament. Mindful of his parents' advice he had then dropped Bosie, for what would the electorate say of an MP who consorted with 'the notorious Lord Douglas'? An indignant Bosie had thereupon compared George in a sonnet ('The Traitor') with Judas Iscariot.

Montagu was a gifted actor and knew how to amuse Olive with clever impersonations of Bosie. To Colonel Custance these skills were of no interest whatever. He attached more importance to the fact that George was heir of an earl and would one day have an annual income of some £30,000.

Bosie invited Olive to dine with him at Kettner's Restaurant, a place he and Oscar had often graced with their presence. It soon dawned on him that Olive had only half-heartedly accepted Montagu's proposal; she thought him 'nice', but she loved Bosie. Assuming, however, that he would catch an American bride, she had felt bound not to reject George.

What a muddle! Bosie thought hard and then came up with a bold suggestion. Would Olive be prepared to marry him secretly? A sober ceremony (he would take care of the paperwork) and then to France for the honeymoon! He assured her it was the only solution. Olive's decision was speedily taken. Yes, she was willing enough and promised to show up on Tuesday morning, 4 March, at nine o'clock sharp at St George's Church, Hanover Square.

The evening before Bosie confided in his mother and his sister, Edith. Sybil was in raptures and gave her son a diamond ring for the bride; Edith consented to be present during the service. Robert Ross and a barrister friend, Cecil Hayes, were also invited, while Olive instructed her maid to smuggle a portmanteau containing a night-dress and toothbrush out of the house.

When on the following morning Custance and his spouse, seated at breakfast, were buttering their toast and sipping their tea, they could not surmise that their daughter was being led to the altar by Lord Alfred Douglas. Their dismay at receiving a telegram in which the newly-wed – now on board of the boat-train to Paris –informed them of their alliance may be more easily imagined than described.

Custance choked. The standard procedure in such cases was to disinherit the bride, but this was impossible, as Olive's grandfather had inalienably bestowed his property on his granddaughter. The Colonel rushed to Scotland Yard, begging to see his son-in-law's 'file'. He evinced genuine surprise on being told there was no such file in existence and returned to Weston Old Hall, his gloomy manor in Norfolk, where he worked off his spleen on his wife, who, as it became clear to him, had not been unaware of Olive's feelings for Bosie.

The news of the marriage spread like wildfire and created an uproar.

The Montagus were highly indignant and showed it, with the exception of George who stoically resigned himself (he would marry an American girl three years afterwards). King Edward let it be known he was highly displeased, although Bosie failed to understand what it had to do with *him*.[14] Others reacted more phlegmatically. Percy Wyndham, for instance, great-uncle of the groom, observed: 'Anything short of murder in the Douglas family is a source of congratulation.'[15]

Olive's parents were faced with a *fait accompli*, and for that reason Custance informed the couple that everything was forgiven, inviting them to spend a few days at Weston. The visit turned out much better than expected. Custance and Bosie got on quite well together, and the latter was taught by the former how to fish. The old man was overjoyed when on 17 November his daughter gave birth to a son, Raymond Wilfrid Sholto, for a son he had never had, while longing for one more than anything else.

Lord and Lady Douglas after some years settled at Lake Farm, an atmospheric old place near Salisbury. Here they spent a happy time. Olive dedicated the third volume of her poems, *The Blue Bird* (1905), to her husband; he hymned her in six marvellous sonnets which she had had illuminated for hanging on the walls of her bedroom.

We catch a glimpse of these halcyon days by glancing at *L'Eclaireur de Nice* of 14 February 1904. It contains an interview with Bosie, written by a French acquaintance, which was sent to me by a Greek lady friend of mine who discovered it by chance. Monsieur Merlet (that was the reporter's name) called on the family in their villa at the Riviera. Lunch was served in the salon overlooking the Mediterranean.

'I listened to the poet of *The City of the Soul*,' Merlet noted, 'and sensed how much the exquisite and delicate man whose dreams found expression in this book must smart under the mediocrity of the age. He has suffered the injustice of fools whom one has to forgive, as they are incapable of comprehending the passions, the illusions and the mysteries of the soul.'

'I have not changed,' Bosie said. 'I have never repudiated what I cherish in art; I have never asked people to approve or disapprove my writings.'

Merlet waxed lyrical about Olive's charms and was shown Raymond, 'a sweet baby with azure eyes and a beautiful smile on his lips'. 'He is', Merlet told his host, 'your masterpiece.'

'Yes, he is,' said Bosie.

Et in Arcadia ego. He had not enjoyed such a tranquillity for a long time. But this peace would not last.

The reviewer of the *Illustrated London News* who in 1902 devoted a small article to a performance of *The Importance of Being Earnest* spoke, it is true, of the 'innocent merriment' presented to the audience, yet scrupulously avoided mentioning the playwright's name.[16] The same discretion prevailed when two years later the magazine reported on the revival of *Lady Windermere's Fan*.[17] Obviously Oscar Wilde remained a controversial figure in England, a circumstance deeply deplored by his literary executor, Robert Ross. He wanted to publish Oscar's collected works to pay off the author's debts and to support his two sons, but he realized that as a preliminary the public had to be persuaded not to perceive Oscar first and foremost as a pathological case. And Ross knew how this change might be effected.

In his archive was kept the manuscript of *De Profundis*, and certain passages, those in which Oscar philosophized on humility, remorse and Christianity, would not fail to impress the British if brought out in a book, unlike the attacks on Bosie which Ross, in consultation with the publisher, Algernon Methuen, wisely decided to leave out. It was important, however, to hide from Bosie the fact that the projected volume was compiled from a letter addressed to him which he had never received; for it was more than probable that he would then try to get an injunction.

Bosie was of course surprised to hear that a posthumous work of Oscar's was in the press. Ross refused to show him the manuscript, declaring that *De Profundis* consisted of fragments from a letter Oscar had written to him (Ross) from gaol – which was also the impression he subsequently created in his preface.[18] The epistle, Ross went on, was marred by vicious criticisms levelled at various friends (including Bosie), but they need not worry, as he had drawn a veil over these gibes.[19] Bosie accepted this explanation, and when the book was launched he reviewed it kindly in a motoring magazine.[20]

The success of *De Profundis* exceeded the most sanguine expectations. The day after the publication of the first edition of 10,000 copies, on 23 February 1905, Methuen informed Ross that the second edition was being prepared; the third followed in March of that year, the twelfth in December 1908.[21] The critics were unanimous in their praise. This greatly troubled Canon Henry Charles Beeching. From his pulpit in Westminster Abbey he warned his flock to be aware of Wilde's 'doctrine of devils', and when he heard that Methuen intended to bring out Oscar's *opera omnia* he urged the publisher in writing to go back on his unholy decision. Methuen replied, expressing his astonishment that, apparently, the spirit of the Spanish Inquisition had not been laid to rest yet; whereat Beeching (author of *The Bible Doctrine of Atonement*) delivered himself of the remark that the Inquisition would have been well advised to burn Oscar Wilde. 'He would have made a good blaze.'[22]

The appearance of *De Profundis* marked the beginning of Oscar's literary rehabilitation in England. On the continent his reputation was undisputed, especially in Germany where a production of *Salomé* in Hedwig Lachmann's translation had been a triumph in 1902 and where three years later Richard Strauss had finished his masterly musical adaptation of the same play.[23] This teutonic appreciation of Oscar's work – ironic if one considers Oscar's aversion to the German empire – yielded royalties which made it possible to pay off the burden of his debts in 1906. Ross was feeling cock-a-hoop – and rightly so.

Bosie, as we have seen, had reviewed *De Profundis*; in the years ahead he would occupy himself with journalistic work on a much larger scale, for in March 1907 he became the editor of a literary weekly, *The Academy*.[24] Its owner was his cousin by marriage, Edward Tennant. His wife, Pamela, had noticed that Bosie began to feel a trifle bored in the country, and at her instigation he was offered the job. Bosie joyfully accepted and moved with his family to London.

The Academy's office was situated in Lincoln's Inn Fields, where Bosie had a secretary, Alice Head, and a tiny errand-boy at his disposal. This lad invariably referred to Bosie as 'the Lord'; when Miss Head asked him where the contributors' ledger was to be found, he would gravely answer: 'The Lord's got it.'[25] The secretary kept a soft spot in her heart for her chief, calling him in her memoirs 'a man of engaging personality'. He gave her a taste for fine poetry, and she remained 'everlastingly grateful for his many kindnesses' (she was less taken with the attentions bestowed on her by the premises' owner, a hoary botanist who showed her 'questionable pictures in old rare books').[26]

Bosie was determined to turn *The Academy* into a first-rate review. He set himself a high standard. One cannot, he argued, love good literature without at the same time hating bad literature. The sphere of literature is an arena, a battlefield; every day horrors are perpetrated in the name of Art, every day the hydra-heads of humbug, cant, hypocrisy, false sentiment and sham pathos rear their horrid shapes. Nothing but rage, the rage of the man who sees his beloved about to be defiled, can provide the strength which can prevail against them.[27] There was no room in *The Academy* for nepotism. The Muses had to be served. *The Academy* did not aim at making a profit. The money-changers were to be chased away from the temple.

Bosie assured himself of the collaboration of people like Richard Middleton, James Elroy Flecker, Frederic Rolfe (alias Baron Corvo), Andrew Lang, Rupert Brooke, Vincent O'Sullivan, Siegfried Sassoon and George Bernard Shaw. He himself wrote articles on poets such as Richard Barnfield, Dante Gabriel Rossetti, François Villon and Oscar Wilde, signing his own verse with his initials. 'Surely the present year, as far as poetry is concerned,' an enthusiastic subscriber commented, 'might be described as 1907 "A.D.".'[28] And Bosie received more compliments from a steadily rising readership: one correspondent described *The Academy* as 'the model of an organ of sane and healthy and fearless criticism'; another complained it was no longer possible for him to cut out the most interesting articles without buying two copies.[29] The paper's prospects looked rosy indeed.

But then Bosie made the mistake of appointing as his assistant editor a man who would exert a disastrous influence, not just on the course of *The Academy* but on Bosie's personal development. 'I made myself as wax / To your fierce seal,' he would later admit in a sonnet[30] addressed to this person. His name was Thomas William Hodgson Crosland.

In Fleet Street he cut a strange figure. He gave the appearance of having slept in his clothes; his eyebrows frowned most of the time. He had an impressive moustache (walrus-type). When angry (and he was angry quite often) the sweat streamed down his face. He was a diabetic with a dicky heart; more than once Bosie was summoned to hospital where his lieutenant was supposed to be dying. Crosland was a spendthrift who daily lunched at Bosie's expense and who borrowed money from all and sundry; twice Bosie had to help him out financially to prevent the bailiff's sequestrating his furniture. In the past Crosland had set up various short-lived periodicals, in one of which, the *English Review*, some lyrics and articles by Bosie had appeared (which had never been paid for). Crosland had published Olive's *Blue Bird*, only to make a hash of its distribution; the volume had not even made it to the *Catalogue of English Books*. Bosie, no frequenter of bars, was occasionally dragged by Crosland to pubs where he did not fit in with the crowd. Conversely, Crosland now and again had to go with Bosie to formal dinners willy-nilly, allowing his boss to rearrange his tie and comb his hair. Crosland was good company, according to Bosie,[31] but his sense of humour was anything but subtle, as is evinced by his satire *The Unspeakable Scot*. Herein the author, himself an alcoholic, upbraided the Highlanders for their excessive consumption of spirits,[32] while begging them earnestly to stay where they were: 'IF WITHOUT SERIOUS INCONVENIENCE TO YOURSELF YOU CAN MANAGE TO REMAIN AT HOME, PLEASE DO.'[33] (Crosland entreated Bosie never to read the book, which proved a phenomenal best-seller.) In the same strain were works bearing titles like *The Egregious English*, *Lovely Woman* and *The Fine Old Hebrew Gentleman*.

Crosland's love of literature was unfeigned. Most of his own poems were second-rate. A married man, he broke a lance for an ethical revival while having a mistress. He prided himself on his business acumen and on one occasion threatened to push an advertiser with whom he had a difference down a lift-well. Crosland was a mischief-maker; one of his colleagues, a specialist in occult sciences, likened him to a poltergeist.[34]

The friendship between Bosie and Crosland – larded with terrible quarrels culminating in a simulated heart-attack on the latter's part – was a mystery to Alice Head. The atmosphere at the editorial office became so tense that she decided to resign.

Meanwhile *The Academy* no longer confined itself to commenting on literary subjects; since Crosland's arrival on the scene, and at his insistence, political matters were tackled as well. This was, with hindsight, a most unfortunate change of course as far as Bosie was concerned. For if ever there was an artist who should have stayed in his ivory tower it was Lord Alfred Douglas. More than any other poet he ought to have written his verses without taking notice of the hurricane lashing his closed window-panes – to use a metaphor of the *Parnassien* Gautier.[35] Instead of bothering over woman's suffrage (which he did not advocate),[36] the policies of the Liberal Prime Minister, Asquith (which he did not advocate), or the intended reform of the House of Lords (which he did not advocate), he should have concentrated on doing what he was cut out for by Dame Nature: writing poetry.

Edward Tennant in the meantime found himself in a quandary. As a Liberal MP and brother-in-law of the Prime Minister he could not bring himself to accept that Bosie, to whom he paid a yearly salary of some £300, should lecture the government on a weekly basis in the columns of *The Academy*. Tennant was eager to get a peerage, but it was hardly to be expected that Asquith would nominate him for a title as long as Tennant's cousin by marriage continued to attack him (Asquith) in a paper Tennant owned. Bosie was therefore requested to refrain in future from passing judgement on politics. When he refused, Tennant announced he would sell *The Academy*.

Bosie was completely taken aback by this. Not so Crosland. He asked, and was granted, permission to negotiate with Tennant, with whom he took a rather hard line. A disagreeable discussion ensued. Finally Tennant decided to hand the paper, together with the sum of £500, to Bosie. He was really fed up with the whole situation.

In his autobiography Bosie lamented the fact that on this occasion Crosland had not conducted himself in a gentlemanly way.[37] Truth compels us, however, to admit that in his capacity of editor of *The Academy* Bosie was also deficient now and again in this respect. He suffered from an excessive flow of adrenalin which sometimes resulted in letters that cannot be considered models of politeness. This irritability would decrease as he grew older and wiser; but even in his sixties and seventies he was still capable of producing letters which showed that he was a chip off the old block. 'Dear Childe,' George Bernard Shaw admonished him in 1941, referring to a letter from Bosie which had appeared in a weekly, 'dear Childe, you really must not be *insolent*. It gives away your class.'[38] Sensible advice.

Bosie had a tiff with GBS in May 1908 when the latter's comedy, *Getting Married*, was slated in *The Academy*. To Shaw this came as a surprise, for up till then the paper had been very complimentary to him; Bosie had labelled him 'the most profound and brilliant of our modern dramatists'.[39] *Getting Married* for all that could not pass muster, according to the anonymous critic; it was simply indecent. Shaw asked Bosie 'who on earth' had been responsible for that article, suggesting he should publicly distance himself from it in the next number to prevent litigation. He even hinted at the dismissal of the reviewer in question. A fine example of socialist ethics! Bosie thought. He answered Shaw that he himself had written the article; legal steps on the part of 'the Nietzsche of Bayswater' he would be looking for with amused interest. There is always the question, Shaw retorted, who is to edit the editor? There are two Douglases: the poet and the hereditary Douglas. The first should be at the helm; for the second is capable of wrecking the paper as well as himself.[40] These words were uncannily prophetic.

It was remarkable, however, that Bosie, who in *The Spirit Lamp* had inveighed against the censor's decision to ban the production of *Salomé*,[41] now maintained in *The Academy* that this same official ought not to have licensed *Getting Married*. These moral objections betrayed the influence, on the one hand, of Bosie's neighbour in Salisbury, the Right Rev. Monsignor Francis Browning Bickerstaffe-Drew, a Catholic priest whom Olive thought 'clever and interesting, as fascinating as the Protestant parsons are dull!',[42] and, on the other, of a man whose comparison of Crosland with a poltergeist we have just quoted: Arthur Machen. Machen, author of horror stories highly regarded by lovers of the genre, wrote in *The Academy* on religion, and these contributions brought Bosie back to the Christian faith he had renounced when at school. He began to view his paper as 'one of the pillars of the Anglican Church',[43] or, to be more precise, of its 'High Church' branch which is more orientated towards Rome than the 'Low Church', which was, and is, slightly suspicious of papist trappings.

While Olive confided to her diary that she often wanted to 'shout out from the house-tops things in praise of beauty and so-called "sin"',[44] her husband allowed Crosland in *The Academy* to slash and even advocate the suppression of 'combustibles' like *The Yoke*, published by John Long.[45] I have read this book by Hubert Wales and can recommend it to those who, like me, enjoy dipping into the 'naughty' novels of our ancestors. The story of Angelica, a forty-year-old spinster who – anxious to shield him from syphilis – receives her ward Maurice (half her age) into her bed, finding her own fulfilment in the process, seems to me unconsciously funny and wholly innocuous.[46] But perhaps I am wrong. A female subscriber to *The Academy*, at any rate, took a more serious view. She wrote to the editor:

> Sir, As one of the 'maidens' for whose sake – partly at any rate – you are taking serious steps to stop the sale of *The Yoke* I offer you my real thanks.
>
> I have not read it, but I have heard it discussed. I know the reputation the author has for dealing with unpleasant topics, and I have seen the book prominently (or otherwise) exhibited for sale – and cheaply.
>
> In a moment of weakness I might have succumbed to the

temptation of the gaily-coloured outside. My story may be that of many other girls who wish to keep as long as possible a mind 'unspotted'. I regret most deeply ever having read – through inadvertence, it is true – one of the shilling series referred to, *The Confessions of a Princess*.

Mr John Long is a real source of danger to girl readers. After reading the above book I determined to write to him, but a girl dislikes discussing such things.[47]

In the end the Commissioner of Police judged that *The Yoke* was not 'an obscene publication within the meaning of the law and statutes applicable to such matters'.[48] And there the matter ended.

Bosie's rather abrupt conversion had far-reaching consequences. He felt guilty about his gay past (which in no way lessened his admiration for Oscar, whose work was continually being praised in *The Academy*) and took a standpoint towards the practitioners of Greek Love which, he thought, was more in keeping with the teachings of Him who had blessed the meek and merciful but which in reality was as unbalanced as his former point of view. Once he had extolled gays as 'the salt of the earth'.[49] Now he looked upon them as the scum of the nation. This intolerance, typical of a neophyte, he subsequently came to regret. 'I wish to repudiate this attitude here and now,' he wrote in his autobiography. 'It is not for me to condemn or judge anyone else.'[50]

Meanwhile a collision with Bobbie was bound to occur. He sporadically contributed to *The Academy*, which was not to the taste of Crosland and Pamela Tennant, who told Bosie that a notorious worshipper of Venus Paidika like Ross should not form part of the *Academy* set. Ross had been increasingly annoyed at the tone of most articles – although in justice to Bosie it must be said that he always allowed authors whose books had been savaged fully to answer their critics – but his indignation may be imagined when he found out that a review of his had been 'corrected' by Crosland, so much so that its drift had been completely altered. When Ross complained, Crosland told him why he would like to dispense with his services in future. That hurt. Ross was not accustomed to being treated like that; as art expert and champion of Oscar he had acquired considerable status. Oscar's artistic rehabilitation – which is evinced by the fact that between November 1909 and September 1910 *The Importance of*

Being Earnest enjoyed a run of 316 performances in London[51] – was chiefly due to *his* efforts. To crown it all, he brought out Oscar's collected works in an edition of twelve handsome volumes. When the first of these had appeared, Bosie (much to Crosland's chagrin) had purred over them in *The Academy*. 'From the purely literary point of view, Oscar was unquestionably the greatest figure of the nineteenth century,' he claimed.

> We unhesitatingly say that his influence on the literature of Europe has been greater than that of any man since Byron died, and, unlike Byron's, it has been all for good. The evil that he did, inasmuch as he did a tithe of the things imputed to him, was interred with his bones, the good (how much the greater part of this great man!) lives after him and will live for ever.[52]

That Bosie's admiration for Oscar did not extend to his literary executor was made plain yet again to Ross on 1 December of that year, 1908. Ross was fêted at the Ritz (a rather maudlin occasion),[53] and Bosie, although he had received an invitation to this banquet at which some two hundred guests were present, failed to turn up. That hurt. Nor did he congratulate Ross on the success of his work. That hurt, too. But Ross could not stomach the fact that whenever he called at 39 Fellows Road, Hampstead, the butler assured him that Lord and Lady Douglas were 'not at home'.

It is ironic that Ross, who in the old days, when Oscar had been alive, had seen Bosie as an impediment, now refused to be dropped by his former rival. A letter he received from him in March 1909, however, quenched any inclination to get closer to its sender. As regards that 'absurd dinner', Bosie wrote, he had not turned up as he did not feel inclined to meet either Frank Harris or Robert Sherard, with whom Oscar had not been on speaking terms when he died, or the Duchess of Sutherland and other people who had no connection whatever with Oscar or literature. That he (Bosie) preferred to keep out of Ross's way could be explained by the fact that, having changed his views, he no longer cared to consort with socialists and sodomites.[54]

Bosie received no answer, although he did learn the recipient's predictable reaction. Ross was furious. *Eh bien! la guerre*. His solicitor advised him not to sue Bosie for libel, fearing his client would suffer the same fate as Oscar, and Ross took this advice. Moreover, he had a better plan. In the autumn he induced the curator of the British Museum to take care of the manuscript of *De Profundis*, stipulating that its contents not be made public for some time; until 1 January 1960, it was agreed. When posterity could read what Oscar Wilde had alleged about Lord Alfred Douglas, he would not be around to justify himself – a prospect that gave Ross inexhaustible pleasure. Vengeance is a dish best served cold.

8

Never Rude,
Except on Purpose

Bosie seldom got parcels from Holland. He was therefore surprised when in the summer of 1908 he received one from The Hague, courtesy of P.C. Boutens. This author was wont to commission Edouard Verbeke, owner of the Saint Catherine's Press in Bruges, to produce limited editions 'both of my own works and other literary productions which might interest my friends, and which are otherwise unobtainable'.[1] Verbeke had already printed *Five Poems of Dante Gabriel Rossetti* in 1905 and Boutens's *Collected Sonnets* in 1907; on 30 June of the following year he put the finishing touches to an impression of *Poems by Lord Alfred Douglas*. The book – 'probably the most coveted of Boutens's private editions'[2] – comprised an unauthorized reprint of *Poems* (1896) and *The City of the Soul* (1899). The packet sent to Bosie contained an inscribed presentation copy, with which he was mightily pleased. 'The book you sent me is altogether charming, and the paper and printing are beautiful,' he wrote to Boutens. 'I am gratified to think that my poems are read by a few connoisseurs in Holland. When you are in London I hope you will give me the pleasure of coming to see me.'[3]

Boutens was not the only continental who brought out Bosie's lyrics: from an article in *The Academy* (which unfortunately does not enter into details) one learns that they had been pirated in Italy and Austria as well.[4]

Bosie earned lavish praise when on 3 June 1909 his *Sonnets* were published by the Academy Publishing Company, printed by the Arden Press on hand-made paper, in bold clear type, bound in stiff boards, with gilt top and marker. The volume, priced at 2s. 6d. net, consisted of nineteen of Bosie's very best poems, chiselled masterpieces which, in my opinion, can stand with those of Platen, Hérédia, even those of

Shakespeare. The *Saturday Review* declared that no man living was capable of writing sonnets 'quite so flawless in their grace and music'.[5] 'These poems,' the Dutch critic P.N. van Eyck noted, 'belong to the most beautiful that have been written in England.'[6] And Harry Count Kessler, who sent a copy to Hugo von Hofmannsthal, raved in an accompanying letter about 'the truly brilliant Alfred Douglas . . . who is publishing stuff here which, to me, seems to be much purer and more imperishable than anything written by Wilde'.[7]

A sound mind belongs in a sound body. Bosie had argued this previously in the *Granta*, the well-known weekly edited by students in Cambridge. The article in question, 'Art and Sport', showed yet again that its author was not weighed down by an inferiority complex. 'To be brutally frank,' Bosie had written, for instance, 'I happen to have written some very good poetry.'[8] Statements like these provided the editor with ammunition to snipe at him in a witty essay which appeared anonymously in the *Granta* on 8 December 1908: 'Celebrities I have not met, yet still am happy [*sic*]. No. 1 – Lord Alfred Bruce Douglas (or the London curry-worry).' It satirized both Bosie's vanity and the zest with which in *The Academy* he went at his contemporaries.

> It is interesting to observe the singular relish with which our hero castigates not only certain offending persons, but large groups of people, even nations, are not safe. In some of his more restless moods I have known him to sweep away the continent of America in a hurricane of petulant damnation. It has been suggested that this comprehensive flagellation is the practice of some mediæval vow which is laid upon the followers of a secret religious brotherhood. On the whole I am inclined to discountenance this view.
>
> I can see ample *raison d'être* for the truculent attitude towards the Universe adopted by the baffling figure – to whom this small tribute is gratefully dedicated – in his capacity as humorist. How can simple orthodox humorists such as Mr Owen Seaman and Mr Hilaire Belloc hope to compete with this dazzling jester, who combines the adventurousness of a Don Quixote with the genial expansiveness of a Scrooge? It may be that he has yet to educate our blunt wits to perceive the finer intricacies of his art, but surely our national sense of the ludicrous can be in no great peril as long as *The Academy* is to be obtained every Friday for threepence.[9]

Bosie was not amused and expressed his displeasure in his paper.[10] When the lampoonist thereupon described him in the columns of the *Cambridge Review* as 'a weekly and quite unconscious contributor to our national gaiety, who should be preserved at any cost',[11] Bosie threatened to sue the printers and editors of the *Review* with an action for libel. The number with the offending skit was hurriedly withdrawn from circulation and apologies tendered.[12]

Such incidents became ever more frequent, since there was a discrepancy between the amount of criticism *The Academy* thought it should pass and the amount of criticism it was willing to take. On 15 May 1909 Crosland announced that by now the magazine had received sufficient apologies – in print, in typescript and handwritten – to paper a wall; and he added that in future slanderers would be taken to court.[13]

A few weeks later Crosland himself was sued because he refused to take back what he had told the Hon. Henry Frederick ('Freddie') Walpole Manners-Sutton. He had called him a coward and a poltroon and a person of no principle and stuck to it. The affair was a direct result of the financial difficulties *The Academy* had got into and which would only increase when in July Bosie and Crosland decided to break with W.H. Smith and Son, the firm which took care of printing and distributing the paper.[14] The pair did not like the ethos of this company (which, they claimed, behaved shabbily towards its competitors);[15] but the receding profits soon made it clear to them that there was a price tag attached to the taking of a moral attitude.

Bosie turned to his friend, Manners-Sutton, a viscount's son who often lunched and dined with the Douglases 'as he seems to eat better with us and it teaches him good manners' (to quote from Olive's diary)[16] and who had repeatedly assured Bosie that he would help him out if ever *The Academy* would have to contend with liquidity problems. Now that it came to the point, however, he cried off. Crosland, delegated by Bosie, was told that a loan was out of the question as long as Bosie was receiving the 'excessive' salary of £15 a week. Moreover, Freddie observed that Olive had been 'a fool' to marry Bosie. This remark, which Crosland reported to his boss, sparked off the quarrel.[17] Bosie sent a furious letter to Manners-Sutton, while Crosland penned an article which appeared in *The Academy* on 19 June. It gave chapter without verse. Mention was made of 'a certain scion of a noble house' – and those in the know were bound to conclude that this was a reference to Manners-Sutton – who was connected with two publishing houses, one of which concentrated on issuing works of a high moral tone, while the other specialized in 'naughty novels'. Freddie demanded that *The Academy* print a paragraph stating that he was not the gentleman alluded to. This did not appeal to Crosland, and when, as we have said, he called him (in writing) an unprincipled coward, Manners-Sutton had had enough. He sued Crosland for libel.

The case, which did not open at the Old Bailey until 10 February 1910, was far from uplifting. Mutual mud-slinging made for 'sensation in court'. Freddie was cross-examined on Maggie Dupont, a virgin under age whom he was supposed to have deflowered; Crosland on his numerous creditors; and Bosie, who appeared as a witness, on his friendship with Oscar. That, however, turned out to be a tactical mistake on the part of the plaintiff's counsel. The Wilde story had nothing whatever to do with the suit, and the effort to rake it up was not appreciated by the jury. Crosland was acquitted.[18]

This was a pyrrhic victory for Bosie. In the first place, Freddie and he remained estranged for a long time (it was thanks to Olive that they were eventually reconciled). Second, the dispute proved to be a financial liability, as the Common Serjeant refused to order the plaintiff to pay the costs of the defence. And, third, Bosie began to acquire a taste for litigation. The ease with which he had parried the attacks of Freddie's counsel – 'Douglas simply ate him, he *ate* him; there's no other word for it,'[19] an onlooker said – gave him a high opinion of himself as a witness. When four months afterwards a new chance to shine as such came his way, he seized the opportunity.

The Rev. Robert Horton had drawn attention in the *Daily News* to the fact that *The Academy* had 'passed into Roman hands' and that Douglas and Crosland should be seen as the mouthpiece of His Holiness the Pope. Bosie was not prepared to lie down under such an allegation and went to court for that reason.

The conflict must be seen in the context of its time. Horton, who believed that a plot was being laid to bring the fatherland under the yoke of the Mother Church, was not the only Englishman afflicted with a hatred of Catholicism in the years preceding the Great War. Oscar's erstwhile advocate, Sir Edward Clarke, felt moved to address some 'vigorous' letters to *The Times*, expressing his concern that 'Roman practices' were permitted 'to continue unchecked' in the Church of England.[20] Blows had been exchanged between demonstrators shouting 'Down with Popery! Go to Rome!' and some 'stalwart young men' forming part of a surpliced, candle-bearing congregation celebrating St Alban's Day in Teddington.[21] In 1908 the Prime Minister had banned a Catholic procession in London at the last minute under pressure from militant Protestants who had threatened to make a slaughter of its participants. In *The Academy* Bosie had fiercely protested against Asquith's surrender to this terrorism,[22] and it was by quoting articles like these – articles which clearly bespoke sympathy for the Catholic faith – that Horton hoped to justify his statements in the *Daily News*. His counsel, Edward Carson, was well known to Bosie; it will be remembered that he had brought Oscar to his knees in the Old Bailey fifteen years ago.

There was no love lost between Carson and Bosie, as became obvious during the cross-examination to which the latter was subjected on 8 June. Bosie emphasized that as an independent editor he felt disparaged by the accusation that he was involved in a popish conspiracy.

'You respect nobody but yourself?' Carson asked him at one point.

'You don't know,' Bosie replied. 'You don't know many people that I do. We don't move in the same circles.'

'I am glad we don't.'

'I ditto that.'

Laughter was heard from the public gallery. The ripostes of Crosland and Arthur Machen (who had pulverized Horton's theological books)[23] raised laughs as well; but it was sad, of course, as the judge remarked in the course of his summing-up, that religious disputes were being fought out in a courtroom as late as 1910. The verdict clearly showed that the suit had baffled the jurors: they found for the defendant but stated in a rider that Horton should have taken more care in ascertaining his facts.[24]

Bosie was instructed to pay Horton's costs and could not raise this sum without selling *The Academy*. He did this with a bleeding heart. The paper quickly went downhill; when in 1911 it reviewed the third edition of *The City of the Soul* (such distinguished work, the critic wrote, is badly needed in a day when tinkers, tailors and pushers of bath-chairs take to 'literature'),[25] the number of subscribers had already dropped dramatically. A few years afterwards, in 1916, *The Academy* was dead and buried.

Meanwhile Bosie, in the middle of the journey of his life, had gone through an inferno.

Gustav Mahler – Joris-Karl Huysmans – Oscar Wilde – Lionel Johnson – John Gray – Aubrey Beardsley – Ernest Dowson – Renée Vivien: what is the connection between these *fin-de-siècle* artists? The answer is that they all converted, in some cases on their death-bed, to the religion which, under the influence of (Neo)Platonic philosophy, uses beauty – the beauty of music, painting and sculpture, the beauty of the word, polished by rhythm and rhyme – to reach out to the divinity; they converted to the Roman Catholic faith.

Bosie took this step, too. It was, he told John Lane, the best thing he had ever done in his life.[26] In his autobiography he stated that it had been his reading *Pascendi*, Pope Pius's encyclical which had come his way while he was editing *The Academy*, that had first convinced him of the validity of the Vatican's claims to apostolic exclusivity;[27] but he did not move in too hurried a manner and waited until May 1911 before joining the Church to which he would cling during the ordeals that were in store for him. The Church would save him from despair – from suicide and madness.

On the other hand, it was his conversion which partly caused his troubles. His father-in-law, a widower for three years, deeply distrusted Rome, as may be gathered from the fact that he had refused to speak to his only sister since her marriage to a Catholic and her adoption of her husband's faith. Custance greatly resented Bosie becoming a Catholic. He was even more displeased at Raymond's becoming one as well.

The soldier and his wife had always shown an excessive interest in their only grandchild. 'Mummy and Daddy were so dreadful about him,' Olive reminded Bosie afterwards, 'they seemed to think we ought to give him up to them.'[28] Custance, who had never forgiven the stork from bringing him nothing but girls (two of them; the younger, Cecil, had died in 1909), had agreed with Bosie to pay Raymond's school fees. The boy often stayed with his grandfather, but this did not satisfy Custance. He wanted to obtain complete custody of him, which Bosie of course did not like. Both men became increasingly quarrelsome. Custance gave Bosie to understand he was a bad parent, and Bosie gave Custance to understand (with difficulty, as the Colonel was hard of hearing) that he should mind his own business. Initially Custance considered making Raymond his heir, provided he would renounce Catholicism, but then he hit upon another tactic to gain control.

Olive was not altogether thrifty. Her father had urged her more than once to mend her ways.

> You chose to run away with Alfred who has nothing and you must now live accordingly. You had no business to take a house and give luncheon and dinner parties which I know you have . . . I utterly decline to be absolutely ruined by my daughter which I very soon would be if I went on paying your debts. If you have not got the money you must not have the things, otherwise it is a certainty you will find yourself in the workhouse.[29]

The Colonel's father had entailed the property on Olive. Custance now suggested to his daughter that she surrender her rights in exchange for an annuity of £600 which he would pay her; after his death she and her son would, as usufructuaries, be assured of a regular income for the rest of their lives. The proposal was as tempting as it was timely, considering that the Douglases had less to spend since Bosie had ceased editing *The Academy*. Suspecting, however, that there was a snag somewhere, Bosie entreated Olive to insist on a signed undertaking from her father concerning the £600. Custance told him not to interfere with the matter, and, when Olive showed up at Weston Old Hall, all the papers had been prepared – with the exception of the document to which Bosie had alluded. Olive, in whose hands a pen was pushed, meekly referred to it. Custance seemed hurt at what he called her 'lack of trust'. He gave her his word. That should suffice. And Olive affixed her signature.

When afterwards Custance ordered her to hand Raymond to him, Bosie announced that he would send the lad to Lady Queensberry; whereupon Custance dropped the mask. 'The moment he takes the boy away,' he wrote to Olive, 'all payments to you will cease.'[30] Sheer blackmail! Bosie thought. And the threat was not vain: Olive was deprived of her income. Bosie bombarded his father-in-law with angry letters and – after Custance had informed him these would be consigned, unopened, to the flames – with telegrams and postcards in which the addressee was called a dishonest and dishonourable man. These messages convinced Custance that he was only doing the right thing. Should his grandson really be raised by someone who expressed himself in such an undignified way?

Bosie, however, insulted Custance with a set purpose. He hoped to entice him to sue him for libel; a court of justice could then decide *who* had been acting in an underhand way here. At first Custance ignored these provocations. Time, he knew, was on his side. Bosie was not well off. He could not manage without Olive's money; surely he would change his tone as his debts and hers accumulated. But when Bosie let it be known that he was going to enlighten Custance's friends and business relations as to what the Colonel had been up to, the latter went to his solicitor and lodged a complaint against Bosie. This happened on 26 February 1913. Although a barrister subsequently assured Bosie he ought to have won his case, and that reading out Custance's letter to Olive, from which we have just quoted, would have sufficed to convince the jury that he, the defendant, had the right on his side,[31] Bosie actually got the worst of it when on 24 April the trial came on.

To understand why, we must retrace our steps and repair ourselves to the office of the publisher, Martin Secker, who in the autumn of 1910 had a meeting there with Arthur Ransome, a young author who had just completed a study of Edgar Allan Poe and who now wished to follow it up with a book on Robert Louis Stevenson. Secker agreed but cabled shortly afterwards, begging him to write a biography of Oscar Wilde. Ransome, not suspecting he was about to stir up a hornets' nest, raised no objections.

A friend advised him to secure the help of Oscar's literary executor, Robert Ross. He turned out to be complaisance itself. To be sure, he was willing to assist Mr Ransome with his research, and he promised him access to archives which had hitherto remained shut. This was a godsend to Ransome, who gratefully dedicated his book, *Oscar Wilde: A Critical Study*, to Ross. He thought him witty, sympathetic and selfless.[32] Ross for his part saw the author as a tool with which he could at long last get even with his arch-enemy, Lord Alfred Douglas, the Adonis who twenty years ago had appropriated Oscar Wilde, relegating him, Bobbie, to limbo.

Ross would later assert that he had not shown Ransome 'any documents or letters reflecting on Douglas' and that he had refused to read the proofs of the book 'on the grounds that I should be unlikely to agree with much that he said'.[33] The amount of truth contained in these statements is nil. 'I am very anxious, when your book comes out, to nurse the press properly and to persuade various editors that it belongs to an entirely different category to the Sherard-Comtesse de Bremont sort of thing,' he wrote to Ransome on 8 June 1911. 'It will be the first serious study of Wilde that has ever appeared, and I want it to be recognised as such.'[34] This is not how one writes about a book one has not read or is not going to read before publication. That Robbie knew at least part of it appears from another letter to the biographer, in the course of which he warmly praised 'the eloquence and excellence' of the introduction: 'It is really admirable,' he said. 'You have adopted a brilliant method of "bringing up the curtain".'[35] The author himself recorded in his memoirs that Ross allowed him to borrow a typescript of *De Profundis*, along with Oscar's letter to Ross in which the sender complained about the mythical betrayal of Bosie who was supposed to have abandoned him at Naples. Ransome's reconstruction of Oscar's downfall and its aftermath was based on this material. How surprised was Bosie to learn from the book, which was published on 16 February 1912, that *De Profundis* 'was not addressed to Mr Ross but to a man to whom Oscar felt that he owed some, at least, of the circumstances of his public disgrace', a man 'whose actions, even subsequent to the trials, had been such as to cause [him] considerable pain'. It was (Ransome went on) this same person – 'whose friendship had already cost [Wilde] more than it was worth . . . whose conduct he had condemned, whose influence he had feared' – who had persuaded the released artist to join him in Naples, and who, 'as soon as there was no money, had left him. "It was," said Wilde, "the most bitter experience of a bitter life!"'[36]

Utterly baffled, Bosie, for the first time since their rupture in 1909, sent a letter to Ross.

It is true that the man Ransome does not mention my name but anyone reading the book carefully with a full knowledge of the circumstances would be led to infer that I was the 'friend' referred to. I now write to ask you whether it is true that the MS. of *De*

Profundis consists of a letter addressed to me, and if so why you have concealed this fact from me for all these years. I should also like to know why you published the letter as a book without my knowledge or consent.

Hitherto I have always been under the impression that *De Profundis* was a letter written by Wilde to *you* but containing abusive or scandalous references to me which you had suppressed. Of course if this latter version of the affair is correct there is no more to be said. But if Ransome's version is correct, matters assume a very different and very serious aspect.[37]

Olive begged her husband to ignore the matter, but, after consulting Crosland he decided to sue Ransome, Secker and the book's printers as well as *The Times* Book Club, which circulated it. He did not ask for damages; he only wished his name to be cleared.

Ransome was flabbergasted and would have preferred to settle things amicably, as distinct from his wife who revelled in the sensation and who, endowed as she was with a fertile imagination, sent a wire to her mother-in-law telling her that a warrant had been issued for Arthur's arrest, adding that he had gone into hiding. Ross (who in *Who's Who* had given 'litigation' as his favourite pastime) could hardly hide his satisfaction, too. This roused Martin Secker's suspicions. He got the impression that Ross, who had volunteered to pay the legal bill for the defence, did this to attain his own goal: to get his revenge on Lord Alfred.[38] Now Secker had just sold back the rights of *Oscar Wilde: A Critical Study* to its author; it sufficed for him (Secker) to apologize to Bosie, who subsequently came to see him and who would become a lifelong friend. Ransome, on the other hand, was pressed by George Lewis Junior, Ross's solicitor, not to throw in the towel. In that case, Lewis argued, Bosie would undoubtedly bring an action against Ross because the latter had handed him (Ransome) a typescript of *De Profundis*.

Those of my readers who did not skip the introduction will remember that in the course of it I quoted one of Robbie's legal advisers, the solicitor E.S.P. Haynes, who once described his client – by then deceased – as 'a very subtle propagandist in his own favour [who had] biassed opinion most unfairly against Douglas'. Ross at this stage was, indeed, carefully preparing a wholesale character assassination. On 10 June 1912 the novelist Marie Belloc Lowndes wrote excitedly in her diary:

I had a long talk with Robert Ross. He told me as a great secret that he had only published a third part of *De Profundis* and that the rest told in the greatest detail the story of Oscar Wilde's trial and his relations with Douglas. He had given the manuscript to the British Museum and it is not to be published for seventy years. I said to him: 'Then you think Douglas was poor Oscar's *âme damnée?*' He assented.

To impart information under the guise of 'a great secret' is the surest way to its gaining the widest possible currency. Marie went on:

I asked him about Frank Harris's book. He told me that he was officially supposed to know nothing about it. Harris asked him to read the proofs. 'If I do, I shall probably not like something in it, and as Wilde's executor I might have to take action.' Apparently Harris's book is simply a long account of Douglas's treachery and of the fact – which is pretty well known already – that many things attributed by the prosecution to Wilde were really done by Douglas.[39]

Harris's book would not be published until 1916, luridly titled *Oscar Wilde: His Life and Confessions*. Ross, again, was feeding an author with information he *knew* to be false – the story of Bosie abandoning Oscar in Naples is a case in point – throwing in some legends of his own invention – telling Harris, for instance, that in 1894 Bosie had been kicked out of Egypt by a scandalized Cromer[40] – and then trying to shield himself from the consequences by pretending not to know the purport of a book he had godfathered.

For Bosie nerve-racking months lay ahead. It had been agreed that the Ransome case would be immediately followed by the action brought by Custance against Bosie; but first the aristocrat had to take a number of blows, which explains why he was not able to enter the arena in top form.

When at the turn of the year he returned home, having been away to visit his sister, he found that the house in Church Row, Hampstead, was partially cleared out and that Olive had disappeared. She had left him a note telling him she had gone to her father. Olive was placed in an awful dilemma, really, being torn between Bosie and the Colonel; the latter held her in a tight grip. 'I went down to Weston penniless and heavily in debt,' she wrote to Sybil afterwards, 'and my father told me he would do nothing for me unless I get him the boy. I am utterly helpless since I made those settlements.'[41] Bosie had, admittedly, put her in a quandary by the less than elegant way he had challenged her father. But had Custance left him any choice? Bosie thought not. Olive's departure was, to him, an act of crass betrayal, nothing more, nothing less. She seems not to have realized how much her decision undermined his position, which it did to such an extent that Custance now thought the time was ripe to start a procedure in the Chancery Court to gain full custody over Raymond. 'Behold, Your House Is Left Unto You Desolate' is the title of a poignant sonnet a disillusioned Bosie wrote in these terrible days.

Meanwhile his money-lenders asked themselves if, after the legal battles which lay ahead of him, he would still be able to pay his debts. To be on the safe side they insisted he discharge all his bills. This he could not possibly do, and he was made bankrupt on 14 January 1913. As a result he was automatically struck off the list of members of White's Club, the oldest and perhaps most exclusive London club, to which he had belonged for more than twenty years. His exclusion was a setback which should not be underestimated; before the Ransome case came up – a case in which in his reputation was at stake – Bosie already knew himself to be *déclassé* in the eyes of those whom he considered to be his peers.

But all this paled into insignificance in comparison with the agony he experienced when he came to read the complete text of *De Profundis*. Ransome had pleaded justification (whereon Bosie had added a claim for damages); his defence was based on a number of letters from Oscar, including the 'encyclical' written in Reading Gaol; and copies of these documents were handed to Bosie before the trial, according to rule. At long last he could take note of the abuse which Oscar – believing that Bosie had completely forgotten him – had hurled at his 'own dear Boy'. After some sixteen years, *De Profundis* had reached its addressee. And Bosie's hair stood on end.

> Deprived of books, of all human intercourse, isolated from every humane and humanising influence, condemned to eternal silence, robbed of all intercourse with the external world, treated like an unintelligent animal, brutalised below the level of any of the brute-creation, the wretched man who is confined in an English prison can hardly escape becoming insane.

This had been pointed out by Oscar, shortly after his release, to the readers of the *Daily Chronicle*, and he had added:

> One of the tragedies of prison life is that it turns a man's heart to stone. The feelings of natural affection, like all other feelings, require to be fed. They easily die of inanition. A brief letter, four times a year, is not enough to keep alive the gentler and more humane affections by which ultimately the nature is kept sensitive to any fine or beautiful influences that may heal a wrecked and ruined life.[42]

De Profundis had clearly shown how much Oscar had suffered under these conditions; the 'amazingly undignified' attacks on Bosie – the adjectives are Shaw's[43] – formed the precipitation, as we have argued, of the hardships he had had to endure behind bars. But a considerable time, more than a decade, would have to pass before Bosie could understand this. He felt betrayed, betrayed by the artist whose memory he had revered, whose charisma he had evoked in a matchless sonnet, whose works he had praised in *The Academy*. The man he had loved and whom, in a letter to his brother Percy written three weeks after Oscar's burial, he had exonerated from cruelty, meanness, hypocrisy and vindictiveness –

> He was always kind and generous and gentle and forgiving. I don't know why I'm inflicting all this on you. I was a little afraid you might think I had changed my mind about him in later life. I never did, and he was the same to me always, my dearest and best friend.[44]

– this man seemed now to have risen from the grave to grab him by the throat and choke him. The whole thing was a nightmare.

Bosie, erroneously believing that Oscar had decreed that after his (Bosie's) death *De Profundis* was to be published in its entirety, was filled now with white-hot hatred of Oscar. The idol had changed into the Devil incarnate.

9

A Fiery Furnace
of Affliction

The public gallery of the King's Bench Division, where the case of *Douglas v. Ransome and Others* opened on 17 April, was packed with curious spectators when the principal actors made their appearance. Women were denied admittance; they were supposed to be too finely strung to attend such a trial. Only Ivy, Ransome's wife, refused to decamp. She had been waiting for this day with inordinate relish.

Military historians are wont to introduce their reconstruction of a battle with an inventory of the forces involved, and following their example we may immediately note that the combatants were not really well matched. A mosquito was to take on an elephant. Bosie, who could not afford a first-class lawyer, was defended by his inexperienced friend Cecil Hayes and a certain Harold Benjamin. Ransome, not richer than Bosie, had been able, thanks to the financial support of Robert Ross, to avail himself of the assistance of two prominent experts, Sir James Campbell, KC (the future Lord Glenavy) and H.A. McCardie, while *The Times* Book Club had turned to Eustache Hills, W.G. Howard Gritten and F.E. Smith, KC (the future Lord Birkenhead), who, 'by [his] intelligence, audacity, driving ambition and sheer gall',[1] had fought his way up. His tongue was razor-sharp.

There are some judges – Bosie wrote in his autobiography – who, when one of the parties in a suit has to struggle against an overwhelming array of 'big counsel', will do their utmost to enable this party properly to put its case to the jury; but Sir Charles John Darling was not one of them.[2] This claim can easily be substantiated. Contemporary reports of the case, those in *The Times*, the *Daily News* and the *Daily Telegraph*, for example, show the extent to which Darling was prejudiced against Bosie. Those reports, however voluminous, were yet far from being complete, for the judge had enjoined the journalists to be as discreet as possible, for the matter which was about to be raked up – the life of Oscar Wilde, whom Darling would later describe as 'a great beast'[3] – was very, very distasteful indeed. A verbatim report of the proceedings 'would do incalculable harm to public morals'.[4]

This injunction sheds light on Bosie's vulnerability. In England homosexuality was considered at the time to be the nadir of depravity; as Oscar Wilde's former lover, Douglas was therefore, in the eyes of the jurors, suspect in advance. His foes were well aware of this fact.

Their principal witness was Oscar himself. After Hayes had argued that it was absurd to suppose that an undergraduate of twenty-one could have 'debauched' a worldly-wise and self-assured man in his late thirties like Oscar Wilde, and after Bosie had stressed that, contrary to what was alleged in Mr Ransome's book, he (Bosie) had not abandoned Oscar, McCardie announced he would establish the evil influence the plaintiff had exercised on the artist. Bosie was shown the manuscript of *De Profundis*, which had been lent for the occasion by the British Museum. Did Lord Alfred recognize the handwriting of Oscar Wilde? Yes, Lord Alfred recognized the handwriting of Wilde. Whereupon McCardie began reading out the unpublished fragments. 'Dear Bosie, After long and fruitless waiting I have determined to write to you myself, as much for your sake as for mine . . .' The public held its breath. What was *this*?

Fifteen minutes had elapsed when Bosie, visibly affected, asked if he could sit down. He could, said Darling, who took over the reading of *De Profundis* from McCardie (who was getting hoarse) and who in turn was relieved by Campbell. It was a long screed.

When on the following day the reading by McCardie of the 'encyclical' had been continued for some time, the judge noted that Bosie was not there. The warders went out in search for him, and when they showed him in Darling asked why he had ventured to absent himself. Bosie answered that he had been under the impression that there was no need for him to be present during the reading of *De Profundis*; had the judge not told him the day before he could understand that he (Bosie) wished to go out?

'I said I did not wonder why you wanted to sit down,' Darling snapped. 'Now, I may tell you this. You are the plaintiff in this case, and if you leave the court again while you are a witness I will give leave for judgment to be entered against you.'[5]

McCardie read on – until the jury declared they had heard enough. Hayes, however, wished the complete text to be read; it would then appear that its tone would gradually become less bitter, showing that Mr Wilde had been a person of moods. But Darling ruled otherwise, and Campbell subjected Bosie to cross-examination.

It was clear that the poet's position had been seriously undermined. From *De Profundis* – lengthily and avidly quoted by the press – he had emerged as an ungrateful, jaded, selfish, *irritating* little brat scribbling doggerel verse, as the louse in Oscar Wilde's fur. With that, Ransome's statements seemed conclusively proven.

Could Bosie defend himself against Oscar's accusations? Yes and no. He possessed letters of his which were able to dispose, for the greater part, of the venom of *De Profundis*. Three examples:

> It is really absurd. *I can't live without you.* You are so dear, so wonderful. I think of you all day long, and miss your grace, your boyish beauty, the bright sword-play of your wit, the delicate fancy of your genius, so surprising always in its sudden swallow-flights towards north or south, towards sun or moon – and, above all, you yourself . . . I have no words for how I love you.

> Dear, dear boy, you are more to me than any one of them has any idea; you are the atmosphere of beauty through which I see life; you are the incarnation of all lovely things.

> How strange to live in a land where the worship of beauty and the passion of love are considered infamous. I hate England; it is only bearable to me because you are here.[6]

But this material – and that is what made Bosie's situation so 'Kafkaesque' – would not, as far as his contemporaries were concerned, *exonerate* him; on the contrary, in view of the nature of the sender's sentiments towards him, it would greatly *incriminate* him. He therefore dared not produce it.

The taboo on homosexuality also explains why Bosie's opponents, in their endeavour to blacken him as much as possible, could avail themselves of pieces one would have expected nowadays Cecil Hayes to have come up with on behalf of his client. Bosie's article which had appeared in the *Revue Blanche*, for instance. It clearly showed that Oscar's condemnation had not left Bosie unmoved; but the fact that in the course of it he described the treatment meted out to his friend as 'barbarous'[7] raised the jurors' eyebrows. From the archive of *Truth* a letter was unearthed, dated June 1895, in which Bosie referred to the Wilde affair as 'the greatest romantic tragedy of the age'.[8] *Romantic?* Oscar's notorious letter to Bosie which Queensberry had managed to obtain, and which had been produced by the Marquess's solicitors to 'save' their client's son 'from the claws of a monster', was now used to besmirch this son. Bosie, incidentally, was completely taken aback by the production of this material, for it had not been mentioned in Ransome's plea of justification. That the defence nevertheless brought it forward was not in keeping with 'the traditions of the Bar'; but Darling saw no ground to interfere.

Campbell availed himself of the tactical advantage of being able to interpret *each* answer of Bosie's to his disadvantage. Did the plaintiff really contribute £360 towards the costs of prosecuting Lord Queensberry? – Well, yes. – Unnatural son! (Campbell would otherwise have called Bosie 'a disloyal friend'.) And did the plaintiff really receive Oscar in a villa at Naples? – Yes. – While the plaintiff *knew* about the ex-convict's lifestyle?

'You must allow me to finish my answer if you wish to get the truth,' Bosie said to Campbell, who was continually interrupting him. 'But perhaps you do not wish it.'

'Will you not be impertinent to the learned Counsel?' Darling barked.

'I am not impertinent,' said Bosie.

'You are impertinent, whether you wish it or not.'

'I accept your Lordship's rebuke, but I thought I was entitled . . .'

'Don't you merely "accept" my ruling!'

'I said I accept your rebuke.'

'You will act upon it.'

'I shall do so. I thought I might explain . . .'

'Will you be silent?' thundered the judge (whose poetical efforts had been laughed at in *The Academy*[9] and who now took the opportunity of getting even with Bosie); 'will you be silent until you are asked another question?'[10]

Campbell read out Oscar's letter to Ross in which the author complained of the fictitious betrayal of the plaintiff, who supposedly had left him to his own devices the moment his (Oscar's) weekly allowance had been stopped.[11] Now this was an accusation Bosie thought he could refute. For at his behest his mother had paid £200 via More Adey to Oscar. Adey appeared as a witness but misrepresented the facts. The £200, he alleged, formed part of a 'debt of honour'. He did not unequivocally state that Bosie had agreed to leaving Oscar on the condition that Lady Queensberry would send Oscar this sum. 'You, too,' Bosie subsequently wrote to Adey, an *intimus* of Robert Ross, 'played the Judas Iscariot to me, your old friend. You deliberately misled the jury. I wish you joy of what you have done.'[12]

It is true that Bosie could prove with the help of his cheque book that he had paid considerable sums of money to Oscar during the final years of the artist's life, but this did not balance the compromising (and wholly irrelevant) facts put forward by the defence. The plaintiff, said Campbell, had not only contributed a 'disgusting article' to the *Revue Blanche*, he had, moreover, 'some most indecent poems'[13] to his discredit. 'Two Loves', for example, which counsel read out. When Hayes remarked that Shakespeare should be glad he was not being interrogated by Campbell about his sonnets, the judge intervened. Surely Mr Hayes was not suggesting that the Bard had been inflicted with the aberrations of Wilde?

At this stage of the trial the members of the jury might have been forgiven for believing they had been empanelled to pass judgment on Bosie's erstwhile sexual activities. The defence had purposely aimed at that; and they still had not played their last trump: a batch of letters from Bosie to Oscar.

Bosie, whose nerves had already been shattered – as may be gathered from the fact that he could not even remember, when asked, in what year his sonnets had appeared – looked up in surprise. These letters had not been mentioned in Ransome's plea of justification, either. 'I am glad you are enjoying Rome so much,' one of them ran. 'It certainly is a lively place, and life there was really better than Naples. I quite agree with you that the boys are far more beautiful there. In fact, I think they come next to English boys.'[14]

When the excitement had died down, Bosie expressed his disgust that these letters were suddenly produced without notice being given.

'If they had been disclosed to you,' Darling queried, 'would you have come here or not?'

'Yes, I would,' Bosie answered.

'What, then, is the unfairness?'

'I think I should have had the opportunity of reading them and knowing how I was to meet the charges.'

'Nobody would have known about them if you had not brought this action!'[15]

Now where did they come from, these missives, for which in Darling's words even a decent pagan of the time of Pericles would have been ashamed? Why, from Robert Ross's collection. He had appropriated Bosie's letters to Oscar after the latter's death and had carefully kept them – or, to be more precise, he had only kept those that could compromise the sender; the rest he had destroyed. Much water had to flow under the bridge before Bosie would be able to forgive him for this.

In his final speech, which followed F.E. Smith's, Campbell claimed that the plaintiff, who in 1895 'had got off scot free', had 'brought this action in the hope of blasting Wilde's reputation' and contrasted Bosie with Oscar's 'real, loyal friends',[16] with Mr Ross in particular, who had set himself the task of rescuing Oscar's works from oblivion.

Then it was the turn of Cecil Hayes. He pointed out that the defence had delivered a plea of justification of sixty-three pages but had failed to call the defendant, Ransome, as a witness to substantiate a single one of the many charges against Bosie.

Campbell rose to protest. That was 'very unfair', he said. It was evident that his client 'could not have proved any of them'. Darling, also, thought that Hayes's remark was neither here nor there. Hayes, according to the judge, had only wanted to put questions to Ransome that he did not care to ask his own witnesses.

And why – Hayes went on – had the defence not called Mr Ross? He had been present throughout the hearing and had been, unlike Ransome, a close friend of Oscar Wilde; *he* might have elucidated what had occurred before and after the writer's downfall. *He* might have explained the court why *De Profundis* had never been sent to Bosie and by what right it had been donated, without the addressee's permission, to the British Museum. The text of this document formed the basis of the defence, but the man who had written it could also not be cross-examined. Mr Ross . . .

Once again Darling interposed. Mr Ross, he said, was not a party to the action; he was 'only Wilde's literary executor', and it was his (Darling's) duty to protect him.[17]

His Lordship considered it his duty, moreover, to wipe the floor with Bosie in his summing-up. He referred to the fact that at present the plaintiff was living apart from his wife and expressed the hope that 'she [didn't] know as much of Lord Alfred Douglas as you and I do'.[18] Bosie, he said, had come into the world 'with advantages such as nobody in this court had had'.[19] But he had made rather a mess of his life and had prevented Oscar from returning to the path of virtue. He was a fatal, a treacherous friend.

This opinion was shared by the jurors, for they found against Bosie. Darling ordered him to pay the costs – some £1,500 – and the room emptied. Crosland was told by the editor of the *Daily Graphic*,

> The case has been a staggering experience for anybody who has an ounce of friendship for Lord Alfred Douglas or the smallest sense of abstract justice. The spectacle of Wilde spitting filth at Lord Alfred from the grave while Ross plays with stolen letters, Campbell bullies, and a pinchbeck Judge 'nobbles' the whole case, is about as unholy a thing as I have ever seen or read about. In the face of Ross and Wilde, Judas begins to look a very old-fashioned person indeed.[20]

As his opponents rubbed in, Bosie lacked the resources to enter an appeal. Besides, another battle lay ahead of him.

On 24 April, two days after the dénouement of the Ransome case, the action for libel which Custance had brought against him took place. But Bosie was quite unable to fight it properly. Dazed, he failed to justify himself. He was therefore found guilty and directed by the Recorder to keep the peace and pay a fine of £500. The Colonel, who had wished Bosie to be put on bread and water, was slightly disappointed. The decision taken by the Chancery Court on 6 May, on the other hand, which decreed that Raymond was to spend the greater part of his holidays with his grandfather, was highly approved of by the veteran.

So Ross and Custance – who shared the same solicitor, if little else – agreed: Bosie had been given what he richly deserved. He would keep quiet in the future.

But in this they were deeply mistaken.

*

Qu'on me donne une heure de bonheur, et je redeviendrai un
excellent chrétien.

Alfred de Vigny, *Chatterton*

In the spring of 1913 Bosie's reputation lay in ruins once again. 'The
Ransome case has done him so much harm,' Olive wrote to her mother-
in-law, 'you don't know what people say.'[21]

There were numerous snubs. Thus *The Times* was requested by
the editor of *The Academy* to insert a paragraph stating that 'Lord
Alfred Douglas [had] had no connexion' with the moribund weekly
'either as editor or contributor' for a considerable time;[22] and when
Elkin Mathews subsequently issued a reprint of Lionel Johnson's
poetical works, Johnson's dedication of 'A Dream of Youth' to Bosie
was tacitly suppressed.

The postman did deliver marks of sympathy at 26 Church Row,
however; there were letters from, among others, Martin Secker and
the journalists William Sorley Brown and Herbert Moore Pim. 'I
would like to write more fully,' Bosie wrote to the latter on 25 April,
'but to [tell] you the truth I am so completely worn out by the strain
of all I have gone through that I can scarcely form the letters of the
words I write.'[23] Of particular interest are two letters signed 'Cherub',
who has been identified as Marcia Lane Foster, a sixteen-year-old
who was to become a wood engraver and illustrator of children's
books. She expressed her indignation at the way Bosie had been
treated, calling him 'the *only* true friend I ever had, and the only *good*
one too,' begging him, a bankrupt, not to send her, a struggling
student, 'any more money, because I know just how you are placed,
and you will want all you can get, you are *much too* good, and if all
the world turned against you, I shall love you all the more'.[24] One can
imagine Bosie sitting in his half-empty house, reading these artless
effusions, sadly smiling and heaving a sigh. Cherub's attempts to
cheer him up sufficed not, however, to pluck the thorn out of his
bosom.

One of the few patricians who did not care a straw about all the
gossip concerning Bosie was the MP George Wyndham, his cousin,
who invited him to his country house to recuperate. It was a fearful
blow to Bosie – yet another one – when George unexpectedly died in
Paris on 8 June.

But meanwhile the poet had gained another ally. The day before he lost the action which Custance had brought against him, the doorbell rang, and a young American lady presented herself. Doris Edwards was her name,[25] and her generosity was as remarkable as her beauty: she had taken her jewels and proposed to sell them so as to enable him to keep his head above water. Bosie – who in his memoirs did not reveal whether he had known her previously or whether she had appeared, a complete stranger, out of the blue – was deeply moved but did not take up her offer. Instead, he sold the few Wilde letters he had not burned, together with his copy of *The Picture of Dorian Gray* and the other books Oscar had autographed for him. These fetched a few hundred pounds, allowing him ostentatiously to plunge into pleasure with his mistress (Doris became his mistress). He didn't care twopence what Olive and Custance thought about that; as far as he was concerned, they could go to the Devil. Olive had been unfaithful to him before, so in his present mood of discontent he persuaded himself he would be a fool to refuse love when it came his way.

'It seems to me that it is a pretty fine thing for a man to undergo the most cruel and brutal persecution, the most unmerited torture and agony of mind and body, and yet to be able to keep from bitterness of thought and word.' Thus Bosie had written in an article from 1908 on François Villon.[26] Alas! He appeared incapable now of emulating his French colleague's dignity and resignation. He was no more prepared to forgive those who had ill-treated him than his boisterous forebears had been. Hit below the belt, he struck back below the belt.

First of all, he wanted to distance himself completely from Oscar. John Long, the publisher who, it will be remembered, had been repeatedly lectured in *The Academy* on the dubious morality of the novels on his list, had approached Bosie, asking him to write down his version of his relations with the author. Bosie signed a contract and received advance royalties but proved incapable of concentrating his thoughts. Whereupon Crosland suggested he leave the writing to *him* (in consideration of a cash payment). And Bosie agreed.

Crosland had viewed with regret how his chief had showered praise on Oscar's works in *The Academy*. He had always detested these works (in so far as he had read them), but as long as Bosie had cherished Oscar's memory the journalist had not ventured to criticize these paeans. Now that Bosie was at odds with his dead friend, Crosland saw his chance, in the capacity of ghost writer, to pillory the 'High Priest of the Decadents'. Although the manuscript was finished in July, the publication of what has been justly termed one of the most unpleasant books of the last hundred years[27] was considerably delayed. For Ross had learned that *De Profundis* was to be extensively quoted (Bosie, of course, had wished to answer the attacks levelled at him in the 'encyclical'), and this, Ross argued, constituted a breach of copyright. The judge to whom he appealed agreed; Bosie was instructed to delete the quotations.[28] The publisher, too, meddled with the contents of *Oscar Wilde and Myself*, which finally appeared in July 1914, a hefty volume running to more than 300 pages.

It makes melancholy reading: a tendentious description of Bosie's 'strictly platonic' relation with Oscar – Bosie would have been unaware of his friend's sexual preferences, and had only stood by him in 1895 because he had been convinced of his 'innocence'[29] – followed by an onslaught as vicious as it was futile on Oscar's poetry and prose, *The Picture of Dorian Gray* being selected as the prime target.[30]

The similarities between *Oscar Wilde and Myself* and *De Profundis* are clear. Both works are the outcome of injured pride, disillusionment and grief. Both works are extremely unfair. And both works are to be seen as the literary equivalent of an instantaneous photograph: Oscar and Bosie came to repudiate what they had said about each other, the first in his conversation and correspondence, the second in his conversation, his correspondence and his subsequent autobiographical writings.[31] Of all the mistakes he had made in his life there was none which Bosie would more deeply deplore than the publication, under his name, of Crosland's indictment of Oscar; he almost had a heart-attack when, many years later, a young friend guilelessly referred to it.[32] 'Partly my reaction against Wilde was due to wounded feelings,' he had previously declared,

> and partly it was due to an imperfect apprehension of Catholic principles. Foolishly and unworthily I allowed my anger at the revelation of his unkind attack on me [in *De Profundis*] to warp my judgment and cloud my sense of justice. I was then a recent convert to Catholicism and like most converts I tried to be more Catholic than the Catholics, and thus by spiritual pride was for the time being deprived of charity. I deeply regret that the book was ever published.[33]

When *Oscar Wilde and Myself* was issued, Bosie was no longer in

London; he had precipitately fled to Boulogne in order to stay out of the hands of the police.

Having slightly recovered from his legal defeats, Bosie, assisted by Crosland, had seized the initiative. He had sworn to avenge himself on Ross and hit at his Achilles' heel: his private life. Ross once averred his reputation was as good as Caesar's wife's had been,[34] but this was not in keeping with Bosie's information. He knew, and shouted from the roof-tops, that Oscar's literary executor habitually transgressed Section 11 of the Criminal Law Amendment Act. Ross, in other words (those of Crosland), was a 'dirty sodomite'.[35]

If something may be learned from history, it is that people do not learn from history. Ross should have ignored these imputations, contained in letters to such notables as the Prime Minister and the Attorney General. He nevertheless walked into the trap which Queensberry had set for Oscar some twenty years ago and resorted to the law.

His timing seemed perfect, as Bosie was at loggerheads with Custance once again. The Colonel had received rather uncomplimentary post from his son-in-law – Bosie had blamed him for his troubles with Olive – whereby the armistice agreed upon in court had been breached. At the time Bosie had promised, on penalty of immediate incarceration, to refrain from censuring the old man. When Custance's solicitor now had a summons served on him, Bosie realized that it was more than likely he would be locked up. If Ross were then to sue him for libel, he would not be allowed bail. Thus he would not be in a position to collect evidence against Ross, would lose his trial and disappear behind bars for a couple of years. An unpleasant prospect! He had therefore hastened to France on 4 March.

Rejoicing, Ross thought the moment had come to sue his enemies: Crosland for conspiracy, Bosie for conspiracy and criminal libel. Crosland was duly arrested in April and made his first appearance at the Old Bailey on 27 June. He really felt in his element there, having told Bosie not to return when the latter had offered to.

So far the two had referred to a single witness, a sixteen-year-old named Garratt who had signed a statement incriminating Ross. This witness, Ross's counsel maintained, had been pressurized by Crosland and Bosie to sully his client by affixing his signature to a trumped-up charge. Ross described his stormy relations with Bosie, pretended to have been 'appalled' on learning about Oscar's sexual tastes; he had 'suggested to him that he should conquer his passions'; insinuated that Bosie had been responsible for Oscar's 'moral deterioration' and furthermore called Bosie's poems 'immoral'.[36] This last remark annoyed the judge, who in his summing-up pointed out to the jurors that they were not supposed to express an opinion on Mr Ross's conduct in life; the issue was whether Garratt had been incited by the defendant and Lord Alfred to commit perjury, or whether both men had honestly believed what the boy had told them about Ross.

The jury needed twenty minutes to deliberate. Crosland was acquitted. The onlookers clapped their hands.

Bosie sailed to England in October, being safe from prosecution for conspiracy as a result of Crosland's triumph in court. It is peculiar that he seems not to have known about the outstanding writ for his arrest on a charge of criminal libel, but it is even more peculiar that Ross, after his disastrous duel with Crosland, should have neglected to withdraw this charge. Anyhow, Bosie was welcomed at Folkestone by Scotland Yard, and brought up before the Police Court.

His fear that the Custance matter would prevent his eventual release on bail proved groundless. Nevertheless George Lewis succeeded in delaying Bosie's departure for a few days. Bosie was brought to Wormwood Scrubs in London, given prison clothes and locked up in a stuffy cell, an experience he vividly described in his autobiography.

> I thought of [Wilde] as I 'went to bed' (a plank bed and no mattress), and said to myself: 'Poor Oscar, however did he manage to stand this for two years?' That was the first time I had had a comparatively soft thought about him since I read the 'unpublished part' of *De Profundis*.[37]

If his adversaries had hoped they could intimidate Bosie, they were disappointed. He energetically prepared his trial and managed, albeit with considerable difficulty, to trace fourteen witnesses whose testimony greatly incriminated the prosecutor during the trial of *Ross v. Douglas*. Detective Sergeant West, for instance, said that 'he knew Mr Ross by sight, and had frequently seen him in Jermyn Street and Piccadilly in the company of young men who were conspicuous by their "get-up" and painted faces'.[38] A soldier who claimed that Ross was indirectly responsible for the death of his brother burst into tears while telling his story.

It is impossible to reconstruct in detail this legal drama, which commenced on 19 November 1914 and dragged on for more than a week. Transcripts of the proceedings have not been kept.[39] The press gave the case a very low profile; events on the continent were, understandably, deemed of greater importance. In the light of the massacres at the Marne, the unravelling of the unholy feud between Bobbie and Bosie must have seemed of little consequence.

Yet for those involved there was much at stake. Bosie ran the risk of being sentenced to two years' imprisonment. Ross, should he lose the case, ran the risk of being arrested for sexual misconduct, just like Oscar in 1895.

As it turned out, neither the one nor the other landed in gaol. One of the jurors had stated on the first day of the trial that he would never bring a verdict against Ross (Bosie thought he had been bribed),[40] and when the other jurymen wished to do just that he was the only one who refused to step into line. This lack of consensus necessitated a new trial, but fortunately it did not come to that. Ross's solicitors suggested a compromise: their client would abandon further prosecution of Bosie (which amounted to a plea of 'guilty' really) and pay his costs (£600). This last was of great importance to the impecunious lord; so he assented.

Unlike Oscar in similar circumstances, Robbie, who had had a hair's breadth escape, was not shunned by the high and mighty. On the contrary, more than three hundred sympathizers, including H.G. Wells,[41] the Prime Minister and the Bishop of Birmingham, signed an illuminated address extolling his generosity and services to literature. This testimonial, accompanied with a round sum, evinces what in fairness to Ross should not go unrecorded: that his treatment of Bosie was not typical of the way he behaved to others. Vyvyan Holland, for instance, Oscar's younger son, described Ross as a second father.[42]

Bosie's treatment of Bobbie has been roundly condemned by all and sundry, and certainly one cannot congratulate him on what he did. But those who express their disgust at 'his bestial behaviour towards Robert Ross so reminiscent of his mad father's hounding of Wilde'[43] tend to overlook that it had been Robbie who had been the first to copy 'Q's' tactics. The Marquess, a practising heterosexual who abhorred gays, had ruined Oscar's reputation by establishing in court that the writer was a practising homosexual. Ross, a practising homosexual, had ruined Bosie's reputation by establishing in court that Bosie had been a practising homosexual and by making it seem that he had left Oscar in the lurch while being perfectly aware of the falsity of this grave charge. But while Queensberry had at least had the courage to make his appearance in the dock and risk a term of imprisonment, Ross tried to keep out of harm's way as much as possible. 'The case seems to me very cleverly conducted by Ransome's counsel,' Max Beerbohm wrote in 1913 after Bosie's action for libel had failed, 'but, as the main part of this cleverness was in keeping Bobbie Ross out of the witness-box, certainly the victory was not of a glorious kind.'[44]

Beerbohm made this observation in a letter to Reginald Turner, who was not a little surprised to discover that his name had been included in the list of signatories to the Ross testimonial without his knowledge or consent.[45] Reggie had incurred Ross's wrath when he had dared privately to reproach Ross for his use of *De Profundis*. That had been the end of their friendship. Turner, living in Florence, wrote to Bosie many years later:

> I think you must know that I have never approved of, or encouraged, or in any way abetted, any attacks on you, and have been bitterly sorry for unprovoked attacks on you. Indeed, many years of my life have been poisoned by that horrible contest, when Queensberry rules were thrown to the wind; and I have never failed to say – and thereby endured much criticism – that you were the provoked and that the production of that unpublished part of *De Profundis* was a disgraceful affair which – I think, indeed, feel sure – would have deeply pained the author.[46]

Two wrongs do not make a right, however, and that Oscar's best friends – fluttering round him as moths flutter round a candle, as a contemporary put it[47] – should have behaved to one another like this is truly deplorable. Neither of them seems to have remembered Oscar's aphorism – 'Always forgive your enemies. Nothing annoys them as much.'

Robert Baldwin Ross died in his sleep, aged forty-nine, on 5 October 1918. His final wish, that his ashes be placed beside those of the writer of *The Happy Prince*, was carried out in 1950.

'Darling Bosie, – I am so glad – and so thankful. It is a splendid triumph!' Thus wrote Lady Douglas to her husband on 11 December

1914, after he had 'settled' with Ross. From the tone of this letter, which ended with the words 'God bless you. Your loving Olive',[48] it may be deduced that the relationship between sender and recipient had considerably improved since the former had suddenly left Bosie to go over to her father's camp. It had been Bosie's keeping house with another woman which decided Olive on arranging a reconciliation. She had phoned him, some months after her departure. And the sound of her voice had 'completely finished'[49] him; he had put a stop to his affair with Miss Edwards. She eventually returned to the United States and remained there. This did not mean, however, that the married couple's separation now came to an end. The time for a reunion did not seem to be ripe yet. But they met occasionally and corresponded regularly, Bosie, as usual, speaking his mind freely. 'I would be only too pleased to go to the war,' he despondently informed her on 2 February 1915, 'and I would be equally pleased to get killed.'[50]

He did not get the opportunity, as the army, in answer to his application for a commission, told him his services were not required. When he thereupon decided to join the ranks of the Foreign Legion, a military friend of his, who *did* know what he was talking about, questioned the wisdom of this resolution. Wasn't it a wee bit hot in the Sahara? On mature consideration Bosie agreed and decided to concentrate on his protracted quarrel with Custance.

It will be remembered that it had been determined in the Chancery Court that Raymond was to spend the greater part of his holidays with his grandfather. Bosie wished to challenge this order in the same court, and the fact that Olive now supported him gave him great confidence that all would end well. Father and mother desired full custody of their own child. The request seemed quite reasonable.

But Bosie's hopes were to be dashed. The Colonel's counsel assured Mr Justice Eve that Lord Douglas was not fit to raise a child and conclusively proved this – at least as far as Eve was concerned – by handing him a copy of *Oscar Wilde and Myself*, drawing his attention to the picture facing page 174. Eve was shocked. A photograph of Raymond! A photograph of Raymond in a book dealing with the career of 'a notorious criminal'![51] The judge declared, references from some distinguished supporters of Lord Douglas notwithstanding, that he did not see his way to vary the order of his colleague. The summons was dismissed with costs.

Bosie had had enough. He took Raymond to Fort Augustus in

Scotland – out of the jurisdiction of the English Chancery Court – let it be known he would stay there indefinitely and bought a house, awaiting Olive, who had announced she would come.

Still Custance did not give up. He secretly contacted his grandson and prevailed on him to be fetched by a private detective. The boy was transported by car to Norfolk one day, and Bosie fell a prey to the most terrible anxiety. Where on earth was Raymond? He had gone out to fish in Loch Ness. Was he drowned? What Bosie had to endure during the space of forty-eight hours is indescribable.

The telegram informing him that Raymond was safely at Weston would have reached him much earlier if it had not been for a gale which had blown down the telegraph wires.[52] Bosie was seething and contemplated having Custance arrested for kidnapping; but when he discovered that Raymond had been privy to the plot, he washed his hands of him. The family reunion did not take place after all.

The years that followed were exceedingly bitter for Bosie, the sonnets he wrote, including the exquisite 'Before a Crucifix', equally sombre. In Shelley's Folly, a charming old place at Lewes in Sussex where he lived with his mother, he spent his days reading hagiographies and books such as Augustine's *De Civitate Dei*. He went for long walks in the surroundings woodlands. He shot at snipe and ducks. And Oscar remained his *bête noire*. He hated the man and his works; and he was not the only one.

In the spring of 1918 a melodrama was staged at the Old Bailey in which Oscar's *Salomé* became the focus of attention and in which Bosie, too, played his part. His performance was not commendable.

The atmosphere in England at that time was very tense indeed. The Great War was dragging on, and its end did not seem to be approaching – on the contrary, since the Russians had made their separate peace with the Central Powers in 1917, the Germans had been able to transfer numerous divisions to the Western front, and on 21 March 1918 General Ludendorff had launched a dangerous offensive. His troops had advanced many miles, as a result of which Paris had come within range of gargantuan guns that pounded the city.

According to the independent MP Noel Pemberton Billing, this unsatisfactory state of affairs could be explained by the fact that the British elite was being massively blackmailed by the German secret service. On 26 January 1918 Billing had claimed in his paper, the *Imperialist*, that the Bavarian Prince, Wilhelm von Wied, owned a black book containing the reports of agents who in England applied themselves to 'spreading debauchery of such lasciviousness as only German minds can conceive and German bodies can execute'. No fewer than 47,000 individuals – cabinet ministers and their wives, privy counsellors, diplomats, poets, publishers, youths of the chorus, bankers and ballerinas – were supposed to have been initiated by these specially trained agents in the delights of 'Sodom and Lesbia',[53] after which the Germans could easily blackmail them.

Equally remarkable was the paragraph that three weeks later appeared in the *Vigilante*, as the *Imperialist* had been renamed since Billing had founded a society advocating an ethical renaissance.

The cult of the clitoris

To be a member of Maud Allan's private performances in Oscar Wilde's *Salomé* one has to apply to a Miss Valetta, of 9 Duke Street, Adelphi. If Scotland Yard were to seize the list of these members I have no doubt they would secure the names of several thousand of the First 47,000.[54]

Who was Maud Allan? 'A lady [who persists] in flopping about stages, clothed only with chaste diaphanousness,' to quote an unimpressed critic.[55] In other words: a dancer. Born in Canada in 1873, she had been a music student in Berlin, where she had earned some extra money by illustrating Dr Penn's *Konversations-Lexicon der Frau* (1900), a sex manual for the fair sex. As a ballerina she had caused a worldwide sensation with her *Vision of Salomé*, for which Marcel Rémy had provided the score. Miss Allan had danced before the King of England; she had also danced before the miners of Kalgoorlie, Australia, who had expressed their delight in their own way: 'Open up yer legs more, darlin',' and 'Get down on yer back again, Maudie.'[56] She aspired to become an actress as well, and when in January 1918 she had been asked by Jack Thomas Grein – a naturalized Englishman of Dutch origin who managed the Independent Theatre – to take the leading part in Oscar's *Salomé*, she had jumped at the offer. Public performances of the play were still prohibited; private ones, however, such as were given by Grein's company, the censor could not prevent.

Maud Allan was not pleased with what the *Vigilante* had written. She rightly interpreted the article's headline as an insinuation that she was a lesbian and sued Billing for libel.

The trial was a farce. Billing, who conducted his own defence, managed to 'prove' that *Salomé* was a work of art that morally corrupted the country. He invoked several expert witnesses: theatrical critics, doctors, a Jesuit and Bosie. Who could better interpret the play's meaning than the man who had known its author, who at his request had translated it into English? Bosie assured the 'intensely bourgeois'[57] members of the jury that Oscar had never written a single line which was not designedly evil, that he had always aimed at undermining virtue, yes, that he had been one of the most powerful pals of the Devil; besides, his bedside book had been Krafft-Ebing's *Psychopathia Sexualis*.

A neutral reporter, the one for the Dutch *Nieuwe Rotterdamsche Courant*, imparted his amazement to his readers. The case, which ended on 4 June 1918, he called 'a concatenation of insanities',[58] Billing and his supporters 'a gang of dangerous maniacs who have egged on one another in their senseless phantasies'.[59] The judge, Darling again, was out of control and ordered the expulsion of numerous persons including, in the course of his summing-up, Bosie, who was cheered by a big crowd as he left the building. It was in part owing to his testimony that poor Maud failed to get a verdict.

The Dutch correspondent thought Bosie's performance absurd, yet 'tragic'. He gave a balanced view of his position.

Lord Alfred Douglas, the [third] son of the late Marquess of Queensberry, is well-known. He is a first-rate poet. He has been the friend of Oscar Wilde who occasioned the latter's downfall in 1895 . . . This unhappy event has ruined Lord Alfred's life. He subsequently repented, broke loose, after Wilde's death in 1900, from the spell which bound his opinions, and got married. And at the same time he has acrimoniously joined issue with [Wilde's] memory. Why? To get on his legs again, some say contemptuously; to receive a humiliating pat on the back from the righteous and the orthodox. Well! I have observed the man in the witness-box, and do not believe this to be a fair judgment. I think his sincerity need not be doubted. On the contrary, the man goes to Court, impelled by a sense of duty, curiously mingled with blind, passionate wrath against what he used to revere, but anyhow equipped with admirable courage to suffer more scorn. For who is more vulnerable than he! And who would, if concerned about his rehabilitation, more anxiously shun cross-examination!

Hume-Williams [Maud Allan's counsel] did nothing but rake up the witness's old sins, and Lord Alfred became increasingly wild and furious. He called the lawyer a thief and a blackmailer who only cared about his fee, who was doing the dirty work for the Germans and the straying sinners with whom they were in league, etc . . .

It was, I repeat, a sad spectacle. Nevertheless, in spite of Lord Alfred's senseless and pathological exaggerations, I kept a feeling of pity for him approximating sympathy.[60]

While the German offensive fizzled out, Bosie's love for Olive revived. Their relationship had reached its lowest ebb in August of the preceding year when Olive, a recent convert to Catholicism, had 'lapsed'; but in October 1918, shortly before the Central Powers laid down their arms, and while Bosie was preparing the publication of his *Collected Poems*, peace was made between the two. It was an emotional scene. 'All the wretchedness of those last seven or eight years rolled away,' Bosie wrote to his wife, 'and I felt towards you just as I used to do when we were first married.'[61] Although they remained on excellent terms for the rest of their lives, and although they met quite regularly, they did not move in together. A lady friend who once expressed her surprise at this was told by a laughing Bosie that it is difficult to live with a poet – and he himself was a *particularly* difficult poet![62]

As for Raymond, he sent his father a letter in 1925 causing great joy. It was an olive branch, an appeal to let bygones be bygones, which did not fall on deaf ears. Custance died soon afterwards, having rejected Bosie's peace overtures.

We have anticipated events. We have yet to relate how Bosie had meanwhile been reconciled with the author with whom his name is inextricably linked. It is a rather dramatic story, this; for while Oscar's temporary unilateral rupture with his lover had been brought about by a stay in one of Her Majesty's gaols, it ironically took a stay in one of His Majesty's gaols to make Bosie venerate Oscar as of old.

10

Liberation Through Incarceration

The simple fact that Bosie was able to buy a copy of the *Evening News* on 4 February 1921 seriously impaired the paper's credibility. For according to a paragraph on its front page he had been found dead in his bed that very morning by his maid: overwork, a chill and heart failure were supposed to have finished the fifty-year-old.

Some error had surely been made. That was the gist of a telephonic message from Bosie and a speedy rectification in later editions of the broadsheet its consequence. The editor, it is true, apologized for the hoax but kept silent on the anonymous obituary describing the career of the 'deceased' to which Bosie had taken exception. And no wonder! It was a denigrating piece in which he was called a degenerate, an eccentric wastrel who in all probability would be remembered for the scandals and quarrels in which he had involved himself rather than for his achievements as a poet.[1] When the *Evening News* failed to withdraw these remarks, Bosie lodged a complaint for libel.

The paper's solicitor happened to be an old acquaintance of his, Sir George Lewis Jr. He hated the poet, had – as legal adviser both to Custance and Ross – had dealings with him more than once and would not miss this opportunity to thwart him for all the world. That is why he advised his clients not to cave in; it would (he pointed out to them) be easy for a barrister, armed with documents from his (Lewis's) archive, to show that the obituarist had actually written with restraint. The editor and proprietors were talked round and pleaded justification, forcing Bosie to enter the arena yet again.

The case opened on 24 November. Women *were* allowed admittance; but when the judge spoke of 'the indelicate nature' of the matters that would come up for discussion, the female members of the jury requested to be allowed not to serve. They left the court, unlike Olive, who had set down next to her husband.

The defence opened its case by recalling that the plaintiff – a *plucked student* – had, when in his twenties, published *perverse lyrics* in a magazine (*The Chameleon*) glorifying *unnatural passions*; had engaged in an *indecent correspondence* with the ill-famed Oscar Wilde; and had *accommodated* him after his release, instead of dropping him like a hot brick (as might have been reasonably expected). Moreover, the plaintiff had subsequently acclaimed this psychopath's works in *The Academy* – and he now objected to what the *Evening News* had written about him? His Lordship's effrontery was almost past belief! Bosie's troubles with his father-in-law were also raked up, and the jurors' expressions became ever more forbidding.

Before Bosie was given the opportunity to fend off this crushing onslaught on his character, his counsel examined two ecclesiastical dignitaries and a homoeopath doctor, friends of Bosie who declared he had been leading a decent, not a decadent, life for many years. He was, in short, a model citizen.

Then came the moment of truth: the model citizen stood up and was questioned at length by his opponents. This verbal duel ended in a complete triumph for Bosie. Never before had he sparkled in the witness box like that; he was quick-witted, amusing, brilliant. The jury, after a short consultation, found for him, awarding him damages to the tune of £1,000. The *Evening News* paid this considerable sum and dismissed the writer of the obituary. That was Arthur Machen, incidentally, formerly on the staff of *The Academy*. It is unclear what had caused him to turn on his old chief in this way; but the fact that in 1943 the latter contributed when a collection was made on behalf of the impoverished Machen shows that Bosie was not as resentful as is often believed.[2]

During the enervating days which lay behind him, Bosie's temperature had sharply risen along with the tension to which he had been exposed, and when, shortly after the trial, he fell victim to a serious attack of influenza it seemed for a while that the *Evening News* would again, and this time rightly, have to announce his death. For weeks he was confined to his bed. This meant the end of *Plain Speech*, the weekly he had founded in October 1921 after being turned out by 'an ignoble intrigue'[3] as editor of the equally ephemeral *Plain English*.

This paper, financed by a wealthy friend of Bosie's brother Percy, differed significantly in one way from the countless magazines displayed in the kiosks of London: its signature was Catholic, but nevertheless great sympathy was expressed for the Ulster Orangemen who since January 1919 had been involved in a civil war with the supporters of Sinn Fein. It is not easy to comprehend Bosie's attitude – Shaw once remarked that, politically, he had 'the brains of a grasshopper';[4] the IRA, at any rate, was not pleased with his journalistic activities and informed him they had put his name on their death-list.

Bosie, a diehard Tory, lambasted not only the Irish nationalists in *Plain English*. The Liberal government, too, was taken to task, as were business tycoons such as Alfred Mond and Ernest Cassel. They were Jewish, with which we touch upon a painful subject: Bosie's anti-Semitism.

When we point out that numerous distinguished contemporaries of Douglas – Heinrich and Thomas Mann, Pierre Louÿs, Alphonse Daudet, Francis Poulenc and Rudyard Kipling, to name but a few – also expressed themselves in an uncomplimentary way about the Jewish race, this is only to draw attention once more to the unpalatable fact that anti-Semitism was a widespread phenomenon in Europe around 1900 which had taken root in intellectual circles as well. The observation that in this respect Bosie was a child of his age is not, of course, advanced in excuse of his attitude, although it should be borne in mind that his strictures in *Plain English* were directed at individuals rather than Jews as such.[5]

Anti-Semitism in pre-war England[6] had been fanned by the likes of Hilaire Belloc and the Chesterton brothers who, while commenting in the *New Witness* on the Marconi Affair (1912–13) and other financial scandals, ceaselessly reminded their readers of the Jewish descent of those involved. The effect created by this propaganda was fairly small thanks to the paper's limited circulation, but, after the shots had been fired in Sarajevo on 28 June 1914, difficult days lay ahead for Jews in the United Kingdom. They were increasingly seen as fifth columnists (the *National Review* stated that 'victory for Germany is for some reason the desideratum of almost the entire Jewish race'),[7] while the profits made by Jewish tailors and shoemakers as the result of the increased demand for boots and uniforms gave rise to jealousy which sometimes manifested itself in rows during which the 'profiteers'' shop windows were smashed. Suspicion grew when in November 1917 the Bolsheviks took power in Russia. They immediately made peace with the Central Powers and liquidated the Tsar, the Tsarina, their daughters and the little Tsarevitch (a massacre which deeply shocked Bosie).[8] The involvement in Communist agitation of Jews such as Lev Trotsky in

Russia, Rosa Luxemburg in Germany and Bela Kun in Hungary fuelled the notion that all Jews, or at least a majority of them, formed part of an international plot.[9] The publication in 1920 of a translation of *The Protocols of the Learned Elders of Zion* provided many Englishmen with convincing proof that this suspicion was founded on fact. The minutes of a secret Jewish confederacy preparing to seize world power had surfaced! There you had it, in black and white: no expedient was eschewed to undermine authority, disrupt the economy, corrupt youth and replace the idealistic aspirations of Christians with scepticism and materialism! The question arises – *The Times* wrote in a piece called 'The Jewish Peril' – whether we have escaped a *Pax Germanica* only to fall into a *Pax Judœica*?[10] Bosie read *The Protocols* as well and initially took them quite seriously. In years to come he would doubt their authenticity.[11] And rightly so, for they were a hoax. In 1921 a correspondent of *The Times* showed in a series of articles that *The Protocols* had been bodily lifted, for the greater part, from an obscure satire by Maurice Joly aimed at the regime of Napoleon III, *Dialogue aux enfers entre Machiavel et Montesquieu, ou la Politique de Machiavel aux* XIX*e siècle* (1864).[12] The plagiarism had been perpetrated about 1905 by an agent of the Russian secret service, who had borrowed his anti-Semitic pamphlet's setting – clandestine meetings of 'the Elders of Zion' – from a penny-dreadful by Hermann Goedsche, *Biarritz*.

Bosie was still convinced of *The Protocols'* trustworthiness when two sensational rumours reached his ears in 1920 on which he wrote at length in *Plain English*. Both rumours, emanating from a generally unreliable source, related to events which had occurred in 1916.

On 31 May of that year a naval battle had erupted near Jutland. From a tactical, but not from a strategic, point of view the Kriegsmarine had got the best of it; for although she had been able to wreak havoc among the Royal Navy, she had failed to run the enemy blockade. This had not prevented the Germans from depicting the fight as a defeat for the Allies, and the surprise of Jellicoe (the admiral who had commanded the British fleet) had been great when his superiors in London had issued a report of the combat which scarcely differed from the German version. The resulting gloomy atmosphere in England had only vanished a few days afterwards with the publication, by the Admiralty, of a more nuanced report.

According to rumour No. 1, a state of panic had been intentionally created at the time so as to enable Jewish speculators to buy, for a mere trifle, government stock which was slumping as a result of the bad news – and to sell it afterwards when its price had risen again, reaping a huge benefit. In this matter Winston Churchill would have been in league with Ernest Cassel. Churchill had drafted the misleading statement. Cassel had made his coup at the Stock Exchange, paying his accomplice the handsome fee of £40,000. One good turn deserves another.

Rumour No. 2 concerned the circumstances under which the Secretary for War, Field Marshal Kitchener, had met his end. Hardly a week after the Battle of Jutland he had, following an invitation from the government at St Petersburg, embarked for Archangel to act as adviser to the Russian general staff. But he never reached his destination. A mine, laid by a German submarine west of the Orkneys, sank the *Hampshire*; an unforeseen gale prevented the use of lifeboats. The composure with which, according to one of the few surviving crew members, the Field-Marshal had drowned contrasted sharply with the commotion the tidings of his death had caused on the home front. People could hardly believe that both the meteorological and the minesweeping service had acquitted themselves of their task as badly as all that, and there were those who doubted the facts of the affair as officially described. Bosie's informant, for one. He claimed that a Jewish saboteur, Nathan by name, had planted a bomb in the *Hampshire*'s hold, for Kitchener was going to give short shrift to the 'Jewish-bolshevist camarilla' which was preparing world revolution, so it had been vitally important to eliminate him.

Bosie, sincerely convinced of the truth of these stories, considered the absence of official reaction to his reporting on them to be yet another indication that he was on the track of a sinister conspiracy. He could not guess that Churchill had been advised to ignore what 'a rag like *Plain English*' was dishing up about him. The publication in 1923, however, of a pamphlet by Bosie entitled *The Murder of Lord Kitchener and the Truth about the Battle of Jutland and the Jews* Churchill could not brook. Six thousand copies had been sold at twopence when Bosie was arrested in November.

The outcome of his trial, which opened at the Central Criminal Court and which attracted widespread interest, was never in doubt. The defendant simply did not have a leg to stand on. It was irrefutably shown that Cassel had not made any transaction at the Stock Exchange at the crucial moment, and that Churchill, far from writing the inaccurate communiqué, had in fact been responsible for the wording of the subsequent one – drafted at the request of the then First Lord of the Admiralty, Lord Balfour. Had Churchill then never received money from Cassel? Oh, yes, *in 1908*, £500. A wedding present. The charges in *Plain English*, the politician said, were utterly groundless.

They originated in the rich imagination of Captain Harold Spencer (ex-Captain Spencer, to be more precise; he had recently been deprived of his rank), who appeared as a witness. He had a curious career as a secret agent behind him, resembling, in the words of Bosie's counsel, 'a Russian romance'.[13] Spencer maintained he had been the one to whom, shortly before the outbreak of war, Wilhelm von Wied had shown the notorious Black Book containing the names of 47,000 VIPs open to blackmail. His (Spencer's) chief had hushed up the affair and had had him locked up in a lunatic asylum, but he had managed to escape on a bicycle, disguised as a nurse. The doctor maintained he had had a sunstroke, but he *had* warned them that they were going to assassinate the Tsar; and as regards the Battle of Jutland, Churchill had told him all about it himself!

Spencer was mentally deranged, and one can only marvel at Bosie's giving credence to his silly stories. He now suffered the consequences. The jury found him guilty of libel, and the judge sentenced him to six months' imprisonment in the second division.

'A moderate sentence,' *The Times* commented.[14]

Bosie was a gourmet – Oscar once referred to his predilection for clear turtle soup, luscious ortolans wrapped in crinkled Sicilian vine leaves and amber-coloured champagne[15] – so that his stay in gaol proved to be, first and foremost, an ordeal from a culinary point of view. A dog, he commented afterwards, would turn up its nose at the fare that was served in Wormwood Scrubs: lumps of stinking meat swimming in lukewarm kitchen grease, rancid cheese, bread as hard as his plank bed, a substance passing for custard.[16] He lost more than eighteen pounds in weight and was sent after seven weeks to the prison hospital by order of the doctor. There he spent the rest of his term, and there he wrote, in a school copy-book, a sequence of sonnets, *In Excelsis*. That its title contrasted with that of Oscar's 'encyclical' was no coincidence, of course.

De Profundis and *In Excelsis* have a peculiar dichotomy in common. Just as in Oscar's letter valuable ethical and aesthetic meditations are marred by unworthy and, for the greater part, unjust tirades against Bosie, so do jeers at the mythical Elders of Zion in some poems of *In Excelsis* detract from the unfolding of impressive Neoplatonic thoughts in others. The sonnets in question, seven in number, are out of place in an anthology; the sestet of one of them, however, gives an impression of the exaltation Lord Alfred felt behind bars.

> My star shone clear, my angel smiled, I went
> Down the white way, I could not break my tryst
> With Scotland's honour in an English gaol.
> My soul fares free, my neck was never bent
> To any yoke except the yoke of Christ,
> This Douglas knee will never bow to Baal.

Oscar had been allowed to leave Reading Gaol carrying the manuscript of *De Profundis* with him; Bosie, on the other hand, was warned that his work, in conformity with tightened regulations, would be confiscated. He therefore memorized it, and on his release went straight to a friend's office where he wrote out the text again.

In Excelsis was published in December 1924 by Martin Secker. In addition to the ordinary edition there was a numbered and signed *édition de luxe* of 100 copies. Crosland, with whom Bosie had definitively broken before his conviction, did not set eyes on the volume; he had died earlier that year.

In the preface to what he considered to be his masterpiece, Bosie declared himself wholly free of rancour; he went so far as to call his imprisonment 'the best thing that ever happened' to him.[17] His stay at Wormwood Scrubs did indeed mark an important watershed in his career: the man who came out of gaol differed greatly from the man who had arrived there five months previously. *Five* months, not six – Bosie had been prematurely released for good conduct, and it was his good conduct that would assure him of the affection of a great many people in the decades ahead.

Rupert Croft-Cooke, a youthful admirer who had feared to meet a sulking poet, was agreeably surprised. Bosie turned out to be easily amused, he spoke of his prison term as a schoolboy would tell his mate about a dressing-down administered by their headmaster, he radiated joy of life and cheerfulness, appreciating wine, music, the beauties of nature, and good company as never before. He himself was good company. He had, according to Croft-Cooke, the very quality which Oscar had not been able to resist in him: he had charm.[18]

This was recognized even by those who, like John Glassco, cared nothing for Bosie's poetry, nor, for that matter, for Bosie himself.

> I was not prepared for his overmastering charm. He was much smaller than I had thought, and the delicate curved nose of the early portraits had developed into a monstrous beak; but he had an irresistible warmth that saved him from insignificance, an inner glow that was simply due to his fondness for people in general. Never was there a more *sociable* man, a man with better manners or more exquisite grace of movement, speech and behaviour. His one desire seemed to be to please – and this ability was so innate, and brought by practice to such a degree of effortless perfection, that it had given him a second nature distinct from his own, a character into which he threw himself with delight. He enjoyed playing the part of Lord Alfred Douglas so much that one was carried away. After a half-hour in his company one was still impressed by the skill and force of the portrayal; and even then, when he tired, there was another mask beneath it that was still more charming and impenetrable.[19]

Glassco, when he met Bosie around 1925, was putting the finishing touches to the ghost-written memoirs of their hostess, Diana Brooke, the exotically styled Dayang Muda of Saràwak. Soon afterwards Bosie was engaged on writing his own memoirs. The book was going to be altogether different from *Oscar Wilde and Myself* as well as from *The Wilde Myth*, which dated from 1917 and which Martin Secker had – wisely – declined to publish. He did publish, and scored a commercial success with, *The Autobiography of Lord Alfred Douglas*, which appeared in the early spring of 1929.

It is an attempt at self-portrayal by a man who was 'his own worst advocate',[20] the story of a hypersensitive, highly strung artist who looked back on a life, numerous chapters of which Miss Prism, no doubt, would have deemed to be 'somewhat too sensational'. Bosie at this stage had not yet fully made his peace with his deceased friend, but he had happily divested himself of his hatred towards him since becoming convinced that Oscar had *not* desired *De Profundis* to be given to the world after the death of his 'own darling Boy'. One senses that Bosie tries to be as fair to Oscar as possible; he admits there had been a sexual side to their friendship, and he repudiates the attack made on Oscar's works in *Oscar Wilde and Myself*. The book is interesting but a failure inasmuch as it paradoxically does not bring out the personality of its author. 'The radiance, generosity, humour and charm which in truth were his'[21] – to quote Croft-Cooke again – are scarcely discernible in its pages. Bosie, talking about his past, could smile at the vicissitudes of his career; but when he took up his pen he became 'obsessed with self-justification'.[22]

Writing the book, which was translated into German and French, certainly did Bosie a lot of good. He became on the whole more relaxed, started referring to Wilde again as 'Oscar', sat down with friends at what used to be their table in the Café Royal and explained that his experiences in Wormwood Scrubs had made him understand how Oscar had come to compose *De Profundis*. Speaking about the author, his eyes would sometimes fill with tears. 'He told us much of Wilde,' a visitor noted down in his diary, 'and after some sherry, said that although the Wilde story had ruined his life, he did not regret him . . .'[23]

The circle was closed. Bosie's last book, *Oscar Wilde: A Summing-Up* (1940), testifies to his reconciliation with the idol of his youth. It is a noble piece of work, and equally noble is what Bosie told a reader who had asked him something about his arch-enemy, Robert Ross:

> I can assure you that I have long ago forgiven him, though it was only some time after I had finished this book (about a week ago) that I got to the point of having two Masses said for his soul by the Franciscans at Oxford. He was at one time a, more or less, devout Catholic, but I am afraid he abandoned his religion years before he died . . . I cherish the hope that in the hour of his death he may have received enlightenment, poor chap. At one time he was one of my greatest friends.[24]

After *In Excelsis* Bosie hardly wrote any poetry but all the more letters. John Betjeman had started a correspondence with him in 1924, which by order of his shocked parents (Mrs Betjeman had steamed open one of Bosie's missives) was abruptly ended. Bosie, surprised at John's silence, subsequently discovered, when John was a student at Oxford, what had happened and how John's father had admonished his son to concentrate on outdoor athletic activities rather than reading 'decadent' verse. Whereupon Bosie presented John with a copy of his *Collected Poems* inscribed: 'Get out into the open air!'[25]

Betjeman, who in the 1930s regularly lunched with Bosie and Olive, remembered the latter as a cheerful matron with a passion for Byron. He thought her as witty as her husband, whom he characterized as 'a vastly entertaining man who gave one a sense of holiday and exaltation whenever one was in his company'; a first-rate raconteur ('What I cannot give in prose is the sparkle of his monologues'); a gentleman with beautiful manners. A phlegmatic, too, at times. John once took him to a performance of *The Importance of Being Earnest*. There was a party afterwards, during which one of the guests, fuddled by champagne, tumbled down, muttering 'Angel face' before losing consciousness. Bosie glanced at the figure outstretched on the carpet. 'Poor fellow, he's ill,' he said. And turned the conversation to the subject of the stage-works of Oscar Wilde.[26]

The commentator of *The Times* who in 1923 had doubted whether Bosie's conviction would make him change his reckless ways[27] was happily proved wrong. The final phase of Bosie's life was going to be free from litigation and tilting at windmills. 'How delightful, after a lifetime of bruising and being bruised, to enjoy the affection even of one's intimate friends!' he once joked at a dinner-table in the hearing of D.B. Wyndham Lewis, the writer, who, recounting this, added: 'His charity was so complete that I cannot remember anything getting under his skin – once so preternaturally thin – except the poetry of Mr T.S. Eliot.'[28]

Good deeds will out. One of the nicest things to be told about Bosie is how he took care of Percy's daughter, Violet. She was placed at a boarding-school in Wales while her father was trying his luck in South Africa. He was searching for gold there; what he found was his death. He passed away in August 1920, and Bosie, who had promised his brother to take the thirteen-year-old under his wing, brought her to his London flat in Hogarth Road. An excellent guardian he proved himself to be, reading to her, before tucking her in bed, from Dickens's novels, improvising nonsense rhymes to amuse her and treating her to lunch occasionally at the Savoy or the Ritz. 'He had great charm,' she recalled, 'and always greeted a lady with a bow, removing his hat. If he was familiar with the lady, he would raise her hand to his lips.'[29]

When Bosie found temporary accommodation in Wormwood Scrubs, Violet's life underwent a dramatic change. She moved to the house of her paternal grandmother and aunt, Edith, in Draycott Place, Chelsea. Here she was, literally, relegated to the attic, a tiny room on the fifth floor. When relatives passed by, she was invariably sent out with a Belgian member of staff. Bosie had always called her 'Lady Violet'; but now this courtesy title was dropped. Violet wanted to know why. She asked her aunt.

'Don't you know?' Edith snappishly answered. 'You're only Percy Queensberry's illegitimate child.'

That news, so brusquely broken, came as a great shock. The identity of her father's mistress has remained a mystery. Sybil's cook, however, seems to have been well posted on the subject. One day she pointed at a yellowed photograph of a posh lady in an evening gown that adorned the scullery wall. 'That's your mother,' she whispered. But she mentioned no name.

Violet felt profoundly miserable. 'Uncle Alfred gave me the only affection I knew as a child,' she said. At seventeen she decided to become a nurse, urged on by an overheard remark from Aunt Edie: 'The sooner she is kicked out to work, the better!'[30] And work she did; during the Second World War she ran a canteen in Burma, catering for some nine hundred soldiers. It was there she met her future husband, of whom she spoke warmly when I had the pleasure of talking to her, a widow, in 1999 during the preparation of *Two Loves*, the documentary film about Bosie in which she played a prominent part. A year after its première she died, aged ninety-four: a frail, delightful woman. When she opened, with shaky hands, a volume of her uncle's poetry, looking for, and then reciting, 'Night Coming into a Garden', we all three – the director Jacqueline van Vugt, the producer Carmen Cobos and I – melted towards her.

The book Violet had taken from her shelves had been published in 1935 by Rich and Cowan in London, forming part of an edition of Bosie's poetical works in two volumes, *Lyrics* and *Sonnets*. They provide further evidence of the extent to which Bosie had 'relaxed', for they included the 'Greek' poems that had not been reprinted, save in pirated editions, since their first appearance in the 1896 volume issued by the Mercure de France. Once Bosie had declared that they 'lend themselves to evil interpretations';[31] now he took the view that 'there [is] really nothing much wrong about these suppressed poems'.[32] They are, in fact, very fine; pieces such as 'Two Loves' and 'In Praise of Shame' form part of what may be called the Gay Canon. Bosie, the devout Roman Catholic, must have had a peculiar, ambivalent feeling towards these early, daring products of his Muse.

Lyrics is adorned with a highly seductive frontispiece, a photograph of Bosie taken in Egypt in 1894. The picture was to wreak havoc down under.

A young, impressionable girl from Australia had bought the book and fallen in love with its contents and with its author. She expressed her feelings in ardent letters which touched Bosie deeply. In replying, he pointed out to her that at sixty-five he no longer resembled the portrait of him she admired so much; but his attempts to quench her passion were unsuccessful. She continued to write to him; he thought it better not to write back. Whereat she killed herself. Her housekeeper informed Bosie about this tragedy, and he was deeply distressed, as Robert Sherard, who chronicled the story,[33] perceived when he paid him a visit at 1 St Ann's Court, Hove, Bosie's address since early 1935.[34]

Relations between Sherard and Bosie had been far from smooth ever since in 1895 the former had prevented the publication of the latter's article in defence of Oscar. Bosie had threatened to shoot the journalist 'like a dog',[35] while Sherard had once expressed the wish to lynch his Lordship.[36] These projects had not been carried out, however, and Bosie's contributing a preface to one of Sherard's books on Oscar Wilde[37] set the seal, as it were, on their reconciliation.

Another frequent guest at Hove was the composer Havergal Brian. Interest in his idiosyncratic music extended to the other world – he, at any rate, claimed to have seen, while working in the depth of night at his *Gothic Symphony*, the shades of Bach, Berlioz and Goethe, a phenomenon to which he 'attached no importance'.[38] A fair number of Brian's symphonies have been released on CD, but we are still waiting for a recording of his Fifth, *Wine of Summer*, an adaptation for baritone solo and orchestra of Bosie's poem of the same name.

Brian had previously been talked out of the idea of setting verse of Bosie's to music by a busybody who had assured him that the poet would never grant his permission. When in 1937 Brian finally approached him, however, the contrary proved to be the case. Bosie was enthusiastic and quite flattered when he heard the work (which would not be premièred until 1969) sung for him in his sitting-room by Brian, who accompanied himself on the piano. The musician, for his part, was highly pleased with the hospitality he received. Bosie would pour the finest claret Brian ever drank and never failed to offer him a Havana to smoke on his way home.[39] Their correspondence has unfortunately been almost entirely lost, unlike the letters exchanged between Bosie and Shaw, which have been edited by Mary Hyde, Viscountess Eccles.

Shaw, who had previously complimented Bosie on his *True History of Shakespeare's Sonnets* (1933), begged him in 1937 to consent to the publication of an English edition of Frank Harris's *Oscar Wilde: His Life and Confessions*. This was a thorny issue.

Others have already commented on the bad taste, the unreliability and venom pervading this biography which appeared in New York, printed by and for the author, in 1916;[40] suffice it to say that most of the nonsense written about Bosie over the years can be traced back to it. An example is the accusation that he had been the one who had introduced Oscar to 'the mysterious world of the homosexual *demi-monde*: the male prostitutes, the brothels – and the blackmailers'.[41] An acquaintance who was shown the book's manuscript found the text 'interlarded with pious sentiments and references to our Saviour'. When asked 'what the devil he meant by dragging in Jesus Christ on every other page', Harris scowled, but in the end he removed most of these devout ejaculations.[42]

The book's style may be gauged from the following extract, a portion of a conversation between Oscar, released from prison, and his biographer to be. Scene: a Parisian bar.

'Don't talk to me of the other sex,' he cried with distaste in voice and manner. 'First of all, in beauty there is no comparison between a boy and a girl. Think of the enormous, fat hips which every sculptor has to tone down, and make lighter, and the great udder breasts which the artist has to make small and round and firm, and then picture the exquisite slim lines of a boy's figure. No one who loves beauty can hesitate for a moment. The Greeks knew that; they had the sense of plastic beauty, and they understood that there is no comparison.'

'You must not say that,' I replied, 'you are going too far; the Venus of Milo is as fine as any Apollo, in sheer beauty; the flowing curves appeal to me more than your weedy lines.'

'Perhaps they do, Frank,' he retorted, 'but you must see that the boy is far more beautiful. It is your instinct, your sinful sex-instinct which prevents you worshipping the higher form of beauty. Height and length of line give distinction; slightness gives grace; women are squat!'[43]

Particularly revolting is Harris's description of Oscar's death. Lying in state, he was supposed to have exploded from the accumulation of gases in his bowels,[44] a morbid piece of fiction which, annoyingly, is repeated even today. It is one of the stories Harris himself came to retract.[45]

These rectifications had been prompted not so much by the scruples of a biographer in search of the truth but rather by the monetary difficulties of a self-styled blackmailer gone downhill. Bosie, who had prevented the book's circulation in England by threatening legal steps, had been approached in 1925 by Harris who had suggested he collaborate on a revised reprint. Inaccuracies in the *editio princeps* Harris had imputed to an ill-disposed informant, since deceased (Robbie Ross); the corrected version of the book, he said, would 'fully rehabilitate' Bosie.

Bosie had had his doubts. He did not trust Harris at all. This is not surprising, for Frank had once swindled him out of £2,000. Afterwards he had tried to extort money from him, threatening to come up with 'revelations' about the Wilde scandal. The two had even come to blows in the Café Royal – a fight 'terrific while it lasted', according to a reporter.[46] But the prospect that his name would be cleared by the man who had smeared it more than anyone else had finally resolved Bosie to take up Harris's offer. In compliance with the latter's request he had therefore annotated a copy of *Oscar Wilde: His Life and Confessions*, pointing out the many errors it contained, and shortly afterwards received the autographed typewritten text of Harris's new preface, in which these were put right. The project had nevertheless foundered when both men had fallen out, and Bosie had contented himself with publishing this foreword on his own.

Now, in 1937, it was Harris's widow who was at the end of her financial tether, and it was for her sake that Bosie magnanimously agreed to a reprint of the biography, edited and introduced by Shaw. Between the two, antipodes in almost every respect, an affectionate correspondence sprang up, Shaw addressing Bosie as 'Childe Alfred', Bosie calling him 'St Christopher'. It was a remarkable friendship.

Equally remarkable was the one which from 1938 linked Bosie to Dr Marie Carmichael Stopes. She was the author of *Prevention of Venereal Disease*, *Sex and the Young*, *Mother, How Was I Born?* and 'Coital Interlocking: A Physiologic Discovery' – 'risky' reading matter for which Bosie had scant sympathy, as she knew full well. Her first letters to him, expressing admiration for his poetry, she therefore signed 'Mary Carmichael'. When in the end she laid her cards on the table, he responded:

> I was astounded to see the signature on your letter this morning. I had not the remotest idea that you were Marie Stopes. It is really very extraordinary because (as you perhaps know) I have in the past criticized you rather strongly [in *Plain English*]. Naturally as a Catholic I disagree with your views about birth control. But now that you have written one so many kind letters and shown so much interest in me and my poetry and my health and my worldly condition, I feel remorseful that I have ever had unkind thoughts about you.[47]

Marie was philanthropically inclined, and when it dawned upon her that Bosie was increasingly beset with financial difficulties she tried to get him a pension. Her petition, signed by fourteen prominent persons including John Gielgud, Harold Nicolson and Virginia Woolf, was rejected, whereupon she and a number of well-wishers took it upon themselves to pay the rent of Bosie's flat when his nephew, Francis, found himself unable to do this.

It was this nephew who informed his uncle that his sonnet 'To Winston Churchill' had been well received by the Prime Minister. The ode, published on 4 July 1941 in the *Daily Mail*, cannot be said to rank with Bosie's best work; but a fine gesture it certainly was, a tribute to a man whose integrity he had previously admitted to having unjustly questioned.[48]

The poet was getting on in years. The mental health of his son, who was a resident in a clinic, worried him deeply. Raymond's was an unhappy life. His career in the army had been of short duration; his marriage, with a grocer's daughter whom he loved, had been opposed on all sides and called off; he rapidly deteriorated after this and was to remain in care, a schizophrenic, until his death in 1964. Olive, Bosie's 'darling mouse-girl' as he called her (somewhat surprisingly, given his horror of mice), declined and passed away on 12 February 1944. Bosie decided to move to her flat in the vicinity of his own – destroying, regrettably, heaps of letters in a fit of depression before clearing out – where he was cared for by her housekeeper, Eileen, a leviathan with wide hips and pendulous breasts at her waistline, sloping shoulders and a large head with a fringe of mangy black hair. Four teeth were all that remained to her.[49] She was quite devoted to Bosie; his conversation, a visitor noted, had lost nothing of his sparkle and vivacity.[50]

When fresh money problems and medical complaints began to deprive him of sleep, Edward and Sheila Colman came to his rescue. They brought him to their place, Old Monk's Farm at Lancing in Sussex, on 1 December 1944. In the following months they prepared for him many a feast of juicy, rich food and choice wines, as the prophet has it. 'Angelic people,' Bosie called them.[51] They kept him company, and they held his hands when, old and worn out, but strengthened by his childlike faith and the last sacraments, he died peacefully in the early morning of 20 March 1945. To his considerable amazement he had reached the age of seventy-four.

The funeral took place three days later. It was a sober ceremony – 'not more than ten of us gathered at his graveside as we buried Oscar's "Rose-lipped youth",' as Sir Donald Sinden remembered.[52] Bosie was interred beside his mother (who had predeceased him by a decade) in the cemetery of the Franciscan Friary in Crawley. 'Douglas, the fighter, the attacker, the quarrelsome spirit, the great artist, the loyal friend, the out-of-time aristocrat, had at last died,' Gerald Hamilton wrote, 'and with his death it seemed to me that one of the most turbulent rivers had at long last found its way to the open sea, that haven of eternal rest.'[53]

'Zeus hath brought an evil doom on us, that even in days to come we may be a song for men that are yet to be.' These words Homer puts into the mouth of the adulterous wife of the King of Sparta, Helen, who admits that by her inconsiderate flight to Troy she has sealed both her lover's fate and her own; words Oscar may well have remembered while serving his term at Reading Gaol. He must have realized that he would never be consigned to oblivion – as the commentator of the *Daily Telegraph* fondly wished him to be[54] – and that the spectacular end of his spectacular career would ensure him a place among the immortals. This certainty is likely to have been of some consolation to him.

The playwright's tragedy inspired numerous playwrights. One of the first, if not the first, was a Dutchman, Adolphe Engers. His *Oscar Wilde*, a drama in five acts, was written as early as 1917. Oscar appears in it under his own name, whereas Bosie is called Lord Harry Douglas. The second act takes place in Sicily, where Oscar owns a villa, and where, dressed 'in a white, fantastic outfit which reminds one of the ancient Romans',[55] he and his boyfriend discuss poetry and beauty, until a shrill noise disturbs them.

HARRY [*starting involuntarily*]: What's that?

WILDE: A boat's steam-whistle. Did it startle you?

HARRY [*smiling*]: Yes! Do you think that's odd?

WILDE: No, you are a sensitive, nervous boy.

HARRY: Where does that ship come from, I wonder?

WILDE: What's that to us?[56]

A lot! On board is Harry's father, who is coming to accuse the author of lewdness ('Every cabby knows the haunts where you're having your orgies with urchins').[57] Act III brings us to the courtroom, Act IV shows us the incarcerated Oscar socializing with a spider, while the final act is situated in 'a vulgar bar'[58] in Paris, where Oscar is scintillating once more –

Whatever I touched I made beautiful, clothing it in a new dress of beauty! I summed up all philosophical systems in one phrase, and all existence in an epigram. A mad lust took hold of me, and I became the spendthrift of my own genius . . .[59]

– before breathing his last in front of asserted riff-raff. Was Engers's play ever produced? Probably not; and a performance seems unlikely these days, as the scenes with Oscar's black servant are politically incorrect.

> WILDE: What book have you there? *Oscar Wilde: An Ideal Husband*. Well, well, are you reading my works?
>
> JOHNY: Yes, Sir, that are very beautiful!
>
> WILDE: Your criticism is most flattering!
>
> JOHNY: I not understand one word of book, but sound very beautiful![60]

The preface to Carl Sternheim's *Oskar Wilde, sein Drama* (1925) is even more politically incorrect. Engers had evinced some sympathy for Bosie; Sternheim portrays him as a blackguard who in the very first scene of the first act threatens to knock Oscar to the ground, abusing him continuously, and who, after the lawsuit, barks at him: 'I do not feel a grain of pity for you, I hate you . . . and have no other wish than to leave you in the lurch . . . *Sauve qui peut!*'[61] Similar caricatures of Bosie may be found in Maurice Rostand's 1934 play[62] and in most of the feature films on Wilde that have been made, including Brian Gilbert's from 1997, starring Stephen Fry: Bosie is 'a nasty shrew', Oscar 'a dumb lamb for the slaughter'.[63] Bosie was no nasty shrew, and Oscar was not a dumb lamb. Oscar, according to Shaw, 'had a ferocious will. He went to the devil his own way in spite of everybody.'[64]

It goes without saying that all these plays and films are based on *De Profundis*, the 'autobiography' of a man who admitted that 'the chance of an epigram [made him] desert truth',[65] the lamentation which has gained Bosie the reputation of being 'the most complete cad in history',[66] as a reviewer described him after reading what was presented as the work's first complete and accurate version, appearing in 1949.

I am convinced that no one would have deplored this opinion more than Oscar himself. A document kept at the William Andrews Clark Memorial Library in Los Angeles which, to the best of my knowledge, has hitherto remained unpublished, proves this yet again. It is a letter which one Frederick William von Herbert dispatched from Shanklin on 18 April 1913 to Bosie's solicitor, George Cran, in which he says that Oscar, after his release, had sent him a letter

> of which I have but a faint recollection, except that I remember vividly Lord Alfred Douglas' name in it, and his complete exoneration, by Mr Wilde, of any fault or blame in past events, in fact I remember Mr Wilde's exact expression, 'guiltless' . . . I do not know, and do not wish to know, any of the parties to the actions now pending; I do not wish to give evidence, and I do not wish my name to be publicly mentioned. Perhaps this statement may help you, in the interests of justice, to build up your case. Yours truly, F.W. von Herbert.

Von Herbert was referring to the case of *Douglas v. Ransome*, in the course of which Oscar's attacks on Bosie, contained in *De Profundis*, were read out, squashing the plaintiff. Von Herbert's letter arrived too late. The trial ended on 22 April; Bosie sent a copy to the judge on the following day.

Oscar exaggerated when he wrote that Bosie had neither part nor lot in his downfall, just as he exaggerated when in *De Profundis* he saddled him with the full responsibility. The truth was more complex. More than one person brought about the catastrophe, and it was Fate that set the catastrophe going by bringing these persons together: Oscar Fingal O'Flahertie Wills Wilde, Alfred Bruce Douglas and John Sholto Douglas, ninth Marquess of Queensberry, protagonists in a powerful tragedy of passion and envy.

Envy! One cannot wholly rid oneself of the impression that the mud which over the years has been slung at Lord Alfred derives in part, consciously or unconsciously, from this feeling. After all, most of us are not really beautiful. Most of us are not of noble birth. Most of us are not so charming as to be capable of charming charming people like Oscar Wilde – *if* we ever meet them, that is. And then we cannot write poetry – at least not as well as to gain the praise of masters like Stéphane Mallarmé.

Bosie was extremely privileged. That irked, and continues to irk.

11

A Testament of Beauty

Legend has it that in the zenith of his youth Bosie was having a drink one day with some friends at the Café Royal when a fellow-poet – a shabbily dressed person with unkempt hair – entered the establishment. Those present were struck by the lack of resemblance between him and Bosie, who was looking, as always, as if he had come out of a bandbox.

'What a contrast!' cried someone.

'Yes,' said a fan of Lord Alfred, 'all the difference between verse – and poetry.'[1]

Aa a prelude to a few concluding observations on Bosie's work, this anecdote seems apposite. After all, a man is mirrored in his style, and the reader of the poems which follow will see straight away that Bosie made sure his lyrics were as polished as his shoes. He had completely mastered the *technique* of his craft. For this reason his work may seem dated in the complimentary sense of the term.

A work of art, he argued, can only pretend to perfection if no traces whatever remain of the effort and trouble the artist has taken.[2] *Ars est celare artem*: art consists in hiding art. Writing a fine poem cost Bosie blood and sweat and tears, which accounts for the fact that his 'output' remained (as he once phrased it) 'wretchedly meagre'.[3]

'We assert that the things in this world are beautiful by participating in form.'[4] These words of the Neoplatonic philosopher Plotinus Bosie took to heart. As to that he was on a par with the German symbolist poet, Stefan George (whom he may have met at Paris once).[5] George believed that 'man can only vanquish evil by *form*. Form is creation, form is principle, form is a precondition. Form also means: discipline, order, regularity, norm. Art conducts what is boundless, it is art which adjusts things.'[6] The ethical component of art, according to Bosie, consists in the artist waging war on the powers of chaos and darkness.[7] Each poem, each statue and each symphony may thus be looked upon as a feat of arms. Chiselling civilizes. Fighting with form gives purpose to life. Bosie considered the Petrarchan sonnet, with two rhymes in the octave arranged ABBAABBA and two or three rhymes in the sestet arranged either CDECDE or CDCDCD, as 'the very quintessence of form',[8] and it is in his sonnets that his mastery is most manifest.

Form, then, is of prime importance (Bosie would have dismissed a term like *art brut* as an oxymoron), but an authentic poet knows how to infuse it with life. It is the combination of fire in the heart and ice in the brain which produces great poetry.[9] Art, to quote a brilliant definition of Antoine Bodar, is stylized emotion. Feeling overpowers the poet and forces him to voice it. This urge to expression, this longing for beauty, is in Bosie's view a question of chromosomes. Either one has the artistic gene, or one hasn't.[10] One's originality is not apparent from one's subject-matter – for there is nothing new under the sun – but from one's ability to vary the perennial themes of Love, Joy, Sorrow, Desire, Regret and the rest.[11]

Bosie's dislike of the verse of most of his contemporaries is not surprising, bearing in mind that in his opinion writing which neither rhymes nor scans cannot be poetry. Moreover, he objected to the 'hideous obscurity'[12] permeating the efforts of the 'moderns'. He allowed that poetry should sometimes deal with the mysterious and the unfathomable but maintained that a sensible person can easily distinguish between that which he cannot understand and that in which there is nothing to be understood;[13] and when he came across lines like these –

> Put it there in there where they have it,
> Put it there in there and they halve it
> Put it there in there there and they have it
> Put it there in there there and they halve it[14]

– he reacted like the child in Andersen's fairy-tale who declared that the Emperor was naked, stark naked. Such frankness did not make him exactly popular in some quarters; it comes as no surprise, Edward Osborn remarked, that Bosie's work is conspicuous by its absence in anthologies like the one in which the fragment just quoted was published: 'It was hardly to be expected that a fraternity of frogs rehearsing their "brekekek koax koax" in a pond, would admit a nightingale to their orgies of noise.'[15]

Bosie's poems – the musicality of which is, of course, shown to full advantage when they are read aloud – require no elaborate exegesis. They are not hermetic, which does not imply that they lack profundity.

In the course of his review of *The City of the Soul*, Lionel Johnson gave a characterization of its author to which little needs be added.

> For him, poetry, the artistic exercise of the imagination, is a safe place of refuge and retirement, a secret citadel, wherein the soul may dwell apart for solace and escape from the pressure of the world. 'The consolation of art' is a familiar affectation with many pretenders to poetry; not so with this poet. His sincerity is evident; it is clear that poetry is to him a serious and real joy, the relief of a quick and sensitive nature, and that the endeavour to write well is both a passion and a comfort. And he does write well, with notable distinction; his manner, vision, interest, attractions are his own. Here is not the impeccable dullness of an accomplished imitator, of the soulless craftsman who has caught some master's style; behind or within these poems there is a personality.[16]

Lord Alfred Bruce Douglas, as we observed before, would have been well advised never to have left his ivory tower. In a life which he himself called 'as melodramatic as any novel by Balzac',[17] he fortunately spent sufficient time there to create a small but important poetic legacy, a testament of Beauty in which his finest qualities shine out. 'For this,' wrote Bernard Shaw, to whom Bosie had sent his collected poems in 1936, 'for this be all thy sins forgiven thee.'[18]

Abbreviations

AD	Lord Alfred Douglas
Autobiography	*The Autobiography of Lord Alfred Douglas* (London: Martin Secker, 1929)
Berg	Henri W. and Albert A. Berg Collection, New York Public Library
Bosie	Rupert Croft-Cooke, *Bosie: The Story of Lord Alfred Douglas, His Friends and Enemies* (London: W.H. Allen, 1963)
Clark	William Andrews Clark Memorial Library, University of California, Los Angeles
CL	*The Complete Letters of Oscar Wilde.* Edited by Merlin Holland and Rupert Hart-Davis (London: Fourth Estate, 2000)
Collected Poems	*The Collected Poems of Lord Alfred Douglas* (London: Martin Secker, 1919)
CP	*The Complete Poems of Lord Alfred Douglas, Including the Light Verse* (London: Martin Secker, 1928)
Doucet	Bibliothèque Doucet, Paris
Douglas	Collection of Lord Gawain Douglas
Holland	Merlin Holland, Irish Peacock and Scarlet Marquess. The Real Trial of Oscar Wilde (London / New York: Fourth Estate, 2002)
Hyde	H. Montgomery Hyde, *Lord Alfred Douglas: A Biography* (London: Methuen, 1984)
Lyrics (1935)	Lord Alfred Douglas, *Lyrics* (London: Rich and Cowan, 1935)
Magdalen	Magdalen College, Oxford
MS Hyde	Collection of Mary Hyde, Viscountess Eccles,

	Department of Manuscripts, British Library, London
Nine Poems	*Nine Poems* (London: privately printed for A.J.A. Symons, 1926)
OC	Olive Custance
OCD	*I Desire the Moon: The Diary of Lady Alfred Douglas (Olive Custance), 1905–1910*, introduced and annotated by Caspar Wintermans (Woubrugge: Avalon Press, 2004)
OW and Myself	Lord Alfred Douglas, *Oscar Wilde and Myself* (London: John Long, 1914)
OW: A Summing-Up	Lord Alfred Douglas, *Oscar Wilde: A Summing-Up* (1940), with an introduction by Derek Hudson, third impression (London: Richards Press, 1961)
Poems (1896)	Lord Alfred Douglas, *Poems* (Paris: Mercure de France, 1896)
Reading	The University of Reading Library Rosenbach Rosenbach Museum and Library, Philadelphia
Ross TS	Typescript of a statement prepared by Robert Ross in late 1913 or early 1914 for his solicitor, Sir George Lewis Jr, including copies of correspondence with Douglas and others, now in the William Andrews Clark Memorial Library, University of California, Los Angeles
Shaw/Douglas	*Bernard Shaw and Alfred Douglas: A Correspondence*, edited by Mary Hyde (London: John Murray, 1982)
Sonnets (1909)	Lord Alfred Douglas, *Sonnets* (London: Academy Publishing Company, 1909)
Sonnets (1935)	Lord Alfred Douglas, *Sonnets* (London: Rich and Cowan, 1935)
Texas	Harry Ransom Humanities Research Center, University of Texas at Austin
The City of the Soul	Lord Alfred Douglas, *The City of the Soul* (London: Grant Richards, 1899)
Trials	H. Montgomery Hyde, *The Trials of Oscar Wilde* (1948) (New York: Dover Publications, 1973)
Without Apology	Lord Alfred Douglas, *Without Apology* (London: Martin Secker, 1938)
Works	[*The Works of Oscar Wilde*, edited by Robert Ross] (London: Methuen, 1908)

Notes to the Text

Introduction

1. *English Review*, 11 November 1905, p. 86. This weekly, founded and edited by T.W.H. Crosland, lasted from October 1905 till February 1906 and should be distinguished from the monthly magazine bearing the same title which Ford Madox Ford started in 1908.
2. AD to Frank Harris, 31 December 1906. MS Texas.
3. Martin Koomen, 'Een tot in het merg verwende ruziezoeker. Biografie van Lord Alfred Douglas', *Vrij Nederland*, 22 June 1985, *Boekenbijlage*, p. 6.
4. J.C.E. Lanters and W. van Maanen, 'Oscar Wilde', in A.G.H. Bachrach et.al., *Moderne encyclopedie van de wereldliteratuur* (Weesp: De Haan/Antwerpen: De Standaard, 1980–84), X, p. 261.
5. Michel van der Plas, 'Een poging tot geluk in ballingschap. Het korte treurige leven van Sebastian Melmoth: Parijs', *Elsevier*, 21 January 1989, p. 92.
6. Martin Koomen, op. cit., p. 6.
7. Martin Greif, *The Gay Book of Days: An Evocatively Illustrated Who's Who of Who Is, Was, May Have Been, Probably Was, and Almost Certainly Seems to Have Been Gay During the Past 5,000 Years* (London: W.H. Allen, 1985), p. 181.
8. Dominic Cavendish, 'We're not yet at this wit's end', *Daily Telegraph*, 10 November 2000.
9. The ode appeared in a privately published booklet, *Oscar Wilde in Belgium. By Danny Cannoot. Member of the O[scar] W[ilde] S[ociety] since 16 September 1993.* [Kortrijk], 2002, p. 32. A note on the following page, written by Rudy Dermaux, informs us that Mr Cannoot 'is an sensitive man who likes very much all what is culture, besides he is a not undeservingly writer himself'.

10. Frank Harris and Lord Alfred Douglas, *New Preface to 'The Life and Confessions of Oscar Wilde'* (London: Fortune Press, 1925), pp. 53–5.

11. Ibid., p. 18.

12. Hugh Kingsmill to Robert Harborough Sherard, 28 October 1933. MS Reading. The solicitor was E.S.P. Haynes.

13. Michel van der Plas, op. cit., p. 95.

14. *The Times*, 18 April 1913; G.W. Sadler, Deputy Manager, the National Provincial Bank, London, to AD, 30 November 1928: MS Magdalen; *Autobiography*, pp. 322–3; *Bosie*, p. 179; Hyde, p. 185.

15. Martin Koomen, op. cit., p. 6.

16. Rory Knight Bruce, 'Oscar Wilde, Bosie and the District Nurse', *Evening Standard*, 6 March 1995.

17. Holland, p. 55.

18. *CL*, [? May–June 1892], p. 526.

19. MS Clark.

Chapter 1

1. And not the eighth, as is stated in various biographies and works of reference. See Hyde, 340, note 5.

2. *Autobiography*, p. 2.

3. *CL* [5 or 6 November 1894], p. 621.

4. AD to Robert Ross, 13 July 1897. Quoted in the *Daily Telegraph*, 25 November 1921.

5. Hugh Trevor-Roper, *A Hidden Life: The Enigma of Sir Edmund Backhouse* (London: Macmillan, 1977), p. 245.

6. *Without Apology*, p. 167.

7. Lionel Johnson, *Ireland, With Other Poems* (Poole/New York: Woodstock Books, 1996), p. 32.

8. Robert Ross, 'Fine Art. Simeon Solomon', *The Academy*, 23 December 1905, p. 1336.

9. William Rothenstein, *Men and Memories* (London: Faber and Faber, 1934), I, p. 147.

10. *OW and Myself*, pp. 36–7.

11. Norman Colbeck, *A Bookman's Catalogue: The Norman Colbeck Collection of Nineteenth-Century and Edwardian Poetry and Belles Lettres in the Special Collections of the University of British Columbia* (Vancouver: University of British Columbia Press, 1987), I, p. 432. My efforts to trace the manuscript of this madrigal, which was

performed during an evening concert given by the College Glee Club in Winchester on 24 July 1893 – part of the '500th Anniversary Celebration of the Opening of the College' – proved unsuccessful. Johnson's text was published in his second volume of verse, *Ireland, With Other Poems* (London: Elkin Mathews, 1897).

12. AD to A.J.A. Symons, 8 July 1935. MS Clark.

13. *CL*, p. 343 (note 3).

14. Sonnet XXVI.

15. 'Mr Wilde has brains, and art, and style, but if he can write for none but outlawed noblemen and depraved telegraph boys, the sooner he takes to tailoring (or some other decent trade) the better for his own reputation and the public morals.' Quoted in H. Montgomery Hyde, *The Cleveland Street Scandal* (London: W.H. Allen, 1976), p. 240. The reviewer referred to a scandal which had erupted a few years previously when it was discovered that a number of aristocrats used to have sex with under-age employees of the General Post Office in a brothel in Cleveland Street.

16. Hesketh Pearson, *Oscar Wilde* (London: Methuen, 1946), p. 147.

17. *Works*, XII, pp.168–9.

18. AD to 'Rachilde', 29 July 1897. Quoted in *Manuscrits et lettres autographes* (Paris: Drouot-Montaigne, 2001), item 75.

19. J.-F. Louis Merlet, 'Passants de la Rivièra: Lord Alfred Douglas', *L'Éclaireur de Nice*, 14 February 1904.

20. AD to A.J.A. Symons, 14 March 1939. MS Clark.

21. *Autobiography*, p. 24.

22. *Works*, XII, p. 183.

23. *Without Apology*, p. 52.

24. Leslie and Sewell Stokes, *Oscar Wilde* (London: Secker and Warburg, 1937), p. 21.

25. 10 December 1893. Quoted in *Bosie*, p. 92.

26. Theodore Wratislaw in *The Artist and Journal of Home Culture*, November 1893. Quoted in G.A. Cevasco, *Three Decadent Poets: Ernest Dowson, John Gray and Lionel Johnson. An Annotated Bibliography* (New York/London: Garland, 1990), p. 188.

27. Lord Alfred Douglas, *Oscar Wilde et quelques autres*. Translated from the English by Arnold van Gennep, second edition, (Paris: Librairie Gallimard, 1930), p. 179.

28. Violet Wyndham, *The Sphinx and Her Circle: A Biographical Sketch of Ada Leverson 1862–1933* (London: André Deutsch,

1963), p. 105.

29. *CL*, p. 685.

30. *OW and Myself*, p. 173. See also Vincent O'Sullivan, *Aspects of Wilde*, with an Opinion by Bernard Shaw (1936), New Edition (London: Constable and Company, 1938), pp. 34–5.

31. *CL*, 2 July 1896, p. 657.

32. *Works*, XII, pp. 15–16.

33. Sonnet XXXVIII.

34. Relationships like the one between Oscar and Bosie – between an artist and a person who stimulates the artist's creativity – are not uncommon, of course. One may think of Dante's veneration for Beatrice, of Boccaccio's for Maria d'Aquino ('Fiammetta'), of Petrarch's love for Laura de Sade, Michelangelo's for Tommasso dei Cavalieri, of Wagner's passion for Mathilde Wesendonck (to which we owe *Tristan und Isolde*), of Leoš Janáček for Kamila Stösslová and of Stefan George's affection for Maximilian Kronberger ('Maximin').

35. *CL*, 20 May 1895, p. 651.

Chapter 2

1. AD to A.J.A. Symons, 14 March 1939; 16 March 1939. MS Clark.

2. Robert Harborough Sherard, *Bernard Shaw, Frank Harris and Oscar Wilde* (London: T. Werner Laurie, 1937), p. 155.

3. A passage from the memoirs of Charles Hirsch, quoted in Peter Mendes, *Clandestine Erotic Fiction in English 1800–1930: A Bibliographical Study* (Aldershot: Scolar Press, 1993), p. 449.

4. Camille Mauclair, *Servitude et grandeur littéraires*. Deuxième édition (Paris: Ollendorf, 1922), pp. 53–4.

5. *CL*, p. 544.

6. Richard Ellmann, *Oscar Wilde* (London: Hamish Hamilton, 1987), p. 261.

7. Lionel Johnson, *Selected Letters*. Edited by Murray Pittock (Edinburgh: The Tragara Press, 1988), p. 14.

8. Ian Anstruther, *Oscar Browning: A Biography* (London: John Murray, 1983), p. 134.

9. *CL*, p. 360.

10. *Autobiography*, p. 72.

11. Reginald Turner to Robert Harborough Sherard, 7 November 1933. MS Reading.

12. 'Jonquil and Fleur-de-Lys'.

13. *Autobiography*, pp. 70–71.

14. George Ives, added note to a diary entry of 19 December 1893. Quoted in John Stokes, *Oscar Wilde: Myths, Miracles and Imitations* (Cambridge: Cambridge University Press, 1996), p. 71.

15. Oscar later alleged in *De Profundis* that as a result of his flying to Bosie's rescue by enlisting the services of Sir George Lewis, he (Oscar) 'began to lose his esteem and friendship, a friendship of fifteen years' standing. When I was deprived of his advice and help and regard I was deprived of the one great safeguard of my life' (*CL*, pp. 701–2). This claim seems very odd to me. Why should a lawyer who, in Oscar's own words, 'knows all about us – and forgives us all' (ibid., p. 134, note 4), adopt such an attitude towards Oscar after getting Bosie out of a scrape? *The Times*, in its obituary of Lewis's son (9 August 1927), wrote: 'People in trouble, in all classes of society, went [to the Lewises] for shrewd personal advice, and the two men, father and son, must have been entrusted with more numerous and more romantic secrets than had ever before fallen to the lot of any firm of solicitors. The father, it was said, knew the history of almost every rascal in Europe, and he was never happier then when he could rescue a victim from the clutches of a blackmailer.'

16. *CL*, pp. 702, 716.

17. AD to Charles Kains-Jackson, 9 April 1894. MS Clark.

18. Bosie showed this valise in 1938 to George Sylvester Viereck. See Francis Queensberry and Percy Colson, *Oscar Wilde and the Black Douglas* (1949) (London/New York: Hutchinson, 1950), p. 147.

19. *CL*, p. 758.

20. E.F. Beresford Chancellor, '*The Spirit Lamp*', *London Mercury*, XXV, No. 148, February 1932, pp. 387–9.

21. A. Hamilton Grant, 'The Raconteur', quoted in E.H. Mikhail, *Oscar Wilde: Interviews and Recollections* (London: Macmillan Press, 1979), I, p. 223.

22. AD, 'An Undergraduate on Oxford Dons', *The Spirit Lamp*, II, No. 3, 18 November 1892, p. 73.

23. Harry Currie Marillier, *University Magazines and Their Makers* (London: Howard Wilford Bell, 1902), p. 59.

24. 'Lines Suggested by Fred. Leslie's Death', *The Spirit Lamp*, III, No. 1, 3 February 1893, p. 17.

25. *The Ephemeral*, No. 1, 18 May 1893, p. 2.

26. Ibid., No. 3, 20 May 1893, p. 23. On the same page may be found an anonymous poem which I should like to rescue from oblivion:

Nature and the Decadent

The wind made voiceful all the willow-trees
That bowed themselves about the level mere;
The waters laughed in myriad ripplings clear;
White clouds in little knots of silken fleece
Rang riot; busy murmurings of bees
Sang summer music in his tirèd ear;
And yet such beauty gave nor joy nor tear:
The décadent saw all and had no ease.
He peered as if amid a gloom of night;
But when his drooping eyes had chanced to stray
Upon a dead fish upturned stomach white,
Near which large frogs plied slimy loves all day,
His withered visage smiled with wan delight,
And his lank soul crawled out to kiss decay.

27. 'Book Reviews. The Mysteries of the Isis', *Morning Post*, 7 March 1912.
28. Hyde, pp. 6–7.
29. Violet Wyndham, *The Sphinx and her Circle: A Biographical Sketch of Ada Leverson 1862–1933* (London: André Deutsch, 1963), p. 111.
30. AD to John Lane, 30 August 1893; 30 September 1893. MS Rosenbach.
31. *Autobiography*, second impression (London: Martin Secker, 1929), p. 160, note.
32. *CL*, p. 574, note 3.
33. 'TO MY FRIEND / LORD ALFRED BRUCE DOUGLAS / THE TRANSLATOR OF / MY PLAY'. Writing to John Lane on 6 July 1906 (MS Texas), Bosie informed the publisher, who was going to reissue the English version of *Salomé*, to omit his name from the title-page. 'Oscar Wilde . . . revised the translation to the extent of taking out from it most of the elements of original work on my part.' Moreover, in a note appended to the second impression of his autobiography (p. 160), he stated that he did not regard the translation of *Salomé* 'which is usually attributed to me . . . as mine at all. I do not claim

it as my translation'. For this reason the book has not been included in my bibliography of Bosie's works.

34. MS Rosenbach.
35. *The Times*, 23 February 1893.
36. *CL*, p. 692.
37. Quoted in *Bosie*, pp. 91–2. Bosie is quoting from Sir Philip Sidney's *Arcadia*.
38. AD to Robert Ross, 20 December 1893. MS Hyde.
39. Alfred Mitchell-Innes to AD, 3 January 1895. MS Magdalen.
40. Robert Hichens, *The Green Carnation* (London: Unicorn Press, 1949), p. xiii.
41. *CL*, p. 696.
42. Carnations dyed green were worn by homosexuals in Paris, a habit adopted by Oscar and his friends. Bosie and/or Oscar were portrayed in numerous novels. We may instance Octave Mirbeau's *Journal d'une femme de chambre* (Paris: Fasquelle, 1900); Baron Jacques d'Adelswärd-Fersen's curious *Lord Lyllian. Messes Noires* (Paris: Léon Vanier, 1905); Julia Frankau's *The Sphinx's Lawyer* (London: Heinemann, 1906), published under the pseudonym 'Frank Danby' and damned as 'irredeemably vulgar' by *The Academy* on 21 April of that year; Ernest La Jeunesse's *Le Boulevard* (Paris: Jean Bosc et Cie, 1906); Abel Hermant's *Cycle de Lord Chelsea* in four volumes (Paris: Nouvelle Revue Française, 1923). In Otto Zarek's *Begierde. Roman einer Weltstadtjugend* (Berlin: Paul Zsolnay Verlag, 1930) we witness the opening in the German capital of a gay club named after Bosie!

Eine Jazzkapelle dröhnte aus einem Parterreraum. Jetzt erst bemerkte Frau Mary, daß unten, an der Bayreuther Straße, ein eigenes Lokal eingebaut war.

'Gehört das auch zu uns?' fragte sie . . .

Etwas nervös antwortete ihr Mann: 'Gewiß, man mußte die Räumlichkeiten ausnutzen. Aber es ist eine Sache für sich – eine "Diele". . . durch Sondervertrag verpachtet . . .'

'Warum heißt sie "Douglas-Diele"?'

'Douglas,' antwortete van Embden mürrisch, 'irgend eine historische Figur, mußt den Pächter fragen. Aber komm jetzt!' Es war ihm unbehaglich zumute; er wußte sehr gut, warum sie 'Douglas-Diele' hieß, und auch, daß ein lebensgroßes Bildnis Oskar

Wildes beim Eingang, neben der Garderobe hing. Im Vorbeigehen
sah er übrigens, daß die Douglas-Diele überfüllt war. [p. 510]

The novel's main characters pay a visit to the establishment
later on:

Als Lilian mit Erwin Bergmann in die Douglas-Diele kam, hatte
dort die Stimmung erst ihren Höhepunkt erreicht. Man tanzte
lebhaft, Männer mit ihren Freunden, jugendlich schlanke
Epheben und beleibte Herren. Erwin lachte, als er dies sah,
lachte laut und wurde übermutig: 'Wage dich nur hinein, Lilian,
man wird dich für einen verkleideten Boy halten, das ist noch
nicht das schlechteste!'

    Aber Lilian lachte nicht. Sie starrte in das Treiben wie in
einen Gespenstertanz. [p. 537]

We may finally mention a truly remarkable novel by a Dutch lady
writing under the pseudonym Floortje Zwigtman, Schijnbewegingen
(Baarn: De Fontein, 2005). It features sixteen-year-old Adrian
Mayfield who gives up his boring job as shop assistant to become
a painter's model and rent boy, crossing the path of Wilde, Douglas,
Ross, Beardsley and a host of others. The story is told with zest
and would make a wonderful feature film.

43. Robert Hichens, op. cit., p. 165.
44. Ibid., p. 1.
45. Ibid.,p. 2.
46. *Yesterday: The Autobiography of Robert Hichens* (London: Cassell, 1947), p. 72.
47. Robert Hichens, *The Green Carnation* (London: Unicorn Press, 1949), p. 3.
48. AD, letter to the editor of the *Star*, published on 16 August 1939.
49. Lady Queensberry had arranged that her son would become an honorary attaché in Constantinople, but when the Ambassador, Lord Currie, learned that Bosie was a bosom friend of Oscar Wilde (of whom he strongly disapproved) the appointment was cancelled. See Hyde, p. 54.
50. Michel van der Plas, 'Oscar Wilde's kwade genius. Bosie: een hopeloos geval', *Elsevier*, 15 December 1984, p. 127.
51. Martin Koomen, 'Een tot in het merg verwende ruziezoeker. Biografie van Lord Alfred Douglas', *Vrij Nederland*, 22 June 1985,

Boekenbijlage, p. 6.

52. Holland, p. 217.

53. Ibid., pp. 217–18.

54. *Without Apology*, p. 247.

55. *CL* [? December 1894], p. 625.

56. John Francis Bloxam to Charles Kains-Jackson, 19 November 1894. MS Clark.

57. *The Chameleon*. A Facsimile Edition (London: Eighteen Nineties Society, 1978), p. 3.

58. *The Letters of John Addington Symonds*, ed. Herbert M. Schueller and Robert L. Peters (Detroit, Michigan: Wayne State University Press, 1969), III, p. 747. The schoolmaster was John Gambril Nicholson (1866–1931), author of *A Garland of Ladslove* and *The Romance of a Choirboy*.

59. Robert Harborough Sherard, *Twenty Years in Paris: Being Some Recollections of a Literary Life* (London: Hutchinson, 1905), p. 458.

60. *The Times*, 26 November 1921.

61. Diary entry of 16 October 1893. Quoted in John Stokes, op. cit., p. 71.

62. AD to Charles Kains-Jackson, 10 September 1893. MS Clark.

63. AD to George Ives, 11 November 1894. MS Clark. See Robin Darwall-Smith, 'Charles Alan Fyffe: A Victorian Tragedy', *University College Record*, XIII, No. 1, 2001, pp. 72–84.

64. *The Chameleon*, p. 58.

65. Ibid., pp. 36, 45.

66. Holland, p. 41; pp. 61–2; pp. 70–73.

67. 'It will do a great deal of harm,' Oscar had said, 'that is good.' See John Stokes, op. cit., p. 74. Bloxam's story was reprinted clandestinely in England more than once, and also appeared in Spanish, Polish, French and German editions, some of which were illustrated and all of which were attributed to Wilde. 'Der ausgezeichnete Kenner Carl Hagemann hat unzweifelhaft recht,' Rainer Maria Schulze [that is, Paul Steegemann] wrote in a note to a German translation, 'wenn er dies vortrefflich gefügte kleine Kunstwerk, dessen Tendenz völlig durch die Form ausgelöst wird, mit aller Entschiedenheit für Wilde in Anspruch nimmt' (*Der Priester und der Messnerknabe*. Hannover: Paul Steegemann Verlag, 1922, pp. 42–3). Heinrich Himmler, the

future Reichsführer-SS, read one of the German editions. He was shocked by the story's apologia for homosexuality, so Bloxam may unwittingly have contributed, in however small a measure, to the ill-treatment of homosexuals in the Third Reich. See Richard Plant, *The Pink Triangle: The Nazi War Against Homosexuals* (New York: Henry Holt, 1986), p. 88.

68. *CL* [early December 1894], p. 625
69. Ibid., pp. 702–3.
70. Clement Scott, 'The Playhouses', *Illustrated London News*, 12 January 1895, p. 35.
71. Quoted in John Stokes, op. cit., p. 77.

Chapter 3

1. Michel van der Plas, 'Oscar Wilde's kwade genius. Bosie: een hopeloos geval', *Elsevier*, 15 December 1984, pp. 127–8.
2. Ibid.
3. *CL* [July–August 1894], p. 598.
4. Ibid. [28 February 1895], p. 634.
5. 'Een tragisch einde', *Algemeen Handelsblad*, 8 April 1895, quoted in *Een pseudo-esthetische zeepbel. Nederlandse reacties op Oscar Wilde. I: 1890–1897*. Ed. Nop Maas (Nijmegen: Uitgeverij Vriendenlust, 1987), p. 38.
6. AD to Robert Ross, 11 February 1895. MS Hyde.
7. *CL* [circa 17 February 1895]. I have slightly changed the sequence of the sentences.
8. *CL*, 28 February 1895, pp. 634–5.
9. *Autobiography*, 103; Shaw/Douglas, 30 May 1931, p. 10.
10. AD to Lord Percy Douglas of Hawick, 11 March 1895. MS Hyde.
11. *Telegraaf*, 6 April 1895 (morning edition).
12. As he recalled in a letter to the editor of the *New Statesman and Nation* which was published on 20 August 1938.
13. Michel van der Plas, op. cit., p. 127.
14. Robert Ross to Lord Percy Douglas of Hawick, 26 May [1895]. MS Douglas.
15. Martin Fido, *Oscar Wilde* (London: Hamlyn Publishing Group, 1984), p. 73.
16. Hesketh Pearson, *The Life of Oscar Wilde* (London: Methuen, 1946), pp. 285–6.
17. *CL*, p. 729.

18. Ibid., pp. 741–2.
19. Hesketh Pearson, op. cit., p. 285.
20. Michel van der Plas, op. cit., p. 128.
21. *CL* [postmark 12 December 1885], p. 272.
22. Ibid., p. 134, note 4.
23. Ibid. [8 September 1894], p. 608.
24. *The Times*, 17, 20, 21, 22 June 1893. Gatty's obituarist, describing him as 'a well-known figure in social and literary circles', made no reference to the case (*The Times*, 9 June 1928).
25. *CL* [? July 1894], p. 594.
26. Ibid., p. 758.
27. Ibid.
28. *Trials*, pp. 232–3, note.
29. *The Times*, 27 April 1931. Clarke's obituarist made no reference to the Wilde trials.
30. Holland, pp. xxvii, 262.
31. *Candid Friend*, 1 June 1901, p. 173.
32. *Trials*, p. 14.
33. Ibid., 112; Holland, p. 91.
34. *CL* [March 1893], 560; *Trials*, 117; Holland, p. 110.
35. At an auction in London one of Oscar's letters fetched £14,300 some years ago (the *Daily Express*, 20 November 1993).
36. *Trials*, p. 129; Holland, p. 170.
37. *Trials*, pp. 132–3; Holland, pp. 207–9.
38. Holland, p. xxxix; Shaw/Douglas, p. 87.
39. *Trials*, 145; Holland, p. 279.

Chapter 4

1. H. Montgomery Hyde, *Oscar Wilde: A Biography* (New York: Farrar, Straus and Giroux, 1975), p. 228.
2. *National Observer*, 6 April 1895. Quoted in *Trials*, p. 156.
3. *Autobiography*, pp. 108–9.
4. 'The Soul of Man Under Socialism', *Works*, VIII, p. 311.
5. Not even Mrs Robinson would have been able to foresee that within a hundred years a plan would be proposed to transform this police station into an Oscar Wilde museum. See *Keynotes: The Newsletter of the Eighteen Nineties Society*. New Series, I, No. 12, June 1992, p. 10.
6. *Works*, V, p. 46.
7. On 8 April 1895 W.E. Henley wrote to Charles Whibley:

'Hyacinthus [Douglas] says that if Apollo [Wilde] goes to quod, he'll take a house by the jug and live there till Apollo comes out. He may chance, if all be true, to find householding unnecessary; for they say the net's to be cast and cast till the pool's empty.' Quoted in John Connell, *W.E. Henley* (London: Constable, 1949), pp. 297–8.

8. *St James's Gazette*, 6 April 1895.

9. George Wyndham to Percy Wyndham, 7 April 1895. MS Hyde.

10. *CL*, 641; pp. 644–5.

11. In a letter to Percy Queensberry, written on 26 April 1895 at the house of the Leversons where he was staying, he announced he would take the eleven o'clock train from Charing Cross on the following day. MS Douglas.

12. H. Montgomery Hyde, *The Cleveland Street Scandal* (London: W.H. Allen, 1976), p. 45.

13. *Telegraaf*, 6 April 1895 (morning edition).

14. *Autobiography*, pp. 119–20.

15. *Trials*, p. 201.

16. *CL*, p. 702.

17. Shaw/Douglas, 16 April 1931, p. 3.

18. Max Beerbohm, *Letters to Reggie Turner*. Ed. Rupert Hart-Davis (London: Rupert Hart-Davis, 1964) [postmark 3 May 1895], p. 102.

19. W. E. Henley to Charles Whibley, *c*. 10 May 1895. Quoted in John Connell, op. cit., pp. 301–2.

20. *The Destruction of Lord Rosebery: From the Diary of Sir Edward Hamilton, 1894–1895*. Ed. David Brooks (London: Historians' Press, 1986), p. 250.

21. The matter is fully discussed in Neil McKenna, *The Secret Life of Oscar Wilde* (London: Century, 2003).

22. *Illustrated Police News*, 1 June 1895.

23. *Trials*, p. 244.

24. Ibid., p. 244.

25. W.T. Stead, 'The Progress of the World. The Conviction of Oscar Wilde', *Review of Reviews*, 1 June 1895, 492; AD, 'Une introduction à mes poèmes, avec quelques considérations sur l'affaire Oscar Wilde', *Revue Blanche*, X, No. 72, 1 June 1896, p. 487; *The Times*, 26 November 1921; Jonathan Gathorne-Hardy, *The Old School Tie: The Phenomenon of the English Public School* (New York: Viking Press, 1978), pp. 156–80; Alisdare Hickson, *The Poisoned Bowl: Sex, Repression and the Public School System* (London:

Bosie aged eight; watercolour by Henry Richard Graves

The real picture of Dorian Gray! The frontispiece of Charterhouse
Press's unauthorized reprint, showing a photogravure of a portrait
signed 'Basil Hallward', which, according to an intriguing note, was
the painting that in 1884 had given Oscar the idea for his book

Oscar and Bosie at Oxford, as immortalized in May 1893 by a contributor to the university magazine *The New Rattle*

Bosie and Oscar, *c.* 1893

Portrait of Bosie by Walter Spindler, reproduced in *Poems* (1896)

Oscar and Bosie in Naples, autumn 1897

Olive Custance, *c.* 1902

Bosie, *c.* 1903

Frontispiece to *The Collected Poems of Lord Alfred Douglas* (1919)

Photograph of Bosie in front of the Old Bailey, taken during the trial of Allan vs. Pemberton-Billing, reproduced on the front page of the *Daily Mirror*, 5 June 1918

Bosie, *c.* 1928

Bosie in the company of Sheila Colman, Easter 1944

Lord Gawain Douglas, Bosie's great-nephew, holding the English
Heritage Blue Plaque that was unveiled on 22 October 2004 at
1 St Ann's Court, Hove, on the 134th birthday of the poet

The Archangel Michael chasing Lucifer and his followers from Heaven; fresco by Spinello of Arezzo (c. 1346–1410) in the S. Agnolo chapel in the Basilica di S. Francesco, Arezzo

Constable, 1995), *passim*.

26. *CL* [? 18 February 1898], p. 1019.

27. *Le Figaro*, 12 April 1895.

28. *OW: A Summing-Up*, p. 32.

29. *CL*, p. 691.

30. A.L. Rowse, *Quiller-Couch: A Portrait of 'Q'* (London: Methuen, 1988), p. 5.

31. Joseph Jerome [Brocard Sewell], *Montague Summers: A Memoir* (London: Cecil and Amelia Woolf, 1965), p. 88. One wonders what Summers's father thought about his son's decadent début, *Antinoüs and Other Poems* (1907), which in 1995 was reprinted by Woolf in London.

32. Dal Young, *Apologia pro Oscar Wilde* (London: William Reeves, 1895), p. 7.

33. *CL*, 1 April 1897, p. 784.

34. Louis Perceau, *Bibliographie du roman érotique au XIXe siècle* (Paris: Georges Fourdrinier, 1930), II, pp. 41–3. The novel in question, written by Alphonse Gallais, was reprinted in 1993, when Patrick Cardon included it in *Dossier Jacques d'Adelswärd-Fersen*, *Cahiers* GKC, No. 21 (Lille: Éditions Gai-Kitsch-Camp).

35. AD to Robert Ross, 4 June 1896. Quoted in the *Daily Telegraph*, 25 November 1921.

36. *Autobiography*, pp. 128–9.

37. *CL*, p. 710ff.

38. *Without Apology*, p. 77.

39. *CL* [? May 1895], pp. 650–51.

Chapter 5

1. *Without Apology*, pp. 224–5.

2. Ross TS.

3. *Bosie*, p. 133.

4. H. Montgomery Hyde, *Oscar Wilde: The Aftermath* (London: Methuen, 1963), p. 5.

5. *CL* [20 May 1895], p. 651.

6. 26 May [1895]. MS Douglas.

7. AD to More Adey, *c.* 30 July 1895; AD to Percy Douglas, 5 August 1895. MS Hyde.

8. Sybil Queensberry to AD, 11 August [1895]. MS Magdalen.

9. Quoted in the *Mercure de France*, CCXCVIII, No. 999–1000, 1 July 1940–1 December 1946, pp. 218–19.

10. *CL* [29 April 1895], pp. 646–7.

11. AD, 'Hymn to Physical Beauty'.

12. AD, *Oscar Wilde: A Plea and a Reminiscence*. Ed. Caspar Wintermans (Woubrugge: Avalon Press, 2002), p. 35.

13. Ibid., p. 33.

14. Ibid., p. 36.

15. Richard Ellmann pulverized Bosie's defence of Oscar as 'futile; Hugues Rebell had done it much better than Douglas could possibly do' (*Oscar Wilde*. London: Hamish Hamilton, 1987, p. 459). Really? Rebell's article is actually much fiercer than Bosie's, lambasting Queen Victoria, advocating the administration of an unspecified number of whip-lashes to, among others, Frank Lockwood, and culminating in an incitement to storm and burn down the prison where Rebell erroneously thought Oscar was held.

16. Robert Sherard, *Oscar Wilde: The Story of an Unhappy Friendship* (London: Hermes Press, 1902), p. 212.

17. 30 November 1895. MS Hyde.

18. AD to Percy Douglas, 5 August 1895; AD to More Adey, 25 August 1895. MS Hyde.

19. *CL*, p. 828 (note).

20. Ibid., p. 722.

21. Ibid., p. 710; p. 756.

22. *Bosie*, 141; Hyde, pp. 100–101. In the course of the trial of *Douglas v. Ransome*, the plaintiff was asked by his counsel:

> 'Why did you not write to [Wilde] when he was in prison?'
>
> 'Because I was particularly told that he did not want me to write to him, because it would be detrimental to him if I wrote him.'
>
> 'If you had not been asked not to write to him, would you have written?'
>
> 'Certainly. I was devoted to him, and ready to do anything for him.' [*Daily Telegraph*, 19 April 1913]

23. *CL*, pp. 683–4; p. 710; p. 721; pp. 725–7; p. 778.

24. 27 September 1896. MS Hyde; Hyde, p. 101.

25. 'Une introduction à mes poèmes, avec quelques considérations sur l'affaire Oscar Wilde', *La Revue Blanche*, X, No. 72, 1 June 1896, pp. 484–90.

26. AD, 'Réponse à quelques journalistes', *La Revue Blanche*, X,

No. 73, 15 June 1896, pp. 552–3: 'Cet article ne m'a valu que des injures et des insultes, quelques sales plaisanteries et des aperçus effrayants sur la dense stupidité et le sordide manque de générosité de beaucoup de gens desquels j'espérais mieux.'

27. *Candid Friend*, 22 June 1901.

28. AD to André Gide [14 February 1896]. MS Doucet. See François J.-L. Mouret, 'Quatorze lettres et billets inédits de Lord Alfred Douglas à André Gide, 1895–1929', *Revue de Littérature Comparée*, XLIX, No. 3, July–September 1975, pp. 487–8.

29. AD to Edmond Jaloux, 16 July 1896. MS Doucet.

30. AD to Edward Strangman, 18 December 1897. MS Hyde.

31. 'Les deux rois', *Les Tentatives passionnées* (Châtillon-sur-Seine: Imprimerie Générale, 1898), pp. 167–77.

32. AD to Rachilde, 26 July 1897. Quoted in *Manuscrits et lettres autographes: Vente aux enchères publiques à Paris le 15 mai 2001* . . . (Paris: Drouot-Montaigne, 2001), item 75.

33. MS Clark.

34. AD to More Adey, 8 February 1897. MS Hyde: 'Had I had the least idea of Oscar's real state of mind towards me, I would never have sent him that unfortunate message about the dedication of my book which brought the actual storm on my head.'

35. *CL* [30 May 1896], pp. 654–5.

36. AD to More Adey, 27 September 1896. MS Hyde.

37. H. Montgomery Hyde expressed his surprise that Bosie did not send a copy of his book to Lady Queensberry (Hyde, p. 99). In March 1952, however, Sotheby and Co. in London offered for sale one of the copies of the *édition de grand luxe* carrying the inscription: 'To my own darling Mamma from her very loving son Bosie. November, 1896, Naples.'

38. Alcanter de Brahm (that is, Marcel Bernhardt), 'Poèmes de Lord Douglas', *La Critique*, III, No. 51, 5 April 1897, p. 75.

39. Ernest La Jeunesse, 'Alfred Bruce Douglas, poète', *Le Journal*, 11 January 1897; Henry-D. Davray, 'Lettres anglaises', *Mercure de France*, XXI, February 1897, pp. 417–18; Charles Guérin, 'Les livres de poésie', *L'Ermitage*, June 1897, pp. 411–12.

40. Stéphane Mallarmé, *Correspondance*. Eds. Henri Mondor and Lloyd James Austin (Paris: Gallimard, 1959–85), XI, p. 171. Cf. IX, p. 101.

41. *CL*, 1 April 1897, p. 780.

42. *Works*, III, p. 115; IV, p. 169; V, p. 130.
43. *CL*, 27 May 1897, pp. 847–55; 23 March 1898, pp. 1045–9.
44. Ibid., p. 684.
45. André Gide, 'Oscar Wilde' (1901). *Œuvres complètes*. Ed . L. Martin-Chauffier (Paris: Nouvelle Revue Française, 1932–9), III, p. 487.
46. *CL*, p. 727.
47. Ibid., p. 685.
48. Ibid., p. 692.
49. 'Brouillé avec les genres et la syntaxe, [Wilde] terminait, un jour, [à Paris], ainsi, l'exposé d'un conte: "A ce moment, la reine, il est mouru!"' Ernest Raynaud, *La Mêlée symboliste (1870–1910). Portraits et souvenirs* (Paris: Nizet, 1971), p. 319.
50. *CL*, p. 725.
51. Ibid., p. 729.
52. 'A Lord of Language', *Vanity Fair*, 2 March 1905, p. 309.
53. *CL*, 2 July 1896, p. 657.
54. *Works*, IX, p. 316.
55. *CL*, 15 June [1897], p. 898.
56. *Bosie*, p. 382.
57. *CL*, 13 May [1897], p. 823.
58. Ibid., 19 May 1897, p. 844.

Chapter 6

1. H. Montgomery Hyde, *Oscar Wilde: A Biography* (New York: Farrar, Straus and Giroux, 1975), p. 178.
2. *Without Apology*, p. 264.
3. *CL*, 23 June [1897], pp. 906–7.
4. Constance Wilde to Carlos Blacker, 20 March 1898. Quoted in *CL*, p. 1041.
5. Ibid., 17 June [1897], p. 902.
6. Ibid., 1 April 1897, p. 782.
7. Ibid.
8. Ross TS. Clark.
9. *CL*, p. 715.
10. André Germain, *Les Fous de 1900* (Paris/Geneva: La Palatine, 1954), p. 24: 'Je possède une lettre de Wilde où il écrit à Douglas, un peu après sa libération: "Notre affection est le sacrement de nos vies."'
11. *CL* [31 August 1897], pp. 932–3.

12. Oscar's youngest son (1886–1967).
13. Quoted (and contradicted) by Derek Hudson in his introduction to *OW: A Summing-Up*, p. ix.
14. *Autobiography*, p. 134.
15. Robert Ross to AD, 23 June [1897]; AD to More Adey, 30 June 1897. TS Hyde.
16. AD to Robert Ross, 13 July 1897. Quoted in the *Daily Telegraph*, 25 November 1921.
17. *Autobiography*, p. 152.
18. *CL*, 10 August [1897], p. 924.
19. AD to More Adey, 15 October 1897. MS Hyde.
20. Michel van der Plas, 'Een poging tot geluk in ballingschap. Het korte treurige leven van Sebastian Melmoth: Parijs', *Elsevier*, 21 January 1989, p. 95.
21. *CL* [23 September 1897], p. 948.
22. Leonard Green to Charles Kains-Jackson, 11 August 1919. TS Texas. The Oxford acquaintance was John Matthew Knapp (1868–1924), at whose house Green was staying when writing his letter.
23. *Autobiography*, p. 154.
24. *CL* [21 November 1897], p. 989.
25. Ibid. [23 November 1897], p. 991; [27 November 1897], p. 994.
26. Oscar subsequently denied having come to any agreement with 'that mischievous foolish woman' (*CL*, [17 March 1898], p. 1038), but Lady Queensberry, writing to More Adey on 18 December 1897 (MS Hyde), acknowledged the receipt of a letter from Wilde, in which he agreed to pocket the £200 in exchange for his pledge 'not to live together' with Bosie.
27. Quoted in *Bosie*, pp. 167–8.
28. *CL* [18 February 1898], p. 1019.
29. Ibid. [? March 1898], p. 1029.
30. Sybil Queensberry to AD, 6 January 1930. MS Magdalen. See also Vincent O'Sullivan, *Aspects of Wilde*, with an Opinion by Bernard Shaw (1936). New Edition (London: Constable and Company, 1938), pp. 90–91. O'Sullivan is right, I think, when in the same book he writes that '[Wilde] was good-natured, kind-hearted, but not large-hearted. He probably never cared for anyone as much as some cared for him. Lord Alfred Douglas was essentially and practically far kinder to Wilde than Wilde ever was to Douglas' (p. 165).

31. *CL*, p. 1035.
32. *OW: A Summing-Up*, pp. 100–101.
33. *CL* [12 or 13 April 1898], p. 1055.
34. AD to Sybil Queensberry, quoted in *Bosie*, p. 168.
35. To adopt George Sylvester Viereck's phrase, used in his introduction to AD, *Perkin Warbeck, and Other Poems* (Girard, Kansas: Haldeman-Julius Company, 1925), p. 11.
36. Quoted in *The City of the Soul*. Third edition (London/New York: John Lane, 1911) [p. 136].
37. Ibid.
38. *Outlook*, 3 June 1899, pp. 587–8.
39. *Some Letters of Lionel Johnson*. Ed. Raymond Roseliep (Notre Dame, Indiana: Department of English, 1953), 13 July 1895, p. 165.
40. *Bosie*, pp. 175–6.
41. *Autobiography*, pp. 122–5.
42. *The Times*, 7 February 1900.
43. AD, 'Some Reflections on the Beauty of Unpunctuality', *The Spirit Lamp*, III, No. 3, 10 March 1893, p. 77.
44. *CL*, p. 1192.
45. 'The only real money of any amount that Oscar got, apart from his allowance and the advances made by various people for possible work, was provided, and provided lavishly, by Bosie Douglas.' Reginald Turner to Robert Harborough Sherard, 29 October 1933. MS Reading.
46. P.N. van Eyck, 'Alfred Bruce Douglas' (1909). *Verzamelde werken* (Amsterdam: Van Oorschot, 1959), III, p. 123.
47. [AD], 'Oscar Wilde's Last Years in Paris', *St James's Gazette*, 3 March 1905. Quoted in AD, *Oscar Wilde: A Plea and a Reminiscence*. Ed. Caspar Wintermans (Woubrugge: Avalon Press, 2002), pp. 43–4.
48. Robert Ross to More Adey, 14 December 1900. Quoted in *CL*, p. 1213.
49. AD to Robert Ross, 29 November 1900. Quoted in the *Daily Telegraph*, 19 April 1913.
50. *OW and Myself*, p. 151.
51. Wilfred Hugh Chesson, 'A Reminiscence of 1898', New York *Bookman*, December 1911. Quoted in *More Letters of Oscar Wilde*. Ed. Rupert Hart-Davis (London: John Murray, 1985), p. 199.

52. *Works*, XII, p. 213.
53. *OW: A Summing-Up*, p. 141.
54. AD to More Adey, 17 December 1900. MS Hyde.

Chapter 7

1. Arthur Conan Doyle, *The Annotated Sherlock Holmes*. Ed. William S. Baring-Gould (London: John Murray, 1968), I, p. 284.
2 . *Autobiography*, p. 211.
3. Jean de Chalon, *Portrait d'une séductrice* (Paris: Éditions Stock, 1976), pp. 108–9.
4. Natalie Clifford-Barney, *Souvenirs indiscrets* (Paris: Flammarion, 1960), p. 61.
5. *Autobiography*, pp. 193–4.
6. MS Hyde.
7. Violet Wyndham, *The Sphinx and Her Circle: A Biographical Sketch of Ada Leverson* (London: André Deutsch, 1963), p. 72.
8. *Who's Who*, Burke's *Landed Gentry* as well as the obituary notice of the Colonel which appeared in *The Times* on 1 October 1925 give his second name as 'Hambleton'; in most books, however, it is spelled – erroneously, it would seem – 'Hambledon'.
9. AD to OC, 2 October 1901. MS Berg.
10. *Washington Post*, 17 December 1901.
11. *New York Herald*, 23 December 1901.
12. MS Doucet.
13. AD to OC, 20 December 1901. MS Berg.
14. *Autobiography*, p. 199.
15 .Elizabeth Longford, *A Pilgrimage of Passion: The Life of Wilfrid Scawen Blunt* (London: Weidenfeld and Nicolson, 1979), p. 373.
16. *Illustrated London News*, 11 January 1902, p. 39.
17. Ibid., 26 November 1904, p. 764.
18. Herein Ross quoted from a letter which Oscar had addressed to him on 1 April 1897: 'Of the many, many things for which I have to thank the Governor there is none for which I am more grateful than for his permission to write fully to A.D. and at as great a length as I desired' (*CL*, pp. 782–3). Now Ross changed 'A.D.' into 'you', making it seem as if Oscar's 'encyclical' had been written to *him*. Cf. Holbrook Jackson, *The Eighteen Nineties: A Review of Art and Ideas at the Close of the Nineteenth Century* (London: Grant Richards, 1913), p. 96: 'During his imprisonment [Wilde] wrote

De Profundis, in the form of a long letter to his friend, Robert Ross.'
19. *The Times*, 25 November 1914.
20. *Motorist and Traveller*, 1 March 1905. The review is reprinted in H. Montgomery Hyde, *Oscar Wilde: The Aftermath* (London: Methuen, 1963), pp. 208–10. Olive referred several times to *De Profundis* in her journal (26 April 1906, 11 January 1907: OCD, pp. 27, 54), and it is evident that she had no inkling it had been lifted from an undelivered letter to her husband.
21. Stuart Mason [that is, Christopher Sclater Millard], *Bibliography of Oscar Wilde* (London: T. Werner Laurie, 1914), pp. 442–51.
22. H. Montgomery Hyde, *Oscar Wilde: The Aftermath* (London: Methuen, 1963), p. 192.
23. Many composers have been inspired by Oscar's writings; the following list is by no means exhaustive. *Salomé* was not only adapted for the musical stage by Strauss but also by Antoine Mariotte (1908). Aleksandr A. Krein's symphonic poem *Salomé* dates from 1913. 'The Birthday of the Infanta' underlay five ballets, by Franz Schreker (1908), Bernhard Sekles (1913), John Alden Carpenter (1918), Miklos Radnai (1918) and Elizabeth Luytens (1932). Alexander Zemlinksy's opera in one act, *Der Zwerg* – a score of ravishing beauty – was based on the same fairy-tale. His composition of *A Florentine Tragedy* dates from 1917 and was followed twelve years afterwards by the version of Richard Flury; René Hirschfeld's was premièred in 1992, bearing the title *Bianca*. Jacques Ibert's *Ballade de la geôle de Reading* for orchestra was finished in 1920. The Czech Jaroslav Křička and the Russian Aleksandr Knaifel both turned 'The Canterville Ghost' into an opera in 1929 and 1966 respectively. Hans Kox wrote the libretto of *Dorian Gray* (1973, revised 1976) himself; Oscar's novel had already inspired three opera composers, to wit Charles Flick-Steger (1930), Hans Schaeuble (1948) and Robert Hanell (1962). The most recent, very successful adaptation dates from 1995 and was made by Lowell Liebermann from New York. *The Importance of Being Earnest* was turned into an opera by Mario Castelnuovo-Tedesco in 1975, a work scored for eight singers, two pianos and percussion. Songs on texts by Wilde have been written by, among others, Charles Griffes and Henry Muldrow. Finally, Jonathan Rutherford selected two fairy-tales, 'The Nightingale and the Rose' and 'The Star Child', as starting point for operas of the same name (1966 and 1985 respec-

tively); in 1985 he composed the cantata *The Young King*.

24. OCD, 20 March 1907, p. 61.

25. Alice M. Head, *It Could Never Have Happened* (London/Toronto: William Heinemann, 1939), p. 42.

26. Ibid., pp. 42–4.

27. AD, 'Poetry and Passion', *The Academy*, 22 June 1907, p. 604.

28. Ibid., 13 July 1907, p. 686.

29. Ibid., 7 September 1907, 878; 31 August 1907, p. 853.

30. 'The Unspeakable Englishman' (1918).

31. *Autobiography*, p. 228.

32. T.W.H. Crosland, *The Unspeakable Scot*, second edition (London: Grant Richards, 1903), p. 162.

33. Ibid., p. 197.

34. Arthur Machen, *Selected Letters: The Private Writings of the Master of the Macabre*. Eds. Roger Dobson, Godfrey Brangham and R.A. Gilbert (Wellingborough, Northamptonshire: Aquarian Press, 1988) [? September 1908], p. 44.

35. Théophile Gautier, *Émaux et camées*. Édition définitive (Paris: Charpentier, 1881), 'Préface' [p. 1].

36. See *The Academy*, 4 July 1908, p. 3, on a demonstration by Emmeline Pankhurst and others: 'Not one married woman in a thousand can walk at a fast pace behind a band on a broiling hot summer's day without producing the effect of ungainliness. The best-looking woman would not come well out of such an ordeal. It is a further proof, if any were needed, that the female Suffragists are not normal women that they consented to *walk* in their procession. The natural womanly woman would have insisted upon being driven.'

37. *Autobiography*, p. 223.

38. Shaw/Douglas, 24 February 1941, p. 136.

39. *The Academy*, 22 June 1907, p. 595.

40. Ibid., 23 May 1908, p. 806; 30 May 1908, p. 830; 6 June 1908, p. 855.

41. *The Spirit Lamp*, IV, No. 1, 4 May 1893, pp. 21–2.

42. OCD, 13 August 1906.

43. *Daily News*, 9 June 1910.

44. OCD, 29 December 1907, p. 78.

45. *The Academy*, 5 September 1908, p. 227.

46. Here are some passages from what Crosland called 'a vile tale':

Then, all at once, she looked up. The strain and stress had vanished; she was calm; she was smiling. More than that, there was something in her face that he had never seen there before, nor in any other woman's – something new and delicious – a slightly quivering light in her soft grey eyes. It made him thrill. With a bound of heart he realized the subtle change that had taken place in their relationship. Hitherto foster-mother and child, guardian and ward; they were now man and woman, as they had stood in Eden.

'Come and sit here,' she said – 'here, very near me, and let us talk.'

He obeyed quietly . He seemed to be walking on air.

'Maurice,' she said, after a slight pause, 'do I seem to you to be *very* old?'

'Good gracious! *no*,' cried Maurice. He forgot for how short a time he could have replied so emphatically. 'Old! You are perfectly lovely, Angelica.'

Angelica blushed with pleasure. 'I used to be good-looking,' she said, 'years ago. But now I have grown grey-haired – and you are so young.' She looked at him a little pensively.

'I'm twenty-two,' said Maurice; 'a very long way from the nursery, dear.' He bent towards her.

'What did you say?' said Angelica.

'A very long way from the nursery,' repeated Maurice.

'I thought you said something else?'

'So I did,' said Maurice, stoutly.

'I like you to say it,' said Angelica; 'I'm glad.' She paused. 'Tell me this: have you ever looked upon me as anything but a sort of mother to you?'

Maurice hesitated.

'Have you?' repeated Angelica.

Suddenly he slipped from his seat, knelt beside her, and took her two hands in his. 'Yes, I have – often, often.'

Angelica drew in her breath. She closed her eyes and dropped her head on the back of the chair. A shiver went through her. The rings on her fingers bit into the flesh. Then, opening her eyes, she spoke very low, 'Could I make up for – for those others?'

'Make up for them? Make up for them?' Maurice repeated the words in a sort of hurried whisper, hardly daring to push them to their utmost meaning. Then, with a gesture of complete self-abasement and homage, he pressed his lips upon the white hands that lay within his own.

He got up. 'Forgive me, ' he said. 'I've been a brute. I don't know what I've been thinking of.'

Angelica looked up. 'You don't understand,' she said.

'Yes, I do,' exclaimed Maurice. 'I know that you are willing to sacrifice yourself to save me. You've brought me up, cared for me, devoted yourself to me all my life – which I've never half returned, never half appreciated – and now, to keep me from harm, you are ready to do even this. Oh, I can't say what I feel. I feel so utterly, horribly little; and you are so splendid.'

'It's not a sacrifice,' cried Angelica, almost passionately. 'I should have less compunction if it were. I want it. I want it more than anything in earth or heaven. But – but – Oh, I'm not sure, I'm not sure.' Again her hands went over her face. And she shook.

Maurice stood perfectly still. For a while he could not fully grasp the wonderful thing that was happening – had happened. Life seemed to have opened a new heaven and a new earth. A paradise undreamt-of lay before him . . .

'I *know* it is right,' he cried. 'I don't care for all the books that were ever written, or all the sermons that were ever preached – I *know* it is right.'

Angelica removed her hands. She smiled at him a little. . . 'Then you may kiss me,' she said.

Maurice paused at the gate of Eden to give a happy laugh. 'Why, I've often kissed you before,' he said.

'But not as you are going to do now,' said Angelica.

With sudden abandon, her arms went out and over him. Her eyes were shining. 'Oh, my dear! my dear!' she cried. All the might of her pent-up womanhood filled the reiteration of the two little words.

Maurice drew her firmly to him and kissed her on the mouth. Then, slowly, his lips travelled downwards; lingered over her neck and shoulder; and stayed there. [*The Yoke*. Third impression. London: John Long, 1907, pp. 135–41]

47. The Academy, 26 September 1908, p. 307.
48. Ibid., 10 October 1908, p. 350.
49. AD, 'Une introduction à mes poèmes, avec quelques considérations sur l'affaire Oscar Wilde', *Revue Blanche*, 1 June 1896, p. 485.

50. *Autobiography*, p. 31.
51. J.P. Wearing, *The London Stage 1900–1909: A Calendar of Plays and Players* (Metuchen, NJ/London: Scarecrow Press, 1981), II, p. 805.
52. 'The Genius of Oscar Wilde', *The Academy*, 11 July 1908, p. 35.
53. Alice M. Head, op. cit., pp. 45–6: 'The tickets were fifteen shillings each, which was a large sum to me in those days, but I determined to go . . . I was inexpressibly puzzled to find that most of the speakers seemed to be so choked with emotion that they could hardly utter their words. On all sides I noticed people apparently ready to dissolve into tears and sobs, and when Robert Ross himself took the floor, the atmosphere was so charged with emotion that I felt ashamed of myself for wanting to laugh. Even after two years on *The Academy* I had no idea what it was all about!'
54. AD to Robert Ross, 1 March 1909. TS Clark.

Chapter 8

1. Quoted in W. Blok, *P.C. Boutens en de nalatenschap van Andries de Hoghe* (Amsterdam: Athenæum – Polak en Van Gennep, 1983), p. 230.
2. A.A.M. Stols, *P.C. Boutens als uitgever* (Utrecht: HES Publishers, 1977), p. 8.
3. AD to P.C. Boutens, 22 January 1909. MS Johan Polak Collection.
4. *The Academy*, 5 December 1908, p. 532.
5. *Saturday Review*, 11 September 1909, p. 321.
6. P.N. van Eyck, 'Alfred Bruce Douglas' (1909). *Verzameld werk* (Amsterdam: Van Oorschot 1959), III, p. 141.
7. *Hugo von Hofmannsthal und Harry Graf Kessler: Briefwechsel 1898–1929*. Ed. Hilde Burger (Frankfurt am Main: Insel Verlag, 1968), 1 January 1910, p. 270.
8. *Granta*, 11 June 1908, p. 20.
9. *Granta*, 8 December 1908, p. 120. The article was written by Raglan H.E.H. Somerset, who had been introduced to Bosie by Ronald Firbank.
10. *The Academy*, 20 February 1909, p. 796.
11. *Cambridge Review*, 4 March 1909, p. 306. Somerset did not have the pluck to admit that he himself had written the article.
12. *The Academy*, 6 March 1909, p. 843; 13 March 1909, p. 867.
13. Ibid., 15 May 1909, p. 101.

14. It has been said that W.H. Smith and Son refused to go on printing *The Academy* after Crosland had criticized the firm (*Bosie*, p. 223; Hyde, p. 163), but the initiative to sever connections had been taken by the editors of the magazine: 'We withdraw the paper from Messrs Smith as a matter of public duty' (*The Academy*, 3 July 1909, p. 267).
15. *The Academy*, 24 July 1909, pp. 341–2.
16. OCD, 12 January 1907, p. 54.
17. *The Times*, 15 February 1910.
18. Ibid., 22, 29 and 31 July 1909; 11, 12, 15 and 16 February 1910.
19. *Autobiography*, p. 234.
20. Obituary of Sir Edward Clarke, *The Times*, 27 April 1931.
21. *Daily News*, 18 June 1907.
22. *The Academy*, 19 September 1908, pp. 275–6; p. 286.
23. Ibid., 16 May 1908, pp. 783–6; 8 August 1908, p. 133.
24. *Daily News*, 9 June 1910.
25. *The Academy*, 14 October 1911, p. 471.
26. AD to John Lane, 13 September 1911. MS Bodleian Library, Oxford.
27. *Autobiography*, p. 246.
28. OC to AD [20 October 1927]. MS Hyde.
29. Custance to OC, 12 April 1905. MS Berg.
30. *Bosie*, 234; Hyde, p. 176.
31. *Autobiography*, p. 254.
32. *The Autobiography of Arthur Ransome*. Ed. Rupert Hart-Davis (London: Jonathan Cape, 1976), p. 142.
33. Ross TS Clark.
34. MS Brotherton Library, University of Leeds, Leeds.
35. 19 August 1911. MS in the same collection.
36. Arthur Ransome, *Oscar Wilde: A Critical Study* (London: Martin Secker, 1912), p. 157; pp. 182–3; p. 196.
37. AD to Robert Ross, 6 March 1912. Ross TS Clark.
38. Secker to Rupert Croft-Cooke. Quoted in *Bosie*, p. 245.
39. *Diaries and Letters of Marie Belloc Lowndes 1911–1947*. Ed. Susan Lowndes (London: Chatto and Windus, 1971), p. 37.
40. Robert Ross to Frank Harris, 17 May 1914. MS Texas. Cf. chapter II, note 39.
41. OC to Lady Queensberry, 31 May 1913. Quoted in *The Times*, 1 July 1915.
42. *CL*, 23 March [1898], pp. 1047–8.

43. Frank Harris, *Oscar Wilde*. With a Preface by Bernard Shaw (London: Constable, 1938), p. xlviii.
44. 19 December 1900. MS Hyde.

Chapter 9

1. Barbara Tuchman, *The Proud Tower* (1966) (London: Macmillan, 1987), p. 372.
2. *Autobiography*, p. 34.
3. *The Times*, 5 June 1918.
4. Ibid., 18 April 1913.
5. Ibid., 19 April 1913.
6. *CL* [? July 1894], p. 594 (Wilde's italics); [31 August 1894], p. 602; [*c.* 9 November 1894] p. 622.
7. Alfred Douglas, 'Une introduction à mes poèmes, avec quelques considérations sur l'affaire Oscar Wilde', *Revue Blanche*, 1 June 1896, p. 486.
8. Quoted in *The Times*, 19 April 1913.
9. *The Academy*, 11 June 1910, p. 555.
10. *Daily Telegraph* and *The Times*, 19 April 1913.
11. Maureen Borland, in her biography of Robert Ross, does not refer to the production of this letter during the Ransome case.
12. AD to More Adey, 23 April 1913. MS Clark.
13. *The Times*, 22 April 1913.
14. Text taken from the *Daily Telegraph*, 25 November 1921. The letter was read out during the Ransome case, but its text was not reported in the papers at the time.
15. *Daily Telegraph*, 19 April 1913.
16. *The Times*, 22 April 1913.
17. Ibid., 23 April 1913.
18. *Daily News*, 23 April 1913.
19. *The Times*, 23 April 1913.
20. Randal Charlton to T.W.H. Crosland, 22 April 1913. Quoted in W. Sorley Brown, *The Life and Genius of T.W.H. Crosland* (London: Cecil Palmer, 1928), p. 300.
21. Quoted in *The Times*, 1 July 1915.
22. Ibid., 23 April 1913.
23. Collection of Julia D. Smith.
24. Marcia ('Madge') Lane Foster, later Mrs Dudley Jarrett, to AD, late April and early May 1913. MS Magdalen. My warmest thanks to

Brendan G. Carroll, who spent a great amount of time to identify her.

25. In his autobiography Bosie did not divulge her name, but it is mentioned in a letter he wrote to Natalie Clifford Barney on 26 February 1930. MS Doucet.

26. 'François Villon', *The Academy*, 4 April 1908, p. 639.

27. *Bosie*, p. 249.

28. 'The case was heard in the Vacation Court before Mr Justice Astbury,' Bosie subsequently wrote. 'The whole proceedings lasted barely five minutes and were conducted in a room (not a court) with a table in it, behind which sat [the Judge], dressed in mufti, while the parties to the case and fifty or sixty other persons crowded into the room pell-mell and anyhow and anywhere' ('Chancery Justice', *Plain English*, I, No. 22, 4 December 1920, p. 507). Ross shortly afterwards established the American copyright of the 'unpublished portions' of *De Profundis* by sending a typescript to Paul Reynolds in New York who printed fifteen copies, of which two were deposited at the Library of Congress. 'It is to be regretted,' says Maureen Borland, 'that [Ross] did not send a copy to Lord Alfred Douglas; if he had, Douglas might have seen it as a gesture of reconciliation' (*Wilde's Devoted Friend: A Life of Robert Ross, 1869–1918*. Oxford: Lennard Publishing, 1990, p. 199). This is an astonishing remark, to put it mildly.

29. *OW and Myself*, pp. 100–101; p. 108; pp. 112–13.

30. Ibid., pp. 269–79.

31. *Autobiography*, pp. 136–8; *Without Apology*, pp. 58–62.

32. Donald Sinden, *A Touch of the Memoirs* (London: Hodder and Stoughton, 1982), pp. 48–50.

33. Robert Harborough Sherard, *Bernard Shaw, Frank Harris and Oscar Wilde*. With a Preface by Lord Alfred Douglas and an additional chapter by Hugh Kingsmill (London: T. Werner Laurie, 1937), p. 12. I have slightly changed the sequence of the sentences.

34. *The Times*, 2 July 1914.

35. T.W.H. Crosland to Robert Ross, 9 January 1914. Quoted in W. Sorley Brown, op. cit., p. 309.

36. *The Times*, 2 July 1914.

37. *Autobiography*, p. 281.

38. *Daily News*, 26 November 1914.

39. I am grateful to Rohinten Mazda who vainly tried to locate the transcript of the trial by contacting David Hamilton of the Court Service,

London, and by paying a visit to the Public Record Office at Kew.

40. AD to OC, 30 November 1914. MS Berg.

41. 'I wish you didn't take up this ugly [that is, pacifist] attitude about the war,' Wells had written to Ross on 6 July 1914. 'It shakes my faith in the harmlessness of homosexuality' (MS Hyde).

42. *Daily News*, 27 November 1914.

43. Timothy d'Arch Smith, *Love in Earnest: Some Notes on the Lives and Writings of English 'Uranian' Poets from 1889 to 1930* (London: Routledge and Kegan Paul, 1970), p. 48. Mr d'Arch Smith, who, rather uncharitably, laments the fact that Bosie did not die at a tender age, has a reference to an action for libel brought by Bosie against the satanist Aleister Crowley, in the course of which Bosie, 'in a fever of agitation and rage, described [one of Oscar's letters to him] in court as "written by a diabolical scoundrel to a wretchedly silly youth"' (p. 53). Mr d'Arch Smith does not tell us if the plaintiff or the defendant was given a verdict; but then the whole case is a figment of his imagination, and Bosie's words were lifted by him from Sir Ellis Hume-Williams's cross-examination of Bosie during Maud Allan's prosecution of Noel Pemberton-Billing. See *The Times*, 3 June 1918.

44. Max Beerbohm, *Letters to Reggie Turner*. Ed. Rupert Hart-Davis (London: Rupert Hart-Davis, 1964) [3 June 1913], p. 227.

45. Ibid. [postmark 25 February 1915], p. 241.

46. Reginald Turner to AD, 3 May 1929. MS Hyde.

47. Mr Justice Coleridge. *The Times*, 28 November 1914.

48. Quoted in *The Times*, 1 July 1915.

49. *Autobiography*, p. 260.

50. Quoted in *The Times*, 1 July 1915.

51. Ibid.

52. *Evening News*, 25 November 1921.

53. Quoted by *The Times*, 30 May 1918.

54. Quoted in *Bosie*, p. 286.

55. *The Academy*, 17 October 1908, p. 365.

56. Felix Cherniavsky, *The Salomé Dancer: The Life and Times of Maud Allan* (Toronto, Ontario: McClelland and Stewart, 1991), p. 222.

57. *Nieuwe Rotterdamsche Courant*, 20 June 1918 (evening edition).

58. Ibid., 6 July 1918 (morning edition).

59. Ibid., 4 July 1918 (evening edition).

60. Ibid., 20 June 1918 (evening edition).

61. AD to OC, 1 November 1918. MS Berg.
62. Marie Carmichael Stopes, *Lord Alfred Douglas, His Poetry and His Personality* (London: Richards Press, 1949), p. 22.

Chapter 10

1. Quoted in *The Times*, 25 November 1921.
2. Aidan Reynolds and William Charlton, *Arthur Machen: A Short Account of His Life and Work* (London: Richards Press, 1963), p. 175.
3. *Autobiography*, p. 305.
4. Shaw/Douglas, 14 November 1940, p. 135.
5. *Bosie*, p. 293; Hyde, p. 249.
6. See Vivian David Lipman, *A History of the Jews in Britain since 1858* (Leicester/London: Leicester University Press, 1990), pp. 80–84.
7. Ibid., p. 141.
8. *Without Apology*, pp. 143–4.
9. Vivian David Lipman, op. cit., pp. 150–51.
10. *The Times*, 8 May 1920.
11. *Sonnets* (1935), p. 73 (note).
12. *The Times*, 16, 17 and 18 August 1921.
13. Ibid., 13 December 1923.
14. Ibid., 14 December 1923.
15. *CL*, pp. 774–5.
16. AD, *In Excelsis* (London: Martin Secker, 1924), pp. 8–9; *Autobiography*, pp. 283–4; p. 311; *Without Apology*, pp. 186–7.
17. AD, *In Excelsis* (London: Martin Secker, 1924), p. 9.
18. Rupert Croft-Cooke, *The Numbers Came* (London: Putnam and Company, 1963), pp. 77–80.
19. John Glassco, *Memories of Montparnasse* (Toronto/New York: Oxford University Press, 1970), p. 203.
20. *Bosie*, p. 14.
21. Ibid., pp. 382–3.
22. Ibid., p. 383.
23. Hyde, p. 314.
24. AD to Dr George Charles Williamson, 22 February 1940. MS Texas. Williamson, interestingly, had been one of the 'Ross signatories'.
25. *Bosie*, p. 344; Bevis Hillier, *Young Betjeman* (London: John Murray, 1988), pp. 116–17.

26. *Bosie*, pp. 339–40; G. Krishnamurti, *The Eighteen Nineties: A Literary Exhibition, September 1973: Supplement to the Catalogue*, with a Foreword by Sir John Betjeman (London: Francis Thompson Society/Enitharmon Press, 1974), pp. 10–11.

27. *The Times*, 14 December 1923.

28. The *Sunday Times*, 31 November 1948.

29. Violet Conaghan-Douglas to the author, 15 May 1995.

30. Rory Knight Bruce, 'Oscar Wilde, Bosie and the District Nurse', *Evening Standard*, 6 March 1995.

31. AD, *Collected Poems* (London: Martin Secker, 1919), pp. 125–6.

32. *Without Apology*, p. 271.

33. Robert Harborough Sherard, *Bernard Shaw, Frank Harris and Oscar Wilde*, with a Preface by Lord Alfred Douglas and an Additional Chapter by Hugh Kingsmill (London: T. Werner Laurie, 1937), p. 157.

34. Thanks to the efforts of Adrian Cooper, an English Heritage Blue Plaque, inscribed 'Lord Alfred Douglas, "Bosie" 1870–1945, Poet and Writer, lived here 1935–1944', was erected here on 22 October 2004.

35. Robert Harborough Sherard, *Oscar Wilde: The Story of an Unhappy Friendship* (London: Hermes Press, 1902), p. 212.

36. Robert Harborough Sherard to an unidentified correspondent (in all likelihood Charles Norton Outcalt), 23 June 1921. Handwritten copy. MS Private.

37. See note 33.

38. Havergal Brian, 'How the "Gothic" Symphony Came to Be Written', *Modern Mystic and Monthly Science Review*, December 1938. Reprinted in Harold Truscott and Paul Rapoport, *Havergal Brian's 'Gothic' Symphony: Two Studies* (Potters Bar, Herts: Havergal Brian Society, 1978), p. 87.

39. Kenneth Eastaugh, *Havergal Brian: The Making of a Composer* (London: Harrap, 1976), pp. 282–4.

40. Robert Harborough Sherard, *Bernard Shaw, Frank Harris and Oscar Wilde* (London: T. Werner Laurie, 1937), *passim*; *Bosie*, pp. 321–4; Rupert Croft-Cooke, *The Unrecorded Life of Oscar Wilde* (London/New York: W.H. Allen, 1972), pp. 2–4.

41. Paul Marijnis, 'De brieven van Oscar Wilde. "Niets, behalve mijn genie"', *NRC Handelsblad*, 13 April 1979, Cultureel Supplement. Cf. Frank Harris, *Oscar Wilde: His Life and Confessions* (New York: Printed and Published by the Author, 1916), II, p. 529.

42. Augustus John, *Chiaroscuro: Fragments of Autobiography*, First Series (London: Jonathan Cape, 1952), p. 129.

43. Frank Harris, op. cit., II, pp. 460–61.

44. Ibid., II, p. 539.

45. Frank Harris and Lord Alfred Douglas, *New Preface to 'The Life and Confessions of Oscar Wilde'* (London: Fortune Press, 1925), pp. 14–15.

46. Hyde, p. 197; Guy Deghy and Keith Waterhouse, *Café Royal. Ninety Years of Bohemia* (London: Hutchinson, 1955), p. 100.

47. Keith Briant, *Marie Stopes: A Biography* (London: Hogarth Press, 1962), p. 202.

48. *Without Apology*, pp. 182–3.

49. Donald Sinden, *A Touch of the Memoirs* (London: Hodder and Stoughton, 1982), p. 47.

50. *Bosie*, p. 373.

51. Hyde, p. 336.

52. Donald Sinden, op. cit., p. 51. H. Montgomery Hyde, who also attended the funeral, said that there were about thirty people present. Hyde, p. 338.

53. Gerald Hamilton, 'A Page from Yesterday: Memories of Lord Alfred Douglas', *World Review*, New Series, No. 1, March 1949, p. 48.

54. *Trials*, p. 17.

55. Adolphe Engers, *Oscar Wilde*. Tragédie in 5 bedrijven naar de gegevens van Dr Fritz Löhner, Bruno Hardt en Dr Franz Martos (The Hague: F.W. de Ruyter van Steveninck [1917]), p. 43.

56. Ibid., p. 47.

57. Ibid.,p. 64.

58. Ibid., p. 144.

59. Ibid., p. 170 (cf. *CL*, p. 729).

60. Ibid., pp. 49–50.

61. Carl Sternheim, *Oskar Wilde, sein Drama* (Potsdam: Gustav Kiepenheuer Verlag, 1925), pp. 70–71. The play received its first and only performance on 31 March 1925 at the Deutsches Theater in Berlin, the author directing.

62. Maurice Rostand, *Le Procès d'Oscar Wilde*. Pièce en trois actes (Paris: Ernest Flammarion, 1934). The première took place in March 1935. See the same author's *Confession d'un demi-siècle* (Paris: La Jeune Parque, 1948), pp. 306–11.

63. 'Voor het voetlicht', *Haags Nieuwsblad*, 9 December 1997.

64. Shaw/Douglas, 25 June 1938, p. 59.
65. *CL* [? April 1891], p. 478.
66. Herbert Read, '"Your Affectionate Friend"', *Listener*, 8 December 1949, p. 1009.

Chapter 11

1. Guy Deghy and Keith Waterhouse, *Café Royal: Ninety Years of Bohemia* (London: Hutchinson, 1955), p. 82.
2. Richard Middleton, *The Pantomime Man* . . . With an Introduction by Lord Alfred Douglas (London: Rich and Cowan, 1933), p. xix.
3. AD to R.N. Green-Armytage, 9 March 1915. MS Columbia University, New York.
4. *Ennead*, I. 6, 'On Beauty' [*The Works of*] *Plotinus*. With an English Translation by A.H. Armstrong (London/Cambridge, Massachusetts: William Heinemann/Harvard University Press, 1966), I, p. 239.
5. H.-J. Seekamp *et al.*, *Stefan George: Leben und Werk: Eine Zeittafel* (Amsterdam: Castrum Peregrini Presse, 1972), p. 55.
6. Antoine Bodar, 'George's omzien naar de moederkerk', *Weten waar de muze woont* (Amsterdam: Heuff, 1998), pp. 21–2.
7. *CP*, p. xv.
8. AD, *The Principles of Poetry* . . . (London: Richards Press, 1943), p. 25.
9. Ibid., p. 21.
10. AD, *Collected Poems* (London: Martin Secker, 1919), p. 120.
11. *The City of the Soul*, third edition (London: John Lane, 1911), pp. viii–ix.
12. AD, *The Principles of Poetry* . . . (London: Richards Press, 1943), p. 20.
13. Ibid., pp. 20–21. A quotation from Coventry Patmore, 'William Blake', *Principle in Art, Religio Poetæ and Other Essays* (London: Duckworth, 1913), p. 74.
14. Quoted in Patrick Braybrooke, *Lord Alfred Douglas: His Life and Work* (London: Cecil Palmer, 1931), p. 262.
15. Quoted in Marie Carmichael Stopes, *Lord Alfred Douglas: His Poetry and His Personality* (London: Richards Press, 1949), p. 26.
16. [Lionel Johnson], 'A Great Unknown', *Outlook*, 3 June 1899, p. 587.
17. AD, 'A Daniel Come to Judgment', *Modern Mystic and Monthly Science Review*, April–May 1937, p. 10.
18. Frank Harris, *Oscar Wilde*, with a Preface by Bernard Shaw (London: Constable, 1938), p. 1.

The Poems

Autumn Days

I have been through the woods to-day
  And the leaves were falling,
Summer had crept away,
  And the birds were not calling.

And the bracken was like yellow gold
  That comes too late,
When the heart is sad and old,
  And death at the gate.

Ah, mournful Autumn! Sad,
  Slow death that comes at last,
I am mad for a yesterday, mad!
  I am sick for a year that is past!

Though the sun be like blood in the sky,
  He is cold as the lips of hate,
And he fires the sere leaves as they lie
  On their bed of earth, too late.

They are dead, and the bare trees weep,
  Not loud as a mortal weeping,
But as sorrow that sighs in sleep,
  And as grief that is still in sleeping.

The Hut, 1890

A Winter Sunset

To my brother Percy

The frosty sky, like a furnace burning,
    The keen air, crisp and cold,
    And a sunset that splashes the clouds with gold;
But my heart to summer turning.

Come back, sweet summer! come back again!
    I hate the snow,
    And the icy winds that the north lands blow,
And the fall of the frozen rain.

I hate the iron ground,
    And the Christmas roses,
    And the sickly day that dies when it closes,
With never a song or a sound.

Come back! come back! with your passionate heat
    And glowing hazes,
    And your sun that shines as a lover gazes,
And your day with the tired feet.

Clouds, 1892

Prince Charming

Buttercup and marigold
    Seems my Prince's hair to be,
Strand and lock and curl and fold,
    Oh! the boy is fair to see.

Yellow, yellow marigold,
    Golden buttercups and daisies,
He is sixteen summers old,
    Daisy-fair my prince's face is.

Jacinth blue and violet
    Is the radiant light that flashes
Through a tangled silken net,
    When he lifts his languid lashes.

Every earthly whiteness seems
    Matched with his obscure and dim;
He is king of all my dreams,
    I am king of love for him.

Oxford, 1892

Two Loves

To 'the Sphinx'

I dreamed I stood upon a little hill,
And at my feet there lay a ground, that seemed
Like a waste garden, flowering at its will
With flowers and blossoms. There were pools that dreamed
Black and unruffled; there were white lilies
A few, and crocuses, and violets
Purple or pale, snake-like fritillaries
Scarce seen for the rank grass, and through green nets
Blue eyes of shy pervenche winked in the sun.
And there were curious flowers, before unknown,
Flowers that were stained with moonlight, or with shades
Of Nature's wilful moods; and here a one
That had drunk in the transitory tone
Of one brief moment in a sunset; blades
Of grass that in an hundred springs had been
Slowly but exquisitely nurtured by the stars,
And watered with the scented dew long cupped
In lilies, that for rays of sun had seen
Only God's glory, for never a sunrise mars
The luminous air of heaven. Beyond, abrupt,
A gray stone wall, o'ergrown with velvet moss,
Uprose. And gazing I stood long, all mazed
To see a place so strange, so sweet, so fair.
And as I stood and marvelled, lo! across
The garden came a youth, one hand he raised
To shield him from the sun, his wind-tossed hair
Was twined with flowers, and in his hand he bore
A purple bunch of bursting grapes, his eyes
Were clear as crystal, naked all was he,
White as the snow on pathless mountains frore,
Red were his lips as red wine-spilth that dyes
A marble floor, his brow chalcedony.
And he came near me, with his lips uncurled
And kind, and caught my hand and kissed my mouth,
And gave me grapes to eat, and said, 'Sweet friend,
Come, I will shew thee shadows of the world

And images of life. See, from the south
Comes the pale pageant that hath never an end.'
And lo! within the garden of my dream
I saw two walking on a shining plain
Of golden light. The one did joyous seem
And fair and blooming, and a sweet refrain
Came from his lips; he sang of pretty maids
And joyous love of comely girl and boy,
His eyes were bright, and 'mid the dancing blades
Of golden grass his feet did trip for joy.
And in his hands he held an ivory lute,
With strings of gold that were as maidens' hair,
And sang with voice as tuneful as a flute,
And round his neck three chains of roses were.
But he that was his comrade walked aside;
He was full sad and sweet, and his large eyes
Were strange with wondrous brightness, staring wide
With gazing; and he sighed with many sighs
That moved me, and his cheeks were wan and white
Like pallid lilies, and his lips were red
Like poppies, and his hands he clenchèd tight,
And yet again unclenchèd, and his head
Was wreathed with moon-flowers pale as lips of death.
A purple robe he wore, o'erwrought in gold
With the device of a great snake, whose breath
Was fiery flame: which when I did behold
I fell a-weeping and I cried, 'Sweet youth,
Tell me why, sad and sighing, thou dost rove
These pleasant realms? I pray thee speak me sooth
What is thy name?' He said, 'My name is Love.'
Then straight the first did turn himself to me
And cried, 'He lieth, for his name is Shame,
But I am Love, and I was wont to be
Alone in this fair garden, till he came
Unasked by night; I am true Love, I fill
The hearts of boy and girl with mutual flame.'
Then sighing said the other, 'Have thy will,
I am the Love that dare not speak its name.'

18 Cadogan Place, September 1892

211

De Profundis

I love a love, but not as other men
    Who tell the world their love for very pride,
For the cold world loves not my love; and when
    My voice would sing my love I needs must hide,
Under a cloak of black ambiguous words,
    The jewelled thoughts and all the scented fancies
That beat against my lips, like prisoned birds
    Caught in a cage when yellow sunlight dances
Without, and the tall trees stretch out green branches.
    Yet well for them they cannot pass the gates
And fly to freedom, for the north wind launches
    Swift shafts of icy death on those he hates:
And as the north wind hates the painted birds
    That sing i' the South, so the unkindly world
Would freeze my fancies and abhor my words.
    Therefore, a ship with never a sail unfurled,
I drift perforce; and never from the lute
    Of mine own lips comes a clear note and strong,
But only broken murmurs; and the fruit
    Of many silent years is like a song
Sung in a prison by the lips of Fear,
    With a hushed voice and a quick glance behind
At what is not. Ah! cruel world and drear!
    And yet – I care not, so my love be kind.

London, November 1892

In Sarum Close

    Tired of passion and the love that brings
    Satiety's unrest, and failing sands
    Of life, I thought to cool my burning hands
    In this calm twilight of gray Gothic things:
    But Love has laughed, and, spreading swifter wings

Than my poor pinions, once again with bands
Of silken strength my fainting heart commands,
And once again he plays on passionate strings.

But thou, my love, my flower, my jewel, set
In a fair setting, help me, or I die,
To bear Love's burden; for that load to share
Is sweet and pleasant, but if lonely I
Must love unloved, 'tis pain; shine we, my fair,
Two neighbour jewels in Love's coronet.

Salisbury, 1893

In Winter

Oh! for a day of burning noon
    And a sun like a glowing ember,
Oh! for one hour of golden June,
    In the heart of this chill November.

I can scarcely remember the Spring's soft breath,
    Or imagine the Summer hazes.
The yellow woods are so damp with death
    That I have forgotten the daisies.

Oh! to lie watching the sky again,
    From a nest of hot grass and clover,
Till the stars come out like golden rain
    When the lazy day is over.

And crowning the night with an aureole,
    As the clouds kiss and drift asunder,
The moon floats up like a luminous soul,
    And the stars grow pale for wonder.

Hatch House, 1893

To Shakespeare

Dedicated to the British
Public on the one hand, and to the
anti-Shakespeare Society on the other

Most tuneful singer, lover tenderest,
Most sad, most piteous, and most musical,
Thine is the shrine more pilgrim-worn than all
The shrines of singers; high above the rest
Thy trumpet sounds most loud, most manifest.
Yet better were it if a lonely call
Of woodland birds, a song, a madrigal,
Were all the jetsam of thy sea's unrest.

For now thy praises have become too loud
On vulgar lips, and every yelping cur
Yaps thee a pæan; the whiles little men,
Not tall enough to worship in a crowd,
Spit their small wits at thee. Ah! better then
The broken shrine, the lonely worshipper.

1893

Apologia

Tell me not of Philosophies,
    Of morals, ethics, laws of life;
Give me no subtle theories,
    No instruments of wordy strife.
I will not forge laborious chains
    Link after link, till seven times seven,
I need no ponderous iron cranes
    To haul my soul from earth to heaven.
But with a burnished wing,
    Rainbow-hued in the sun,

I will dive and leap and run
In the air, and I will bring
Back to the earth a heavenly thing,
    I will dance through the stars
    And pass the blue bars
Of heaven. I will catch hands with God
    And speak with Him,
    I will kiss the lips of the seraphim
    And the deep-eyed cherubim;
I will pluck of the flowers that nod
    Row upon row upon row,
In the infinite gardens of God,
To the breath of the wind of the sweep of the lyres,
    And the cry of the strings
    And the golden wires,
    And the mystical musical things
That the world may not know.

Oxford, April 1893

Hymn to Physical Beauty

Sweet Spirit of the body, archetype
    Of lovely mortal shapes, where is thy shrine?
        Long have I wandered over dales and hills,
    Seeking in vain, and now these eyes of mine,
        That were like stars, are like to running rills,
So sad am I; come, for the fruits are ripe,
    The yellow fruits that wait thee, a white dove
        For thee is caged, I have a thousand roses
        Both white and red; come, ere the hot day closes
Its languid eyes, and lead me to thy grove.

Alas! I hear no voice, I see no sign,
    Art thou then dead? Nay, but that cannot be,
        For yesterday, when the broad sun at noon
    Stood in the burning heavens, I chanced to see
        A lad that bathed; his face was like the moon,

His flesh was honey-pale, his locks were fine
    As silk new spun and stained with saffron stains.
      So fair he was, I thought on young Narcisse,
      Dead for desire of a shadow's kiss,
    And to my shepherd's lute I sang these strains.

        I know a boy who every day
        Leaps in the lake in summer weather.
        His lips are like fresh flowers in May,
        His feet are silver on the heather.

        His eyes are blue as sunny seas,
        His hair is like the golden money,
        His shoulder cheats the honey bees,
        So like it is to golden honey.

Thou needs must live, seeing he is so fair,
    For all his beauty is but part of thee.
      Alas! I fear me, in this dreary land,
    Thou art disdained, there is no galaxy
      Of worshippers, no priest with pious hand
Twines chaplets for thine altars; greedy care
    For wealth, the barter of dull merchandise,
      And sad-faced gods, have maimed or marred men's souls,
      Their eyes for beauty are but sightless holes,
    Spurned in the dust uranian passion lies.

Dull fools decree the sweet unfruitful love,
    In Hellas counted more than half divine,
      Less than half human now; the untrammelled shapes
    Of glorious nakedness, the curve and line
      Of sun-browned youth, must hide, for human apes
Have found God's image shameful. Go, white dove,
    Wither, red rose, the world is sad and brown,
      For Pan is dead, and in Apollo's courts
      The noisy rabble brawls, the shy resorts
    Of nymphs and fauns are tainted with the town.

Oh! radiant thing (I will not say divine,
    Thou art more gracious and more beautiful
        Being human merely), they who worshipped thee,
    Thy gods, are dead; once were thy temples full
        Of gifts; thou hadst more images than He
Who died for men, around thy glorious shrine
    Fair flowers were strewn: the wine-red lips of boys
        Kissed the flute's lips for thee, to thee did rise
        The passionate incense of sweet lovers' sighs,
And songs that told of lovers' passionate joys.

Those days are fled, and now the sickly age
    Is dotard, and its bleared and glazing eyes
        Are wellnigh blind to beauty; yet, I know
    That in some hearts a wakening spirit cries
        And strives for freedom, we are not so low
That there is none of us to scorn the rage
    Of Caliban, and dare to drink his full
        Of thy gold cup; and in this sad late day
        There be some faithful found who dare to say:
'We needs must love what is most beautiful.'

Come down and save us; let the world reborn
    Be glad again. Our hearts are barren fountains,
        Come down like rain. Ah! do I sleep or wake?
    Methinks I hear thy feet upon the mountains;
        And ere the red sun stoops and drinks the lake,
Haply my aching eyes shall see thy dawn.

Oxford, 1893

Night Coming into a Garden

To Fanny Zæssinger

Roses red and white,
    Every rose is hanging her head,
Silently comes the lady Night,
    Only the flowers can hear her tread.

All day long the birds have been calling,
    Calling shrill and sweet,
They are still when she comes with her long robe falling,
    Falling down to her feet.

The thrush has sung to his mate,
    'She is coming! hush! she is coming!'
She is lifting the latch at the gate,
    And the bees have ceased from their humming.

I cannot see her face as she passes
    Through my garden of white and red;
But I know she has walked where the daisies and grasses
    Are curtseying after her tread.

She has passed me by with a rustle and sweep
    Of her robe (as she passed I heard it sweeping),
And all my red roses have fallen asleep,
    And all my white roses are sleeping.

Goring, 1893

Night Going out of a Garden

To Charles Fleming

Through the still air of night
   Suddenly comes, alone and shrill,
Like the far-off voice of the distant light,
   The single piping trill
Of a bird that has caught the scent of the dawn,
   And knows that the night is over;
(She has poured her dews on the velvet lawn
   And drenched the long grass and the clover),
And now with her naked white feet
   She is silently passing away,
Out of the garden and into the street,
Over the long yellow fields of the wheat,
   Till she melts in the arms of the day.
And from the great gates of the East,
   With a clang and a brazen blare,
Forth from the rosy wine and the feast
   Comes the god with the flame-flaked hair;
The hoofs of his horses ring
   On the golden stones, and the wheels
Of his chariot burn and sing,
   And the earth beneath him reels;
And forth with a rush and a rout
   His myriad angels run,
And the world is awake with a shout,
   'He is coming! The sun! The sun!'

Goring, 1893

In an Ægean Port

I saw the white sails of the silver ships
Bend to the bay's blue waters; ivory
And bars of gold, a prince's treasury,
The sailors brought; and odorous oil that drips
From the full cask, as the broad galleon dips
And rises to the swell; and I saw thee
In thy white tunic gowned from neck to knee,
And knew the honey of thy sugar lips.

Rarer than all the hoarded merchandise
Heaped on the wharves, more precious than fine pearls,
Than all the loot and pillage of the deep
More enviable, oh! food to my starved eyes
(That gaze unmoved on wanton charms of girls),
Fair as the lad on Latmian hills asleep.

London, August 1893

The Sphinx

To Reginald Turner

I gaze across the Nile; flamelike and red,
The sun goes down, and all the western sky
Is drowned in sombre crimson: wearily
A great bird flaps along with wings of lead,
Black on the rose-red river. Over my head
The sky is hard green bronze, beneath me lie
The sleeping ships; there is no sound, or sigh
Of the wind's breath – a stillness of the dead.

Over a palm tree's top I see the peaks
Of the tall pyramids; and though my eyes
Are barred from it, I know that on the sand

Crouches a thing of stone that in some wise
Broods on my heart; and from the darkening land
Creeps Fear and to my soul in whisper speaks.

British Agency, Cairo, January 1894

In Praise of Shame

Unto my bed last night, methought there came
Our lady of strange dreams, and from an urn
She poured live fire, so that mine eyes did burn
At sight of it. Anon the floating flame
Took many shapes, and one cried, 'I am Shame
That walks with Love, I am most wise to turn
Cold lips and limbs to fire; therefore discern
And see my loveliness, and praise my name.'

And afterwards, in radiant garments dressed,
With sound of flutes and laughing of glad lips,
A pomp of all the passions passed along,
All the night through; till the white phantom ships
Of dawn sailed in. Whereat I said this song,
'Of all sweet passions, Shame is loveliest.'

London, February 1894

A Prayer

To Lionel Johnson

Often the western wind has sung to me,
There have been voices in the streams and meres,
And pitiful trees have told me, God, of Thee:
And I heard not. Oh! open Thou mine ears.

The reeds have whispered low as I passed by,
'Be strong, O friend, be strong, put off vain fears,
Vex not thy soul with doubts, God cannot lie:'
And I heard not. Oh! open Thou mine ears.

There have been many stars to guide my feet,
Often the delicate moon, hearing my sighs,
Has rent the clouds and shown a silver street;
And I saw not. Oh! open Thou mine eyes.

Angels have beckoned me unceasingly,
And walked with me; and from the sombre skies
Dear Christ Himself has stretched out hands to me;
And I saw not. Oh! open Thou mine eyes.

Clouds, 1894

Lust and Hypocrisy

My love and life have taught me late two things
That I have been most dull and slow in learning,
Even to the foolishness of quick returning,
When I had almost learned, on fanciful wings
To my old folly. These: that of all kings
That are most fierce in slaying and in burning,
Lust is the strongest, friendship overturning
And scorning love and sweet imaginings.

This, too, I know: that smooth Hypocrisy
Rules in the land, and there is not one man
But owes to it, having wherewith to pay,
Only ill words of other men. Ah me!
When will God come, and, with his fearful fan,
Purge this rank harvest and turn night to day?

London, 1894

Impression de Nuit

To the memory of Count Louis de Laveaux

See what a mass of gems the city wears
Upon her broad live bosom! row on row
Rubies and emeralds and sapphires glow.
See! that huge circle like a necklace, stares
With thousand of bold eyes to heaven, and dares
The golden stars to dim the lamps below,
And in the mirror of the mire I know
The moon has left her image unawares.

That's the great town at night: I see her breasts,
Pricked out with lamps they stand like huge black towers.
I think they move! I hear her panting breath.
And that's her head where the tiara rests.
And in her brain, through lanes as dark as death,
Men creep like thoughts ... The lamps are like pale flowers.

London, 1894

A Ballad of Hate

Here's short life to the man I hate!
(Never a shroud or a coffin board)
Wait and watch and watch and wait,
He shall pay the half and the whole,
Now or then, or soon or late.
(Steel or lead or hempen cord,
And the devil take his soul!)

Nights are black and roads are dark,
(Never a shroud or a coffin board)
But a moon-white face is a goodly mark,
And a trap is a trap for a man or a mole,
And a man is dead when he's stiff and stark.
(Steel or lead or hempen cord,
And the devil take his soul!)

He shall not be shrived or sung.
Never a shroud or a coffin board.)
Man to grave and beast to hole,
Earth to earth, and dung to dung!
(Steel or lead or hempen cord,
And the devil take his soul!)

London, September 1894

The Image of Death

To More Adey

I carved an image coloured like the night,
Winged with huge wings, stern-browed and menacing,
With hair caught back, and diademed like a king.
The left hand held a sceptre, and the right
Grasped a sharp sword, the bitter marble lips
Were curled and proud; the yellow topaz eyes

(Each eye a jewel) stared in fearful wise;
The hard fierce limbs were bare, and from the hips
A scourge hung down. And on the pedestal
I wrote these words, 'O all things that have breath,
This is the image of the great god Death,
Pour ye the wine and bind the coronal!
Pipe unto him with pipes and flute with flutes,
Woo him with flowers and spices odorous,
Let singing boys with lips mellifluous
Make madrigals and lull his ear with lutes.
Anon bring sighs and tears of harsh distress,
And weeping wounds! so haply ye may move
A heart of stone, from breasts of hate suck love,
Or garner pity from the pitiless.'

Clouds, 1894

Rondeau

If he were here, this glorious sky,
This sweet blue sea, these ships that lie
On the bay's bosom, like white sheep
On English fields, these hours that creep
Golden in summer's panoply,
This wind that seems a lover's sigh,
Would make a heaven of peace as high
As God's great love, a bliss as deep,
If he were here.

This great peace does but magnify
My great unrest that will not die,
My deep despair that may not reap
One poppy, one poor hour of sleep,
Nor aught but pain to wake and cry,
'If he were here!'

Sorrento, August 1895

225

To Sleep

Ah, Sleep, to me thou com'st not in the guise
Of one who brings good gifts to weary men,
Balm for bruised hearts and fancies alien
To unkind truth, and drying for sad eyes.
I dread the summons to that fierce assize
Of all my foes and woes, that waits me when
Thou mak'st my soul the unwilling denizen
Of thy dim troubled house where unrest lies.

My soul is sick with dreaming, let it rest.
False Sleep, thou hast conspired with Wakefulness,
I will not praise thee, I too long beguiled
With idle tales. Where is thy soothing breast?
Thy peace, thy poppies, thy forgetfulness?
Where is thy lap for me so tired a child?

Capri, 1895

In Memoriam
Francis Archibald Douglas
Viscount Drumlanrig

Killed by the Accidental Explosion of his gun,
October 18, 1894

Dear friend, dear brother, I have owed you this
Since many days, the tribute of a song.
Shall I cheat you who never did a wrong
To any man? No, therefore though I miss
All art, all skill, in this short armistice
From my soul's war against the bitter throng
Of present woes, let these poor lines be strong
In love enough to bear a brother's kiss.

Dear saint, true knight, I cannot weep for you,
Nor if I could would I call back the breath
To your dear body; God is very wise,
All that this year had in its womb He knew,
And, loving you, He sent His Son like Death,
To put His hand over your kind gray eyes.

October 1895

Væ Victis!

To Matthew Prichard

Here in this isle
The summer still lingers,
And Autumn's brown fingers
So busy the while
With the leaves in the north,
Are scarcely put forth
In this land where the sun still glows like an ember,
In mid-November.

In England it's cold,
And the yellow and red
Of October have fled;
 And the sun is wet gold
 Like an emperor weeping,
When Death goes a-reaping
All through his empire, merciless comer,
 The dead things of summer.

The sky has cried so
That the earth is all sodden,
With dead leaves in-trodden,
 And the trees to and fro
 Wave their arms in the air,
 In despair, in despair:
They are thinking of all the hot days that are over,
 And the cows in the clover.

Here the roses are out,
And the sun at high noon
Make the birds faint and swoon.
 But the cricket's about
 With his song, and the hum
 Of the bees as they come
To feast at the honey-board laden and groaning,
 Makes musical droning.

But vainly, alas!
Do I hide in the south,
Kiss close with my mouth
 Red flowers, green grass,
 For Autumn has found me
 And thrown her arms round me.
She has breathed on my lips and I wander apart,
 Dead leaves in my heart.

Capri, November 16, 1895

Sonnet,

Dedicated to those French men of letters
(Messrs Zola, Coppée, Sardou and others)
who refused to compromise their spotless reputations
or imperil their literary exclusiveness
by signing a merciful petition in favour of Oscar Wilde

Not all the singers of a thousand years
Can open English prisons. No. Though hell
Opened for Thracian Orpheus, now the spell
Of song and art is powerless as the tears
That love has shed. You that were full of fears,
And mean self-love, shall live to know full well
That you yourselves, not he, were pitiable
When you met mercy's voice with frowns or jeers.

And did you ask who signed the plea with you?
Fools! It was signed already with the sign
Of great dead men, of God-like Socrates,
Shakespeare and Plato and the Florentine
Who conquered form. And all your petty crew
Once, and once only, might have stood with these!

Naples, February 1896

The Garden of Death

To Ernest La Jeunesse

There is an isle in an unfurrowed sea
That I wot of, whereon the whole year round
The apple-blossoms and the rosebuds be
In early blooming; and a many sound
Of ten-stringed lute, and most mellifluous breath
Of silver flute, and mellow half-heard horn,
Making unmeasured music. Thither Death
Coming like Love, takes all things in the morn
Of tenderest life, and being a delicate god,
In his own garden takes each delicate thing
Unstained, unmellowed, immature, untrod,
Tremulous betwixt the summer and the spring:
The rosebud ere it come to be a rose,
The blossom ere it win to be a fruit,
The virginal snowdrop, and the dove that knows
Only one dove for lover; all the loot
Of young soft things, and all the harvesting
Of unripe flowers. Never comes the moon
To matron fulness, here no child-bearing
Vexes desire, and the sun knows no noon.
But all the happy dwellers of that place
Are reckless children, gotten on Delight
By Beauty that is thrall to Death; no grace,
No natural sweet they lack, a chrysolite
Of perfect beauty each. No wisdom comes
To mar their early folly, no false laws
Man-made for man, no mouthing prudence numbs
Their green unthought, or gives their license pause;
Young animals, young flowers, they live and grow,
And die before their sweet emblossomed breath
Has learnt to sigh save like a lover's. Oh!
How sweet is Youth, how delicate is Death!

Paris, about 1896

Rejected

Alas! I have lost my God,
    My beautiful god Apollo.
Wherever his footsteps trod
    My feet were wont to follow.

But oh! it fell out one day
    My soul was so heavy with weeping
That I laid me down by the way;
    And he left me while I was sleeping.

And my soul awoke in the night,
    And I bowed my ear for his fluting,
And I heard but the breath of the flight
    Of wings, and the night-birds hooting.

And Night drank all her cup,
    And I went to the shrine in the hollow,
And the voice of my cry went up:
    'Apollo! Apollo! Apollo!'

But he never came to the gate,
    And the sun was hid in a mist,
And there came one walking late,
    And I knew it was Christ.

He took my soul and bound it
    With cords of iron wire,
Seven times round He wound it
    With the cords of my desire.

The cords of my desire,
    While my desire slept,
Were seven bands of wire
    To bind my soul that wept.

And He hid my soul at last
    In a place of stones and fears,
Where the hours like days went past
    And the days went by like years.

And after many days
    That which had slept awoke,
And desire burnt in a blaze,
    And my soul went up in the smoke.

And we crept away from the place
    And would not look behind,
And the angel that hides his face
    Was crouched on the neck of the wind.

And I went to the shrine in the hollow
    Where the lutes and the flutes were playing,
And cried: 'I am come, Apollo,
    Back to thy shrine, from my straying.'

But he would have none of my soul
    That was stained with blood and with tears,
That had lain in the earth like a mole,
    In the place of great stones and fears.

And now I am lost in the mist
    Of the things that can never be,
For I will have none of Christ
    And Apollo will none of me.

Paris, April 1896

St Martin's Summer

Now dallies at the gate my loitering youth
 Equipped to go, now while it waits for thee,
 Ere my late roses wither utterly,
Pluck where thou wilt the comely and the couth.

Take all my garden, and if the flowers be few
 Under thy feet, look up and see above thee
 The red tree-blossoms; and, Love, if thou approve me,
Will haply plant fresh lilies and renew
 Dead, withered roses, seeing how much I love thee.

Paris, 1896

Plainte Éternelle

The sun sinks down, the tremulous daylight dies.
 (Down their long shafts the weary sunbeams glide.)
 The white-winged ships drift with the falling tide,
Come back, my love, with pity in your eyes!

The tall white ships drift with the falling tide.
 (Far, far away I hear the seamews' cries.)
 Come back, my love, with pity in your eyes!
There is no room now in my heart for pride.

Come back, come back! with pity in your eyes.
 (The night is dark, the sea is fierce and wide.)
 There is no room now in my heart for pride,
Though I become the scorn of all the wise.

I have no place now in my heart for pride.
 (The moon and stars have fallen from the skies.)
 Though I become the scorn of all the wise,
Thrust, if you will, sharp arrows in my side.

Let me become the scorn of all the wise.
   (Out of the East I see the morning ride.)
   Thrust, if you will, sharp arrows in my side,
Play with my tears and feed upon my sighs.

Wound me with swords, put arrows in my side.
   (On the white sea the haze of noonday lies.)
   Play with my tears and feed upon my sighs,
But come, my love, before my heart has died.

Drink my salt tears and feed upon my sighs.
   (Westward the evening goes with one red stride.)
   Come back, my love, before my heart has died,
Down sinks the sun, the tremulous daylight dies.

Come back! my love, before my heart has died.
   (Out of the South I see the pale moon rise.)
   Down sinks the sun, the tremulous daylight dies,
The white-winged ships drift with the falling tide.

France, about 1896

Ode to My Soul

Rise up, my soul!
Shake thyself from the dust.
Lift up thy head that wears an aureole,
Fulfil thy trust.
Out of the mire where they would trample thee
Make images of clay,
Whereon having breathed, from thy divinity
Let them take mighty wings and soar away
   Right up to God.
Out of thy broken past
Where impious feet have trod
Build thee a golden house august and vast
Whereto these worms of earth may some day crawl.
Let there be nothing small

Henceforth with thee;
Take thou unbounded scorn of all their scorn,
    Eternity
Of high contempt: be thou no more forlorn
But proud in thy immortal loneliness,
And infinite distress:
And, being 'mid mortal things divinely born,
Rise up, my soul!

Paris, 1896

The Travelling Companion

Into the silence of the empty night
I went, and took my scornèd heart with me,
And all the thousand eyes of heaven were bright;
But Sorrow came and led me back to thee.

I turned my weary eyes towards the sun,
Out of the leaden East like smoke came he.
I laughed and said, 'The night is past and done';
But Sorrow came and led me back to thee.

I turned my face towards the rising moon,
Out of the south she came most sweet to see,
She smiled upon my eyes that loathed the noon;
But Sorrow came and led me back to thee.

I bent my eyes upon the summer land,
And all the painted fields were ripe for me,
And every flower nodded to my hand;
But Sorrow came and led me back to thee.

O Love! O Sorrow! O desired Despair!
I turn my feet towards the boundless sea,
Into the dark I go and heed not where,
So that I come again at last to thee.

France, 1896

Ode to Autumn

Thou sombre lady of down-bended head,
And weary lashes drooping to the cheek,
With sweet sad fold of lips uncomforted,
And listless hands more tired with strife than meek;
Turn here thy soft brown feet, and to my heart,
Unmatched to Summer's golden minstrelsy,
Or Spring's shrill pipe of joy, sing once again
    Sad songs, and I to thee
Well tuned, will answer that according part
That jarred with those young season's gladder strain.

Give me thy empty branches for the biers
Of perished joys, thy winds to sigh my sighs,
Thy falling leaves to count my falling tears,
And all thy mists to dim my aching eyes.
There is no comfort in thy lips, and none
In thy cold arms, nor pity in thy breast,
But better 'tis in gray hours to have grief,
    Than to affront the sun
With sunless woe, when every flower and leaf
Conspires to make the season merriest.

The drip of rain-drops on the sodden earth,
The trampled mud-stained grass, the shifting leaves,
The silent hurrying birds, the sickly birth
Of the red sun in misty skies, the sheaves
Of rotting ruined corn, the sudden gusts
Of angry winds, the clouds that fly all night
Before the stormy moon, thy desolate moans,
    All thy decays and rusts,
Thy deaths and dirges, these are tuned aright
To my unquiet soul that sorrow owns.

But ah! thy gentler mood, the honeyed kiss
Of thy faint watery sunshine, thy pale gold,
Thy dark red berries, and the ambergris
That paints the lingering leaves, while on the mould

Their dead make bronze and sepia carpetings
That lightly rustle in thy quiet breath.
These are the shadows of departed smiles,
    The ghosts of happy things;
These break again the broken heart, the whiles
Thou goest on to winter, I to death.

France, October 1896

Spring

Wake up again, sad heart, wake up again!
(I heard the birds this morning singing sweet.)
Wake up again! The sky was crystal clear,
    And washed quite clean with rain;
And far below my heart stirred with the year,
Stirred with the year and sighed. O pallid feet
Move now at last, O heart that sleeps with pain
    Rise up and hear
The voices in the valleys, run to meet
The songs and shadows. O wake up again!

Put out green leaves, dead tree, put out green leaves!
(Last night the moon was soft and kissed the air.)
Put out green leaves! The moon was in the skies,
    All night she wakes and weaves.
The dew was on the grass like fairies' eyes,
Like fairies' eyes. O tree so black and bare,
Remember all the fruits, the full gold sheaves;
    For nothing dies,
The songs that are, are silences that were,
Summer was Winter. O put out green leaves!

Break through the earth, pale flower, break through the earth!
(All day the lark has sung a madrigal.)
Break through the earth that lies not lightly yet

    And waits thy patient birth,
Waits for the jonquil and the violet,
The violet. Full soon the heavy pall
Will be a bed, and in the noon of mirth
    Some rivulet
Will bubble in my wilderness, some call
Will touch my silence. O break through the earth.

Rome, March 1897

The Poet and the Moon

I

Once as a boy when he slept
In a little uncurtained room,
The moon came by and crept
To where he lay in the gloom.

II

In the heat of the summer night
He had thrown off gown and cover,
And his limbs were as naked and white
As the limbs of her Latmian lover.

III

So she wrapped him in silver silk,
A soft transparent shroud
Of nacre and opal and milk
Till he shone like a star through a cloud.

IV

And she poured her diaphanous beams
Into his parted lips
And the light swam into his dreams
Like the sailing of silver ships.

V

And she burned with a soft white flame
And kissed him over and over,
Till the dawn blushed red for shame
And the stars grew faint above her.

VI

Then she sailed away to the sea
On the wings of a wind from the south,
But she left her kisses with me
And the moonlight in my mouth.

Lake, near Salisbury, 1908
(First version: July 1897)

Wine of Summer

The sun holds all the earth and all the sky
From the gold throne of this midsummer day.
In the soft air the shadow of a sigh
Breathes on the leaves and scarcely makes them sway.
The wood lies silent in the shimmering heat,
Save where the insects make a lazy drone,
And ever and anon from some tree near,
    A dove's enamoured moan,
Or distant rook's faint cawing harsh and sweet,
Comes dimly floating to my listening ear.

Right in the wood's deep heart I lay me down,
And look up at the sky between the leaves,
Through delicate lace I see her deep blue gown.
Across a fern a scarlet spider weaves
From branch to branch a slender silver thread,
And hangs there shining in the white sunbeams,
A ruby tremulous on a streak of light.
    And high above my head
One spray of honeysuckle sways and dreams,
With one wild honey-bee for acolyte.

239

My nest is all untrod and virginal,
And virginal the path that led me here,
For all along the grass grew straight and tall,
And live things rustled in the thicket near:
And briar rose stretched out to sweet briar rose
Wild slender arms, and barred the way to me
With many a flowering arch, rose-pink or white,
    As bending carefully,
Leaving unbroken all their blossoming bows,
I passed along, a reverent neophyte.

The air is full of soft imaginings,
They float unseen beneath the hot sunbeams,
Like tired moths on heavy velvet wings.
They droop above my drowsy head like dreams.
The hum of bees, the murmuring of doves,
The soft faint whispering of unnumbered trees,
Mingle with unreal things, and low and deep
    From visionary groves,
Imagined lutes make voiceless harmonies,
And false flutes sigh before the gates of sleep.

O rare sweet hour! O cup of golden wine!
The night of these my days is dull and dense,
And stars are few, be this the anodyne!
Of many woes the perfect recompense.
I thought that I had lost for evermore
The sense of this ethereal drunkenness,
This fierce desire to live, to breathe, to be;
    But even now, no less
Than in the merry noon that danced before
My tedious night, I taste its ecstasy.

Taste, and remember all the summer days
That lie, like gold reflections in the lake
Of vanished years, unreal but sweet always;
Soft luminous shadows that I may not take
Into my hands again, but still discern
Drifting like gilded ghosts before my eyes,

Beneath the waters of forgotten things,
    Sweet with faint memories,
And mellow with old loves that used to burn
Dead summer days ago, like fierce red kings.

And this hour too must die, even now the sun
Droops to the sea, and with untroubled feet
The quiet evening comes: the day is done.
The air that throbbed beneath the passionate heat
Grows calm and cool and virginal again.
The colour fades and sinks to sombre tones,
As when in youthful cheeks a blush grows dim.
    Hushed are the monotones
Of doves and bees, and the long flowery lane
Rustles beneath the wind in playful whim.

Gone are the passion and the pulse that beat
With fevered strokes, and gone the unseen things
That clothed the hour with shining raiment meet
To deck enchantments and imaginings.
No joy is here but only neutral peace
And loveless languour and indifference,
And faint remembrance of lost ecstasy.
    The darkening shades increase,
My dreams go out like tapers – I must hence.
Far off I hear Night calling to the sea.

Villerville, near Trouville, August 1897

Sonnet on the Sonnet

To see the moment holds a madrigal,
To find some cloistered place, some hermitage
For free devices, some deliberate cage
Wherein to keep wild thoughts like birds in thrall;
To eat sweet honey and to taste black gall,
To fight with form, to wrestle and to rage,
Till at the last upon the conquered page
The shadows of created Beauty fall.

This is the sonnet, this is all delight
Of every flower that blows in every Spring,
And all desire of every desert place;
This is the joy that fills a cloudy night
When, bursting from her misty following,
A perfect moon wins to an empty space.

Naples, 1897

The City of the Soul

I

In the salt terror of a stormy sea
There are high attitudes the mind forgets;
And undesired days are hunting nets
To snare the souls that fly Eternity.
But we being gods will never bend the knee,
Though sad moons shadow every sun that sets,
And tears of sorrow be like rivulets
To feed the shallows of Humility.

Within my soul are some mean gardens found
Where drooped flowers are, and unsung melodies,
And all companioning of piteous things.
But in the midst is one high terraced ground,
Where level lawns sweep through the stately trees
And the great peacocks walk like painted kings.

II

What shall we do, my soul, to please the King?
Seeing he hath no pleasure in the dance,
And hath condemned the honeyed utterance
Of silver flutes and mouths made round to sing.
Along the walls red roses climb and cling,
And oh! my prince, lift up thy countenance,
For there be thoughts like roses that entrance
More than the languors of soft lute-playing.

Think how the hidden things that poets see
In amber eves or mornings crystalline,
Hide in the soul their constant quenchless light,
Till, called by some celestial alchemy,
Out of forgotten depths, they rise and shine
Like buried treasure on Midsummer night.

III

The fields of Phantasy are all too wide,
My soul runs through them like an untamed thing.
It leaps the brooks like threads, and skirts the ring
Where fairies danced, and tenderer flowers hide.
The voice of music has become the bride
Of an imprisoned bird with broken wing.
What shall we do, my soul, to please the King,
We that are free, with ample wings untied?

We cannot wander through the empty fields
Till Beauty like a hunter hurl the lance.
There are no silver snares and springes set,
Nor any meadow where the plain ground yields.
O let us then with ordered utterance,
Forge the gold chain and twine the silken net.

IV

Each new hour's passage is the acolyte
Of inarticulate song and syllable,
And every passing moment is a bell,
To mourn the death of undiscerned delight.
Where is the sun that made the noon-day bright,
And where the midnight moon? O let us tell,
In long carved line and painted parable,
How the white road curves down into the night.

Only to build one crystal barrier
Against this sea which beats upon our days;
To ransom one lost moment with a rhyme
Of passionate protest or austere demur,
To clutch Life's hair, and thrust one naked phrase
Like a lean knife between the ribs of Time.

Naples, 1897

A Triad of the Moon

I

Last night my window played with one moonbeam,
And I lay watching till sleep came, and stole
Over my eyelids, and she brought a shoal
Of hurrying thoughts that were her troubled team,
And in the weary ending of a dream
I found this word upon a candid scroll:
'The nightingale is like a poet's soul,
She finds fierce pain in miseries that seem.'

Ah me, methought, that she should so devise!
To seek for pain and sing such doleful bars,
That the wood aches and simple flowers cry,
And sea-green tears drench mortal lovers' eyes,
She that is made the lure of those young stars
That hang like golden spiders in the sky.

II

That she should so devise, to find such lore
Of sighful song and piteous psalmody,
While Joy runs on through summer greenery
And all Delight is like an open door.
Must then her liquid notes for evermore
Repeat the colour of sad things, and be
Distilled like cassia drops of agony,
From the slow anguish of a heart's bruised core?

Nay, she weeps not because she knows sad songs,
But sings because she weeps; for wilful food
Of her sad singing, she will still decoy
The sweetness that to happy things belongs.
All night with artful woe she holds the wood,
And all the summer day with natural joy.

III

My soul is like a silent nightingale
Devising sorrow in a summer night.
Closed eyes in blazing noon put out the light,
And Hell lies in the thickness of a veil.
In every voiceless moment sleeps a wail,
And all the lonely darknesses are bright,
And every dawning of the day is white
With shapes of sorrow fugitive and frail.

My soul is like a flower whose honey-bees
Are pains that sting and suck the sweets untold,
My soul is like an instrument of strings;
I must stretch these to capture harmonies,
And to find songs like buried dust of gold,
Delve with the nightingale for sorrowful things.

Naples, 1897

Ennui

Alas! and oh that Spring should come again
Upon the soft wings of desired days,
And bring with her no anodyne to pain,
And no discernment of untroubled ways.
There was a time when her yet distant feet,
Guessed by some prescience more than half divine,
Gave to my listening ear such happy warning,
    That fresh, serene, and sweet,
My thoughts soared up like larks into the morning,
From the dew-sprinkled meadows crystalline.

Soared up into the heights celestial,
And saw the whole world like a ball of fire,
Fashioned to be a monster playing ball
For the enchantment of my young desire.
And yesterday they flew to this black cloud,
(Missing the way to those ethereal spheres)
And saw the earth a vision of affright,
    And men a sordid crowd,
And felt the fears and drank the bitter tears,
And saw the empty houses of Delight.

The sun has sunk into a moonless sea,
And every road leads down from Heaven to Hell,
The pearls are numbered on youth's rosary,
I have outlived the days desirable.
What is there left? And how shall dead men sing
Unto the loosened strings of Love and Hate,
Or take strong hands to Beauty's ravishment?
    Who shall devise this thing,
To give high utterance to Miscontent,
Or make Indifference articulate?

Venice, April 1898

The Legend of Spinello of Arezzo

Spinello of Arezzo, long ago
A cunning painter, made a large design
To grace the choir of St Angelo.
Therein he pictured the exploits divine
Of the Archangel Michael, beautiful
Exceedingly, in wrath most terrible,
Until at last that holy place was full
Of warring angels; and that one who fell
From the high places of the highest Heaven
Into the deep abyss of lowest Hell,
He pictured too, in mad disaster driven
Before the conquering hosts of Paradise.
And him the painter drew in uncouth shape,
A foul misshapen monster with fierce eyes,
Of hideous form, half demon and half ape.

And lo! it fell out as he slept one night,
His soul, in the sad neutral land of dreams
That lies between the darkness and the light,
Was 'ware of one whose eyes were soft as beams
Of summer moonlight, and withal as sad.
Dark was his colour, and as black his hair
As hyacinths by night, his sweet lips had
A curve as piteous as sweet lovers wear
When they have lost their loves; so fair was he,
So melancholy, yet withal so proud,
He seemed a prince whose woes might move a tree
To find a tearful voice and weep aloud.
He spoke, his voice was tunable and mellow,
But soft as are the western winds that stir
The summer leaves, and thus he said, 'Spinello,
Why dost thou wrong me? I am Lucifer.'

Hatch House, 1898

Palmistry

I saw in dreams a bed within a chamber
Whereon the moon had cast a curious ray,
And one that slept whose hair was like fine amber
With head down drooped like flower at close of day.
And as he slept I scarcely heard his sighing,
And in the moon the motes moved with his breath
Scarcely at all, like weary white moths flying
On soft vague wings towards desired death.
One tired hand lay on the coverlet,
Whereon, as from a mountain seen, were lines
(Like to the little streams in meadows set)
Which God has made for everlasting signs
Of the eternal roads of Life and Death,
Of Joy and Woe and Danger and Desire,
Of Love that goeth out or tarrieth,
Of Hate and Hope, and Sin that burns like fire.
And lo! from out the hemispheres of night,
With veilèd face, on swift and soundless feet,
That came which is the Mysteries' acolyte
And sits beside the undesired seat
Of Fatal things, which marked his hand and went
As it had come, an undiscernèd road.
Then on his palm my eager eyes intent
Espied a cross, O lamentable load!
Laid on his hand that slept. The sleeper stirred
And softly moaned; and, prisoned in a mesh,
Methought I saw his soul, a frightened bird,
Behind the eternal barriers of flesh.
At length his body quickened with slow sighs
And broke the bondage of his sleeping-place.
He turned his head and opened wide his eyes,
And looked at me – and lo! 'twas mine own face.

The Dead Poet

I dreamed of him last night, I saw his face
All radiant and unshadowed of distress,
And as of old, in music measureless,
I heard his golden voice and marked him trace
Under the common thing the hidden grace,
And conjure wonder out of emptiness,
Till mean things put on beauty like a dress
And all the world was an enchanted place.

And then methought outside a fast locked gate
I mourned the loss of unrecorded words,
Forgotten tales and mysteries half said,
Wonders that might have been articulate,
And voiceless thoughts like murdered singing birds.
And so I woke and knew that he was dead.

Paris, 1900–1901

The Traitor

Cast out, my soul, the broken covenant,
Forget the pitiable masquerade,
And that ignoble part ignobly played.
Let us take shame that such a mummer's rant
Of noble things, could pierce the adamant
Of Pride wherewith we ever were arrayed,
And being with a kiss once more betrayed,
Let not our tears honour that sycophant.

Let him, on graves of buried loyalty,
Rise as he may to his desired goal;
Ay and God speed him there, I grudge him not.
And when all men shall sing his praise to me
I'll not gainsay. But I shall know his soul
Lies in the bosom of Iscariot.

1901

Dies Amara Valde

Ah me, ah me, the day when I am dead,
And all of me that was immaculate
Given to darkness, lies in shame or state,
Surely my soul shall come to that last bed
And weep for all the whiteness that was red,
Standing beside the ravished ivory gate
When the pale dwelling-place is desolate
And all the golden rooms untenanted.

For in the smoke of that last holocaust,
When to the regions of unsounded air
That which is deathless still aspires and tends,
Whither, my helpless soul, shall we be tossed?
To what disaster of malign Despair,
Or terror of unfathomable ends?

1901

Forgetfulness

Alas! that Time should war against Distress,
And numb the sweet ache of remembered loss,
And give for sorrow's gold the indifferent dross
Of calm regret or stark forgetfulness.
I should have worn eternal mourning dress
And nailed my soul to some perennial cross,
And made my thoughts like restless waves that toss
On the wild sea's intemperate wilderness.

But lo! came Life, and with its painted toys
Lured me to play again like any child.
O pardon me this weak inconstancy.
May my soul die if in all present joys,
Lapped in forgetfulness or sense-beguiled,
Yea, in my mirth, if I prefer not thee.

1901

Premonition

If Love reveal himself, to haggard eyes,
Compact of lust and curiosity,
And turn a pallid face away from thee
To seek elsewhere a harlot's paradise;
If Faith be perjured and if Truth be lies,
And thy great oak of life a rotten tree,
Where shall we hide, my soul, how shall we flee
The eternal fire, the worm that never dies?

O born to be rejected and denied,
Scorn of the years and sport of all the days,
Must the gray future still repeat the past?
O thrice betrayed and seven times crucified,
Is there no issue from unhappy ways,
No peace, no hope, no loving arms at last?

La Brague, 1903

To a Silent Poet

Where are the eagle-wings that lifted thee
Above the ken of mortal hopes and fears,
And was it thou who in serener years
Framed magic words with such sweet symmetry?
Didst thou compel the sun, the stars, the sea,
Harness the golden horses of the spheres,
And make the winds of God thy charioteers
Along the roads of Immortality?

Art thou dead then? Nay, leave the folded scroll,
Let us keep quiet lips and patient hands,
Not as sheer children use, who would unclose
The petals of young flowers, but paying toll
At that high gate where Time, grave gardener, stands
Waiting the ripe fulfilment of the rose.

1905

Rewards

From the beginning, when was aught but stones
For English Prophets? Starved not Chatterton?
Was Keats bay-crowned, was Shelley smiled upon?
Marlowe died timely. Well for him, his groans
On stake or rack else had out-moaned the moans
Of his own Edward; and that light that shone,
That voice, that trumpet, that white-throated swan,
When found he praise, save for 'his honoured bones'?

Honour enough for bones! but for live flesh
Cold-eyed mistrust, and ever watchful fear,
Mingled with homage given grudgingly
From cautious mouths. And all the while a mesh
To snare the singing-bird, to trap the deer,
And bind the feet of Immortality.

1906–1908

The Green River

I know a green grass path that leaves the field
And, like a running river, winds along
Into a leafy wood where is no throng
Of birds at noon-day, and no soft throats yield
Their music to the moon. The place is sealed,
An unclaimed sovereignty of voiceless song,
And all the unravished silences belong
To some sweet singer lost or unrevealed.

So is my soul become a silent place.
Oh may I wake from this uneasy night
To find a voice of music manifold.
Let it be shape of sorrow with wan face,
Or Love that swoons on sleep, or else delight
That is as wide-eyed as a marigold.

1906

To Olive

I

When in dim dreams I trace the tangled maze
Of the old years that held and fashioned me,
And to the sad assize of Memory
From the wan roads and misty time-trod ways,
The timid ghosts of dead forgotten days
Gather to hold their piteous colloquy,
Chiefly my soul bemoans the lack of thee
And those lost seasons empty of thy praise.

Yet surely thou wast there when life was sweet,
(We walked knee-deep in flowers) and thou was there,
When in dismay and sorrow and unrest,
With weak bruised hands and wounded bleeding feet,
I fought with beasts and wrestled with despair
And slept (how else?) upon thine unseen breast.

253

II

I have been profligate of happiness
And reckless of the world's hostility,
The blessèd part has not been given to me
Gladly to suffer fools, I do confess
I have enticed and merited distress,
By this, that I have never bowed the knee
Before the shrine of wise Hypocrisy,
Nor worn self-righteous anger like a dress.

Yet write you this, sweet one, when I am dead:
'Love like a lamp swayed over all his days
And all his life was like a lamp-lit chamber,
Where is no nook, no chink unvisited
By the soft affluence of golden rays,
And all the room is bathed in liquid amber.'

III

Long, long ago you lived in Italy,
You were a little princess in a state
Where all things sweet and strange did congregate,
And in your eyes was hope or memory
Or wistful prophecy of things to be;
You gave a child's blank 'no' to proffered fate,
Then became grave, and died immaculate,
Leaving torn hearts and broken minstrelsy.

But Love that weaves the years on Time's slow loom
Found you again, reborn, fashioned and grown
To your old likeness in these harsher lands;
And when life's day was shadowed in deep gloom
You found me wandering, heart-sick and alone,
And ran to me and gave me both your hands.

IV

My thoughts, like bees, explore all sweetest things
To fill for you the honeycomb of praise,
Linger in roses and white jasmine sprays,
And daffodils that stand in yellow rings.
In the clear air they moan on muted strings,
And the blue sky of my soul's summer days
Shines with your light, and through pale violet ways,
Birds bear your name in beatings of their wings.

I see you all bedecked in bows of rain,
New showers of rain against new-risen suns,
New tears against new light of shining joy.
My youth, equipped to go, turns back again,
Throws down its heavy pack of years and runs
Back to the golden house a golden boy.

V

When we were Pleasure's minions, you and I,
When we mocked grief and held disaster cheap,
And shepherded all joys like willing sheep
That love their shepherd; when a passing sigh
Was all the cloud that flecked our April sky,
I floated on an unimagined deep,
I loved you as a tired child loves sleep,
I lived and laughed and loved, and knew not why.

Now I have known the uttermost rose of love;
The years are very long, but love is longer;
I love you so, I have no time to hate
Even those wolves without. The great winds move
All their dark batteries to our fragile gate:
The world is very strong, but love is stronger.

VI

When I am dead you shall not doubt or fear,
Or wander nightly in the halls of gloom.
The moon will shine into my empty room,
And in the narrow garden flowers will peer,
While you look through your window. Scarce a tear
Will drench your child's blue eyes, while on my tomb,
Where the red roses wake and break and bloom,
The stars gaze down eternal and austere.

And I, in the dark ante-room of Death,
Will wait for you with ever-outstretched hands
And ears strained for your little timid feet;
And in the listening darkness, when your breath
Pants in distress, my arms will be like bands
And all my weakness like your winding-sheet.

Silence

This is deep hell, to be expressionless,
To leave emotion inarticulate,
To guess some form of Love or Joy or Hate
Shadowed in an imperial loveliness
Behind the hurrying thoughts that crowd and press,
To track, to follow, to lie down, to wait,
And at the last before some fearful gate
To stand eluded and companionless.

Oh, if proud summer's high magnificence
And all the garnered honey of sweet days,
And sweets of sweeter nights, cannot prevail
Against this spell of tongue-tied impotence,
How shall we sing, my soul, when skies are pale,
And winter suns shed melancholy rays?

1907

A Christmas Carol

When Christ was born in Bethlehem
    The stars, cold wells of liquid light,
    Sunk in the deep blue veil of night,
Were jewels for His diadem.

The moon, a globe of opal fire,
    Wove Him a garment of pale gold,
    A shining raiment meet to hold
The body of the world's desire.

Then night and dawn together blent
    Melted into a purple band;
    While hushed to silence sea and land
Waited the awful sacrament.

And He was born our Prince to be,
    And land and sea did so rejoice,
    That the whole world became a voice
In tune with heavenly harmony.

1907

Beauty and the Hunter

Where lurks the shining quarry, swift and shy,
Immune, elusive, unsubstantial?
In what dim forests of the soul, where call
No birds, and no beasts creep? (the hunter's cry
Wounds the deep darkness, and the low winds sigh
Through avenues of trees whose faint leaves fall
Down to the velvet ground, and like a pall
The violet shadows cover all the sky).

With what gold nets, what silver-pointed spears
May we surprise her, what slim flutes inspire
With breath of what serene enchanted air? —
Wash we our star-ward gazing eyes with tears,
Till on their pools (drawn by our white desire)
She bend and look, and leave her image there.

1908

The Poet

They gave him scorn and hate and the fierce rod
Of bitter words, they strangled him with lies,
But from his lips there came no meaner cries
Than these that were the very songs of God.
They made his years a Hell-scorch'd period,
And he but smiled and cast his conquering eyes
Along the level lawns of Paradise
Where late the luminous feet of angels trod.

There the ripe fruits are stars upon the trees,
And in the air that is like yellow wine
Ever the birds of rapture soar and sing
Their silver songs in magical sweet keys,
And round about him in a golden line
The shining seraphim stand wing to wing.

1909

Proem

For the Third Edition of *The City of the Soul*

How have we fared, my soul, across the days,
Through what green valleys, confident and fleet,
Along what paths of flint with how tired feet?
Anon we knew the terror that dismays
At noon-day; and when night made dark the ways
We bought delight and found remembrance sweet.
Though in our ears we heard the wide wings beat
Ever we kept dumb mouths to prayer and praise.

Yet never lost or spurned or cast aside,
And never sundered from the love of God,
Through how-so wayward intricate deceits,
Lured by what shining toys, our charmed feet trod,
On the swift winds we saw bright angels ride,
And strayed into the moon-made silver streets.

1909

A Christmas Sonnet

Late, as I slept worn with life's cares and jars,
I had a vision of an angel bright,
Who told me: 'Christ was born a living Light
To lead men's souls from where, behind the bars
Which are the Flesh, they hide their wounds and scars.'
Whereat he smiled on me and took strong flight
Through the deep sapphire darkness of the night,
Beyond the scattered gold-dust of the stars.

Higher he flew and higher till his eyes,
If haply he looked down, might scarce descry,
Like a faint shining mist, the Milky Way.
And so before the gates of Paradise
He vanished from my aching sight. And I
Wept and awoke – and it was Christmas day.

1909

Behold, Your House Is Left Unto You Desolate

Alas, for Love and Truth and Faith, stone dead,
Borne down by Hate to death unnatural,
Stifled and poisoned! From the empty hall
To the dismantled chamber where the bed
Once held its breathing warmth, the soundless tread
Of sad ghosts goes by night. Timid and small
One creeps and glides; I saw her shadow fall
Behind me on the floor uncarpeted.

Poor wistful semblance of too weak remorse,
Why have we met in your forsaken room,
Where the pale moon looks in on emptiness
And holds a lamp to ruin? Fragile force,
You come too late, my cold heart is a tomb
Where love lies strangled in his wedding dress.

26 Church Row, 1913

Stones for Bread

Ah, woe to us who look for asphodel
Where asphodel is not, and bitter woe
To us who bid the barren gardens blow
With fabulous flowers; who hear the silver bell
Chiming from some enchanted citadel,
When flower and bell and citadel lie low
In the lost dust of dreams. Naked we know,
Through fire and ice, the fall from Heaven to Hell.

We clothed with white and shining loveliness
The soul of the belovèd. And anon
We saw it gleam, red hate, behind her eyes.
The imagined loyalty of friends was less
Than the least benefit we fed it on.
Daily our hope is born and daily dies.

1913

Before a Crucifix

What hurts Thee most? The rods? the thorns? the nails?
The crooked wounds that jag Thy bleeding knees?
(Can ever plummet sound such mysteries?)
It is perchance the thirst that most prevails
Against Thy stricken flesh, Thy spirit quails
Most at the gall-soaked sponge, the bitter seas
O'erflow with this? *'Nay, is is none of these.'*
Lord, Lord, reveal it then ere mercy fails.

Is it Thy Mother's anguish? *'Search thine heart.*
Didst thou not pray to taste the worst with Me,
O thou of little faith.' Incarnate Word,
Lord of my soul, I know, it is the part
That Judas played; this have I shared with Thee
(By wife, child, friend betrayed). *'Thy prayer was heard.'*

November 1916

The Unspeakable Englishman

You were a brute and more than half a knave,
Your mind was seamed with labyrinthine tracks
Wherein walked crazy moods bending their backs
Under grim loads. You were an open grave
For gold and love. Always you were the slave
Of crooked thoughts (tortured upon the racks
Of mean mistrust). I made myself as wax
To your fierce seal. I clutched an ebbing wave.

Fool that I was, I loved you; your harsh soul
Was sweet to me: I gave you with both hands
Love, service, honour, loyalty and praise;
I would have died for you! And like a mole
You grubbed and burrowed till the shifting sands
Opened and swallowed up the dream-forged days.

1918

Lighten Our Darkness

England, 1918

In the high places lo! there is no light,
The ugly dawn beats up forlorn and grey.
Dear Lord, but once before I pass away
Out of this Hell into the starry night
Where still my hopes are set in Death's despite,
Let one great man be good, let one pure ray
Shine through the gloom of this my earthly day
From one tall candle set up on a height.

Judges and prelates, chancellors and kings,
All have I known and suffered and endured,
(And some are quick and some are in their graves).
I looked behind their masks and posturings
And saw their souls too rotten to be cured,
And knew them all for liars, rogues and knaves.

On a Showing of the Nativity

See where she lies, pale and serene and mild,
Our little Virgin meek and innocent,
The wistful oval of her face down-bent
Upon the wonder of her new-born child.
How frail the stable seems, how fierce and wild
(Outside the intangible angel circle) blent
In fearful hordes the infernal armament,
The dark battalions of the unreconciled!

I saw the vision of our House of Bread,
In liquid fire it floated on the air,
In the blue deeps of night its shining trail
Was suddenly in milky radiance shed;
Against the hope which God hath planted there
Even the gates of Hell shall not prevail.

1918

House of Bread

There is a ghostly stable in my heart,
Frailly devised and fashioned out of dreams
Whose patient masons were infrequent gleams
Of immaterial visions. In the mart
Where Passions are made slaves, I bought a part
Of that wherewith I builded. On slow streams
Of tears, whose fountains were vouchsafèd beams,
The rest came floating – Holy as Thou art,

Child of all light, celestial Excellence,
Enwombed in grace-bestowed Virginity
Which is Her image consecrated there,
Be born in this rude house, where broken sense
Is gold straw for Thy feet. So shall it be
A transubstantial mansion built of air.

1920

To a Certain Judge

Master of dubious arts, the sophist's cloak
Rests all too aptly on your cynic mind.
Justice we know is never quite so blind,
Under her hoodwinked eyes, as simple folk
Simply suppose. A deft judicial spoke
Thrust in her wheel, a crooked push behind,
Invisibly bestowed, are, in their kind,
Cantrips that cozen, jury-fogging smoke.

England expects, when ministerial boots
Accite subservience to the lingual task,
Vigour and zeal. Your ludship's verbal grace
Outshines the varnish that your tongue salutes.
Red-robed automaton, behind your mask
You hide (too obviously) a leering face.

Wormwood Scrubs, January 1924

In Excelsis

To Alfred Rose

I

Torment of body, torment of the mind,
Pain, hunger, insult, stark ingratitude
Of those for whom we fought, detraction rude
But sanctimonious, cruel to be kind
(Truly for bread a stone): all these we find
In this our self-appointed hell whose food
Is our own flesh. To what imagined good
Have we thus panted, beaten, bound and blind?

God knows, God knows. And since He knows indeed,
Why there's the answer: who would stay outside
When God's in prison? Who would rather choose
To warm himself with Peter than to bleed
With Dismas penitent and crucified,
Facing with Christ the fury of the Jews?

II

I follow honour, brokenly content,
Though the sick flesh repine, though darkness creep
Into the soul's unfathomable deep,
Where fear is bred: though from my spirit spent
Like poured-out water, the mind's weak consent
Be hardly wrung, while eyes too tired to weep
Dimly discern, as through a film of sleep,
Squalor that is my honour's ornament.

Without, the fire of earth-contemning stars
Burns in deep blueness, like an opal set
In jacinth borders underneath the moon.
The dappled shadow that my window bars
Cast on the wall is like a silver net.
My angel, in my heart, sings 'heaven soon.'

III

I have within me that which still defies
This generation's bloat intelligence,
Which is the advocate of my defence
Against the indictment of the world's assize.
Clutching with bleeding hands my hard-won prize,
Immeasurably bought by fierce expense
Of blood and sweat and spirit-harnessed sense,
I keep the steadfast gaze of tear-washed eyes.

And this discernment, not inherited,
But grimly conned in many cruel schools,
Unravels all illusion to my sight.
In vain, for me with wings, the snare is spread.
Folly imputed by the mouth of fools
Is wisdom's ensign to a child of light.

IV

When death, the marshal of our settled state,
Shall beckon us to our appointed end,
To what remembrances shall be the trend
Of those last thoughts that gather at the gate?
What profit then that this was delicate,
Or that breathed flowers? Shall they not rather tend
To recollected woe as to a friend,
For pleasures are but hostages to fate?

What bitterness shall then be left in these,
As insult, calumny, the truth abjured,
The dock, the handcuff and the prison cell,
Detraction bartered for forensic fees,
And, else, a thousand wrongs bravely endured
And sovereign against the gates of hell?

V

O none, if grace enrich the soul's release
With covenanted joy's presentiment,
Sweet presage of fruition's deep content
Which is the complement of hope's increase,
The harvest of delight, sorrow's surcease,
The untransmutable extreme consent
Of will and spirit ultimately blent
In diapason of perpetual peace.

But who can so set up his reason's throne
Above the accident of mortal hap,
As to embrace disparagements and mocks,
Encounter suffering without a groan,
Lie like a nurseling in affliction's lap
And realise the saintly paradox?

VI

Not I, alas, at any rate, not yet;
Prisoned in flesh the willing spirit wars,
Glimpses a transient lustre through the bars
And beats her wings in vain against the net.
In vain her evocated hosts beset
The citadel that lies beyond the stars;
The guarded walls stand up like beetling scaurs,
Though white desire o'er-leap the parapet.

Perfection's fortress is impregnable,
But her saint-trodden way allures us still.
She bids us cherish what our senses hate,
And entertain where we would fain repel;
And love at last constrains the inconstant will
To make the bitter choice deliberate.

VII

For such is love, a great good every way,
Bearing all toil, making all burdens light:
To its internal vision the dark night
Shows clear and shining as the dawn of day:
Being born of God it still denies to stay
With less than God, but evermore takes flight
To the belov'd on wings as swift as sight,
A torch, a vivid flame, a lucent ray.

Could love compel the appertinent retinue
Of all our essence to some bridge of air,
Spanning the gulf of that estranging sea
Which hides the lover from the loved one's view,
How happy then were we who lothly wear
This earthy vesture of mortality.

VIII

But so to use oneself as to entice
The visit of such love, so dignified
With such a sovereignty, may scarce betide
Us, the sad outcast heirs of paradise.
Hardly the merchant paid the exceeding price
Of that one pearl whose lustrous sheen outvied
The zenith of his longing, else denied
To any less than utter sacrifice.

And how shall we, unemptied of desire
Of all created things, command our Lord
Or open hopeful casements to the Dove?
Nay, but the spark pre-vents consuming fire,
The seedling predicates the harvest's hoard,
From depth to height love corresponds to love.

IX

And we bereft, diswinged, a very clod
Of sense-afflicted earth, uncomforted,
Cheated of dreams, whose flatteries have fled
Long since, fierce disillusion's iron rod;
We whose entrammelled feet yet dully plod
The bitter road that saints were wont to tread,
Fulfilled of joy, by angel hosts bestead,
Or led like children by the hand of God, –

We have this love, and having it possess
The last reversion of felicity.
For what, but love of God, could so enforce
This furious will to seize on bitterness,
Revoke the lease of nature, and decree
With sweetness irremediable divorce?

Epilogue

Follow the star. The unseen sighing wings
Beat in the soul's night in the forest's gloom.
Follow the star, the Child is in the womb
That shall be born, the lamp is lit that swings
Over joy's cradle. Who is this that sings
In the heart's garden where red roses bloom?
The moth-soft fleece is woven on God's loom,
The web of peace is spun, ye holy Kings.

Follow the star and enter where it rests,
Be it on palace or on lowly shed.
What house is this whose hideous bolt and bar
Groan on the opening? Who are these pale guests,
These creeping shadows? Whither am I led?
What iron hold is here? *Follow the star.*

This sonnet-sequence was written in Wormwood Scrubs Prison.
Begun on February 5 and finished
on Good Friday, April 18, 1924

To — with an Ivory Hand Mirror

Look in this crystal pool, and you will see
(Haloed in gold, enshrined in ivory)
What Heaven's unopened windows hid from me.

Whence this enchantment, weaving spells that bind
With sightless cords my visionary mind?
What angel, dark or shining, lurks behind?
Eyes of the flesh still bind, unfolded scroll
Hiding its mystery! God knows the whole.
I guess your face the shadow of your soul.

Limpsfield, 1927

Oxford Revisited

Alas! what make you here, poor ghost that goes
Where your swift feet of youth so lightly went?
Time has borne down that gracious argument
Which was your advocate where Isis flows
Through Christ Church meadows. Sublimate your woes
Among these happy children whose consent
Holds out kind hands; accept the treasure lent,
Unconquered sweetness, death-defying rose.

Would yet this sweetness find an echoed home
Where the dream-builded city's semblance lies
Beyond the stars, could but its silver bell
Out-chime the iron knell of miscalled doom,
How would not Death come kindly with mild eyes
Shining like invocated Uriel?

May 17, 1932

Winston Churchill

Not that of old I loved you over-much,
Or followed your quick changes with great glee,
While through rough paths of harsh hostility
You fought your way, using a sword or crutch
To serve occasion. Yours it was to clutch
And lose again. Lacking the charity
Which looks behind the mask, I did not see
The immanent shadow of 'the Winston touch'.

Axe for embedded evil's cancerous roots,
When all the world was one vast funeral pyre,
Like genie smoke you rose, a giant form
Clothed with the Addisonian attributes
Of God-directed angel. Like your sire
You rode the whirlwind and outstormed the storm.

1941

The Wastes of Time

If you came back, perhaps you would not find
The old enchantment, nor again discern
The altered face of love. The wheels yet turn
That clocked the wasted hours, the spirit's wind
Still fans the embers in the hidden mind.
But if I cried to you, 'Return! return!'
How could you come? How could you ever learn
The old ways you have left so far behind?

How sweetly, forged in sleep, come dreams that make
Swift wings and ships that sail the estranging sea,
Less roughly than blown rose-leaves in a bowl,
To harboured bliss. But oh! the pain to wake
In empty night seeking what may not be
Till the dead flesh set free the living soul.

February 1934

Translations from the French of Charles Baudelaire

Harmonie du soir

Voici venir les temps où vibrant sur sa tige
Chaque fleur s'évapore ainsi qu'un encensoir;
Les sons et les parfums tournent dans l'air du soir;
Valse mélancolique et langoureux vertige!

Chaque fleur s'évapore ainsi qu'un encensoir;
Le violon frémit comme un cœur qu'on afflige;
Valse mélancolique et langoureux vertige!
Le ciel est triste et beau comme un grand reposoir.

Le violon frémit comme un cœur qu'on afflige,
Un cœur tendre, qui hait le néant vaste et noir!
Le ciel est triste et beau comme un grand reposoir;
Le soleil s'est noyé dans son sang qui se fige.

Un cœur tendre, qui hait le néant vaste et noir,
Du passé lumineux recueille tout vestige!
Le soleil s'est noyé dans son sang qui se fige;
Ton souvenir en moi luit comme un ostensoir!

Harmonie du soir

Now is the hour when, swinging in the breeze,
Each flower, like a censer, sheds its sweet.
The air is full of scents and melodies,
O languorous waltz! O swoon of dancing feet!

Each flower, like a censer, sheds its sweet,
The violins are like sad souls that cry,
O languorous waltz! O swoon of dancing feet!
A shrine of Death and Beauty is the sky.

The violins are like sad souls that cry,
Poor souls that hate the vast black night of Death;
A shrine of Death and Beauty is the sky.
Drowned in red blood, the Sun gives up his breath.

This soul that hates the vast black night of Death
Takes all the luminous past back tenderly,
Drowned in red blood, the Sun gives up his breath.
Thine image like a monstrance shines in me.

Paris, 1898 or 1899

Le Balcon

Mère des souvenirs, maîtresse des maîtresses,
O toi, tous mes plaisirs! ô toi, tous mes devoirs!
Tu te rappelleras la beauté des caresses,
La douceur du foyer et le charme des soirs,
Mère des souvenirs, maîtresse des maîtresses!

Les soirs illuminés par l'ardeur du charbon,
Et les soirs au balcon, voilés de vapeurs roses.
Que ton sein m'était doux! que ton cœur m'était bon!
Nous avons dit souvent d'impérissables choses
Les soirs illuminés par l'ardeur du charbon.

Que les soleils sont beaux dans les chaudes soirées!
Que l'espace est profond! que le cœur est puissant!
En me penchant vers toi, reine des adorées,
Je croyais respirer le parfum de ton sang.
Que les soleils sont beaux dans les chaudes soirées!

La nuit s'épaississait ainsi qu'une cloison,
Et mes yeux dans le noir devinaient tes prunelles,
Et je buvais ton souffle, ô douceur! ô poison!
Et tes pieds s'endormaient dans mes mains fraternelles.
La nuit s'épaississait ainsi qu'une cloison.

Je sais l'art d'évoquer les minutes heureuses,
Et revis mon passé blotti dans tes genoux.
Car à quoi bon chercher tes beautés langoureuses
Ailleurs qu'en ton cher corps et qu'en ton cœur si doux?
Je sais l'art d'évoquer les minutes heureuses!

Ces serments, ces parfums, ces baisers infinis,
Renaîtront-ils d'un gouffre interdit à nos sondes,
Comme montent au ciel les soleils rajeunis
Après s'être lavés au fond des mers profondes?
— O serments! ô parfums! ô baisers infinis!

Le Balcon

Mother of Memories! O mistress-queen!
Oh! all my joy and all my duty thou!
The beauty of caresses that have been,
The evenings and the hearth remember now,
Mother of Memories! O mistress-queen!

The evenings burning with the glowing fire,
And on the balcony, the rose-stained nights!
How sweet, how kind you were, my soul's desire.
We said things wonderful as chrysolites,
When evening burned beside the glowing fire.

How fair the Sun is in the evening!
How strong the soul, how high the heaven's tower!
O first and last of every worshipped thing,
Your odorous heart's-blood filled me like a flower.
How fair the sun is in the evening!

The night grew deep between us like a pall,
And in the dark I guessed your shining eyes,
And drank your breath, O sweet, O honey-gall!
Your little feet slept on me sister-wise.
The night grew deep between us like a pall.

I can call back the days desirable,
And live all bliss again between your knees,
For where else can I find that magic spell
Save in your heart and in your Mysteries?
I can call back the days desirable.

These vows, these scents, these kisses infinite,
Will they like young suns climbing up the skies
Rise up from some unfathomable pit,
Washed in the sea from all impurities?
O vows, O scents, O kisses infinite!

Paris, 1899

Recueillement

Sois sage, ô ma Douleur, et tiens-toi plus tranquille.
Tu réclamais le Soir; il descend; le voici:
Une atmosphère obscure enveloppe la ville,
Aux uns portant la paix, aux autres le souci.

Pendant que des mortels la multitude vile,
Sous le fouet du Plaisir, ce bourreau sans merci,
Va cueillir des remords dans la fête servile,
Ma Douleur, donne-moi la main; viens par ici

Loin d'eux. Vois se pencher les défuntes Années,
Sur les balcons du ciel, en robes surannées;
Surgir du fond des eaux le Regret souriant;

Le Soleil moribond s'endormir sous une arche,
Et, comme un long linceul traînant à l'Orient,
Entends, ma chère, entends la douce Nuit qui marche.

Recueillement

Peace, be at peace, O thou my heaviness,
Thou calledst for the evening, lo! 'tis here,
The City wears a sombre atmosphere
That brings repose to some, to some distress.
Now while the heedless throng make haste to press
Where pleasure drives them, ruthless charioteer,
To pluck the fruits of sick remorse and fear,
Come thou with me, and leave their fretfulness.

See how they hang from heaven's high balconies,
The old lost years in worn clothes garmented,
And see Regret with faintly smiling mouth;
And while the dying sun sinks in the skies,
Hear how, far off, Night walks with velvet tread,
And her long robe trails all about the south.

1900

La Beauté

Je suis belle, ô mortels! come un rêve de pierre,
Et mon sein, où chacun s'est meurtri tour à tour,
Est fait pour inspirer au poëte un amour
Éternel et muet ainsi que la matière.

Je trône dans l'azur comme un sphinx incompris;
J'unis un cœur de neige à la blancheur des cygnes;
Je hais le mouvement qui déplace les lignes,
Et jamais je ne pleure et jamais je ne ris.

Les poëtes, devant mes grandes attitudes,
Que j'ai l'air d'emprunter aux plus fiers monuments,
Consumeront leurs jours en d'austères études;

Car j'ai, pour fasciner ces dociles amants,
De purs miroirs qui font toutes choses plus belles:
Mes yeux, mes larges yeux aux clartés éternelles!

La Beauté

Fair am I, mortals, as a stone-carved dream,
And all men wound themselves against my breast,
The poet's last desire, the loveliest.
Voiceless, eternal as the world I seem.
In the blue air, strange sphinx, I brood supreme
With heart of snow whiter than swan's white crest,
No movement mars the plastic line – I rest
With lips untaught to laugh or eyes to stream.

Singers who see, in trancèd interludes,
My splendour set with all superb design,
Consume their days, in toilful ecstasy.
To these revealed, the starry amplitudes
Of my great eyes which make all things divine
Are cristal mirrors of eternity.

New York, 1902

Notes to the Poems

The title of each poem is followed by the title of the book in which it first appeared. Poems marked with an asterisk were not reprinted by Bosie until 1935, in *Lyrics* and *Sonnets*, although they were included in the pirated editions edited by P.C. Boutens (1908), George Sylvester Viereck (1925) and E. Du Perron (1928).

Evident misprints, of which there are quite a few – 'All my life has been poisoned and embittered by printers who are certainly the enemies of the human race,' Bosie once complained in an undated letter to Martin Secker (MS Texas) – have been silently corrected.

Many poems in the volume published by the Mercure de France in 1896 were dedicated to individual friends and relations. These dedications were omitted in subsequent editions, but they have been restored here, as they throw an interesting light on the circles frequented by Douglas.

A collection of poetical manuscripts and typescripts, which in 1899 was sent by Bosie to his cousin Wilfrid Blunt (who acted as his go-between with the publisher Grant Richards), and which is now kept at the West Sussex County Record Office, Chichester, provides valuable information as to the precise dating of lyrics which first appeared in *The City of the Soul*, Bosie's memory being at fault more than once when he came to affix dates to his early poems while seeing his work through the press in the late 1920s and 1930s.

I have availed myself of the Authorized Version of the Bible as far as my references to the Scriptures are concerned.

Dedication (p. 5)
(*Sonnets* (1909)
An adaptation of the sonnet which Bosie had written as the dedication of his first volume of verse, *Poems* (1896). It had been suppressed by

order of Wilde (see p. 78), but its text has survived (TS Magdalen):

To Oscar Wilde

> What shall I say, what word, what cry recall,
> What god invoke, what charm, what amulet,
> To make a sonnet pay a hopeless debt,
> Or heal a bruised soul with a madrigal?
> O vanity of words! my cup of gall
> O'erflows with this, I have no phrase to set,
> And all my agony and bloody sweat
> Comes to this issue of no words at all.
>
> This is my book, and in my book my soul
> With its two woven threads of joy and pain,
> And both were yours before they were begun.
> Oh! that this dream would like a mist unroll,
> That I might look upon your face again,
> And hear your kind voice say: 'This was well done.'

The new version appeared with the title 'A Dedication' in *The Academy*, LXXVI, No. 1922, 6 March 1909, p. 845.

4 winged / wing'd
5 at all, / at all:

Autumn Days (p. 207)

Poems (1896)

Bosie stated that this poem had appeared in the *Oxford Magazine*, but it has not been traced there.

The Hut: A country house belonging to Lady Queensberry, some two miles from Bracknell in Berkshire. In his younger years Bosie often stayed there during the summer holidays.

In the *Wimbledon and Merton Annual*, 1904, pp. 52–5, a setting of this poem by Liza Lehmann appeared, with the title 'Autumn Woods'. The same text was set to music in 1987 by the Dutch composer Aart de Kort.

A Winter Sunset (p. 208)

Poems (1896)

Percy Sholto, Lord Douglas of Hawick and Tibbers (1868–1920), was the brother with whom Bosie felt the greatest affinity. His career was summed up by *The Times* obituarist on 3 August 1920 as follows:

A Rover in Many Lands

. . . He entered the Navy, but, after a few years as a midshipman, spent in the Mediterranean and the Pacific, he left the Service and went to the Canadian North-West to learn ranching. Tiring of this, he purchased a horse and made his way to the borders of Alberta and Montana, where he managed a roadside house. His customers, to use his own description, were 'made up of whisky smugglers, miners, and cowboys'. Later, he returned to England, and for a brief period held a commission in the Militia battalion of the King's Own Scottish Borderers. He soon went abroad again, however, and after a few months in Ceylon set sail for Australia with David Carnegie, the explorer.

The Coolgardie gold rush had just started when they reached Melbourne, and the two men at once set off for the fields, landing at Albany with a joint capital of 30 shillings. Their gold-seeking venture was successful, and each made a comfortable fortune. The Marquess returned to London, and engaged in financial enterprises with varying success – 'a very rich man one day, poor the next,' he wrote in an autobiography; 'the Stock Exchange knew more than I did'. On more than one occasion he figured in the Bankruptcy Court. In 1911 he went to America, and worked as a reporter on Chicago and New York newspapers.

The Marquess was twice married. His first wife, by whom he had two sons and a daughter, was the daughter of the Rev. T. Walters, vicar of Boyton, Cornwall. He married her in 1893, while engaged in his Australian goldmining venture. She died in 1917, and in the following year he married Mrs Mary Louise Morgan, of Cardiff.

*Prince Charming (p. 209)

Poems (1896)

First appeared in *The Artist or, Journal of Home Culture*, XV, No. 172, April 1894, p. 102. *The Artist* was a magazine which published poems that were distinctly gay. Bosie, writing to its former editor,

Charles Kains-Jackson, on 16 May 1894 (MS Clark), referred to it as 'our only organ of expression'.

*Two Loves (pp. 210–11)

Poems (1896)

First appeared in *The Chameleon*, I, No. 1, December 1894, pp. 26–8.

'The Sphinx' was Oscar's nickname for Ada Leverson *née* Beddington, a friend as witty as she was loyal who contributed to *Punch*. Her marriage with the businessman Ernest Leverson was not a happy one; when he emigrated to Canada in 1907 she remained in London where she wrote novels which were well received by the public. See Violet Wyndham, *The Sphinx and Her Circle: A Biographical Sketch of Ada Leverson 1862–1933* (London: André Deutsch, 1963).

The poem's title is taken from Shakespeare's sonnet CXLIV, which opens: 'Two Loves I have of comfort and despair, / Which like two spirits do suggest me still: / The better angel is a man right fair, / The worser spirit a woman, colour'd ill.'

The concluding line, 'I am the Love that dare not speak its name,' has gained immortality, Charles Gill's cross-examination of Oscar about its meaning inspiring the latter to come up with a description of Greek Love which has proved a source of pride and encouragement to countless homosexuals. The speech was reproduced by Johannes Gaulke in his essay 'Die Homoerotik in der Weltliteratur' which appeared in Adolf Brand's pioneer gay monthly magazine, *Der Eigene. Ein Blatt für männliche Kultur, Kunst und Litteratur*, II [that is, IV], No. 2, February 1903, p. 129. Jean Cocteau quoted Bosie's most famous line at the head of one of his early – apparently unpublished – poems (see Francis Steegmuller, *Cocteau: A Biography*. London: Macmillan, 1970, p. 36). Gerald Hamilton, a friend of Bosie, put the last nine lines of 'Two Loves' at the head of Chapter 8 of his gay novel *The Desert Dreamers: A Romance of Friendship*, which was published under the pseudonym 'Patrick Weston' (London: At the Sign of the Tiger Lily, 1914). The playwright Maurice Rostand gave further currency to the poem by quoting bits of it in *Le Procès d'Oscar Wilde*, which was first put on stage in 1935. Dr Charles Fouqué, contributing a volume about homosexuality to the Collection d'Études Psycho-Sexuelles, called it, significantly, *L'Amour qui n'ose pas dire son nom* (Paris: Éditions des Deux Sabots, [1948]). He printed Rostand's partial translation of Bosie's poem, attributing the lines to the French author: 'J'ai voulu choisir, pour introduction à cet ouvrage que j'entends écrire avec une tristesse grave, cette magnifique poésie de Maurice Rostand' (p. 8)!

When in 1977 *Gay News* published a poem by James Kirkup entitled 'The Love that Dares to Speak Its Name', the magazine was successfully prosecuted by Mary Whitehouse for blasphemous libel.

Dominique Fernandez's *L'Amour qui ose dire son nom: art et homosexualité* was published by Stock in Paris in 2001.

The Dutch poet Sander Waalkamp prefixed Bosie's celebrated line to 'Nachtwake' in *Beelden* (Leiden: privately printed, 2002).

Reverberations of Bosie's lyric continue to be heard, even in the House of Commons. On 26 November 2003 Michael Howard, the leader of the Opposition, in the course of the Queen Speech's debate, spoke of 'the tax that dare not speak its name'.

In *The Watchman and Other Poems* (Toronto: McClelland [1916]) by Lucy Maud Montgomery may be found a piece called 'Two Loves' which betrays more than a nodding acquaintance with Bosie's poem. I am grateful to Merlin Holland for drawing my attention to this.

18 Cadogan Place. The London address of Lady Queensberry.

2	a ground, / a ground
4	flowers / buds
19	sun-rise / sunrise
21	moss / moss,
22	Uprose. And / Uprose; and
25	a youth; / a youth,
36	shew / show
37	See, / See
46	joy. / joy;
47	lute, / lute
57	tight, / tight
62	Was fiery flame: / Was like curved flame:
63	a-weeping and I cried, / a-weeping, and I cried:
73	Then sighing said the other, / Then, sighing, said the other:
74	Love / love

*De Profundis (p. 212)

Poems (1896)

The title is taken from Psalm 130: 'Out of the depths have I cried unto thee, o Lord.'

In Sarum Close (pp. 212–13)

Poems (1896)

Sarum: Salisbury in the county of Wiltshire. In this city, which boasts a magnificent cathedral, Lady Queensberry owned a house in the close.

When Bosie sent the text of this poem to Oscar, he received the following letter from him (*CL*, [January 1893], p. 544) :

> My Own Boy, Your sonnet is quite lovely, and it is a marvel that those rose-leaf lips of yours should have been made no less for music of song than madness of kisses. Your slim gilt soul walks between passion and poetry. I know Hyacinthus, whom Apollo loved so madly, was you in Greek days.
>
> Why are you alone in London, and when do you go to Salisbury? Do go there to cool your hands in the grey twilight of Gothic things, and come here whenever you like. It is a lovely place – it only lacks you; but go to Salisbury first.
>
> Always, with undying love, yours
Oscar

The letter was stolen and used to blackmail Oscar, who, when its text was read out in the course of his libel action against Queensberry, alleged that it was really a 'prose poem'. To substantiate this claim he referred to *The Spirit Lamp*, IV, No. 1, 4 May 1893, to which his erstwhile friend, the French poet and novelist Pierre Louÿs, had obligingly contributed the following.

Sonnet

A Letter Written in Prose Poetry by Mr Oscar Wilde to a Friend,
And Translated into Rhymed Poetry
By a Poet of No Importance

Hyacinthe! Ô mon cœur! Jeune dieu doux et blond!
Tes yeux sont la lumière de la mer! Ta bouche
Le sang rouge du soir où mon soleil se couche . . .
Je t'aime, enfant câlin, cher aux bras d'Apollon.
Tu chantais, et ma lyre est moins douce, le long
Des rameaux suspendus que la brise effarouche,
A frémir, que ta voix à chanter, quand je touche
Tes cheveux couronnés d'acanthe et de houblon.

Mais tu pars! tu me fuis pour les portes d'Hercule;
Va! rafraîchis tes mains dans le clair crépuscule
Des choses où descend l'âme antique. Et reviens,

Hyacinthe adoré! Hyacinthe! Hyacinthe!
Car je veux voir toujours dans les bois syriens
Ton beau corps étendu sur la rose et l'absinthe.

The poem was reprinted in Pierre Louÿs, *Poèmes*, édition définitive, établie par Yves-Gérard le Dantec (Paris: Albin Michel, 1945), I, p. 204.

'In Sarum Close' 'is an example of what I call the "art-for-art's sake" heresy', Bosie commented in *Sonnets* (1935). 'It lacks sincerity and is therefore merely an exercise in verse.' Besides, the poem was 'slightly marred by a faulty arrangement of rhymes in the sestet', which was also the case with 'To Shakespeare', 'The Sphinx' and 'Impression de Nuit'. 'This fault is due to the fact that at the time when I wrote them I was influenced by the sonnets of Rossetti which are far from being models of perfection so far as form is concerned.'

In Winter (p. 213)

Poems (1896)
Hatch House. A place of Lady Queensberry in Tisbury, Wiltshire.

To Shakespeare (p. 214)

Poems (1896)
The anti-Shakespeare Society: Robbie Ross once got a rise out of Bosie by facetiously suggesting the founding of an association bearing that name, 'to combat exaggerated Bardolatry' (*CL*, p. 782, note 3).

Apologia (pp. 214–215)

Poems (1896)
First appeared in *The Spirit Lamp*, IV, No. 2, 6 June 1893, p. 99, with the title 'Apologia pro classe sua (A Fragment)'.

1	Tell me not of Philosophies, / Talk not to me of broad philosophies,
3	subtle / cautious
8	heaven. / Heaven.
13	thing, / thing.
16	heaven. / Heaven
18	seraphim / Seraphim

19   cherubim; / Cherubim,
24   cry / song

*Hymn to Physical Beauty (pp. 215–17)
Poems (1896)
Shelley wrote a 'Hymn to Intellectual Beauty'.

13–16   the untrammelled shapes
     Of glorious nakedness, the curve and line
          Of sun-browned youth, must hide, for human apes
     Have found God's image shameful.

This is not an exaggeration. Henry Tuke, a homosexual painter settled in Falmouth whose work strongly appealed to Bosie (as is shown by a letter he wrote to Charles Kains-Jackson on 9 April 1894: MS Clark), specialized in fine depictions of scantily dressed or naked boys and young men which earned him the disapproval of the *Cornish Echo* which thundered in 1899: 'Mr Tuke seems to find nothing so congenial to his mind as to tackle a subject everybody else would shrink from. Masterly as is [his] work, one cannot help feeling regret that he does not give his attention to a more acceptable subject.' Quoted in Emmanuel Cooper, *The Life and Work of Henry Scott Tuke 1858–1929* (London: Gay Men's Press, 1987), p. 43.

18   Pan is dead. Plutarch relates that during the reign of Tiberius an Egyptian pilot, Thamus, was called, while sailing to Italy and passing the island of Paxi, by a voice, saying: 'When you come opposite Palodes, announce that Great Pan is dead.' Thamus

> made up his mind that if there should be a breeze, he would sail past and keep quiet, but with no wind and a smooth sea about the place he would announce what he had heard. So, when he came opposite Palodes, and there was neither wind nor wave, Thamus from the stern, looking toward the land, said the words as he had heard them: 'Great Pan is dead.' Even before he had finished there was a great cry of lamentation, not of one person, but of many, mingled with exclamations of excitement. As many persons were on the vessel, the story was soon spread in Rome.

Plutarch's *Moralia*, with an English translation by Frank Cole Babbitt

(London: William Heinemann, 1936), V, 'Obsolence of Oracles' (419), pp. 401–3.

The line 'Pan, Pan is dead' is often repeated in Elizabeth Browning's poem 'The Dead Pan' (1844).

7   Caliban: a misshapen, extremely uncivilized creature appearing in Shakespeare's *Tempest*.

Night Coming into a Garden (p. 218)

Poems (1896)

First appeared in *La Revue Blanche*, X, No. 71, 15 May 1896, pp. 467–8.

Fanny Zæssinger was an actress. She made her début in May 1895 and served as model for the painter Charles Léandre. See Paul Léautaud, *Journal littéraire* (Paris: Mercure de France, 1954–66), I, p. 14 (note); p. 60; and Jean-Paul Goujon, *Jean de Tinan* (Paris: Plon, 1991), pp. 178–82.

Written in The Cottage, Goring-on-Thames, where Oscar was staying from June till September 1893, working on *An Ideal Husband*.

Night Going out of a Garden (p. 219)

Poems (1896)

Charles Fleming: Possibly Charles James Nicol Fleming (b. 1868). An undergraduate of Queen's College, Oxford, he took his BA degree in 1891 (*Literae Humaniores*). From 1893 to 1900 he was Assistant Master at Fettes. He subsequently entered the Civil Service, spending some years in Egypt and Sudan, before becoming Inspector of Schools, Scottish Education Department, in 1903.

17   the god with the flame-flaked hair: Helios, the sun-god.

This poem was set to music in 1954 by the American composer John Duke.

*In an Ægean Port (p. 220)

Poems (1896)

First appeared in *The Artist or, Journal of Home Culture*, XIV, No. 167, October 1893, p. 311, with the title 'A Port in the Ægean'.

On 31 August 1893 Bosie wrote to the magazine's editor, Charles Kains-Jackson (MS Clark):

> I wrote [this sonnet] about a week ago and I think you will
> agree that I have improved. I was so fascinated by the expres-
> sion 'sugar lips' used of a boy in one of [Richard] Burton's
> translations that I wrote a sonnet on purpose to bring it in.

14   the lad on Latmian hills: Endymion, a beautiful young
shepherd of divine ancestry, plunged into eternal sleep on mount
Latmus in Caria; the lover of the moon-goddess, Selene.

In *Sonnets* (1935) the last three lines of the sestet read as follows:

> More enviable. Green pastures for young eyes,
> Visible dream of tender unripe girls,
> Moon-rapt on Latmian hills, where are thy sheep?

The Sphinx (pp. 220–21)

Poems (1896)

Reginald Turner (1869–1970), who nursed Oscar during his last days,
was an illegitimate son of Lionel Lawson. See Stanley Weintraub,
Reggie: A Portrait of Reginald Turner (New York: George Braziller,
1965). The poet and critic Richard Aldington wrote the following in
his memoirs, first published in 1940:

> Reggie was a wrinkled ugly little man, with a habit of batting his
> eyelids like an owl. When he talked he waved his hand contin-
> uously, and began nearly every sentence with 'however'. He
> wrote a lot of bad novels which nobody read, except Reggie
> himself, and he frequently shed tears over the affecting produc-
> tions of his genius. He also collected and preserved every new
> book of memoirs which mentioned him. People knew of this
> innocent mania and, I am glad to say, went out of their way to
> gratify it, for he was a kindly warm-hearted creature, and his
> devotion to Oscar in those bitter days of persecution was a noble
> deed. This book won't join the collection, for poor Reggie is dead.
> His is the only funeral to which I have ever sent a wreath. I did
> that for his own sake and because of what he did for Oscar [*Life
> for Life's Sake. A Book of Reminiscences*. London: Cassell,
> 1968, pp. 342–3].

This poem was set to music by Aart de Kort in 1987.

*In Praise of Shame (p. 221)

Poems (1896)

First appeared in *The Chameleon*, I, No. 1, December 1894, p. 25.

'Shame' was a code-word for homosexuality in the 1890s, and the term carried the same connotation in 'Aubade', one of the pieces to be found in Montague Summers's *Antinous and Other Poems* (1907; reprint: London: Cecil Woolf, 1995, p. 57):

> We worship Love, adore him,
> Low in the dust before him
> We bow down, and implore him,
> > Give thanks for our sweet shame.

After his conversion to Christianity Bosie felt bound to refer 'enquirers about [the sonnet's] meaning to the last verse of the second chapter of the book of Genesis', complaining about 'wooden-headed lawyers' who 'on at least two occasions [had] entirely misinterpreted [the poem] in the Law Courts'. Methinks his Lordship did protest too much. 'In Praise of Shame' remains, when all is said and done, a fine homosexual lyric which it took a great deal of courage to publish under one's own name in the latter years of the reign of Queen Victoria.

1   Unto my bed last night methought there came / Last night unto my bed methought there came

A Prayer (p. 222)

Poems (1896)

Lionel Pigot Johnson (1867–1902), 'a delightful fellow' (*Autobiography*, 57), poet and literary critic who introduced Bosie to Oscar in 1891. He published *The Art of Thomas Hardy* (1894), *Poems* (1895, containing 'A Dream of Youth' which was dedicated to Bosie) and *Ireland, with Other Poems* (1897). Johnson exercised great influence on W.B. Yeats. See George A Cevasco, *Three Decadent Poets: Ernest Dowson, John Gray and Lionel Johnson: An Annotated Bibliography* (New York: Garland, 1990). Adrian Earle, whom Bosie once thought of making his literary executor, acquired numerous manuscripts of Johnson as well as some letters from Bosie to him (Lionel). The whereabouts of these papers are unknown. Bosie, writing to Earle on 18 March 1943 (MS Clark), expressed regret that the letters which Johnson had written to him (Bosie) had 'simply disappeared. I am sure I never destroyed them. Probably someone stole them!'

The poem was set to music in 1987 by Aart de Kort.

Clouds: The country house at East-Knoyle, Salisbury, of Bosie's grand-uncle, Percy Scawen Wyndham.

Lust and Hypocrisy (pp. 222–3)

Poems (1896)

3   Even to the foolishness of quick returning: It was only in the pocket edition of *Sonnets* (1943) that this line was printed correctly; in previous editions it read 'Even unto the foolishness of quick returning'. 'Even' should be pronounced as a monosyllable, 'E'en'.

Impression de Nuit (p. 223)

Poems (1896)

First appeared in *La Revue Blanche*, X, No. 71, 15 May 1896, p. 469.

'Written in Charles Gatty's flat on the top floor of the building which was replaced by the Hyde Park Hotel' (*CP*).

Count Louis de Laveaux: perhaps Comte Louis-Ernest de la Vaulx (died 1895).

3   sapphires / amethysts

A correction only made in *Sonnets* [pocket edition] (London: Richards Press, 1943). See Marie Carmichael Stopes, *Lord Alfred Douglas, His Poetry and His Personality* (London: The Richards Press, 1949), pp. 35–6.

*A Ballad of Hate (p. 224)

Poems (1896)

First appeared anonymously in the *Pall Mall Gazette*, 5 September 1894, 2, with the title 'A Ballad of Hating', and subsequently in *La Revue Blanche*, X, No. 71, 15 May 1896, pp. 466–7, the title being followed by the words '(Dedicated to my Father)'.

The Image of Death (pp. 224–5)

Poems (1896)

William More Adey (1858–1942): Friend of Robert Ross – with whom he ran the Carfax Gallery – and Oscar. Published a translation of Henrik Ibsen's *Brand* in 1891 and edited the *Burlington Magazine* from 1911 to 1919. He died in a lunatic asylum.

19   breasts of hate: This phrase is to be found in Algernon Charles Swinburne's poem 'A Cameo' from *Poems and Ballads* (1866).

*Rondeau (p. 225)

Poems (1896)

To Sleep (p. 226)

Poems (1896)

In Memoriam: Francis Archibald Douglas, Viscount Drumlanrig (p. 227)

Poems (1896)
When this sonnet was reprinted in *The City of the Soul* in 1899 it appeared under the title 'In Memoriam. (D). Oct. 18, 1894'.

Væ Victis! (p. 227–8)

Poems (1896)
So dated in a MS in the Rare Book and Manuscript Library, Columbia University, New York.

Matthew Stewart Prichard was born in 1865. He was educated at Marlborough College, Wiltshire, and at New College, Oxford, taking his BA in 1887 and a second-class honours degree in 1889. A connoisseur of art, he formed part of the circle of Edward Perry Warren. During the First World War he was incarcerated in a civilian prisoners' camp near Berlin where he organized classes in history, languages, aesthetics and philosophy. A correspondent of *The Times*, writing on 19 October 1936, shortly after Prichard's death, called him 'a strange, original personality . . . He was a natural ascetic, would have been quite at ease in a garment of camel's hair, and preferred a dish of raw vegetables to the most delicate fare.' Additionally he preferred the company of his own sex, once turning down an invitation to attend a party with the words: 'No. There are women. I shall tremble' (David Sox, *Bachelors of Art: Edward Perry Warren and the Lewes House Brotherhood*. London: Fourth Estate, 1991, p. 170).

Væ victis! 'Woe to the vanquished!' Words supposed to have been spoken by the Gallic general Brennus. In 390 or 387 BC his troops were besieging Rome. Senators who had come up with a huge amount of gold to buy off the enemy accused the invaders of using debased weights; whereat Brennus angrily threw his sword in the scale, which then balanced in the Gauls' favour.

Sonnet, Dedicated to Those French Men
of Letters . . . (p. 229)

In 1895 the American poet Stuart Merrill, who was living in Paris, appealed to French writers to sign a petition to Queen Victoria in favour of the imprisoned Wilde. Its text ran as follows (*La Plume*, No. 159, 1 December 1895, p. 559):

A Sa très excellente Majesté la Reine

Madame,

Les soussignés, agissant uniquement au nom de l'human-ité et de l'art, sans se préoccuper de la culpabilité du condamné, seraient heureux de voir accorder à M. Oscar Wilde une grâce complète, sinon une large commutation de peine.

Nous sommes, avec la plus profonde vénération, Madame, de Votre Majesté, les très respectueux serviteurs.

Merrill's initiative did not meet with the response he had hoped for. Emile Zola, author of the cycle of twenty novels, *Les Rougon-Macquart*, wondered: 'De qui émane la pétition? De quel élan? Veut-on se servir de notre nom pour se tailler une carte-réclame sur le dos du prisonnier?' Victorien Sardou, who wrote historical show-pieces like *Fédora* and *La Tosca* for Sarah Bernhardt, told to reporters: 'C'est une boue trop immonde pour que je m'en mêle, de quelque façon que ce soit.' François Coppée showed very bad taste indeed when announcing he would only sign the petition as member of the Society for the Prevention of Cruelty to Animals (*La Plume*, No. 161, 1 January 1896, pp. 8–10). How ironic, therefore, that in 1903 Monsieur Coppée's reputation was tarnished when it transpired that Baron Jacques d'Adelswärd-Fersen, to whose volume of poems *Ébauches et débauches* (1901) he had contributed a short, if glowing, preface, was an assiduous lover of boys and young men!

Bosie had sent his sonnet to Merrill on 17 February 1896 (MS Texas): 'It explains itself, so I need add no more than express to you my deep-felt thanks for your generous efforts on behalf of one who

is dearer to me than any thing or person in the world.' He sent it to
André Gide and to the editor of *The Savoy*, Arthur Symons, as well.
It was not published, however, and did not appear in any edition of
his works, although he quoted the sestet from memory in *Without
Apology* (p. 270); he had forgotten the text of the octave.

12–13   the Florentine / Who conquered form: Michelangelo

The Garden of Death (p. 230)

Poems (1896)

Ernest La Jeunesse was the pseudonym of the journalist, carica-
turist, novelist and playwright Ernest-Henri Cohen (1874–1917),
who enthusiastically reviewed Bosie's *Poems* (1896) in *Le Journal*
on 11 January 1897. He had, according to Bosie, 'an impish sense
of humour, a great deal of erudition, and a real gift of wit. He kept
one laughing all the time' (*Without Apology*, 278). His turgid novel
Le Boulevard (Paris: Jean Bosc et Cie, 1906) features a character
called Odin Howes who is clearly modelled on Oscar. See Jean-
Paul Goujon, Ernest La Jeunesse.' *L'Étoile-Absinthe*, 23ème et 24è
Tournées, 1984, pp. 49–52.

Rejected (pp. 231–233)

Poems (1896)

*St Martin's Summer (p. 233)

Poems (1896)

St Martin of Tours (*c.* 316–97) is patron of tavern-keepers. In
Amiens he cut his cloak in two, giving half of it to a benumbed beg-
gar. His feast is on 11 November, during a time of year which is
often characterized by mild weather and which in England is known
as St Martin's Summer.

Plainte Éternelle (pp. 233–4)

Poems (1896)

First appeared in *La Revue Blanche*, X, No. 71, 15 May 1896,
pp. 465–6.

6   seamews' / sea-mews

Ode to My Soul (pp. 234–5)

Poems (1896)

The Travelling Companion (p. 235)

The City of the Soul

Ode to Autumn (pp. 236–7)

The City of the Soul

Spring (pp. 237–8)

The City of the Soul

The Poet and the Moon (pp. 238–9)

Nine Poems (1926)

First appeared in *The Academy*, LXXV, No. 1900, 3 October 1908, p. 317, with the title 'Minion of the Moon' (cf. *The First Part of King Henry the Fourth*, Act I, Scene 2), and the following quotation: 'Those who look too long at the moon become mad; but those upon whom the moon looks are poets.'

This poem, dated 1908 by Bosie, was in fact written as early as July 1897, as is evinced by a typescript at the West Sussex Record Office. Bosie made changes before publishing it in *The Academy* but returned to the original version when printing it in book form.

1	Once as a boy when he slept / The boy lay down and slept
2	In a little uncurtained room, / In an uncurtained chamber,
3	The moon came by and crept / Thither the young moon crept
4	To where he lay in the gloom. / Down a ladder of amber.
6	He had thrown off gown and cover, / He threw off gown and cover;
7	And his limbs were as naked and white / And his limbs were naked and white
8	As / Like
9	silk, / silk
10	A soft transparent shroud / In a soft transparent shroud
13	her diaphanous beams / diaphanous beams
17	a soft white flame / a white-hot flame,

Wine of Summer (pp. 239–41)

The City of the Soul

This lyric inspired Havergal Brian to write his Symphony No. 5 for baritone and orchestra in 1937. 'The Douglas poem is a lovely inspiration and completely reflected in my music,' the composer wrote in 1969, the year of the symphony's première. 'The opening theme is a genuine vocal theme and, added with the orchestra, sometimes in unison and always with chameleon changes, seems to me to make it a work easily grasped' (Kenneth Eastaugh, *Havergal Brian: The Making of a Composer*. London: Harrap, 1976, p. 283).

Sonnet on the Sonnet (p. 242)
The City of the Soul

The City of the Soul (pp. 242–4)
The City of the Soul
The title of this series of sonnets, which in 2000 was set to music by the Dutch composer Marijn Simons, is possibly derived from the first line of the LXXVIIIth strophe of the Fourth Canto (1818) of Byron's *Childe Harold's Pilgrimage*: 'Oh, Rome! my country! City of the Soul!'

II (p. 243)
13–14 they rise and shine / Like buried treasure on Midsummer night: A typescript of this poem in the West Sussex Record Office has the following note: 'According to an old tradition, on Midsummer night buried treasure rises to the surface of the earth and shines.'

IV (p. 244)
12   of passionate protest or austere demur
Sonnets (1935) has the following note by Bosie: 'In all previous versions the fourth line of the sestet of this sonnet was printed:

Or, if fate cries and grudging gods demur

I have now restored the line to what I originally wrote. Wilde did not like it, and I altered the phrase to please him, but I think my own original version is the better line and makes better sense, though it makes "passionate" only two syllables.'

A Triad of the Moon (pp. 244–5)
The City of the Soul

On 1 October 1897 or thereabouts Oscar wrote to Robbie Ross (*CL*, p. 950): 'Bosie has written three lovely sonnets, which I have called "The Triad of the Moon" – they are quite wonderful.'

Ennui (p. 246)
The City of the Soul
In a MS at the West Sussex Record Office the poem has the title 'Spring'.

The Legend of Spinello of Arezzo (p. 247)
The City of the Soul
It was about two years before his death that Spinello of Arezzo (*c*. 1346–1410) painted the fresco in the Sant'Agnolo chapel in the Basilica di San Francesco, Arezzo, which inspired Bosie's poem. Giorgio Vasari tells us that the artist enjoyed picturing Lucifer as repulsive as possible, and that the Prince of Darkness upbraided him for this in a nightmare. Spinello was so terrified that, 'half mad, with staring eyes, he slipped into the grave' (*Lives of the Painters, Sculptors and Architects*, translated by Gaston du C. de Vere. London: Everyman's Library, 1996, I, p. 223).

Palmistry (p. 248)
Nine Poems (1926)
First appeared in *The Academy*, LXXII, No. 1829, 25 May 1907, p. 501. Bosie dated this poem 1906, but the presence of a TS in the West Sussex Record Office inclines me to think that it was written about 1898.

1   a bed / a room

14   Of Joy and Woe and Danger and Desire,: By a strange oversight, this line is not included in either *Nine Poems* or any subsequent edition.

The Dead Poet (p. 249)
Sonnets (1909)
The first version of this celebrated poem, dated 10 December 1900, was quoted by Frank Harris in *Oscar Wilde: His Life and Confessions* (New York: The Author, 1916), II, p. 588.

To Oscar Wilde

I dreamed of you last night. I saw your face
All radiant and unshadowed of distress,
And as of old, in measured tunefulness,
I heard your golden voice and marked you trace
Under the common thing the hidden grace,
And conjure wonder out of emptiness,
Till mean things put on Beauty like a dress,
And all the world was an enchanted place.

And so I knew that it was well with you,
And that unprisoned, gloriously free,
Across the dark you stretched me out your hand.
And all the spite of this besotted crew
(Scrabbling on pillars of Eternity),
How small it seems! Love me made understand.

The second version first appeared in the *Candid Friend*, II, No. 43, 22 February 1902, p. 657, with the title 'Ad Memoriam', and subsequently in the *English Review*, I, No. 13, 13 January 1906, p. 285, with the title 'Ad Memoriam O.W.'

1   night, / night:
3   And as of old, in music measureless, / And, as of old, in measured tunefulness,
13   singing birds. / singing-birds:

The definitive version was printed in *The Academy*, LXXIII, No. 1846, 21 September 1907, p. 917.

Numerous translations of this poem have been made. The version of the Dutch writer P.C. Boutens was first published in *Carmina* (Amsterdam: P.N. van Kampen en Zoon, [1912]), pp. 188–9:

De Doode Dichter

'k droomde vannacht van hem: 'k zag zijn gelaat
Stralend en zonder schijn of schaûw van wee,
En hoorde als altijd de muziek dier zee,
Zijn gouden stem. Hij wekte in veil geraad

Verholen gratie waar zijn ooglicht glee.
Uit niets bezwoer hij wonders overdaad.
Tot 't minste ding in schoonheid ging verwaad,
En heel de weerld was één bekoorde steê.

Dan, leek mij, buiten dicht gesloten poort
Rouwde ik om woorden ongeboekt verloren,
Verschald verhaal, geheimnis half gehoord,

Wondren verstoken van der wereld ooren,
Gedachten stom als vogelen vermoord –
En waakte en wist hem dood gelijk tevoren.

The first French version of the poem seems to have been
written by Lucie Delarue-Mardrus; it appeared in her biog-
raphy *Les Amours d'Oscar Wilde* (Paris: Flammarion, 1929), pp.
121–2.

L'autre nuit j'ai rêvé de lui, revu sa face
Rayonnante et sans rien des ombres du malheur.
Sa voix, musique d'or, comme aux jours de bonheur
Parlait, et je voyais se révéler la grâce
Que cache au fond de soi la chose la plus basse
Et le vide obéir aux signes du charmeur,
Et robe, la beauté revêtir la laideur,
Et le monde roulait, enchanté dans l'espace.

Puis ce fut cette porte aux lourds verrous fermés,
Et je portais le deuil de mots inexprimés,
De mystères non dits, de chansons sans pareilles,
Le deuil d'une voix tue au moment des merveilles,
Oiseaux assassinés lorsqu'ils chantaient encore.
Alors me réveillant, je sus qu'il était mort.

Elsie McCalman's German version of the poem appeared in
her translation of Bosie's autobiography, *Freundschaft mit Oscar
Wilde* (Leipzig: Paul List Verlag, 1929), p. 69:

Der Tote Dichter

Ich träumte heute nacht von ihm. Ich sah
Sein Antlitz licht und aller Qualen bloss,
Und wie dereinst, in Wohllaut grenzenlos,
Hört' ich die goldne Stimme klar und nah.

Und alle Schönheit war mit einmal da,
Alles Gewohnte stand beglänzt und gross,
Und Wunder sprossten aus der Öde Schoss,
Und Wunder war's, was aller Welt geschah.

Dann wie verjagt auf grausames Gebot
Kniet' ich und klagte um verwehtes Wort,
Um Leidenschaft, die stumm ins Nichts verloht,

Traumblüten, die verwelkt, eh' sie noch rot,
Singvögelstimmen, ohne Laut verdorrt.
So wacht' ich auf und wusste, er war tot.

The following was published in Lord Alfred Douglas, *Poèmes*,
translated by Francis d'Avilla (Fabienne Hillyard), p. 7.

Le Poète mort

L'autre nuit j'ai rêvé. Je voyais son visage
Qui brillait, radieux, sans voile de douleur,
Et comme au temps passé, musicale langueur,
J'entendais sa voix d'or et suivais le sillage

Où de l'infirmité la grâce se dégage,
Où naît du merveilleux de la moindre fadeur,
De Beau vêtue ainsi que d'autours enchanteurs,
Et l'Univers devint un radieux mirage.

Et je songeais, devant de hauts portails fermés,
Traînant en moi le deuil des mots inexprimés,
Et le morne regret des choses oubliés,
Des mots divins tués dans leur sublime essor,
Rossignols égorgés, ô muettes pensées!
Alors, me réveillant, je sus qu'il était mort.

The most recent translation, by Christa Schuenke, was published in Caspar Wintermans, *Lord Alfred Douglas – ein Leben im Schatten von Oscar Wilde* (Munich: Karl Blessing Verlag, 2001), p. 309.

Tod des Dichters

Im Traum heut hab ich sein Gesicht gesehn,
Ganz hell und klar, und nicht umwölkt von Gram.
Und so wie früher ich Musik vernahm:
Die goldene Stimme lockt' hervor, was schön
Ist im Alltäglichen. Sein Dichterwort
Hat Wunder aus dem Nichts heraus vollbracht
Und das gemeinste Ding noch schön gemacht:
Die ganze Welt war ein verwunschner Ort.

Trauernd um Worte, die nie aufgeschrieben,
Stand ich vor einem fest verschlossenen Tor,
Um Sagen, denen das Vergessen droht,
Geheimnisse, die ungelüftet blieben,
Gedanken, stumm, wie toter Vögel Chor.
Und so erwachend, wusst ich, er war tot.

The sonnet was set to music by the American singer and composer Henry Muldrow in 2000.

The Traitor (p. 249)

Sonnets (1909)
First appeared in the *English Review*, I, No. 8, 9 December 1905, p.180.
Reprinted in *The Academy*, LXXII, No. 1833, 22 June 1907, p. 597.
Written about George Montagu (see p. 103).

Dies Amara Valde (p. 250)

Sonnets (1909)
First appeared in the *Candid Friend*, I, No. 1, 1 May 1901, p. 8, with the title 'Sonnet.'

1	Ah me, ah me, / Ah me! Ah me!
3	darkness / Darkness
4	bed / bed,
6	gate / gate,
7	desolate / desolate,

10   air / air,

14   terror / Terror

The sonnet was reprinted in the *Candid Friend*, II, No. 49, 5 April 1902, p. 891, in the course of a short article on Bosie's marriage, by the weekly's editor, Frank Harris. 'Lord Alfred Douglas,' he wrote, 'is a poet of the highest and rarest sense of the word. He has written, in my poor opinion, the best sonnets that have been written in English since Keats went silent. If I were asked to select the best twenty sonnets in English, the best from Shakespeare and Milton and Keats and Wordsworth, I should certainly include this one of Lord Alfred Douglas' among the best.'

The poem's definitive version appeared subsequently in *The Academy*, LXXIII, No. 1842, 24 August 1907, p. 813.

Forgetfulness (p. 250)

Sonnets (1909)

First appeared in *The Academy*, LXXV, No. 1889, 18 July 1908, p. 53.

12–14 See Psalm 137, pp. 5–6: 'If I forget thee, O Jerusalem, let my right hand forget her cunning. If I do not remember thee, let my tongue cleave to the roof of my mouth; if I prefer not Jerusalem above my chief joy.'

11   O pardon me this weak inconstancy. / You shall forgive me this inconstancy!

12   May my soul die if in all present joys, / May my soul perish – in all present joys

Premonition (p. 251)

Sonnets (1909)

First appeared in *The Academy*, LXXV, No.1887, 4 July 1908, p. 5, with the title 'Before the Dawn' and bearing the date November 1898, which does not seem to be correct in view of the fact that the sonnet was not published in *The City of the Soul*. The title was changed in *Collected Poems* (1919), which gives 1903 as the date of composition.

To a Silent Poet (p. 251)

Sonnets (1909)

First appeared in *The Academy*, LXXII, No. 1825, 27 April 1907, p. 405.

10   hands, / hands;

13   gardener, / gardener
  'Written about myself' (*CP*).

Rewards (p. 252)

Sonnets (1909)

First appeared in the *English Review*, I, No. 12, 6 January 1906, p. 265.

2   Prophets / prophets
3   Was Keats bay-crowned, was Shelley smiled upon? / And
         were not Keats and Shelley spat upon?
4   timely. Well / timely; well
5   On stake or rack / On rack and stake
6   light / sun
7   That voice, that trumpet, that white-throated swan, / The
         great delight, that glory, that white swan
8   praise, / praise
9   bones! / bones,
10   Cold-eyed mistrust, and ever watchful fear, / Scorn and
         contempt and watchful hate and fear,
11   homage / homage,
12   From cautious mouths. And all the while a mesh / From
         gaping foolish mouths; and then a mesh
13   To snare the singing-bird, to trap the deer, / To snare a
         singing bird or trap a deer,
14   And bind the feet of Immortality. / And – the revenge of
         mediocrity!

The definitive version was printed in *The Academy*, LXXV, No. 1897, 12 September 1908, p. 245.

2   Chatterton: Thomas Chatterton (1752–70) forged the lit-
         erary works of a fictitious fifteenth-century monk, Thomas
         Rowley, whose manuscripts he claimed to have discov-
         ered in a Bristol church. Seven years after Chatterton had
         killed himself, *The Rowley Poems* appeared in print,
         fomenting a heated debate about their authenticity or
         otherwise.

4   Marlowe: The playwright Christopher Marlowe (1564–93),
         whose *Tragical History of Doctor Faustus* was greatly
         admired by Goethe, was killed in a tavern in Deptford,
         shortly before he was to have been interrogated by the

authorities about 'his damnable opinions and judgment of relygion and scorne of Gods worde'.

6   his own Edward: This own Edward: A reference to Marlowe's tragedy *Edward the Second* (1593). Its hero, the English king who mounted the throne in 1307, came under the baneful influence of his lover, Peers Gaveston, 'who furnished his court with companies of iesters, ruffians, flattering parasites, musicians, and other vile and naughtie ribalds, that the King might spend both daies and nights in iesting, plaieng, banketing, and such other filthie and dishonorable exercises'. A rebellion of the nobility was the result; Gaveston was liquidated in 1312. Eventually the Queen, too, turned against her husband. Eight months after his abdication he was brutally murdered at Berkeley Castle (1327):

They kept him down and withall put into his fundament an horne, and through the same they thrust up into his bodie an hot spit, or (as others have) through the pipe of a trumpet a plumbers instrument of iron made verie hot, the which passing into his intrailes, and being rolled to and fro, burnt the same, but so as no appearance of any wound or hurt outwardlie might be once perceived. His crie did moove manie within the castell and towne of Berkley to compassion. [*Holinshead's Chronicles: England, Scotland and Ireland*, with a new introduction by Vernon F. Snow. New York: AMS, 1976, III, 547, p. 587]

6–7   that light that shone, / That voice, that trumpet, that white-throated   swan: Shakespeare. The swan has been of old a symbol of poetry,   and is as such often depicted as an attribute of Apollo.

8   'his honoured bones': A quotation from John Milton's poem 'On Shakespear' (1630):

What needs my *Shakespear* for his honour'd Bones,
The labour of an age in piled Stones.
Or that his hallow'd reliques should be hid
Under a Star-ypointing *Pyramid?*

The Green River (p. 253)

Sonnets (1909)

First appeared in the *English Review*, I, No. 15, 27 January 1906, p. 325.

2	running river, / flowing river
3	leafy / lonely
5	the moon. The / the moon; the
7	unravished / untroubled
9	Oh may I wake / O! let me wake
10	a voice of music manifold. / some loveliness, unsung, untold,
12	sorrow / Sorrow
13	delight / Delight

The definitive version was published in *The Academy*, LXXII, No. 1834, 29 June 1907, p. 621. The poem was set to music by two composers: John Alden Carpenter (1876–1951) and Robert Fairfax Birch (b. 1917).

To Olive (pp. 253–6)

Sonnets (1909)

This series of love poems is printed in the order adopted by Bosie.

I (p. 253)

Written on 4 May 1906. First appeared in *Vanity Fair*, LXXVII, 16 January 1907, p. 70.

1	tangled / winding
2	old / young
3	to / at
4	time-trod / Time-trod
9	there / near
10	here, / there
14	despair / Despair

The poem was then published in *The Academy*, LXXIII, No. 1837, 20 July 1907, p. 693.

10	here, / there

II (p. 254)

First appeared in *Vanity Fair*, LXXVII, 23 January 1907, 101; reprinted in *The Academy*, LXXIII, No. 1837, 20 July 1907, p. 693.

III (p. 254)

Lord Gawain Douglas owns the MS of the first version of this poem, inscribed 'To my darling beloved little girl. A sonnet for her birthday. Feb. 7, 1904'.

2	a little princess in a state / a Princess in a little state
3	sweet and strange did congregate, / strange and sweet did congregate.
4	And in your eyes was hope or memory / You laughed and played a little wistfully,
5	Or wistful prophecy of things to be; / And often gazed upon the dreaming sea;
6	proffered fate, / promised fate,
9	But Love that weaves the years on Time's slow loom / And then you slept, waiting to be my wife
10	Found you again, reborn, fashioned and grown / All the long centuries behind the door
11	To your old likeness in these harsher lands; / Of your carved tomb; till rising from that bed
12	And when life's day was shadowed in deep gloom / You came before the spring; you came when life
13	You found me wandering, heart-sick and alone, / Walked in late winter darkness, just before
14	And ran to me and gave me both your hands. / The first pale primrose raised a silken head.

The sonnet was published in *Vanity Fair*, LXXVII, 6 March 1907, p. 295.

1	Italy, / Italy –
2	princess / Princess
3	congregate, / congregate.
4	hope or memory / far-oft memory
5	prophecy / prescience
6	fate, / Fate,
9	Love / Love,
10	again, / again
11	likeness / semblance

The definitive version was subsequently printed in *The Academy*, LXXIII, No. 1837, 20 July 1907, p. 693.

IV (p. 255)

First appeared in the *English Review*, I, No. 11, 30 December 1905, p. 246.

I have restored the commas in the first line which were left out in all editions of Bosie's poetry.

3   Linger in roses and white jasmine sprays, / Linger in pinks and honeysuckle sprays

4   yellow / golden

5   clear / sweet

11   joy. / joy;

13   its heavy pack of years / his heavy pack of years,

The poem was then published in *The Academy*, LXXIII, No. 1836, 13 July 1907, p. 669, bearing the subtitle 'A Rainbow Sonnet'.

3   Linger in roses and white jasmine sprays, / Linger in pinks and honey-suckle sprays

4   And marigolds that stand in yellow rings / And daffodils that stand in golden rings

9   see / saw

V (p. 255)

First appeared in *The Academy*, LXXV, No. 1901, 10 October 1908, p. 341, with the title 'Love and the World'.

VI (p. 256)

First appeared in *The Academy*, LXXV, No. 1890, 25 July 1908, p. 77.

Silence (p. 256)

Sonnets (1909)

First appeared in *The Academy*, LXXIII, No. 1838, 27 July 1907, p. 717.

The first line of this sonnet – a manuscript of which is kept at the Harry Ransom Humanities Research Center, the University of Texas, Austin – is printed correctly only in the edition of 1909; in subsequent editions what should be a decasyllabic line is changed into an eleven-syllabled one: 'This is a deep hell, to be expressionless.'

4   an / some

5   press, / press.

7   fearful gate / fast-locked gate

9   Oh, / Oh

A Christmas Carol (p. 257)

Nine Poems (1926)

First appeared in *The Academy*, LXXIII, No.1859, 21 December 1907, p. 261. It was quoted in full in *Vanity Fair*, LXXVIII, 25 December 1907, p. 805, and described as 'one of the best things we have read for a long time . . . For heavenly beauty that takes the breath with childish simple appeal, it may be compared with the "Anunciation [*sic*]" of Rosetti [*sic*].'

Beauty and the Hunter (p. 257)

Sonnets (1909)

First appeared in *The Academy*, LXXIV, No. 1869, 29 February 1908, p. 505.

'This is pure Catholic mysticism, though I did not know it when I wrote it two or three years before I became a Catholic' (*CP*).

The Poet (p. 258)

Appeared in *The Academy*, LXXVI, No. 1927, 10 April 1909, p. 965, and has not been reprinted so far.

Proem (p. 259)

The City of the Soul, Third Edition (London: John Lane, 1911)

First appeared in *The Academy*, LXXVI, No. 1919, 24 April 1909, p. 29, with the title 'The Ransomed'.

3   feet? / feet!
11   deceits, / deceits

A Christmas Sonnet (p. 259)

Nine Poems (1926)

First appeared in *The Academy*, LXXVII, No. 1964, 25 December 1909, p. 869.

Written in Olive's bed on 19 December 1909 (AD to OC, 20 December 1909. MS Berg).

Behold, Your House Is Left Unto You Desolate (p. 260)

Collected Poems (1919)

The title is derived from Matthew XXIII, p. 38.

Stones for Bread (p. 260)

CP

First appeared in *Plain English*, I, No. 1, 10 July 1920, 4 with the title 'The Years Which the Locust Hath Eaten' (derived from Joel VII, 9). The new title refers to Matthew VII, 9.

1   asphodel: An immortal flower which, according to the ancient Greeks, blossomed in Elysium.

2   not, / not;

4   fabulous / fabled

8   ice, / ice

10   belovèd. And anon / belovèd and anon

Before a Crucifix (p. 261)

Collected Poems (1919)

Written in November 1916 and privately printed on a single leaf, with the following quotation of the mystic, Anna Catharina Emmerich (1774–1824) following Bosie's name: 'Rien dans toute la Passion n'affliges [*sic*] aussi profondèment [*sic*] le Sauveur, que le trahison de Judas.'

14   (By wife, child, friend betrayed): In *CP* and subsequent editions this line reads: (So many times betrayed)

The Unspeakable Englishman (p. 261)

Collected Poems (1919)

A sonnet about T.W.H. Crosland, author of *The Unspeakable Scot* (London: Grant Richards, 1902).

Lighten Our Darkness (p. 262)

Collected Poems (1919)

11   quick = alive

On a Showing of the Nativity (p. 262)

Collected Poems (1919)

First appeared in *The Irishman*, 5 January 1918, p. 7.

9   House of Bread: The translation of Bethlehem.

14   Even the gates of Hell shall not prevail: Cf. Matthew XVI, p. 18: And I say also unto thee, That thou art Peter, and upon this rock I will build my church; and the gates of hell shall not prevail against it.'

12   I have adopted the semi-colon which is placed after 'shed' in *The Irishman*, and which was replaced by a comma in the

various editions of Bosie's poetry.

14   prevail. / prevail . . .

House of Bread (p. 263)

Nine Poems (1926)

First appeared in *Plain English*, I, No. 25, 25 December 1920, p. 578, with the title 'Christmas'.

    'House of Bread' is the translation of 'Bethlehem'.

8   immaterial / insubstantial

9   floating – / floating. –

10   light, / Light,

11   A transubstantial mansion built of air. / Ringed round with wings that beat the enchanted air.

To a Certain Judge (p. 263)

Nine Poems (1926)

An acrostic: the first letters of the fourteen lines make up the name Mr Justice Avory. Sir Horace Edmund Avory (1851–1935) was the judge who on 13 December 1923 sentenced Bosie to six months' imprisonment for libelling Winston Churchill. Bosie wrote this poem in gaol.

In Excelsis (I–IX; Epilogue) (pp. 264–8)

In Excelsis (London: Martin Secker, 1924)

First appeared in the *London Mercury*, X, No. 60, October 1924, pp. 568–74, bearing the motto: 'For honour peereth in the meanest habit.' Shakespeare, *Taming of the Shrew*. Sonnets I, XV and XVI were left out by the editor, Sir John Squire.

Alfred Rose (1878–193-?) got talked about in 1898 when as a monk belonging to an Anglican brotherhood he was condemned to no less than three years' imprisonment for stealing valuable books belonging to Canon Deedes (see Edward Marjoribanks, *The Life of Sir Edward Marshall Hall*. London: Victor Gollancz, 1929, pp. 110–13). It is not clear when exactly he got to know Bosie, but when the latter was incarcerated it was Rose who arranged that Bosie be given a school copy-book, in which *In Excelsis* was written; and it was at the office of Rose that Bosie wrote out the text of his sonnet-cycle after this copy-book had been confiscated by the authorities (it is still kept by the Home Office!). In 1927 a quarrel ensued when

Bosie discovered that Rose had stolen and sold some of his manu-
scripts.

Rose is the compiler of the posthumously published *Registrum
librorum eroticum* (London: Privately printed for subscribers, 1936),
which was issued under the pseudonym 'Rolf S. Reade'.

I (p. 264)

4 cruel to be kind: Cf. *Hamlet*, III, iv.

5 (Truly for bread a stone): Cf. Matthew VII, 9.

11–14 Cf. Luke XXII, 55.

13 Dismas: The penitent murderer who was crucified with
Jesus. Luke does not mention his name (XXIII, 40–43), but
it may be found in the apocryphal Gospel of Nicodemus. St
Dismas is the patron of those who are condemned to death;
his feast is on 25 March.

III (p. 265)

11 Cf. Proverbs, I, 17: 'But a net is spread in vain before they
eyes of them that have wings.' '"Wings" here means
"prayer"' (note of Douglas).

IV (p. 265)

8 fate? / Fate?

VII (p. 267)

'The octave of this sonnet comes almost verbatim from St Thomas à
Kempis' *The Imitation of Christ*' (note of Douglas). The passage in
question runs as follows:

> Love is a great thing and a good, and alone maketh heavy bur-
> dens light, and beareth in like balance things pleasant and
> unpleasant; it beareth a heavy burthen and feeleth it not, and
> maketh bitter things to be savoury and sweet. The noble love
> of Jesus perfectly printed in the soul maketh a man do great
> things, and stirreth him always to desire perfection, growing
> more and more in grace and goodness. Love will always have
> the mind upward to God, and will not be occupied with love of
> the world . . . Such a lover flieth high, he runneth swiftly, he is
> merry in God, he is free in soul, he giveth for all, and hath all

in all; for he resteth in one high Goodness above all things, of Whom all Goodness floweth and proceedeth. [Book III, 'The Inward Speaking of Christ to a Faithful Soul, 5. Of the Marvellous Effect of the Love of God']

VIII (p. 267)

11   Or open hopeful casements to the Dove? An allusion to the story of Noah's ark, Genesis VIII, 8–12.

IX (p. 268)

11   For what, but love of God, / For what but love of God

Epilogue (p. 268)

1   *Follow the star:* The star of Bethlehem, which led the Wise Men from the East to the manger where Jesus was born (Matthew II, 2; 9).

To — with an Ivory Hand Mirror (p. 269)

CP

A poem about Ivor Goring, who called himself 'the reincarnation of Dorian Gray'. He went to America in 1927, embarking upon a theatrical career.

In Limpsfield, Surrey, Lady Queensberry owned a place called St Martin's.

Oxford Revisited (p. 269)

Sonnets (1935)

First appeared in the *Cherwell*, XXXV, No. 6, 4 June 1932, p. 129, and again there – because of a few misprints – in No. 7, 11 June 1932, p. 155, with the title 'A Sonnet. By Lord Alfred Douglas (In Memory of his Recent Visit to Oxford)'.

4   Isis: The Thames

12   Uriël: One of the arch-angels. His name, which means 'Light of God', is mentioned in the apocryphal Books of Enoch.

6   Among / Amongst

7   hands; accept the treasure lent, / hands. Accept the treasure lent:

9   this / that

11   could / would

12   doom, / doom;

13   kindly with mild eyes / kindly, with mild eyes

'I am cheered by the thought that actually I am still an under-graduate as I never took my degree!' Bosie, giving an account to his visit to Oxford, wrote to a friend on 25 May 1932. 'I stayed with young Richard Rumbold at Christ Church. He had a party for the "leading undergraduates", from the literary point of view, to meet me, the editors of the university papers, the *Isis* and *Cherwell*, [the] secretary of the Oxford University Dramatic Society (the OUDS), etc. etc., about 20 of them. They were all awfully nice to me and Rumbold tells me I made a great hit with them . . . I enjoyed it all immensely' (Hyde, p. 292).

Winston Churchill (p. 270)
Sonnets [pocket edition] (London: Richards Press, p. 1943)
First appeared on the front page of the *Daily Mail*, 4 July 1941.

13   your sire: John Churchill, Duke of Marlborough (1650–1722), Churchill's forebear, who in 1704 defeated the French at Blenheim (Hochstädt) in Bavaria during the War of the Spanis Succession. This victory was commemorated a year later by Joseph Addison (1672–1719) in 'The Campaign'; Bosie's sonnet   alludes to the following lines:

'Twas then great MARLBRÔ's mighty soul was prov'd,
That, in the shock of charging hosts unmov'd,
Amidst confusion, horror and despair,
Examin'd all the dreadful scenes of war;
In peaceful thought the field of death survey'd,
To fainting squadrons sent the timely aid,
Inspir'd repuls'd battalions to engage,
And taught the doubtful battel where to rage.
So when an Angel by divine command
With rising tempests shakes a guilty land,
Such as of late o'er pale *Britannia* past,
Calm and serene he drives the furious blast;
And, pleas'd th'Almighty's orders to perform,
Rides in the whirl-wind, and directs the storm.

(*The Miscelleaneous Works of Joseph Addison*. Edited by A.C. Gutkelch. London: Bell, 1914, I, p. 165.)

3   rough paths / grim paths
4   a sword / the sword
9   evil's / Evil's
10   all the world / the whole world
13   sire / Sire
14   outstormed / out-stormed

The Wastes of Time (p. 271)

Sonnets (1935)

First appeared in *Nash's Pall-Mall Magazine*, XCIII, No. 493, 15 June 1934, p. 20.

The title echoes Shakespeare's sonnet XII:

> Then of thy beauty do I question make,
> That thou among the wastes of time must go

Translations from the French of Charles Baudelaire

Harmonie du soir (p. 273)

The City of the Soul

A TS of this poem with autograph corrections is kept at the West Sussex Record Office.

1   when, swinging in the breeze, / when swinging in the breeze
2   Each flower, like a censer, / Each flower like a censer
5   Each flower, like a censer, / Each flower like a censer
10   Death; / Death.
12   blood, / blood
13   Death / Death,
14   tenderly, / tenderly.
15   Sun / sun

Le Balcon (p. 275)

The City of the Soul

A TS of this poem with autograph corrections is kept at the West Sussex Record Office.

2   Oh! / O!

7	And, on the balcony, the rose-stained nights! / And on the balcony the rose-stained nights.
11	the Sun / the sun
12	heaven's tower! Subsequent editions have heaven's high tower!
14	heart's-blood / heart's blood
15	How fair the Sun is in the evening! / How fair the sun is in the evening.
22	your knees, / thy knees
24	Mysteries? / Mysteries.
27	skies / skies,
30	O vows, O scents, O kisses infinite! / These vows, these scents, these kisses infinite.

Recueillement (p. 277)

Sonnets (1909)

Dated 26 August 1899, it appeared in the *Outlook*, IV, No. 83, 2 September 1899, p. 131.

1	O thou my heaviness, / oh thou my Heaviness!
2	calledst / called'st
2	here, / here;
3	City / city
5	the heedless throng make haste / the wretched herd makes haste
6	Where pleasure drives them, / Where Pleasure drives it,
7	sick remorse and fear / sick Remorse and Fear,
8	with me, / with me
9	See how they hang / See! how they lean
10	garmented, / garmented;
11	mouth; / mouth.
2	the dying sun sinks in the skies, / the dying Sun sinks to the seas,
14	And her long robe trails all about the south. / And her dark shroud trails all about the South.

The poem appeared in *The Academy*, LXXIII, No. 1839, 3 August 1907, p. 741.

1	heaviness, / Heaviness
5	make haste / makes haste
10	garmented, / dressed

12   skies, / West

The definitive version was first printed in *Collected Poems* (1919).

La Beauté (p. 279)

Sonnets (1909)

First appeared in *The English Review*, I, No. 17, 10 February 1906, p. 364.

3   loveliest. / loveliest;
5   supreme / supreme,
6   crest, / crest;
7   line – / line,
8   laugh / laugh,
9   Singers who see, in trancèd interludes, / Singers that see, in ravished interludes,
11   ecstasy. / ecstasy;
13   which / that
15   eternity. / Eternity.

The definitive version appeared in *The Academy*, LXXII, No. 1831, 8 June 1907, p. 549.

   'Written in New York at the request of Natalie Barney' (*CP*).

Index of First Lines

Ah me, ah me, the day when I am dead, 250

Ah, Sleep, to me thou com'st not in the guise, 226

Ah, woe to us who look for asphodel, 260

Alas! and oh that Spring should come again, 246

Alas, for Love and Truth and Faith, stone dead, 260

Alas! I have lost my God, 231

Alas! that Time should war against Distress, 190

Alas! what make you here, poor ghost that goes, 269

And we bereft, diswinged, a very clod, 267

But so to use oneself as to entice, 267

Buttercup and marigold, 209

Cast out, my soul, the broken covenant, 249

Dear friend, dear brother, I have owed you this, 227

Each new hour's passage is the acolyte, 244

Fair am I, mortals, as a stone-carved dream, 279

Follow the star. The unseen sighing wings, 268

For such is love, a great good every way, 267

From the beginning, when was aught but stones, 252

Here in this isle, 227

Here's short life to the man I hate!, 224

How have we fared, my soul, across the days, 259

I carved an image coloured like the night, 224

I dreamed I stood upon a little hill, 210

I dreamed of him last night, I saw his face, 249

If Love reveal himself, to haggard eyes, 251

If he were here, this glorious sky, 225

I follow honour, brokenly content, 264

If you came back, perhaps you would not find, 271

I gaze across the Nile; flamelike and red, 220
I have been profligate of happiness, 254
I have been through the woods to-day, 207
I have within me that which still defies, 265
I know a green grass path that leaves the field, 253
I love a love, but not as other men, 212
In the high places lo! there is no light, 262
In the salt terror of a stormy sea, 242
Into the silence of the empty night, 235
I saw in dreams a bed within a chamber, 248
I saw the white sails of the silver ships, 220
Last night my window played with one moonbeam, 244
Late, as I slept worn with life's cares and jars, 259
Long, long ago you lived in Italy, 254
Look in this crystal pool, and you will see, 269
Master of dubious arts, the sophist's cloak, 263
Most tuneful singer, lover tenderest, 214
Mother of Memories! O mistress-queen, 275
My love and life have taught me late two things, 222
My soul is like a silent nightingale, 245
My thoughts, like bees, explore all sweetest things, 255
Not all the singers of a thousand years, 229
Not I, alas, at any rate, not yet, 266
Not that of old I loved you over-much, 270
Now dallies at the gate my loitering youth, 233
Now is the hour when, swinging in the breeze, 273
Often the western wind has sung to me, 222
Oh! for a day of burning noon, 213
Once as a boy when he slept, 238
O none, if grace enrich the soul's release, 266
Peace, be at peace, O thou my heaviness, 277
Rise up, my soul!, 234
Roses red and white, 218
See what a mass of gems the city wears, 223
See where she lies, pale and serene and mild, 262
Spinello of Arezzo long ago, 247
Sweet Spirit of the body, archetype, 215
Tell me not of Philosophies, 214
That she should so devise, to find such lore, 245

The fields of Phantasy are all too wide, 243
The frosty sky, like a furnace burning, 208
There is a ghostly stable in my heart, 263
There is an isle in an unfurrowed sea, 230
The sun holds all the earth and all the sky, 239
The sun sinks down, the tremulous daylight dies, 233
They gave him scorn and hate and the fierce rod, 258
This is deep hell, to be expressionless, 256
Thou sombre lady of down-bended head, 236
Through the still air of night, 219
Tired of passion and the love that brings, 212
Torment of body, torment of the mind, 264
To see the moment holds a madrigal, 242
Unto my bed last night, methought there came, 221
Wake up again, sad heart, wake up again!, 237
What hurts Thee most? The rods? the thorns? the nails?, 261
What shall I say, what word, what cry recall, 282
What shall we do, my soul, to please the King?, 243
When Christ was born in Bethlehem, 257
When death, the marshall of our settled state, 265
When I am dead you shall not doubt or fear, 256
When in dim dreams I trace the tangled maze, 253
When we were Pleasure's minions, you and I, 255
Where are the eagle-wings that lifted thee, 251
Where lurks the shining quarry, swift and shy, 257
You were a brute and more than half a knave, 261

Bibliography

Works of Lord Alfred Douglas

Poetry, satires, nonsense rhymes

Poems. Paris: Published by the Mercure de France, XV, rue de l'Échaudé-Saint-Germain, XV, MDCCCXCVI.Colophon: 'Achevé d'imprimer le trente octobre mil huit cent quatre-vingt-seize par l'imprimerie Vve Albouly pour le Mercure de France.'
With French prose translations by Eugène Tardieu. Frontispiece portrait of the author by Walter Spindler.

A thousand copies at 3 fr. 50 were printed. There were, besides, an *édition de luxe* at 10 fr. and an *édition de grand luxe* at 25 fr. of twenty and five copies respectively.

Reissued, with cancelled title-page: Paris: MCMVII. I have only come across one copy of this reissue; it is to be found at the library of the University of Wisconsin, Madison. Who was responsible for this venture is unknown.

A single letter from Douglas to the Mercure de France appears to have survived; it bears the date 14 June 1907, is kept at the firm's archive and runs as follows: 'Monsieur, Je vous prie de vouloir bien m'envoyer dans un bref delai le compte des exemplaires de mon livre *Poèmes par Lord Alfred Douglas* que vous avez publié il y a quelques années. Veuillez agréer, Monsieur, l'expression de mes sentiments distingués. [Signed] Lord Alfred Douglas.' The letter bears a manuscript note, presumably by Alfred Vallette: 'Compte fourni le 19 vi 1907 (compte au 30 juin 1906).'

On 5 December 1908 *The Academy* quoted from an article by 'Jacob Tonson' (that is, Arnold Bennett) which had appeared in the *New Age*: 'Of course I had to admit that Lord Alfred Douglas, before he began to cut capers in the hinterland of Fleet Street, had been a poet. I have an early and unprocurable volume of his that, to speak mildly, is not for sale.' Douglas – or perhaps it was T.W.H. Crosland – countered: 'Of the edition of a thousand copies issued by the *Mercure de France* about nine hundred have been sold and the remainder are on sale, and can be obtained by writing to the *Mercure de France* or to any bookseller in London or Paris; . . . so that when "Jacob Tonson" asserts that he possesses an unprocurable volume he makes a serious blunder, and when he says that the book is not for sale he makes a blunder of an even more serious nature.'

Perkin Warbeck and Some Other Poems. London: printed at the Chiswick Press, MDCCCXVII.
Privately printed. The edition was limited to fifty copies.

Tails with a Twist. The Verses by 'Belgian Hare'. The Pictures by E.T. Reed, Author of *Pre-historic Peeps*, *Mr Punch's Animal Land*, &c. London: Edward Arnold, 37 Bedford Street [1898].
Published in November 1898, price 3s. 6d.

The Duke of Berwick. A Nonsense Rhyme by the Belgian Hare, Author of *Tales with a Twist*. Illustrated by Toni Ludovici. London: Leonard Smithers and Co., 5 Old Bond Street, W. [1899].
Contains ten tinted plates. Published in December 1899, price 5s.

The City of the Soul. London: Grant Richards, 9 Henrietta Street, Covent Garden, W.C., 1899.
Five hundred copies were printed. Published anonymously in May 1899, price 5s.

The City of the Soul. Second Edition. London: Grant Richards, 9 Henrietta Street, Covent Garden, W.C., 1899.
Five hundred copies were printed. Published on 8 January 1900 (AD to Wilfrid Blunt, 12 January 1900, MS Sussex), with the author's name on recto title page.

The Placid Pug and Other Rhymes. By the Belgian Hare (Lord Alfred Douglas), Author of *Tails with a Twist* and *The Duke of Berwick*. With Illustrations by P.P. London: Duckworth and Co., 3 Henrietta Street, Covent Garden, 1906.
Published in November 1906, price 3s. 6d.

The Pongo Papers and The Duke of Berwick. Illustrations by David Whitelaw. London: Greening and Co.. Ltd, 1907.
Published in October 1907, price 2s. 6d.

Poems.
Colophon: 'This book contains Lord Alfred Douglas' *Poems* (Édition du Mercure de France, MDCCCXCVI), together with the other poetry by the same author, as found in the volume *The City of the Soul* (London, Grant Richards, 1899). The book was seen through the press by P.C. Boutens, and printed in forty copies for private circulation. Completed on 30 June 1908 by the St Catherine Press Ltd, Bruges, Belgium.'

Sonnets by Lord Alfred Douglas, Author of *The City of the Soul*. [With a Note by T.W.H. Crosland.] London: Academy Publishing Company, MDCCCCIX.
Five hundred copies were printed. Published in June 1909, price 2s. 6d.

Sonnets by Lord Alfred Douglas, Author of *The City of the Soul*. [With a Note by T.W.H. Crosland.] Second edition. London: Academy Publishing Company, MDCCCCIX.
Five hundred copies were printed. Published in December 1909, price 2s. 6d.

The City of the Soul. [Third edition.] London: John Lane, The Bodley Head / New York: John Lane Company, MCMXI.
Published in September 1911, price 5s.
 Reissued with cancelled title-page: London: Martin Secker, xvii Buckingham Street, Adelphi, n.d.

The Rhyme of F double E. [Boulogne: 1914].
Published in July 1914.
 A satire on F.E. Smith, subsequently Lord Birkenhead (1872–1930).

To A Certain Judge. [Galashiels, Scotland: 1915].
One hundred copies were printed. One leaf.
 A satirical sonnet on Sir Reginald More Bray (1842–1923), to be distinguished from another sonnet bearing the same title which was written in 1924.

Before a Crucifix. [Galashiels, Scotland: Printed by Robert Dawson and Son, 1916].
One leaf.

All's Well With England. [Galashiels, Scotland: Printed by Robert Dawson and Son, 1916.]
Five hundred copies were printed. One leaf.

The Rossiad. London: [Galashiels, Scotland: Printed and Published by Robert Dawson and Son] 1916.
Published in February 1916, price 1s. 6d.
    A satire on Robert Ross. The title is derived from Charles Churchill's *The Rosciad* (1761).

The Rossiad. Second Edition. Galashiels, Scotland: Printed and Published by Robert Dawson and Son [1916].

The Rossiad. Third Edition. Galashiels, Scotland: Printed and Published by Robert Dawson and Son [1916].

Eve and the Serpent. Galashiels, Scotland: Printed and Published by Robert Dawson and Son [1917].
Published in June 1917, price 1s. 6d.
    A satire on Sir Harry Trelawney Eve (1856–1940), with whom Douglas had dealings in 1915.

Eve and the Serpent. Second Edition, Containing Postscript of Startling News. Galashiels: Printed and published by Robert Dawson and Son [1917].

Collected Poems. London: Martin Secker, xvii Buckingham Street, Adelphi, 1919.
Frontispiece portrait. Published in October 1919, price 7s. 6d. Besides the ordinary edition there was a signed *édition de luxe* limited to two hundred copies which was published in August 1920, price 21s.
    Dedication: 'To my Mother.'

The Rossiad. Fourth Edition. Galashiels, Scotland: Printed and Published by Robert Dawson and Son [1921].

The Devil's Carnival. Galashiels, Scotland: Printed and Published by Robert Dawson and Son [1922].
A political poem, dated 26 June 1922, written after the murder four days previously of Field Marshal Sir Henry Wilson who had been dispatched by the IRA.

In Excelsis. London: Martin Secker, 1924.
Published in December 1924, price 5s. Besides the ordinary edition there was a numbered and signed édition de luxe limited to one hundred copies, price 21s.
     Dedication: 'To Alfred Rose.'

The Duke of Berwick and Other Rhymes. London: Martin Secker, 1925.
Published in November 1925, price 5s.

The Duke of Berwick and Other Rhymes. New York: A.A. Knopf, 1925.

Perkin Warbeck, and Other Poems. With an Introduction by George Sylvester Viereck. Girard, Kansas: Haldeman-Julius Company [1925] (Little Blue Book No. 788).
Frontispiece portrait. A pirated edition.
     From Viereck's introduction, called 'The Genius of Alfred Douglas', we may quote the following:

> Douglas in *Oscar Wilde and Myself* assumes towards Wilde's erotic vagaries an attitude difficult to reconcile with his 'Hymn to Physical Beauty' extolling 'the sweet unfruitful love / In Hellas counted more than half divine'. In many of his poems, Lord Alfred plays with Greek fire. We need not, in spite of this contradiction, condemn Douglas as a hypocrite. Psycho-analysis has shown that it is possible to love and to hate at the same time with perfect sincerity, that certain emotions like certain mathematical formulae may be prefixed by both a plus and a minus sign. Douglas may not himself realize that whatever may be his intellectual convictions, he is at heart a Pagan. His Paganism is more joyous than Swinburne's. Wilde was an Irish Protestant with a middle-class conscience, and pronounced Catholic leanings who vainly tried to make himself believe he was a Greek. Douglas is a Greek who vainly imagines himself a Catholic. The boot

does not fit. It is easy to discern under the monkish gown the cloven hoof of Pan! [p. 11]

The City of the Soul, and Other Sonnets. With an Introduction by George Sylvester Viereck. Girard, Kansas: Haldeman-Julius Company [1925] (Little Blue Book No. 789).
A pirated edition.

Nine Poems. London: Privately printed for A.J.A. Symons, 1926.
Colophon: 'Of these poems, which have never before been printed in any book, fifty copies have been printed, privately. This is No . . . Set Up February 17th, 1926.'

Selected Poems. London: Martin Secker, 1926 (New Adelphi Library, Volume IX).
Published about May 1926, price 3s. 6d.

The Duke of Berwick. London: Martin Secker, 1926 (New Adelphi Library, Volume XIV).
Published in July 1926, price 3s. 6d.

Collected Satires. London: Fortune Press, 1926.
Colophon: 'This Edition Consists of Five Hundred and Fifty Copies on Vergé de Mongolfier à la Forme.'
   Published in November 1926, price 10s. 6d. In addition there was a numbered and signed édition de luxe limited to 250 copies, price 30s.
   Dedication: 'I dedicate this book / To the whole company of Rosencrantz and Guildenstern in General / And in particular / To all my false friends (whose name is legion) . . .'

[*Poems*]. The Augustan Books of Modern Poetry. Edited by Edward Thompson. [London: Ernest Benn, 1926.]
A selection. Published in November 1926, price 6d.

Complete Poems, Including the Light Verse. London: Martin Secker, Number Five John Street, Adelphi, 1928.
Published in December 1928, price 10s. 6d.

Two Loves and Other Poems. [Maastricht: A.A.M. Stols] 1928.

Colophon: 'Printed in Garamond Roman and Italic type on Dutch antique laid paper in September 1928. This edition is limited to fifty copies (not for sale).'

A pirated edition: Douglas's 'decadent' poems, seen through the press by E. Du Perron.

Sonnets. London: Rich and Cowan, 1935.
Frontispiece: facsimile. Published in November 1935, price 7s. 6d.

There was a signed *édition de luxe* of fifty copies, price 42s.

Reissued with cancelled title-page: London: Richards Press Ltd, 8 Charles Street, St James's Square, 1943.

Lyrics. London: Rich and Cowan, 1935.
Frontispiece portrait. Published in November 1935, price 7s. 6d. There was a signed *édition de luxe* of fifty copies, price 42s.

Reissued with cancelled title-page: London: Richards Press Ltd, 8 Charles Street, St James's Square, 1943.

Poèmes. Traduits par Francis d'Avilla [Fabienne Hillyard]. Paris: Albert Messein, Éditeur, 19, Quai Saint-Michel, 19, 1937.
Price 6 fr.

Contains a facsimile letter from Douglas to the translatress.

Sonnets [pocket edition]. London: Published by the Richards Press Ltd, at No. 8 Charles Street, St James's Square, S.W. [1943].
Published in October 1943, price 2s. 6d.

Sonnets [pocket edition]. London: Published by the Richards Press Ltd, at No. 8 Charles Street, St James's Square, S.W. [1947].
Price 2s. 6d.

Hymn to Physical Beauty. [Amsterdam] Sub Signo libelli, 1976.
Embellished with a linocut representing a naked youth, made by the publisher, Ger Kleis.

Colophon: 'This poem was printed in Bembo roman and italic in May 1976 on a Boston-handpress. The edition is limited to 20 copies on Gaubert Japon and 10 copies on Zerkall-Bütten. This is number . . .'

Price fl. 30,-. A much sought-after book, which in 1999 sold for fl. 650,-.

De Profundis and Other Poems. [Amsterdam]: Sub signo libelli, 1976.
With a frontispiece. Contains Douglas's homo-erotic verse.

Colophon: 'This selection was composed in Bembo and printed on a Boston-handpress by Ger Kleist in June 1976. The drawing was made by Bob van Blommestein. The edition is limited to 18 copies on Zerkall-Bütten and 16 copies on Van Gelder Vergé. This is number . . .'

Price fl. 30,-.

Collected Poems. New York: AMS Press, 1976.
A facsimile reprint of the 1919 edition.

Collected Satires. New York: AMS Press, 1976.
A facsimile reprint of the 1926 edition.

Tails with a Twist. Animal Nonsense Verse. Illustrated by Brian Robb. London: B.T. Batsford, 1979.

The Dead Poet. Amsterdam: Riba-pers, 1983.
Contains the following poems: 'In Praise of Shame', 'A Song', 'The Dead Poet'. The edition is limited to eighteen copies.

Colophon: '*The Dead Poet* werd op 7 januari 1983 gezet uit de Garamond en gedrukt op de proefpers van 't Schuurtje te Hoofddorp. Het tweede eerste exemplaar werd gemaakt voor Moniek Sakkers, of all sweet passions de heerlijkste volgens de meest broze en langoureuse direkteur van de Riba-pers.'

Gedichten. Geselecteerd en van een inleiding voorzien door Caspar Wintermans. [The Hague: 1988.]
Frontispiece portrait.

A pirated edition.

Limitation: 'Deze bundel verschijnt in een oplage van 15 exemplaren. Dit is nummer . . .'

'Two Loves' and Other Poems: A Selection. East Lansing, Michigan: Bennet and Kitchel, 1990.
Edited by William Whallon.

Seven Sonnets. The Hague: 1992.
A pirated edition, limited to seven copies, edited by Caspar Wintermans.

The City of the Soul. Oxford: Woodstock Books, 1996 (Decadents, Symbolists, Anti-Decadents: Poetry of the 1890s. A series of facsimile reprints chosen and introduced by R.K.R. Thornton and Ian Small). A reprint of the first (anonymous) edition of 1899.

    Price £25.

Lyrics and Sonnets [2001].
Colophon: 'This edition consists of one hundred copies printed by Richard Healy on the hand-press at Right-Hand Press, Southbourne-on-Sea. The poems were set in Narrow Bembo Italic – cast specially for this edition, with Centaur capitals. The prefatory matter was set in Centaur roman. Papier d'Arches, from the mill at Montval, was used. Binding by Frank Brown of Dorchester. This copy is number . . .'

    Price £65.99.

Prose

Letters to My Father-in-Law. No. 1 – No. 2. [Boulogne: 1914].

Oscar Wilde and Myself. With photogravure portrait of the author and thirteen other portraits and illustrations and also facsimile letters. London: John Long, Norris Street, Haymarket.
Dedication: 'To my Mother, Sybil, Marchioness of Queensberry.'

    Written for the greater part by T.W.H. Crosland. The book was subsequently repudiated by Douglas.

    Published in July 1914, price 10s. 6d.

Oscar Wilde and Myself. With a portrait of the author and thirteen other portraits and illustrations, also facsimile letters. New York: Duffield and Company, 1914.

Salomé, A Critique, The Beauty of Unpunctuality, an Essay, and Three Poems. Bruno Chap Books, Vol. II, No. 3, New York: Guido Bruno, September 1915, pp. 39–50.
An unauthorized reprint of articles and poems by Douglas that had appeared in *The Spirit Lamp*. Page 50 has the following note:

> There was a time when Lord Alfred Douglas would have laughed at
> the idea that he would write a book explaining away his friendship

with Oscar Wilde [*Oscar Wilde and Myself*]. As editor of *The Spirit Lamp*, a magazine published by James Thornton, High Street, Oxford, and edited by Lord Alfred Douglas, he seemed to be a diligent imitator of his friend Oscar. He imitated his style in prose and in poetry. Whenever he received a contribu-tion from Oscar Wilde it was the main and leading feature of the issue.

I collected a few essays and a few poems from this interesting, short-lived, literary publication and believe they will throw an important sidelight on Lord Alfred Douglas.

In the Matter of Raymond Douglas, an Infant; Before Mr Justice Peterson, May 3rd, 1916. Lord Alfred Douglas's Speech [London: Westminster Press, 411a Harrow Road, W, 1916].
An exceedingly rare pamphlet. There is a copy at the New York Public Library.

Oscar Wilde et moi. Traduit de l'anglais par William Claude. Paris: Émile-Paul frères, éditeurs, 100, rue du Faubourg Saint-Honoré, 100, Place Beauvau, 1917.
A translation of *Oscar Wilde and Myself*.

Oscar Wilde et moi. Traduit de l'anglais par William Claude. Deuxième édition. Paris: Émile-Paul frères, éditeurs, 100, rue du Faubourg Saint-Honoré, 100, Place Beauvau, 1917.

'The Wilde Myth'. 1917.
Unpublished. A set of proofs is at the Harry Ransom Humanities Research Center, Texas University, Austin.

Fashionable Intelligence about the 'Morning Post'. Galashiels: Robert Dawson and Son [1918].
Published in June 1918, price 1s.

'A Touching Ceremony'. With Apologies to Lord and Lady Bathurst and the 'Morning Post'. Galashiels: Robert Dawson and Son [late 1918].
This pamphlet can be dated by a reference to the silver wedding of the Earl and Countess Bathurst, which took place in 1918; a reference to Christopher Millard's serving a term of imprisonment (he was released on 28 December of that year); and by the fact that Robert Ross is spoken of as deceased.

Striking Tribute to a Solicitor: Sir George Lewis Honoured. Dedicated to the London Papers which printed Accounts of the Robert Ross Testimonial. Galashiels: Published by Robert Dawson and Son, 40 High Street [1918 or 1919].
Price 1d.

Oscar Wilde and Myself. Cheap Edition with a new Preface. London: John Long Ltd, Norris Street, Haymarket,1919.
Published in June 1919, price 6s.

Wilde Oszkár és én. Forditotta Kosztolányi Dezso. Budapest: A Kultúra Könyvkiadó és Nyomda R.-T., Kiadása, VI., Teréz-Körut 5, 1919.
A Hungarian translation of *Oscar Wilde and Myself.*

An Appeal to Friends and Supporters of Plain English and Plain Speech. London [?], 1 January 1922.
A pamphlet which I have not been able to see. It was recently offered on the internet.

The Murder of Lord Kitchener and the Truth about the Battle of Jutland and the Jews. Speech made by Lord Alfred Douglas at the Memorial Hall, Farringdon Street, London. Reprinted from *The Border Standard* [Galashiels: John McQueen and Son, 1923].
Published in October 1923, price 2d. 30,000 copies were printed, of which some 6,000 had been sold when Douglas was arrested on 6 November.

Oscar Wilde y yo. Con varias illustraciones. Traducido directamente de la edición inglesa por R. Cansino-Assens. Madrid: Biblioteca Girelda (Colección de escritores extranjeros), 1925.
A Spanish translation of *Oscar Wilde and Myself.*

The Autobiography of Lord Alfred Douglas. London: Martin Secker, 1929.
Dedication: 'To William Sorley Brown.'
    Nine portraits. Published in March 1929, price 21s.

The Autobiography of Lord Alfred Douglas. Second impression. London: Martin Secker, 1929.
Nine portraits. Published in April 1929, price 21s. Page 160 contains an

added note about Douglas's translation of Oscar Wilde's *Salomé*.

Freundschaft mit Oscar Wilde. Mit acht Bildtafeln. Mit einem Vorwort von Franz Blei. Leipzig: Paul List Verlag, 1929.
A translation of *The Autobiography of Lord Alfred Douglas* by Elsie McCalman.
 Franz Blei's interesting preface ends as follows:

> Wer [diese Erinnerungen des Lord Douglas] mit einiger Aufmerksamkeit liest, wird deren zeitweilige Dissonanz mit dem Gedanken sich erträglich machen müssen, daß hier nicht ein leichtsinniger Mensch sich recht-fertigt oder zu bereuen vorgibt, und sich mit den Erbärmlichkeiten des Tages herumschlägt, um sich sozial zu rehabilitieren, sondern daß der Dichter von einem Band sehr schöner Gedichte sich dagegen wehrt, nichts als Episodenfigur eines Skandals gewesen zu sein und darüber mit dem vergessen zu werden, was sein unsterbliches ist – nicht die zu Gott gerettete Seele, sondern ihre Emanationen, die Gedichte. Aus Schutt und Trümmern eines Lebens reckt sich ein Arm, eine Hand hoch, in der etwas leuchtet wie ein köstliches Geschmeide, das verschenkt sein will: man soll um dieser Gabe willen sich nicht scheuen vor dem, der sie reicht.

Oscar Wilde et quelques autres. Traduit de l'Anglais par Arnold van Gennep. [Paris] Librairie Gallimard, 43, rue de Beaune (VIIe) [1930] (Les contemporains vus de près).
Three portraits. A partial translation of *The Autobiography of Lord Alfred Douglas*, with an extra chapter: 'Mes fréquentations littéraires à Paris', pp. 177–82. The book ran into at least six editions. Price 15 fr.
 Limitation: 'Il a été tiré de cette édition trois cent quatre-vingt-dix-sept exemplaires sur alfa, dont dix-sept exemplaires hors commerce marqués de *a* à *q*, trois cent cinquante exemplaires numérotés de 1 à 350 et trente exemplaires d'auteur hors commerce numérotés de 351 à 380.'

The Autobiography of Lord Alfred Douglas. Second Edition. London: Martin Secker, 1931.
Frontispiece portrait. Published in October 1931, price 8s. 6d.
 Preface to the new edition, pp. ix–xiv.

My Friendship with Oscar Wilde, Being the Autobiography of Lord Alfred

Douglas. New York: Coventry House, 1932.

Portraits. Contains a 'Preface to the American Edition', pp. 7–9.

Limitation: 'One thousand copies only have been printed of this edition, of which the first hundred have been signed by the author. This is number...'

The True History of Shakespeare's Sonnets. London: Martin Secker, No. 5 John Street, Adelphi, 1933.

Dedication: 'To Olive.'

Frontispiece portrait of the Bard. Published in March 1933, price 8s. 6d.

A Letter from Lord Alfred Douglas on André Gide's Lies about Himself and Oscar Wilde. Set Forth with Comments by Robert Harborough Sherard (Knight of the Legion of Honour). Calvi (Corsica): Vindex Publishing Co., 1933.

Price 1d.

Without Apology. London: Martin Secker, Publisher to the Richards Press, 8 Charles Street, St James's Square [1938].

Reminiscences. Published in April 1938, price 10s. 6d.

Without Apology. Toronto: Ryerson Press, 1938.

Oscar Wilde: A Summing-Up. London: Duckworth, 1940.

Two portraits and a facsimile letter from Wilde to the author.

Published in February 1940, price 6s.

Ireland and the War Against Hitler. London: Richards Press, 8 Charles Street, St James's Square, 1940.

Published in October 1940, price 2s.

Quotes extensively from H. De Montmorency's *Sword and Stirrup: Memories of an Adventurous Life* (London: G. Bell and Sons, 1936).

The Principles of Poetry: An Address Delivered by Lord Alfred Douglas before the Royal Society of Literature on September 2nd, 1943. London: Published by the Richards Press Ltd, at 8 Charles Street, St James's Square, S.W., 1943.

A thousand copies were printed. Published in November 1943, price 2s. 6d.

Oscar Wilde: A Summing-Up. With an Introduction by Derek Hudson. London: Richards Press, 1950.
Frontispiece portrait and a facsimile letter from Wilde to the author.
    Published in October 1950, price 12s. 6d.

Oscar Wilde: A Summing-Up. With an Introduction by Derek Hudson. Third printing. London: Richards Press, Royal Opera Arcade, Pall Mall [1961].
Frontispiece portrait and a facsimile letter from Wilde to the author.

Oscar Wilde: A Summing-Up. With an Introduction by Derek Hudson. London: Icon Books, 1962.
Frontispiece portrait.

The True Story of Shakespeare's Sonnets. Port Washington: Kennikat Press, 1970.
A facsimile reprint of the 1933 edition.

The Autobiography of Lord Alfred Douglas. Freeport, New York: Books for Libraries Press, 1970.
A facsimile reprint of the 1931 edition.

The Autobiography of Lord Alfred Douglas. St Clair Shores, Michigan: Scholarly Press, 1971.
A facsimile reprint of the 1929 edition.

Oscar Wilde: A Summing-Up. Folcroft, PA: Folcroft Library Editions, 1977.

Oscar Wilde and Myself. New York: AMS Press, 1977.
A facsimile reprint of the American edition of 1914.

Con Oscar Wilde. La riposta al *De Profundis* dell' 'amore proibito' di Oscar Wilde. Milan: Gammalibri, 1982.
An Italian translation of *Oscar Wilde and Myself*. Price L.9,000.

The Autobiography of Lord Alfred Douglas. Reprint Services Corporation, 1994.

Halcyon Days: Contributions to The Spirit Lamp. Selected and Introduced by Caspar Wintermans. Francestown, New Hampshire:

Typographeum, 1995.
Frontispiece. Contains: 'An Undergraduate on Oxford Dons', 'Concerning Rulers', '*Salomé*: A Critical Review' and 'Gray and Gold'.

Colophon: 'One hundred copies of this book have been printed and bound by R.T. Risk at Francestown, New Hampshire. Completed in September 1995.'

Price $50.

Oscar Wilde: A Plea and a Reminiscence. Introduced and annotated by Caspar Wintermans. Woubrugge: Avalon Press, 2002.
With frontispiece portrait and facsimile. Contains 'Oscar Wilde' (1895) and 'Oscar Wilde's Last Days in Paris' (1905).

Colophon: '*Oscar Wilde: A Plea and a Reminiscence* was set in Van Dijck and printed at the Avalon Press by Jan Keijser in an edition of 250 copies on Oud Hollands.' Price   75.

In preparation:
Un cri du cœur et son écho. Lord Alfred Douglas et la Revue Blanche. Introduction and notes by Caspar Wintermans (Woubrugge: Avalon Press).
A reprint of 'Une introduction à mes poèmes avec quelques considérations sur l'affaire Oscar Wilde' and 'Réponse à quelques journalistes', the articles which Douglas had published in the *Revue Blanche* in June 1896, along with the reactions his campaign for Oscar evoked in the French press.

Articles

This list does not claim to be complete. Not all Douglas's contributions to *The Academy* and *Plain English* were signed, yet some of them may be safely attributed to him because he referred to them as his own in his correspondence or his autobiographical writings – 'Dr Clifford's Government' (*The Academy*, 19 September 1908) being a case in point. I regret to say that I was not able to study a complete file of *Plain English*. John Cooper kindly looked at a rare set of *Plain Speech* kept in the New York Public Library and provided me with a list of Douglas's articles which appeared in its vitriolic columns.
'An Undergraduate on Oxford Dons'. *The Spirit Lamp*, II, No. 3, 18

November 1892, pp. 69–73.

Arguing persuasively that 'an ugly bearded Don with a black gown and an important air' is less interesting to behold than 'a merry boy with a fresh face under his straw hat and a flower in his coat'. Reprinted in: Lord Alfred Douglas, *Halcyon Days: Contributions to* The Spirit Lamp. Selected and Introduced by Caspar Wintermans (Francestown, New Hampshire: Typographeum, 1995).

'Gray and Gold'. *The Spirit Lamp*, III, No. 1, 3 February 1893, pp. 18–22.

A story set in Oxford. 'The doctors said the Dean died of heart disease, and the golden-haired boy went to his funeral.' Reprinted in *Halcyon Days*.

'Tout vient à qui sait attendre'. *The Spirit Lamp*, III, No. 2, 17 February 1893, pp. 34–42.

An article on the ideal waiter.

'Essays I Have Shown Up. No. 1. – What Is the True Method of Ethics?' *The Spirit Lamp*, III, No. 3, 10 March 1893, pp. 56–9.

'Some Reflections on the Beauty of Unpunctuality'. *The Spirit Lamp*, III, No. 3, 10 March 1893, pp. 74–7.

Noting 'the alarming and dangerous prevalence of baldness, seriousness and solid common-sense' among the punctual.

'*Salomé:* A Critical Review'. *The Spirit Lamp*, IV, No. 1, 4 May 1893, pp. 20–27.

A glowing article on Wilde's play. Reprinted in *Halcyon Days*.

'Concerning Rulers'. *The Spirit Lamp*, IV, No. 1, 4 May 1893, p. 29–35.

A parody of the dialogues of Plato. Reprinted in *Halcyon Days*.

'In Memoriam John Addington Symonds'. *The Spirit Lamp*, IV, No. 1, 4 May 1893, pp. 44–5.

A tribute to the author of *A Problem in Greek Ethics* (1883) and *The Renaissance in Italy* (1875–86), who had been sending affectionate letters to Bosie recently 'which came like a sunbeam in mid-winter'. 'Alas! he had not finished his work, there was more to do; there were chains he might have loosened, and burdens he might have lifted; chains on the limbs of lovers and burdens on the wings of poets.'

'Oscar Wilde'.
An article which was written in August 1895 for the *Mercure de France*. Owing to the intervention of Robert Harborough Sherard it was not published. The manuscript of the original, English version has been lost; the manuscript of the French translation, once part of the collection of Count Alain de Suzannet, is kept at the Library of the University of Princeton, New Jersey. Typescripts of Christopher Sclater Millard's re-translation into English are at Princeton and in the William Andrews Clark Memorial Library, Los Angeles.

A new English version appeared in: Lord Alfred Douglas, *Oscar Wilde: A Plea and a Reminiscence*. Introduced and Annotated by Caspar Wintermans (Woubrugge: Avalon Press, 2002).

'Une introduction à mes poèmes, avec quelques considérations sur l'affaire Oscar Wilde'. *La Revue Blanche*, X, No. 72, 1 June 1896, pp. 484–90.
The typescript of an (incomplete) English retranslation, made in 1913 by M. Didier, is to be found at the William Andrews Clark Memorial Library, Los Angeles.

'Réponse à quelques journalistes'. *La Revue Blanche*, X, No. 73, 15 June 1896, pp. 552–3.
Reacting to the avalanche of abuse engendered by his article published two weeks before. 'J'étais assez naïf pour croire que "les gens cultivés, les hommes de lettres," à qui, comme je l'ai dit, mon article était spécialement adressé, s'ils n'avaient jamais lu Platon, avaient du moins entendu parler de lui et possédaient quelques notions de sa doctrine.'

The typescript of an English re-translation, made in 1913 by M. Didier, is to be found at the William Andrews Clark Memorial Library, Los Angeles.

'William Morris'. *La Revue Blanche*, XI, No. 81, 15 October 1896, pp. 378–9.
A tribute to the designer and writer (1834–96) who had inspired the Arts and Crafts Movement and who had founded the Kelmscott Press. 'Né à l'époque peut-être la plus basse, la plus sordide et la plus laide que l'Angleterre ait jamais vue, c'est-à-dire *the Victorian age*, il tourna ses efforts

contre la hideur de la vie, opposant son socialisme poétique et impraticable au monstre du négoce qui tyrannisait sa patrie.'

'Oscar Wilde's Last Years in Paris'. *The St James's Gazette*, 2 March 1905, pp. 5–6, and 3 March 1905, pp. 5–6.
Reprinted (without permission) in [Anonymus], *The Trial of Oscar Wilde from the Shorthand Reports* (Paris [Charles Carrington], 1906), pp. 113–26, and (with permission) in Lord Alfred Douglas, *Oscar Wilde: A Plea and a Reminiscence*. Introduced and Annotated by Caspar Wintermans (Woubrugge: Avalon Press, 2002).

'Lesser Lights'. *English Review*, I, No. 4, 11 November 1905, pp. 86–7.
An article commisserating with the fate of impecunious peers.

'Birth and Sport'. *English Review*, I, No. 6, 25 November 1905, pp. 132–3.
An effort to point out to 'the youth of the upper and leisured class' that 'sport and art are so far from being incompatible that they have ever been associated in the highest, and therefore rarest, type of gentleman'.

'Plain and Coloured'. *The Academy*, LXXII, No. 1812, 26 January 1907, pp. 89–90.
A review of ten books of verse. 'Mr William Stevens has rashly ornamented his volume with his own portrait, thereby providing the reviewer with evidence that he has reached an age when he can no longer have any valid excuse for imagining that he can write poetry.'

'A Literary Causerie. Beowulf, Burns and Co.'. *The Academy*, LXXII, No. 1814, 9 February 1907, pp. 142–3.
A review of Kate Warren (ed.), *A Treasury of English Literature* (London: Constable, 1907).

'Some Protests and an Appreciation'. *The Academy*, LXXII, No. 1816, 23 February 1907, p. 190.
A review of six volumes of verse.

'Inspired Journalism'. *The Academy*, LXXII, No. 1819, 16 March 1907, p. 271.
On the writings of Maurice Maeterlinck.

'Shirts and Shekels'. *The Academy*, LXXII, No. 1820, 23 March 1907, pp. 293–4.
Setting out that the greatest artists in history were, more often than not, exceedingly poor.

'Nursery Rhymes'. *The Academy*, LXXII, No. 1822, 6 April 1907, p. 341.

'The Blessed Damozel'. *The Academy*, LXXII, No. 1823, 13 April 1907, pp. 365–6.
On Dante Gabriel Rossetti.

'A Neglected Poet'. *The Academy*, LXXII, No. 1824, 20 April 1907, pp. 388–9.
An article on the work of 'Michael Field' (the pseudonym of Katherine Harris Bradley and her niece Edith Emma Cooper), 'perhaps the greatest of our living lyric poets who are actually writing at this time'.

'Mr St John Hankin's Comedy at the Court'. *The Academy*, LXXII, No. 1826, 4 May 1907, pp. 442–3.
A review of a new production of *The Return of the Prodigal* (1905).

'A Great Elizabethan Poet'. *The Academy*, LXXII, No. 1828, 18 May 1907, pp. 487–8.
An article on Richard Barnfield 'whose sonnets have been compared from the nature of their subject-matter to those of Shakespeare'.

'Mad Dogs'. *The Academy*, LXXII, No. 1831, 8 June 1907, pp. 555–6.
Taking issue with a certain Father Ignatius who in the course of one of his sermons delivered himself of the following statement: 'The nude in art is diabolical and pagan, and it is the duty of the Church to protest. There is no high art in stripping off clothes. Nude art ought to swept out of the country.'

'Poetry and Passion'. *The Academy*, LXXII, No. 1833, 22 June 1907, pp. 603–4.
'The measure of one's love for good poetry and for good music is the hatred, the violent hatred, one feels for bad poetry and bad music.'

'Drama. The Irish Players Again'. *The Academy*, LXXII, No. 1833, 22 June 1907, pp. 610–11.

A review of the Abbey Theatre Company of Irish Players' production of plays by Lady Gregory and W.B. Yeats.

'The Fool's Reproach'. *The Academy*, LXXIII, No. 1835, 6 July 1907, pp. 653–4.
An article about a highly critical review in *The Times* of Wilfrid Blunt's *Secret History of the English Occupation of Egypt: Being a Personal Narrative of Events* (London: T. Fisher Unwin, 1907).

'Mr Whibley's Byron'. *The Academy*, LXXIII, No. 1836, 13 July 1907, pp. 678–9.
A review of the *Selected Poems of Lord Byron*. With an Introduction by Charles Whibley (Edinburgh: T.C. and E.C. Jack [1907]).

'A False Prophet'. *The Academy*, LXXIII, No. 1841, 17 August 1907, pp. 800–801.
A review of R. Henderson Bland's *Moods and Memories* (London: Greening and Co., 1907).

'Mr Wilfrid Blunt and *The Times*'. *The Academy*, LXXIII, No. 1857, 7 December 1907, pp. 223–5.
Discussing Blunt's privately published pamphlet of that title, which forms 'A Memorandum as to the attitude of the *Times* newspaper in Egyptian affairs'.

'The Revival of *Arms and the Man*'. *The Academy*, LXXIV, No. 1861, 4 January 1908, p. 324.
A review of a new production of Bernard Shaw's play.

'Tantæne animis coelestibus iræ?' *The Academy*, LXXIV, No. 1870, 7 March 1908, pp. 538–9.
An article on *The Academy*'s course.

'The Limit'. *The Academy*, LXXIV, No. 1871, 14 March 1908, pp. 563–4.
A review of T.H. Warren's *The Death of Virgil: A Dramatic Narrative* (London: Murray, 1907), upbraiding the President of Magdalen and Vice-Chancellor of the University of Oxford for 'staining fair white paper' with 'verse which would disgrace a fourth-form school-boy'.

'François Villon'. *The Academy*, LXXIV, No. 1874, 4 April 1908, pp. 638–9.

'Mrs Dearmer's New Book'. *The Academy*, LXXIV, No. 1875, 11 April 1908, pp. 662–3.
A review of Jessie Mabel Dearmer's *The Alien Sisters* (London: Smith Elder, 1908).

'*The Times*, Mr Murray, and Mr Wilfrid Blunt'. *The Academy*, LXXIV, No. 1880, 16 May 1908, p. 781.

'For Shame, Mr Shaw!' *The Academy*, LXXIV, No. 1881, 23 May 1908, p. 806.
A review of *Getting Married*.

'Can You Not Manage?' *The Academy*, LXXIV, No. 1882, 30 May 1908, p. 830.
Shaw's reaction to Douglas's review of *Getting Married*, and Douglas's comments.

'Socialism and Suffragitis'. *The Academy*, LXXIV, No. 1882, 30 May 1908, pp. 831–2.
'The Socialists are blighting and spoiling all that is fine and noble and lovely in this country.'

'The Shaving of Patshaw'. *The Academy*, LXXIV, No. 1883, 6 June 1908, p. 855.
The sequel of the Shaw–Douglas controversy.

'Art and Sport'. *Granta*, Special May Week Number, 11 June 1908, pp. 19–20.
'The complete gentleman of this 20th century should be no less well equipped mentally than the complete gentleman of the Elizabethan age.'

'The Genius of Oscar Wilde'. *The Academy*, LXXV, No. 1888, 11 July 1908, 35.
A review of Wilde's collected works, published by Methuen.

'Dr Clifford's Government'. *The Academy*, LXXV, No. 1898, 19 September 1908, pp. 275–6.

An article protesting against the suppression of a procession planned to celebrate the Catholic Eucharistic Congress in London.

'Heterodoxy'. *The Academy*, LXXV, No. 1899, 26 September 1908, pp. 301–2.
On G.K. Chesterton.

'The Poetry of Oscar Wilde'. *The Academy*, LXXVI, No. 1916, 23 January 1909, pp. 702–3.
'At his worst he was always an accomplished master of his craft, and at his best he was a great poet whose immortality is assured as long as the English language exists.'

'"Jupiter, What a Mess!"'. *The Irishman*, 5 January 1918, 7–8; 12 January 1918, pp. 9–10.
A withering review of T.W.H. Crosland's *The English Sonnet* (London: Martin Secker, 1917).

'The "Dream" of Padraic Pearse'. *The Irishman*, 19 January 1918, pp. 7–8.
A review of Padraic H. Pearse, *The Story of a Success: Being the Record of St Enda's College, September, 1908, to Easter, 1916*. Edited by Desmond Ryan. (Dublin/London: Maunsel, 1917.)

'Poetry'. *Plain English*, I, No. 3, 24 July 1920, p. 57.
A review of a volume of verse by Samuel J. Looker.

'Christian Charity and the Jews'. *Plain English*, I, No. 4, 31 July 1920, pp. 78–9.
'There is such a thing as Christian Charity even in relation to the Jews, and Christian Charity forbids us to join in wholesale and indiscriminate abuse and vilification of an entire race.'

'A Call for Mr Winston Churchill'. *Plain English*, I, No. 8, 28 August 1920, p. 169.
Referring to Churchill as 'the only man among our leading politicians who possesses the brain and the pluck' to give the 'one vigorous kick to bring about [the Bolsheviks'] complete collapse'.

'Robert Ross, Asquith and Co.' *Plain English*, I, No. 10, 11 September 1920, pp. 218–19.

About the testimonial to Robert Ross.

'*Plain English* and the *Jewish Guardian*'. *Plain English*, I, No. 19, 13 November 1920, pp. 434–5.
Challenging the *Jewish Guardian* to take *Plain English* – 'which is not an anti-Semitic paper' – to court.

'H.G. Wells Frightens a Crippled Newspaper Seller'. *Plain English*, I, No. 21, 27 November 1920, pp. 483–4.
Drawing attention to the fact that the author, 'whose publications and writings have been adversely criticised in *Plain English*, has interfered with the sale of the paper by threatening the newspaper seller whose "pitch" is right outside the National Liberal Club'.

'Chancery Justice'. *Plain English*, I, No. 22, 4 December 1920, pp. 506–7.
Reflections on the Chancery Court.

'Enemies Within the Gates'. *Plain English*, II, No. 26, 1 January 1921, pp. 6–7.
Accusing the Catholic Bishop of Northampton of supporting Sinn Fein.

'A Bishop Out of His Province'. *Plain English*, II, No. 27, 8 January 1921, pp. 26–7.
A tiff with the Bishop of Northampton, incidentally 'a subscriber of *Plain English* almost from our first number'.

'Still Alive – and Kicking'. *Plain English*, II, No. 32, 12 February 1921, p. 127.
About the obituary notice devoted by the *Evening News* to Douglas, supposedly deceased. 'We have ample evidence that a good many people . . . feel that if we are not dead we ought to be, and very soon shall be. For example, we have received a pamphlet from "The Cremation Society of England" setting forth in eloquent language the advantages of cremation "as a method of disposing of the dead in a sanitary, reverent and innocuous manner".'

'Impeach Churchill'. *Plain English*, II, No. 33, 19 February 1921, p. 45.

'America Demands Jutland Money'. *Plain English*, II, No. 34, 26 February 1921, pp. 166–7.
Referring to Winston Churchill as 'the manipulator of the false Jutland report'.

'*Henri IV* at the Court Theatre'. *Plain English*, II, No. 36, 12 March 1921, pp. 212–13.
Words of praise for the production; and some reflections on the character of Falstaff.

'Prosecute and be D—d!' *Plain English*, II, No. 37, 19 March 1921, p. 226.
Inviting the Public Prosecutor to institute proceedings against *Plain English* for libelling Winston Churchill.

'A Triumph for Decency'. *Plain English*, II, No. 41, 16 April 1921, pp. 306–7.
Referring to the Lord Mayor's decision to seize and destroy copies of Cyril Scott's *Autobiography of a Child* (London: Kegan Paul, Trench, Trübner and Co., 1920): '"I find that this book deals with certain unnatural practices and much of it is obscene. I regret that such an old and respectable firm should have published it."'

'Ourselves and the *Evening News*'. *Plain English*, II, No. 44, 7 May 1921, pp. 368–9.
Giving copies of the 'Statement of Claim' and the 'Defence' in the action brought against Associated Newspapers Ltd.

'A Personal Statement'. *Plain English*, II, No. 50, 18 June 1921, p. 486.
Declaring that, pending the result of his action against the *Evening News*, Douglas is retiring from the editorship of *Plain English*. 'It is not my fault, nor is it even, rightly considered, my misfortune, that my whole life has been staged as an allegorical drama of the soul's passage from darkness to light, and that again and again I have been forced before the public eye to defend not only myself but certain large and eternal principles for which I would willingly lay down my life.'

'Plain English for Our Readers'. *Plain English*, II, No. 51, 25 June 1921, p. 506.

Expressing thanks for letters received 'from all over the world' which 'generally take the form of congratulations on our "courage"', yet pointing out that 'moral support is not everything, and there is such a thing as material support'.

'The Levities of Mr Oscar Levy'. *Plain English*, II, No. 51, 25 June 1921, pp. 507–8.
Criticizing this German philosopher, a resident in England, for endorsing the opinion of Lunacharsky, the Soviet Minister for Education, that 'Christ, if He should ever visit the earth again, would immediately join the Bolshevist party'.

'Who Is on Our Side?' *Plain English*, III, No. 52, 2 July 1921, p. 526.
Asking for financial support to keep the paper going.

'Their Majesties and the Asquiths'. *Plain English*, III, No. 53, 9 July 1921, p. 546.
Regretting the fact that the King and Queen have been lunching with the Asquiths. 'We implore His Majesty to think twice before he again offends and disheartens all his most devoted friends and supporters.'

'Is the Empire Doomed?' *Plain English*, III, No. 54, 16 July 1921, pp. 566–7.
Aye.

'The Author of Sherlock Holmes'. *Plain English*, III, No. 54, 16 July 1921, pp. 568–9.
About Sir Arthur Conan Doyle's spiritualistic propaganda, of which Douglas does not approve. Nor does the article evince great admiration for the fictional detective, 'who for some extraordinary reason appears to spend most of his time, when at home, in a dressing-gown'.

'An Excommunicated Murderer'. *Plain English*, III, No. 55, 23 July 1921, pp. 586–7.
About Eamon de Valera.

'Looking After the Pence'. *Plain English*, III, No. 55, 23 July 1921, pp. 587–8.
Appealing for funds to enable the paper 'to continue [its] struggle against treason, anarchy, falsehood and filth'.

'Slinging Mud at Shakespeare'. *Plain English*, III, No. 56, 30 July 1921, pp. 606–7.
Dismissing 'the Frank Harris school of criticism of Shakespeare'.

'The King and Northcliffe'. *Plain English*, III, No. 57, 6 August 1921, pp. 627–8.
Rejoicing in the fact that it has been established 'that the King had nothing whatever to do with the surrender to De Valera'.

'Our Dismal Dukes'. *Plain English*, III, No. 58, 13 August 1921, p. 646–7.
'We tell the Duke of Portland that he and the great, wealthy landowners of Great Britain are to blame for all the misfortunes that have overtaken the country in the last twenty years, including the war with Germany, which never would have happened at all if they had done their duty instead of living entirely for pleasure and "the social round".'

'Inge on Miracles'. *Plain English*, III, No. 58, 13 August 1921, pp. 647–8.
Taking issue with the opinions on the supernatural of Dean William Ralph Inge (1860–1954).

'A Wilderness of Monkeys'. *Plain English*, III, No. 61, 3 September 1921, pp. 706–8.
About Darwin's theory of evolution. '[It] is utterly devoid of foundation. It is not only untrue, but is has been *proved* to be untrue and grossly false.'

'Questions for the *Daily Express*'. *Plain English*, III, No. 62, 10 September 1921, pp. 725–6.
About the troubles in Ireland.

'An Appeal to the Duke of Northumberland'. *Plain English*, III, No. 62, 10 September 1921, pp. 727–8.
Begging His Grace, who had '[come out] some months ago with a tremendous flourish of trumpets,' announcing 'he was going to "save the country" and "combat the revolution"', to explain his apparent withdrawal from the political scene.

'The Jewish Star Chamber'. *Plain English*, III, No. 63, 17 September 1921, pp. 746–8.
About the plight of the editor of the authorized English translation of

Nietzsche's works, who was ordered to leave England where he had been living since 1894. 'It is a curious irony of circumstance that . . . it is to *Plain English* that Dr Oscar Levy, a German Jew and an enemy of Christianity, comes for a fair hearing against monstrous injustice. He does not appeal in vain.'

'An Open Letter to the Duke of Northumberland'. *Plain English*, III, No. 64, 24 September 1921, pp. 766–8.
'You may or may not forgive me for telling you that the attitude you have taken up is, in my opinion, altogether unworthy of your name, your family traditions, and your race.'

'Our Last Number?' *Plain English*, III, No. 65, 1 October 1921, pp. 787–8.
Requesting 'one rich man to risk twenty or thirty thousand pounds to establish *Plain English* as a permanence . . . It is quite on the cards that, unless help is forthcoming, this will be the last number to appear.'

'An Undenominational Christian'. *Plain English*, III, No. 66, 8 October 1921, pp. 809–11.
Replying to a letter from Commander H.M. Fraser inviting Douglas 'to consider that there are many thousands – perhaps millions – of good, honest (if fat-headed) Britons who look on Roman Catholics with as much suspicion as on the Jew. That is putting it mildly.'

'Pity the Poor Millionaire'. *Plain English*, III, No. 67, 15 October 1921, p. 827.
Reflecting on letters received, one of which contains the following lamentation: 'I don't think this nation is worth saving; nothing matters but ape-like lust, gambling and amusement.'

'The Truth About *Plain English*'. *Plain Speech*, I, No. 1, 22 October 1921, pp. 4–5.
'*Plain English* does not appear this week under my editorship. A company of persons who are responsible for putting a receiver in its offices, have, it appears, decided to bring it out as usual under some other editorship. As I am still legally the Editor of *Plain English* and have neither resigned my position nor been removed from it by the two directors of the North British Publishing Company (of whom I am one), this creates a situation which must be pretty well unprecedented in the history of journalism . . . The deflection of *Plain English* has been to me the worst calamity that has

befallen me in a life whose record is a long series of almost incredible calamity.'

'What Does It All Mean?' *Plain Speech*, I, No. 2, 29 October 1921, p. 21.
z'The Apostle of Birth Control'. *Plain Speech*, I, No. 3, 5 November 1921, p. 37.

'The Hideous Prohibition Heresy'. *Plain Speech*, I, No. 4, 12 November 1921, p. 54.

'The Wooden Heads of Old England'. *Plain Speech*, I, No. 5, 19 November 1921, p. 70.

'Casting the Children's Bread to Bolsheviks'. *Plain Speech*, I, No. 6, 26 November 1921, p. 86.

'Literary Criticism'. *Plain Speech*, I, No. 7, 3 December 1921, pp. 98-9.

'My Action Against the Northcliffe Press'. *Plain Speech*, I, No. 7, 3 December 1921, p. 101.

'Lloyd George Once More Exploits the King'. *Plain Speech*, I, No. 8, 10 December 1921, p .116.

'The Breaking Point of Ulster's Loyalty'. *Plain Speech*, I, No. 9, 17 December 1921, p. 133.

'The Jews, the Britons and the *Morning Post*'. *Plain Speech*, I, No. 10, 24 December 1921, p. 149.

'Pray for the Devil! By Order'. *Plain Speech*, I, No. 11, 31 December 1921, p. 165.

'Oscar Wilde – Catholic and Poet'. *Carmina*, No. 5, March 1931, pp. 124–5.
This article appeared in the magazine issued by the Catholic Poetry Society of which the Hon. Evan Morgan was the Honorary President. Its object was

'to revivify Catholic culture in England; to stimulate a Renaissance of Catholic thought in the arts, more especially in literature, and to encourage interest amongst the Catholic population of Great-Britain and the English-speaking world'. Associates included G.K. Chesterton, Compton Mackenzie, Father John Gray (one of Oscar's closest friends before Douglas appeared on the scene), Katharine Tynan and Douglas. The membership fee was 10s. 6d. per annum for Catholics, while non-Catholics had to pay 12s. 6d.!

'English Benedictines. Personal Statement'. *Carmina*, No. 11, May 1932, pp. 328–9.
The inclusion in Maurice Leahy's *Anthology of Contemporary Catholic Poetry* (London: Cecil Palmer, 1931) of a Douglas sonnet written more than fifteen years ago has raised some eyebrows because of its strictures of the Abbot of the Monastery and College of Fort Augustus. Douglas regrets the compiler's choice of the poem. 'The feelings which inspired [it] have long ceased to exist . . . I have always had the deepest reverence and regard for the Glorious Order of Saint Benedict and I number valued friends among the order who figure daily in my prayers.'

'Oscar Wilde in Relation to the Catholic Church'. *Carmina*, No. 11, May 1932, pp. 329–32.
Amplifying his first article in *Carmina* on the subject. 'While his libel action against my father was pending, he said to me one day, "If I win this case, and of course I shall win it, I think we really must be received into the *dear* Catholic Church." . . . I replied, rather brutally: "Well, if you *don't* win the action we certainly won't be received anywhere else!" This made him very angry, I remember.'

'A Daniel Come to Judgment'. *Modern Mystic and Monthly Science Review*, I, No. 4, April–May 1937, pp. 10–11.
Autobiographical.

'The Post-Victorians – But Not Necessarily the Moderns'. *Catholic Herald*, 20 May 1938.
A review of Herbert Palmer's *Post-Victorian Poetry* (London: J.M. Dent and Sons, 1938).
'Poems Are Made'. *Weekly Review*, 15 September 1938.
A favourable review of Cecil Floersheim's *Collected Poems* (Hove:

Combridges, 1938), containing a typical dig at 'the "poems" of Messrs Dash and Asterisk (no real names please) and their disciples'.

[Review of Geoffrey Masefield's *I Am Not Armed* (London: Duckworth, 1938) and Lord Dunsany's *Mirage Water* (London: Putnam, 1938.] *Weekly Review*, 19 January 1939, pp. 472–3.

'Memories of My Childhood'. *Border Standard*, 30 November 1940. Reprint of a fragment from Bosie's *Autobiography*.

Prefaces, correspondence, etc.

Frank Harris / Lord Alfred Douglas, *New Preface to 'The Life and Confessions of Oscar Wilde'*. London: Fortune Press, Twelve Buckingham Palace Road [1925].
According to *The English Catalogue of Books* this work was published in February 1926, price 5s. From Douglas's correspondence with Reginald Caton, the publisher (kept at the William Andrews Clark Memorial Library), it emerges, however, that the book was already out in December 1925. An *édition de luxe* limited to 225 numbered and signed copies was published in July 1926, price 21s.

Frank Harris / Lord Alfred Douglas, *New Preface to 'The Life and Confessions of Oscar Wilde'*. Second Edition. London: Fortune Press, Twelve Buckingham Palace Road [1927].
Published in October 1927, price 7s. 6d. Contains Douglas's 'Note to the Second Edition', pp. 5–11.

Frank Harris / Lord Alfred Douglas, *Neue Vorrede zu: Oscar Wilde, 'eine Lebensbeichte'*. Berlin: Globus Verlag G.m.b.H. [1928].

Horatio Bottomley, *Songs of the Cell* [With an Introduction by Lord Alfred Douglas]. London: William Southern, Bolt Court, Fleet Street, E.C. 2, 1928.
Published in November 1928, price 2s.

Dame Ethel Smyth, Lord Berners, Harold Nicolson [*et al.*], *Little Innocents: Childhood Reminiscences*. Preface by Alan Pryce-Jones. London: Cobden-Sanderson, 1932.

Contains Lord Alfred Douglas, 'Winning the Steeplechase at Winchester', pp. 19–22, price 6s.

Richard Middleton, *The Pantomime Man*. Edited, with a Foreword, by John Gawsworth [that is, Terence I.F. Armstrong]. Introduction by Lord Alfred Douglas. London: Rich and Cowan, Maiden Lane, Strand, 1933.
Frontispiece portrait. Published in September 1933, price 7s. 6d.

Robert Harborough Sherard, *Oscar Wilde Twice Defended from André Gide's Wicked Lies and Frank Harris's Libels, to Which Is Added a Reply to George Bernard Shaw, a Refutation of Dr G. J. Renier's Statements, a Letter to the Author from Lord Alfred Douglas, an Interview with Bernard Shaw by Hugh Kingsmill* [that is, Hugh Kingsmill Lunn]. Chicago: Argus Book Shop, 1934.

Robert Harborough Sherard, *Bernard Shaw, Frank Harris and Oscar Wilde*. With a Preface by Lord Alfred Douglas and an Additional Chapter by Hugh Kingsmill. London: T. Werner Laurie Ltd, Cobham House, Water Lane, E.C. 4, 1937.
Published in January 1937, price 18s.

Robert Harborough Sherard, *Bernard Shaw, Frank Harris and Oscar Wilde*. With a Preface by Lord Alfred Douglas. New York: Greystone Press, 1937.

Leslie and Sewell Stokes, *Oscar Wilde* [A Play in Three Acts with a Preface by Lord Alfred Douglas]. London: Martin Secker and Warburg Ltd, 1937.
Published in February 1937, price 3s. 6d. or 2s. 6d. sewed.

John Piper, *Brighton Aquatints*. Twelve Original Aquatints of Modern Brighton with Short Descriptions by the Artist and an Introduction by Lord Alfred Douglas. London: Duckworth, 3 Henrietta Street, W.C. 2, 1939.
Published in December 1939, price 21s.

Frances Winwar, *Oscar Wilde and the Yellow Nineties*. With a Foreword by Lord Alfred Douglas. New York: Garden City, Harper and Brothers, 1941.

ALFRED DOUGLAS: A POET'S LIFE AND HIS FINEST WORK

'There would be no object in pinning down all the minor errors in Miss Winwar's book; e.g . . . my father's whiskers were not red but very dark brown, almost black, as was his hair. Not that it matters.'

Marie Carmichael Stopes, *Wartime Harvest: Poems*. With a Preface by the Lord Alfred Douglas and a Letter by George Bernard Shaw. London: Alexander Moring, De la Mare Press, 2A Cork Street, Bond Street, W.1, 1944, price 5s.

Frank Harris / Lord Alfred Douglas, *New Preface to 'The Life and Confessions of Oscar Wilde'*. London: Printed for the Homosexual Society of London, 1961.

François J.-L. Mouret (ed.), 'Quatorze lettres et billets inédits de Lord Alfred Douglas à André Gide, 1895-1929'. *Revue de Littérature Comparée*, XLIX, No. 3, July–September 1975, pp. 483–502.

Mary Hyde (ed.), *Bernard Shaw and Alfred Douglas: A Correspondence*. London: John Murray, 1982.

Mary Hyde (ed.), *Bernard Shaw and Alfred Douglas: A Correspondence*. New Haven: Ticknor and Fields, 1982.

Mary Hyde (ed.), *George Bernard Shaw und Alfred Douglas: 'Seien Sie nicht so undankbar, mir zu antworten.' Briefwechsel*. Aus dem Englischen von Ursula Michels-Wenz. Frankfurt am Main: Suhrkamp, 1986.

Discography

Poems of Lord Alfred Douglas. Recited by Lord Gawain Douglas. Privately issued. This CD may be ordered by writing to Lord Gawain Douglas: gasfdouglas@yahoo.co.uk

Works by Other Authors (Selection)

Anonymous, *The Trial of Oscar Wilde from the Shorthand Reports* (Paris: Privately printed [Charles Carrington], 1906).

Barney, Natalie Clifford, *Souvenirs Indiscrets* (Paris: Flammarion, 1960).

Beerbohm, Max, *Letters to Reggie Turner*. Edited by Rupert Hart-Davis (London: Rupert Hart-Davis, 1964).

Beresford Chancelor, E., '*The Spirit Lamp*'. *The London Mercury*, XXV, No. 148, February 1932, pp. 387–9.

Blow, Simon, *Broken Blood: The Rise and Fall of the Tennant Family* (London/Boston: Faber and Faber, 1987).

Bolitho, Hector, 'T.E. Lawrence and Lord Alfred Douglas'. *Theatre World*, LVI, No. 428, September 1960, pp. 30–31.

Borland, Maureen, *Wilde's Devoted Friend. A Life of Robert Ross, 1869–1918* (Oxford: Lennard Publishing, 1990).

Braybrooke, Patrick, *Lord Alfred Douglas, His Life and Work*. With an Essay by James M. Mills ['The Poetry of Lord Alfred Douglas'] (London: Cecil Palmer, 1931).

Briant, Keith, *Marie Stopes: A Biography*. With a Foreword by the Right Honourable R.A. Butler CH, MP (London: Hogarth Press, 1962).

Brown, William Sorley, *The Genius of Lord Alfred Douglas. An Appreciation*. (Galashiels: The Author, 1913).

——, *Lord Alfred Douglas: The Man and the Poet* (Galashiels: John McQueen and Son [1918]).
'I had not been an hour in his presence before I realised that I had never before met anyone who was more approachable or who had a greater charm of manner. The absence of vanity, affectation and patronising conduct was

most marked, and I was made to feel very much at home . . . If he has a fault, I should say that it consists in his being too chivalrous and too kind-hearted.'

——, *The Life and Genius of T.W.H. Crosland* (London: Cecil Palmer, 1928).

Bruce, Robert Knight, 'Oscar Wilde, Bosie and the District Nurse'. *Evening Standard*, 6 March 1995.
An interview with Violet Conaghan-Douglas, the niece of the poet.

Cecil, David, *Max: A Biography of Max Beerbohm* (New York: Atheneum, 1985).

Cevasco, George A., *The 1890s: An Encyclopedia of British Literature, Art and Culture* (New York/London: Garland Publishing, 1993).

Chalon, Jean, *Portrait d'une séductrice* (Paris: Éditions Stock, 1976).
A biography of Natalie Clifford Barney.

The Chameleon, I, No. 1 (December 1894). A Facsimile Edition. Introduction by H. Montgomery Hyde. 'On *The Chameleon:* An Essay' by Timothy d'Arch Smith (London: Eighteen Nineties Society, 1978).

Cherniavsky, Felix, *The Salomé Dancer: The Life and Times of Maud Allan* (Toronto, Ontario: McClelland and Stewart, 1991).

Chester, Lewis, Leitch, David and Simpson, Colin, *The Cleveland Street Affair* (London: Weidenfeld and Nicolson, 1977).

Colson, Percy and Douglas, Francis, *Oscar Wilde and the Black Douglas* (1949) (London / New York: Hutchinson and Co., 1950).

Connell, John, *W.E. Henley* (London: Constable, 1949).

Croft-Cooke, Rupert, *The Glittering Pastures* (London: Putnam and Co., 1962).

——, *Bosie: The Story of Lord Alfred Douglas, His Friends and Enemies* (London: W.H. Allen, 1963).

——, *The Numbers Came* (London: Putnam and Co., 1963).

——, *Feasting with Panthers. A New Consideration of Some Late Victorian Writers* (London: W. H. Allen, 1967).

——, *The Unrecorded Life of Oscar Wilde* (London/New York: W.H. Allen, 1972).

Crosland, Thomas William Hodgson, *The Unspeakable Scot* (1902) (London: Grant Richards, 1903).

——, *Collected Poems* (London: Martin Secker, 1917).

Custance, Olive (Lady Olive Douglas), *The Blue Bird* (London: Marlborough Press, 1905).

——, *The Inn of Dreams* (London/New York: John Lane, 1911).

——, *The Selected Poems of Olive Custance*. Edited by Brocard Sewell (London: Cecil Woolf, 1995) (The Poets of the 1890s).

——, *Opals (1897) with Rainbows (1902)* (Poole/New York: Woodstock Books, 1996) (Decadents, Symbolists, Anti-Decadents. Poetry of the 1890s. A Series of Facsimile Reprints Chosen and Introduced by R.K.R. Thornton and Ian Small).

——, *I Desire the Moon: The Diary of Lady Alfred Douglas (Olive Custance), 1905–1910*. Introduced and annotated by Caspar Wintermans (Woubrugge: Avalon Press, 2004).
An edition limited to 195 copies. Published in June 2005.

Darwall-Smith, Robin, 'Charles Alan Fyffe: A Victorian Tragedy'. *University College Record*, XIII, No. 1, 2001, pp. 72–84.

Delarue-Mardrus, Lucie, *Les Amours d'Oscar Wilde* (Paris: Flammarion, 1929) (Collection 'Leurs Amours').

Eastaugh, Kenneth, *Havergal Brian. The Making of a Composer* (London: Harrap, 1976).

Egremont, Max, *The Cousins: The Friendship, Opinions and Activities of Wilfrid Scawen Blunt and George Wyndham* (London: Collins, 1977).

Ellis, Stewart M., *Mainly Victorian* (London: Hutchinson and Co., 1925).

Ellmann, Richard, *Oscar Wilde* (London: Hamish Hamilton, 1987).

Eyck, P.N. Van, 'Alfred Bruce Douglas' (1909). *Verzameld werk* (Amsterdam: Van Oorschot, 1959), III, pp. 120–43.

Fido, Martin, *The Dramatic Life and Fascinating Times of Oscar Wilde* (1973) (London: Hamlyn Publishing Group, 1984).

Fryer, Jonathan, 'Sheila Colman'. *Independent*, 27 November 2001. An obituary of Douglas's friend and literary executrix, born Sheila Crouch, who died aged eighty-two. 'Those who had dealings with her quickly began to understand that within this *petite* woman, always so immaculately dressed and exquisitely polite, there were veins of steel.'

Germain, André, *Les Fous de 1900* (Paris/Genève: La Palatine, 1954).

Gertz, Elmer, *Odyssey of a Barbarian: The Biography of George Sylvester Viereck* (Buffalo, New York: Prometheus Books, 1978).

Goodman, Jonathan, *The Oscar Wilde File* (London: Allison and Busby, 1988)

Goujon, Jean-Paul, *Tes blessures sont plus douces que leurs caresses: Vie de Renée Vivien* (Paris: Régine Desforges, 1986).

Grassal, Georges *see* Rebell, Hugues

Greshoff, Jan, *Alfred Douglas en Oscar Wilde* (Arnhem: Hijman, Stenfert Kroese en Van der Zande, 1921). A Dutch pamphlet in defence of Lord Alfred. 'Voor jonge menschen is de keus tusschen Oscar Wilde en Alfred Douglas niet moeilijk. Zij staan geheel aan Douglas' zijde. Zij verachten even fel en even standvastig het snobisme, het æsthetisme, waarin de menschelijkheid verloren gaat, de luiheid, de nutteloosheid, de immoraliteit en het gebrek aan gemeenschapszin. Zij verlangen naar gezondheid, daden, orde en het bereid zijn tot een offer.'

Hall, Ruth, *Marie Stopes: A Biography* (London: André Deutsch, 1977).

Harris, Frank [Article announcing Douglas's marriage], *Candid Friend*, II, No. 49, 5 April l902, pp. 890–91.

——, *Oscar Wilde: His Life and Confessions* (New York City: Printed and Published by the Author, 3 Washington Square, 1916). Two vols.

——, The same, with the title: *Oscar Wilde: His Life and Confessions*. Including the hitherto unpublished *Full and Final Confession* by Lord Alfred Douglas and *My Memories of Oscar Wilde* by Bernard Shaw (Garden City, New York: Garden City Publishing Co., 1930).
Contains a new preface by Harris, in the course of which he quotes a letter which Douglas had written to him on 20 March 1925 (MS Texas). Also new is Harris's account of yet another conversation he claims to have had with Oscar on the subject of Bosie's poetry:

> 'He takes himself so seriously,' said Oscar, 'his little verses make me laugh.'
> 'But surely,' I said, 'you see Oscar, that his poetry is extraordinary. Some of his sonnets rank with the best ever written. Take the one on you. It's better than anything you have done in the way of poetry.' . . .
> Oscar laughed loudly: 'I don't think I overrate my work, but nothing that any Douglas has done, or ever will do, can compare with my poetry; sheer brains separate the second-rate from the first rate.' [p. xl]

The sonnet in question, 'The Dead Poet', was written shortly *after* Wilde's death!

——, The same, with the title: *Oscar Wilde*. [Edited and] With a Preface by Bernard Shaw (London: Constable and Company, 1938).

Hawkey, Nancy J., 'Olive Custance Douglas: An Annotated Bibliography of Writings About Her'. *English Literature in Transition*, XV, No. 1, 1972, pp. 49–56.

Head, Alice M., *It Could Never Have Happened* (London/Toronto: William Heinemann, 1939).

Hichens, Robert, *The Green Carnation* (1894) (London: Unicorn Press, 1949).

——, *Yesterday. The Autobiography of Robert Hichens* (London: Cassell and Company, 1947).

Hillier, Bevis, *Young Betjeman* (London: John Murray, 1988).

Hoare, Philip, *Wilde's Last Stand: Decadence, Conspiracy and the First World War* (London: Duckworth, 1997).

Holland, Merlin, *The Wilde Album* (London: Fourth Estate, 1997).

——, *Irish Peacock and Scarlet Marquess: The Real Trial of Merlin Holland.* Foreword by Sir John Mortimer (London/New York: Fourth Estate, 2003).

Holland, Vyvyan, *Son of Oscar Wilde* (London: Rupert Hart-Davis, 1954).

Hyde, Harford Montgomery, *The Trials of Oscar Wilde* (1948) (New York: Dover Publications, 1973).

——, *Cases That Changed the Law* (London: William Heinemann, 1951).

——, *Oscar Wilde: The Aftermath* (London: Methuen and Co. 1963).

——, *Oscar Wilde: A Biography* (New York: Farrar, Straus and Giroux, 1975).

——, *The Cleveland Street Scandal* (London: W.H. Allen, 1976).

——, *Lord Alfred Douglas: A Biography* (London: Methuen, 1984).

——, *Christopher Sclater Millard (Stuart Mason), Bibliographer and Antiquarian Book Dealer* (New York/Amsterdam: Global Academic Publishers, 1990).

Jackson, Holbrook, *The Eighteen Nineties: A Review of Art and Ideas at the Close of the Nineteenth Century* (London: Grant Richards, 1913).

Jacoby, H., 'Lord Alfred Douglas et Oscar Wilde'. *Les Nouvelles Littéraires*, 11 May 1929.
An interview with Douglas. 'Je tiens à proclamer aujourd'hui que Wilde fut un très grand écrivain, un grand poète, et que les traverses de notre amitié n'ont jamais dérobé à mes yeux l'éclat de son génie. Il a droit à une plus belle place que celle que lui font actuellement les critiques littéraires en Angleterre.'

Jay, Karla, *The Amazon and the Page: Natalie Clifford Barney and Renée Vivien* (Bloomington/Indianapolis: Indiana University Press, 1988).

Johnson, Lionel, *Poems* (London: Elkin Mathews/Boston: Copeland and Day, 1895).

——, 'A Great Unknown'. *Outlook*, 3 June 1899, pp. 587–8.
A glowing review of Douglas's *City of the Soul* (1899). 'Among crowds of clever versifiers here comes a poet. Need we say more?'

——, *Some Letters of Lionel Johnson*. Edited by Raymond Roseliep (Notre Dame, Indiana: Department of English, 1953).

——, *Selected Letters of Lionel Johnson*. Edited by Murray Pittock (Edinburgh: Tragara Press, 1988).

Kettle, Michael, *Salomé's Last Veil: The Libel Case of the Century* (London: Granada Publishing/Hart-Davis, MacGibbon, 1977).

La Jeunesse, Ernest, 'Alfred Bruce Douglas, poète'. *Le Journal*, 11 January 1897.
A review of Douglas's *Poems* (1896). 'C'est sincère, c'est beau, cela veut de l'admiration, de la sympathie – et du respect.'

Le Gallienne, Richard, 'From a Crowded Book-Shelf'. *The Realm*, 14 December 1894.
A review of, among other publications, *The Chameleon*. Its contributors are described as 'a few persons whose youth has been depressed by exceptionally æsthetic surroundings'.

Lemonnier, Léon, *La Vie d'Oscar Wilde* (Paris: Éditions de la Nouvelle Revue Critique, 1931).

Longford, Elizabeth, *A Pilgrimage of Passion: The Life of Wilfrid Scawen Blunt* (London: Weidenfeld and Nicolson, 1979).

Machen, Arthur, *Selected Letters: The Private Writings of the Master of the Macabre*. Edited by Roger Dobson, Godfrey Brangham and R.A. Gilbert (Wellingborough, Northamptonshire: Aquarian Press, 1988).

McKenna, Neil, *The Secret Life of Oscar Wilde* (London: Century, 2003).

Mason, Stuart [Millard, Christopher Sclater], *Oscar Wilde Three Times Tried* (London: Ferrestone Press, 1912) (Famous Old Bailey Trials of the Twentieth Century).

——, *Bibliography of Oscar Wilde*. With a Note by Robert Ross (London: T. Werner Laurie, 1914).

Maxwell, Herbert, *A History of the House of Douglas from the Earliest TimesDown to the Legislative Union of England and Scotland* (London: Freemantle and Co., 1902). Two vols.

Mazumdar, Maxim, *Oscar Remembered* (Toronto: Personal Library, 1977). A dramatic monologue.

Merlet, J.F. Louis, 'Passants de la Rivièra. Lord Alfred Douglas'. *L'Éclaireur de Nice*, 14 February 1904.
An interview.

Merrill, Stuart, ['Lettre à Léon Deschamps'], *La Plume*, No. 158, 15 November 1895, pp. 508–9.

——, 'L'Affaire Oscar Wilde'. *La Plume*, No. 159, 1 December 1895, pp. 559–60.

——, 'Pour Oscar Wilde. Épilogue'. *La Plume*, No. 161, 1 January 1896, pp. 8–10.
Articles about the failed attempt to induce French authors to sign a petition for Wilde's release.

Mikhail, E.H. (ed.), *Oscar Wilde. Interviews and Recollections* (London: Macmillan Press, 1979). Two vols.

Millard, Christopher Sclater *see* Mason, Stuart

Murray, Douglas, *Bosie: A Biography of Lord Alfred Douglas* (London: Hodder and Stoughton, 2000).

Nelson, James G., *Publisher to the Decadents: Leonard Smithers in the Careers of Beardsley, Wilde, Dowson*. With an Appendix on Smithers and the Erotic Book Trade by Peter Mendes and a Checklist of Smithers's Publications by James G. Nelson and Peter Mendes (University Park, Pennsylvania: Pennsylviana State University Press, 2000).

Osborn, E.B., 'Books of the Day'. *Morning Post*, 17 January 1936.
A review of Douglas's *Sonnets* and *Lyrics* (1935), written by a former contributor to *The Spirit Lamp*. 'His poetry is himself, first and last, and its lasting beauty and passion will always appeal to that giant heart of memories and tears which is England's.'

O'Sullivan, Vincent, *Aspects of Wilde*. With an Opinion by Bernard Shaw (1936) (London: Constable and Co., 1938).

Paterson, Gary H., 'Lord Alfred Douglas: An Annotated Bibliography of Writings About Him'. *English Literature in Transition*, XXII, No. 3, 1980, pp. 168–200.

Pearson, Hesketh, *The Life of Oscar Wilde* (London: Methuen and Co., 1946).

Polak, Johan, *Oscar Wilde in Nederland. Een flard verlaat fin de siècle*

(Maastricht: Gerards en Schreurs, 1988).

'Rachilde' [Vallette, Marguerite], 'Questions brûlantes'. *La Revue Blanche*, XI, No. 78, 1 September 1896, pp. 193–200.
An article in which the writer breaks a lance for Douglas, who had been attacked in the French press after the publication, in the *Revue Blanche*, of his defence of Wilde. 'Oui, fatalement, irrémédiablement, lord Alfred Douglas devait crier son amour pour cela seul qu'il fut marqué bien avant sa naissance, du sceau des reprouvés . . . ou des élus. Et voici, à mon humble avis, pourquoi, lorsqu'il lui était possible, après tout, de garder le silence, il a crié si fort: parce que, fidèle et désespéré, désirant s'entourner d'un cercle de flammes à jamais isolateur, rêvant de se murer, lui aussi, dans sa prison infamante, il tenait noblement à se séparer de vos estimes de gens vertueux.'

——, 'Oscar Wilde et lui'. *Mercure de France*, CXXVIII, No. 1, 1 July 1918, pp. 59–68.
A review of the French translation of *Oscar Wilde and Myself*. 'J'ai tout lu, j'ai bien lu ce livre froid, correctement écrit, de Lord Alfred Douglas. J'ai eu les dénégations qu'il fallait, soulevée par le dégoût de certaines petites choses, *si femme* dans le mauvais sens du mot. Mais il demeure le déni de justice.'

Ransome, Arthur, *The Autobiography of Arthur Ransome*. Edited, with Prologue and Epilogue, by Rupert Hart-Davis (London: Jonathan Cape, 1976).

Rebell, Hugues [Grassal, Georges], 'Défense d'Oscar Wilde'. *Mercure de France*, XV, No. 8, August 1895, pp. 182–90.
An inflammatory article. 'La seule manière d'obtenir la grâce de Wilde, ce serait de recommencer pour Pentonville ce qu'on fit pour la Bastille en 1789 . . . Ah! il y aurait une belle et noble expédition à entreprendre . . . Avec quel joie je verrais Pentonville en flammes! Et ce n'est pas seulement a cause de Wilde que je me réjouirais, mais à cause de nous tous, artistes et écrivains païens, qui en sommes de droit les prisonniers honoraires.'

Reynolds, Aidan and Charlton, William, *Arthur Mache: A Short Account of His Life and Work*. With an Introduction by D.B. Wyndham Lewis (London: Richards Press, 1963).

Roberts, Brian, *The Mad Bad Line: The Family of Lord Alfred Douglas* (London: Hamish Hamilton, 1981).

Ross, Margery (ed.), *Robert Ross, Friend of Friends: Letters to Robert Ross, Art Critic and Writer, Together with Extracts from His Published Articles* (London: Jonathan Cape, 1952).

Rothenstein, William, *Men and Memories* (1931) (London: Faber and Faber Ltd, 1934). Three vols.

Rowse, A.L., *Quiller-Couch: A Portrait of 'Q'* (London: Methuen, 1988).

Secker, Martin, 'Publisher's Progress: 2. From my Unpublished Memoirs'. *Cornhill Magazine*, No. 1079, Spring 1974, pp. 256–63.

Secrest, Meryle, *Between Me and Life: A Biography of Romaine Brooks* (New York: Doubleday and Co./Garden City, 1974).

Sewell, Brocard, *Olive Custance, Her Life and Work* (London: Eighteen Nineties Society, 1975) (Makers of the Nineties, Edited by G. Krishnamurti).

Sherard, Robert Harborough, *Oscar Wilde: The Story of an Unhappy Friendship*. With Portraits and Facsimile Letters (London: Privately printed. Hermes Press, 1902).

——, *André Gide's Wicked Lies about the Late Mr Oscar Wilde in Algiers in January, 1895, as Translated from the French and Broadcast by Dr G.J. Renier*. Minutely Examined and Commented Upon by Robert Harborough Sherard, Chevalier de la Légion d'Honneur. With a Frontispiece by Fernand Mouren (Calvi [Corsica]: Vindex Publishing Company, 1933).
A curious pamphlet in which the Nobel Prize laureate is taken to task, Sherard even doubting the veracity of the Frenchman's amorous feats as related in *Si le grain ne meurt:*

> Gide describes how vastly superior are the delights of Sodomy to those of Onanism and goes on to describe his own virile perfor-

mance on that night of nights [in Algiers]. The particular passage
. . . is so filthy that . . . I have turned it into Latin of sorts. Here it
is: – 'Mohammedo abito, postea, ossa tremens gaudio, diu mansi.
Et quanquam per illum, summa voluptate jam quintum fructus
eram, libidinosam delectationem egomet renovavi sæpenumero. Et
ad hospitium reditus usque ad matutinas horas ejus repercussiones
extendi.' He concludes by relating how 'at daybreak I rose and ran,
yes, really ran in my sandals far beyond Mustapha, feeling from the
night I had passed no fatigue whatever, but on the contrary a spright-
liness, a kind of lightness of soul and body which did not leave me
the whole of that day.'

Can Renier honestly maintain that he believes this story? If so,
he runs contrary to the score of eminent medical men whom I have
consulted. And not medical men alone. Here is what a retired Indian
judge who has had to investigate the sordid details of hundreds of
cases of unnatural offences wrote to me, after I had submitted my
Latin version to him, ripest of scholars, with the question whether
Petronius would have passed it: 'I admire your friend Gide. He must
be a strong [sic] built man, a Monsieur Douze-Fois, as Casanova
would say. I have the best authority for saying that the inhabitants
of the cities of the plain are reduced to absolute inertia after two
visits to the Temple of Venus Præpostera.' [p. 9]

Sinden, Donald, *A Touch of the Memoirs* (London: Hodder and
Stoughton, 1982).

Smith, Timothy d'Arch, *Love in Earnest: Some Notes on the Lives and
Writings of English 'Uranian' Poets from 1889 to 1930* (London:
Routledge and Kegan Paul, 1970).

[Somerset, Raglan H.E.H.,] 'Celebrities I Have Not Met, Yet Still Am
Happy. No. 1. – Lord Alfred Bruce Douglas (or the London Curry-
worry) '. *Granta*, 8 December 1908, pp. 119–20.

This benign, unostentatious nobleman conceals a dangerously
attractive personality. Every gracious line that flows so blithely from
his pen is instinct with a warm and generous nature; and yet – and
yet some deep irrational instinct, some wild stirring of the profound
mechanism for protection that (we are told) is the world-old inher-

itance of every living thing, forbids the unchecked enthusiasm that might spring all too readily to acclaim this irridescent and enticing litterateur.

——, 'The Granta and The Academy'. Cambridge Review, 4 March 1909, pp. 305–6.

Stokes, John, 'Wilde at Bay: The Diaries of Georges Ives'. English Literature in Transition 1880–1920, XXVI, No. 3, 1983, pp. 175–86.

——, Oscar Wilde: Myths, Miracles, and Imitations (Cambridge: Cambridge University Press, 1996).

Stols, A.A.M., Bibliographie van het werk van P.C. Boutens 1894–1914 (Maastricht: Boosten en Stols, 1925).

Stopes, Marie Carmichael, Lord Alfred Douglas, His Poetry and His Personality (London: Richards Press, 1949).

Stratford, John, 'The Poetry of Lord Alfred Douglas'. Book and Magazine Collector, No. 133, April 1995, pp. 66–77.

Symonds, John Addington, The Memoirs of John Addington Symonds. Edited and introduced by Phyllis Grosskurth (London: Hutchinson, 1984).

Vallette, Marguerite see 'Rachilde'

Weeks, Jeffrey, Coming Out: Homosexual Politics in Britain, from the Nineteenth Century to the Present (London/Melbourne/New York: Quartet Books, 1977).

Weintraub, Stanley, Reggie: A Portrait of Reginald Turner (New York: George Braziller, 1965).

Wilde, Oscar, De Profundis (London: Methuen and Co., 1905).

—— [Works. Edited by Robert Ross] (London: Methuen, 1908). Fourteen vols.

——, *The Letters of Oscar Wilde*. Edited by Rupert Hart-Davis (London: Rupert Hart-Davis, 1962).

——, *More Letters of Oscar Wilde*. Edited by Rupert Hart-Davis (London: John Murray, 1985).

——, *The Complete Letters of Oscar Wilde*. Edited by Merlin Holland and Rupert Hart-Davis (London: Fourth Estate, 2000).

[Wilson, J.H.], *Gentle Criticisms on British Justice*. By I. Playfair. Part I. [London: Privately printed, 1895].
An exceedingly rare pamphlet in defence of Oscar Wilde, the sequel of which seems not to have been published. A quotation:

> To none of his children has this 'loving father' [i.e. the Marquess of Queensberry] shown so intense an animosity as to his son, LORD ALFRED DOUGLAS, whose persistent devotion to his broken-hearted mother, and whose chivalrous attempts to defend her from the utterly incredible persecutions of her cruel enemy, seem to act on this man's mind as a 'poisonous mineral' on the digestive system. Our 'affectionate parent's' pretence to object to the friendship of OSCAR WILDE with his son, was a masterpiece of cynical hypocrisy, but well carried out. This desire to ruin his gifted son had long been a passion with him (in addition, of course, to a great many other passions), and to accomplish this generous purpose, while dealing the most crushing blow that could possibly be inflicted on any mother, and riding off through all as the 'affectionate father', 'the loving parent', and 'anxious relative', etc., and winning the loud support of British judges and juries, and the almost hysterical admiration both of the press and the mob, both of rulers and rabble, was a fine stroke of art. Hypocrisy has many distinguished sons in this favoured land, but this gentleman is her Senior Wrangler. To him she indeed owes a monument. [10]

Wintermans, Caspar, *Alfred Douglas: De boezemvriend van Oscar Wilde*. Met een voorwoord van Gerrit Komrij en een keuze uit de poëzie van Alfred Douglas (Amsterdam/Antwerpen: De Arbeiderspers, 1999) (Open Domein Nr. 36).

———, *Lord Alfred Douglas: Ein Leben im Schatten von Oscar Wilde*. Aus dem Niederländischen von Christiane Kuby und Herbert Post. Mit einer Auswahl von Douglas Gedichten, aus dem Englischen übertragen von Christa Schuenke (München: Karl Blessing Verlag, 2001).

Wood, Gregory, *A History of Gay Literature* (New Haven/London: Yale University Press, 1998).

Wyndham, Violet, *The Sphinx and Her Cycle: A Biographical Sketch of Ada Leverson 1862–1933* (London: André Deutsch, 1963).

Young, Dal, *Apologia pro Oscar Wilde* (London: William Reeves, 1895). A pamphlet written by a composer who did not make it into *Grove's Dictionary of Music and Musicians*. 'The crime with which we are dealing is a bodily act, therefore the first evidence we want is that of doctors. I have asked several doctors, and have always been told that they know of no bodily harm which this act does to either of the parties taking part in it' (p. 42).

Index

Academy, The, 107–8, 113, 115–21, 127, 132, 136–7, 150

Adam, Paul (1862–1920), 77

Addison, Joseph (1672–1719), 313

Adelswärd-Fersen, Baron Jacques d' (1880–1923), 68, 181, 294

Adey, More (1858–1942), 20, 75, 77, 81, 88–9, 97, 133, 293

Albemarle Club, London, 45, 54

Aldington, Richard (1892–1962), 290

Alençon, Émilienne d' (1869–1946), 32

Algiers, 45, 80

Allan, Maud (1873–1956), 145–7, 202

Andersen, Hans Christian (1805–75), 170

Andrien, Eileen, 164

Annan, Dumfries, 21

Antinoüs, 100

À Rebours (Huysmans), 29

Archangel, 153

Arnold, Edward Augustus (1857–1942), 91

Asquith, Herbert Henry, Earl of Oxford and Asquith (1852–1928), 109–10, 119, 141

Astbury, Sir John Meir (1860–1939), 201

Athens, 39

Augustine, St, 144

Avenue Kléber, Paris, 91

Avory, Sir Horace Edmund (1851–1935), 310

Babbacombe, 29

Bach, Johann Sebastian (1685–1750), 160

Backhouse, Sir Edward Trelawney (1873–1944), 23

Balfour, Arthur James (1848–1930), 154

Balzac, Honoré de (1799–1850), 171

Barney, Natalie Clifford (1876–1972), 100, 103, 316

Barnfield, Richard (1574–1627), 62, 108

Battersea, Lady Constance, *née* de Rothschild (1843–1931), 31

Beardsley, Aubrey Vincent (1872–98), 28, 37–8, 120

Beeching, Henry Charles (1859–1919), 107

Beerbohm, Henry Maximilian ('Max') (1872–1956), 28, 36, 63, 81, 142

Begierde (Zarek), 181–2
Belloc, Joseph Hilaire Pierre
    (1870–1953), 116, 151
Bennett, Arnold (1867–1931), 321
Benjamin, Harold, 129
Berkeley Hotel, London, 42
Berlioz, Hector (1803–69), 160
Berneval-sur-Mer, 83–4
Bernhardt, Sarah (1843–1923), 37,
    294
Betjeman, Sir John (1906–84),
    157–8
Biarritz (Goedsche), 152
Bible Doctrine of Atonement, The
    (Beeching), 107
Bickerstaffe-Drew, Right Rev.
    Monsignor Count Francis
    Browning (1858–1928), 111
Billing, Noel Pemberton
    (1880–1948), 144–6, 202
Birkenhead, Lord *see* Smith, F.E.
Bloxam, John Francis (1873–1928),
    42–4, 183–4
Blunt, Wilfrid (1840–1922), 281
Blue Bird, The (Custance), 105, 108
Bodar, Antoine (1944), 170
Borland, Maureen, 200–201
Boulogne, 139
Boutens, Pieter Cornelis
    (1870–1943), 115, 281, 299
Boyton, 41
Brand, Adolf (1874–1945), 284
Bremont, Comtesse de (d. 1922),
    123
Brian, Havergal (1876–1972),
    160–61, 296
Brinkel, Bernardus Gerhardus
    Franciscus *see* Michel van de Plas
British Museum, 114, 130

Brooke, Diana (Gladys), the Dayang
    Muda of Saràwak, 156
Brooke, Rupert (1887–1915), 108
Brown, William Sorley (1889–1942),
    136
Browning, Elizabeth *née* Barrett
    (1806–61), 288
Bruges, 115
Burne-Jones, Edward (1833–98), 39
Burton, Sir Richard Francis
    (1821–90), 289
Byron, Lord George Noel Gordon
    (1788–1824), 113, 158, 296

Cadogan Hotel, London, 57
Cadogan Place, London, 92
Café Royal, London, 31, 33, 48,
    157, 162, 169
Cairo, 38
Cambridge, 32
Cambridge Review, 117
Campbell, Sir James Henry Mussen,
    Lord Glenavy (1851–1931),
    129–35
Cannoot, Danny, 18
Capri, 76
Carnegie, David, 283
Carson, Edward Henry
    (1854–1935), 54–7, 64
Cassel, Sir Ernest (1852–1921),
    151, 153–4
Catullus, 62
Chameleon, The, 42–5, 55, 57, 61,
    80, 150
Chansons de Bilitis (Louÿs), 28
Chantilly, 94–5
Chatterton, Thomas (1752–70), 304
Chesterton, Cecil Edward
    (1879–1918), 151

Chesterton, Gilbert Keith (1874–1936), 151

Churchill, John, Duke of Marlborough (1650–1722), 313

Churchill, Sir Winston (1875–1965), 153–4, 163

Church Row, Hampstead, 125

Clarke, Sir Edward (1841–1931), 52–4, 56–7, 60–61, 63, 118

Cobos, Carmen (1964), 159

Cocteau, Jean (1889–1963), 284

Collected Sonnets (Boutens), 115

Colman, Edward (1902–88), 164

Colman, Sheila, *née* Sanderson Crouch (1919–2001), 164

Conaghan, Jo, 159

Conaghan, Violet, *née* Douglas (1907– 2001), 19, 158–9

Constantinople, 182

Cooper, Adrian (1973), 204

Coppée, François (1842–1908), 294

'Corvo, Baron', pseudonym of Rolfe, Frederick William (1860–1913), 108

Cran, George R., 167

Crawley, Sussex, 164

Criminal Law Amendment Act (1885), 34, 139

Croft-Cooke, Rupert (1903–79), 155–7

Cromer, Lord Evelyn Baring (1841–1917), 38, 125

Crosland, Thomas William Hodgson (1865–1924), 19, 108–13, 117–19, 135, 137–40, 155

Crowley, Aleister (1875–1947), 202

Custance, Cecil (1876–1909), 120

Custance, Colonel Frederic Hambleton (1844–1925), 101, 103–5, 120–22, 125, 135, 137, 139, 143–4, 149

Custance, Olive Eleanor *see* Douglas, Lady Olive

*Cycle de Lord Chelsea (*Hermant), 181

Daily Chronicle, 80, 127

Daily Graphic, 135

Daily Mail, 163

Daily News, 118, 129

Daily Telegraph, 129

'Danby, Frank', pseudonym of Frankau, Julia, *née* Davis (1864–1916), 181

Darling, Charles John (1849–1936), 129–35, 146

Daudet, Louis Marie Alphonse (1840–97), 151

'd'Avilla, Francis', pseudonym of Hillyard, Fabienne, 300

De Civitate Dei (St Augustine), 144

De Grey, Constance Gladys, Lady (1859–1917), 83

Delarue-Mardrus, Lucie (1880–1945), 299

Dialogue aux enfers entre Machiavel et Montesquieu ou la Politique de Machiavel aux XIXe siècle (Joly), 152

Dickens, Charles John Huffham (1812–70), 158

Dieppe, 20, 82, 84

Douglas, Lord Alfred Bruce ('Bosie') (1870–1945), *passim*
  Life:
    birth and early youth, 21–2
    at public school, 22–3
    in Oxford, 24–5
    meets Oscar Wilde, 27

homosexual relations, 34

edits *The Spirit Lamp*, 35–6

translates *Salomé*, 37–8

portrayed in *The Green Carnation* (Hichens), 39

quarrels with father, 41–2

part played in the trial of Wilde versus Queensberry, 47–51

stays in England after Wilde's arrest, 60

forced departure to France, 60

defends Wilde publicly, 71–2

his article for the *Mercure de France*, 74–5

his article in the *Revue Blanche*, 77

described in *De Profundis*, 79–81

reunited with Wilde, 86

with Wilde in Naples, 87–9

back in England, 91

tries to reconcile with his father, 93–4

supports Wilde financially, 95

mourns Wilde, 96–7

in love with Olive Custance, 100

in the USA, 101–3

his runaway match with Olive Custance, 104–5

reviews partial publication of *De Profundis*, 106

edits *The Academy*, 107–19

friendship with T.W.H. Crosland, 108–9

quarrel with Edward Tennant, 109–10

criticizes Shaw, 110–11

conversion, 111–12

quarrel with Ross, 112–14

quarrel with Manners-Sutton, 117–18

sues Horton, 118–19

becomes a Roman Catholic, 120

quarrel with father-in-law, 120–22

sues Ransome, 124, 129–35

quarrel with wife, 126

bankruptcy, 126

reads full text of *De Profundis* for the first time, 126–7

hatred for Wilde, 127

takes a mistress, 137

witness in the trial of Allan versus Billing, 144–7

reconciliation with Olive, 147

sues the *Evening News*, 149–50

edits *Plain English* and *Plain Speech*, 150–54

convicted for libelling Winston Churchill, 153–4

in prison, 154–5

reconciliation with Wilde, 157

forgives Ross, 157

takes care of his niece, Violet, 158

friendship with Havergal Brian, 160–61

relations with Frank Harris, 162

friendship with Shaw, 163

friendship with Mary Stopes, 163

dies, 164

posthumous reputation, 166–7

reputation as poet, 169–71

Works:

Autobiography, 19, 156

City of the Soul, The, 91, 105, 115, 119

Collected Poems, 147, 158

Duke of Berwick, The, 92–3

In Excelsis, 155, 157

Lyrics, 159–60

Murder of Lord Kitchener and the Truth about the Battle of Jutland and the Jews, The (pamphlet), 153

Oscar Wilde: A Summing-Up, 19, 157

Oscar Wilde and Myself, 19, 138, 143, 156

Poems, 79, 115, 189

Poems (Boutens edition), 115

Sonnets, 115–16

Sonnets (1935 edition), 159

Tails with a Twist, 91

True History of Shakespeare's Sonnets, The, 161

Wilde Myth, The, 156

Without Apology, 19

Poems:

'Before a Crucifix', 144

'Behold, Your House Is Left Unto You Desolate', 126

'The Dead Poet', 95

'In an Ægean Port', 78

'Night Coming into a Garden', 159

'In Praise of Shame', 78

'Prince Charming', 92

'Rondeau', 73

'The Traitor', 103

'Two Loves', 43, 62, 92, 133

'Væ Victis!' 73

'Wine of Summer', 160, 296

'Winston Churchill', 163

Douglas, Rev. Lord Archibald ('Archie') (1850–1938), 94

Douglas, Lady Edith (1874–1942), 21, 104, 159

Douglas, Lady Olive Eleanor, *née* Custance (1874–1944), 97, 99, 100–105, 111, 117–18, 120–21, 125, 135–7, 142–4, 147, 158, 164

Douglas, Raymond Wilfrid Sholto (1902–64), 105, 120–21, 126, 143–4, 147

Douglas, Lord Sholto (1872–1942), 21

Douglas, Violet *see* Conaghan Douglas, Violet

Dowson, Ernest Christopher (1867–1900), 28, 120

Draycott Place, London, 159

Duke, John (1899–1984), 289

Duke Street, London, 100

Dupont, Maggie, 118

Earle, Adrian, 291

Edgcumbe, Richard, 94

Edward VII, King (1841–1910), 40, 51, 71, 101, 105

Edwards, Doris, 137, 143

Éclaireur de Nice, 105

Egregious English, The (Crosland), 109

Eigene (Brand), 284

Eileen *see* Andrien, Eileen

Eliot, Thomas Stearns (1888–1965), 158

Ellmann, Richard (1918–87), 188

Engers, Adolphe (1888–1945), 165–6

English Review, 17, 108

Ephemeral, 36

Eve, Sir Harry Trelawney (1856–1940), 143

Evening News, 149–50

Farquharson, Henry R., 52

Fellows Road, Hampstead, 113

Fine Old Hebrew Gentleman, The (Crosland), 109

Five Poems of Dante Gabriel Rossetti, 115

Flecker, James Elroy (1884–1915), 108

Fleming, Charles James Nichols (b. 1868), 289

Florence, 142

Folkestone, 140

Fort Augustus, Scotland, 143

Fortnightly Review, 50

Foster, Marcia ('Cherub') Lane, subsequently Mrs Dudley Jarrett (b. 1897), 136

Frankau, Julia, *née* Julia Davis *see* Danby, Frank

Fry, Stephen, 166

Fyffe, Charles Alan (1845–1892), 43

Garratt, Charles, 139–40

Gatty, Charles Tindall (1851–1928), 52, 292

Gautier, Théophile (1811–72), 109

Gay News, 284

George, Stefan (1868–1933), 169

Getting Married (Shaw), 110–11

Gide, André (1869–1951), 77, 80, 294

Gielgud, Sir John (1904–2000), 163

Gilbert, Brian, 166

Gill, Charles Frederick (1851–1923), 61–3, 284

Glassco, John (1909–81), 156

Goedsche, Hermann Ottomar Friedrich (1815–78), 152

Goethe, Johan Wolfgang (1749–1832), 160

Goring, Oxfordshire, 29

Goring, Ivor, 312

Grainger, Walter, 55

Grand Café, Paris, 95

Granta, 116

Gray, John (1866–1934), 28, 99, 120

Green Carnation, The (Hichens), 39, 41

Grein, Jakob Thomas ('Jack') (1862–1935), 145

Gritten, W.G. Howard, 129

Hadrian, 100

The Hague, 115

Hamilton, Sir Edward (1847–1908), 64

Hamilton, Gerald (1888–1945), 164, 284

Hampstead, London, 113, 125

Harris, Frank (1855–1931), 18, 50, 57, 95, 113, 125, 161–2, 302

Hayes, Cecil, 104, 129–34

Haymarket Theatre, London, 45

Head, Alice Maud (1886–1981), 107, 109, 198

Headlam, Rev. Stewart Duckworth (1847–1924), 63

Heinemann, William (1863–1920), 77

Herbert, Frederick William von, 166–7

Hérédia, José-Marie de (1842–1905), 115

Hermant, Abel (1862–1950), 181

Hichens, Robert Smythe (1864–1950), 38–40, 77

Hickey, Charles (b. *c.* 1873), 20

High Street, Oxford, 35

Hills, Eustache, 129

Hillyard, Fabienne *see* 'D'Avila, Francis'

Hofmannsthal, Hugo von (1874–1929), 116

Hogarth Road, London, 158

Holburn Viaduct Restaurant, London, 57

Holland, Cyril (Wilde's eldest son) (1885–1915), 25

Holland, Merlin (Wilde's grandson) (b. 1945), 53, 285

Holland, Vyvyan Beresford (Wilde's younger son) (1886–1967), 25, 85, 141

Holloway Prison, London, 60

Homburg, 40

Homer, 164

Hors-nature, Les ('Rachilde'), 77

Horton, Rev. Robert Forman (1855–1934), 118–19

Hôtel de l'Athénée, Paris, 32

Hove, 160

Hume-Williams, Sir Ellis (1855–1934), 147, 202

Humphreys, Son and Kershaw (solicitors), 49–50, 52

Huysmans, Joris-Karl (1848–1907), 29, 120

Hyde, Mary, *née* Morley Crapo, Viscountess Eccles (1912–2003), 86, 161

Illustrated London News, 53, 106

Illustrated Police News, 65

Imitation of Christ (Kempis), 311–12

Imperialist, 144–5

Ives, George Cecil (1867–1950), 43, 45

Jaloux, Edmond (1878–1949), 77

Jellicoe, John Rushworth, Viscount (1859–1935), 152

Johnson, Lionel Pigot (1867–1902), 25, 32, 36, 44, 92, 120, 136, 171, 291

Joly, Maurice (1831–78), 152

Journal d'une femme de chambre (Mirbeau), 181

Kains-Jackson, Charles (1857–1933), 283, 288–9

Keats, John (1795–1821), 302

Kempis, Thomas à (1397–1471), 311

Kessler, Harry Klemens Ulrich, Count (1868–1937), 116

Kettner's Restaurant, London, 104

Kinmount House, Dumfries, 21

Kipling, Rudyard (1865–1936), 151

Kirkup, James (b. 1918), 284

Kitchener, Lord Horatio Herbert (1850–1916), 153

Knapp, John Matthew (1868–1924), 191

Koomen, Martin, 19, 41

Kort, Aart de, 282, 290–91

Krafft-Ebing, Richard von (1840–1902), 146

Kun, Bela (1886–1938), 152

Labouchère, Henry (1831–1912), 71–2

Lachmann, Hedwig (1869–1918), 107

La Jeunesse, Ernest (1874–1917), 77, 181, 294–5

Lake Farm, near Salisbury, 105

Lancing, Sussex, 164

Lane, John Lane (1854–1925), 37–8, 92, 120

Lang, Andrew (1844–1912), 108
Lehmann, Liza (1862–1918), 282
Leverson, Ada Esther, *née*
  Beddington ('The Sphinx')
  (1862–1933), 28, 44, 60, 64, 77,
  284
Leverson, Ernest David (1850–1922),
  50, 64, 76–7, 81, 284
Lewes, Sussex, 144
Lewis, Dominic Bevan Wyndham
  (1891–1969), 158
Lewis, Sir George Henry
  (1833–1911), 34, 49, 179
Lewis, Sir George James Graham
  (1868–1927), 124, 149, 179
Liebermann, Lowell, 194
Lincoln's Inn Fields, London, 107
Lippincott's Monthly Magazine, 26
Little College Street, London, 56, 80
Lockwood, Sir Frank (1847–97),
  64–5
London, 22–3, 29, 37, 50, 75, 91,
  140, 150, 158–9
Long, John (b. 1864), 111–12, 137
Lord Lyllian (d'Adelswärd-Fersen),
  181
Louÿs, Pierre (1870–1925), 28, 80,
  151, 286
Lovely Woman (Crosland), 109
Lowndes, Marie Belloc
  (1868–1947), 124–5
Ludendorff, General Erich
  (1865–1937), 144
Ludovici, Anthony M. (1882–1971),
  92–3
Luxemburg, Rosa (1870–1919), 152
Luxor, 38

McCalman, Elsie, 300

McCardie, Sir Henry Alfred
  (1869–1933), 129–31
Machen, Arthur (1863–1947), 111,
  119, 150
Magdalen College, Oxford, 24, 34,
  36
Mahler, Gustav (1860–1911), 120
Mallarmé, Stéphane (1842–98), 79,
  167
Mann, Heinrich (1871–1950), 151
Mann, Thomas (1875–1955), 151
Manners-Sutton, Henry Frederick
  Walpole, Viscount Canterbury
  (1879–1918), 117–18
Marlowe, Christopher (1564–93), 304
Mason, Charles Spurier
  (1868–1940), 80
Mathews, Charles Elkin
  (1851–1921), 136
Maturin, Rev. Charles Robert
  (1780–1824), 83
Mavor, Sidney Arthur (1876–1952),
  61
Melmoth the Wanderer (Maturin), 83
Mémoires du baron Jacques (Gallais,
  Alphonse), 68
Mercure de France, 68, 74
Merlet, Jean-François Louis
  (1878–1942), 105
Merrill, Stuart (1863–1915), 80,
  293–4
Methuen, Sir Algernon Methuen
  Marshall (1856–1924), 106
Metropolitan Club, Washington,
  102–3
Michelangelo (1475–1564), 62, 294
Milton, John (1608–74), 302, 305
Middleton, Richard Barham
  (1882–1911), 108

Mirbeau, Octave Henri Marie
    (1850–1917), 77, 181
Mond, Sir Alfred (1868–1930), 151
Montagu, George Charles, Earl of
    Sandwich (1874–1962), 103–5
Monte Carlo, 50
Montgomery, Fanny Charlotte, *née*
    Wyndham (1821–93), 73
Montgomery, Lucy Maud
    (1874–1942), 285
Morning Post, 36
Muldrow, Henry, 195, 302

Naples, 18, 76, 86–7, 90, 123,
    132–3
Napoleon III (1808–73), 152
National Observer, 59, 64
Nelson, Major James Osmond
    (1859–1914), 79
Newgate Prison, London, 78
New Witness, 151
New York, 102
Nicolson, Harold (1886–1968), 163
Nieuwe Rotterdamsche Courant,
    146

Opals (Douglas), 100
Orkneys, 154
Osborn, Edward Bolland
    (1866–*c.* 1939), 170
Oscar Wilde (Engers), 165–6
Oscar Wilde: A Critical Study
    (Ransome), 122–4
*Oscar Wilde: His Life and
    Confessions* (Harris), 18, 125
Oskar Wilde (Sternheim), 166
O'Sullivan, Vincent (1868–1940),
    108, 191
Outlook, 92

Owen, Wilfred (1893–1918), 19
Oxford, 24, 36, 42–3, 157

Paillard Restaurant, Paris, 39
Paris, 28, 32, 37, 39, 49, 71, 75–7,
    90–91, 96, 100, 144, 165, 169, 181
Parkinson, Major W.H. (d. 1894),
    43–4
Parnell, Charles Stewart (1846–91),
    51
Pascendi (Pius X), 120
Pater, Walter Horatio (1839–94), 28
Pearson, Hesketh (1887–1964), 51
Pentagram, 23
Pentonville Prison, London, 72
Pericles, 134
Perron, Edgar Du (1899–1940), 281
Pigott, Edward F. Smyth (1826–95), 37
Pigott, William *see* 'Wales, Hubert'
Pim, Herbert Moore (1883–1950),
    136
Pius X (Sarto, Giuseppe)
    (1835–1914), 120
Plain English, 150–54, 163
Plain Speech, 150
Plas, Michel van der, pseudonym of
    Brinkel, Bernardus Gerhardus
    Franciscus, 41, 47, 51
Platen-Hallermünde, August, Count
    (1796–1835), 115
Plato, 36, 62
Plotinus, 169
Plutarch, 288
Poe, Edgar Allan (1809–49), 122
Portland, Maine, 102
'Pougy, Liane de', pseudonym of
    Chassaigne, Anne-Marie,
    subsequently Princess Ghika
    (1869–1950), 32

Poulenc, Francis (1899–1963), 151
Prichard, Matthew Stewart
    (1865–1936), 293
'Priest and the Acolyte, The'
    (Bloxam), 44, 183–4
Procès d'Oscar Wilde (Rostand), 166,
    284
*Protocols of the Learned Elders of
    Zion*, 152
Psychopathia Sexualis
    (Krafft-Ebing), 146
Punch, 28

Queensberry, Francis Archibald
    Douglas, Viscount Drumlanrig
    (1867–94), 21, 40–41, 64, 78
Queensberry, Lord Francis, eleventh
    Marquess of (1896–1954), 163
Queensberry, Lord John Sholto
    Douglas, ninth Marquess of ('Q')
    (1844–1900), 17–18, 21–4,
    33–4, 36, 40–42, 45, 47–54,
    56–7, 59, 63–8, 74, 76, 79, 84,
    93–4, 132, 141–2, 167
Queensberry, Lord Percy Sholto,
    tenth Marquess of ('Turts')
    (1868–1920), 21, 41, 49, 57,
    63–5, 73, 94, 127, 150, 158,
    282–3
Queensberry, Lady Sibyl, *née*
    Montgomery, Marchioness of
    (1844–1935), 21–4, 28, 60,
    73, 84, 87–90, 92, 104, 121,
    125, 133, 159, 189, 282,
    286–7
Quiller-Couch, Sir Arthur
    (1863–1944), 67

'Rachilde', pseudonym of Vallette,

Marguerite, *née* Eymery
    (1860–1953), 77
Raleigh Hotel, Washington, 102
Ransome, Arthur S. (1878–1967),
    122–4, 129–30
Ransome, Ivy, 124, 129
Reading Prison, 79, 126, 155
'Rebell, Hugues', pseudonym of
    Crassal, Georges (1868–1905),
    74
Rémy, Marcel (1865–1906), 145
Reni, Guido (1575–1642), 83
Renaissance, The (Pater), 28
Retté, Adolphe (1863–1930), 80
Retz, Gilles de (1404–40), 67
Revue Blanche, 77, 85, 132–3
Ribblesdale, Lord Thomas Lister
    (1854–1925), 83
Richards, Grant (1872–1948), 91–2,
    281
Ritz Hotel, London, 113, 158
Robinson, Mrs, pseudonym of
    Adelaide Shore, 52
Rodin, Auguste (1840–1917), 92
Rolfe, Frederick William *see* 'Corvo,
    Baron'
Rome, 89, 133
Rose, Alfred (b. 1878), 311–12
Rosebery, Lord Archibald Primrose
    (1847–1929), 40, 65
Ross, Robert Baldwin ('Bobbie' or
    'Robbie') (1869–1918), 18–20,
    32–4, 36–8, 48–9, 51, 57, 60,
    68, 73, 75–8, 81–91, 94–6, 104,
    106–7, 112–14, 122–5, 129,
    134–5, 138–42, 149, 157, 162,
    193, 287
Rossetti, Dante Gabriel (1828–82),
    108

Rostand, Maurice (1891–1968), 166, 284

Rothenstein, Sir William (1872–1945), 28

Rouen, 73, 86

Rumbold, Richard William John Nugent (1912–62), 313

St Ann's Court, Hove, 160

St George's Church, Hanover Square, London, 104

St James's Gazette, 26, 92

St James's Place, London, 61

St James Theatre, London, 45

St Petersburg, 153

Sade, Donatien Alphonse François, Marquis de (1740–1814), 67

Salisbury, 105, 111

Sardou, Victorien (1831–1908), 294

Sassoon, Siegfried (1886–1967), 108

Saturday Review, 32, 45, 116

Savoy, 294

Savoy Hotel, London, 61, 158

Schopenhauer, Arthur (1788–1860), 29

Schuenke, Christiana, 301

Schijnbewegingen (Zwigtman), 182

Scotsman, 92

Scot's Observer, 26

Seaman, Owen (1861–1936), 116

Secker, Martin (1882–1978), 122, 124, 136, 155

Shakespeare, William (1564–1616), 22, 25–6, 30, 62, 116, 133, 302, 314

Shaw, George Bernard (1856–1950), 63, 108, 110, 127, 151, 161–3, 166, 171

Shelley, Percy Bysshe (1792–1822), 37

Shelley's Folly, Lewes, 144

Sherard, Robert Harborough (1861–1943), 31, 33, 43, 64, 75, 113, 123, 160

Silverpoints (Gray), 28

Simons, Marijn, 296

Sinden, Sir Donald (b. 1923), 164

Smith, Sir Frederick E., first Lord Birkenhead (1872–1930), 129, 134

Smith, Timothy d'Arch (1936), 202

Smith and Son, W.H., 117, 199

Smithers, Leonard (1861–1907), 87, 92–3, 95

Sodoma (Bazzi, Giovanni) (*c.* 1477–1549), 83

Solomon, Simeon (1840–1905), 24

Sorrento, 73

Spencer, Captain Harold Sherwood (b. 1890), 154

Sphinx's Lawyer ('Frankau'), 181

Spindler, Walter (1878–1940), 79

Spinello of Arezzo (*c.* 1346–1410), 297

Spirit Lamp, The, 35–7, 42, 94, 111, 286

Squire, Sir John Collings (1884–1958), 310

Stenbock, Count Erik (1860–95), 36

Sternheim, Carl (1878–1942), 166

Stevenson, Robert Louis (1850–94), 122

Stopes, Dr Marie Carmichael (1880–1956), 163

Strauss, Richard (1864–1949), 107

Summers, Alphonsus Joseph-Mary Augustus Montague (1880–1948), 67

Sutherland, Mary, Duchess of, *née* Michell (1848–1912), 113

Swinburne, Algernon Charles
    (1837–1909), 37, 292
Symonds, John Addington
    (1840–93), 36
Symons, Arthur (1865–1945), 295

Tardieu, Eugène (b. 1851), 78
Tarn, Pauline Mary *see* 'Vivien,
    Renée'
Taylor, Alfred Waterhouse Somerset
    (b. 1862), 50, 56, 61, 63, 65, 80
Tennant, Edward Priaulx, Lord
    Glenconner (1859–1920), 107,
    109–10
Tennant, Pamela, *née* Wyndham,
    Lady Glenconner (1871–1928),
    112
Theocritus, 62
Thornton, James, 35
Times, The, 94, 118, 129, 136, 152,
    154, 158
Tite Street, Chelsea, 25, 35, 47
To-Day, 44
Torquay, 29
Tour d'amour, La ('Rachilde'), 77
Trotsky, Lev, pseudonym of Leib
    Bronstein (1879–1940), 151
Truth, 132
Tuke, Henry Scott (1858–1929), 288
Turner, Reginald (1869–1938), 32,
    34, 57, 82, 87, 95, 142, 290
Two Loves (documentary film), 159

Unspeakable Scot (Crosland), 109

Vallette, Alfred (1858–1935), 74,
    77, 321
Vallette, Marguerite, *née* Eymery see
    'Rachilde'

Venice, 100
Verlaine, Paul (1844–96), 28
Verbeke, Edouard, 115
Verzamelde sonnetten (Boutens), 192
Victoria, Queen (1819–1901), 26,
    40, 71, 83, 293
Viereck, George Sylvester
    (1884–1962), 325
Vigilante, 145
Villon, François (1431–64), 108, 137
Virgil, 62
'Vivien, Renée', pseudonym of Tarn,
    Pauline Mary (1877–1909), 100,
    120
Voisin Restaurant, Paris, 39
Vught, Jacqueline van (1970), 159

'Waalkamp, Sander', pseudonym of
    Waal, Sander van der (1974), 285
'Wales, Hubert', pseudonym of
    Pigott, William (1870–1943), 111
Warren, Sir Thomas Herbert
    (1853–1930), 34
Washington, 102
Wells, Herbert George (1866–1946),
    141
West, Detective-Sergeant, 140
Westminster Palace, London, 57
Weston, Norfolk, 104, 105, 121,
    125, 144
Wied, Wilhelm Friedrich Heinrich
    von (1876–1945), 144, 154
White's Club, London, 126
Wilde, Constance, *née* Lloyd
    (1857–98), 25, 57, 84, 87–8,
    90–91
Wilde, Cyril *see* Holland, Cyril
Wilde, Lady Jane Francesca, *née*
    Elgee (1826–96), 63–4

Wilde, Oscar Fingal O'Flaherty
Wills (1854–1900), *passim*
Life:
his literary career before his
meeting with Bosie, 25–6
his remarkable personality, 27–8
accuses Bosie of distracting him,
29
meeting with Queensberry, 33
sexual relations with Bosie, 34
indiscretion, 34–5
suggests Bosie translate *Salomé*,
37
quarrels with Bosie about the
quality of the translation, 37–8
his account of his meeting in
Paris with Bosie after the
latter's return from Egypt, 39
portrayed in *The Green Carnation*
(Hichens), 39–40
harassed by Queensberry, 42
contributes to *The Chameleon*, 43
his subsequent account of the
episode, 44–5
at the height of his fame, 44–5
sues Queensberry for criminal
libel, 45
his motives for suing
Queensberry, 47–9, 51–3
loses his case against
Queensberry, 53–6
arrest, 57
reputation blasted, 59
in Holloway Prison, 60
his first trial, 61–3
his second trial, 63–5
sentenced to two years' hard
labour, 65
his love letters to Bosie, 68–9

wrecked by his incarceration,
72–3
finds a scapegoat in Bosie, 73
forbids publication of Bosie's
apology for him in the *Mercure
de France*, 75
made bankrupt, 76
forbids Bosie to dedicate a
volume of poems to him, 77
writes *De Profundis*; its veracity
and therapeutic effect, 79–82
released from gaol, 82
in Berneval, 83
meets Bosie in Rouen, 86
with Bosie in Naples, 87–9
in Paris, 90
wrongfully accuses Bosie of
having abandoned him, 90
complains about Bosie's lack of
financial support, 94–5
death, 95–6
growing reputation as the result of
the partial publication of *De
Profundis*, 106–7
Works:
The Ballad of Reading Gaol, 67,
81, 87, 91
A Florentine Tragedy, 29, 48
De Profundis, 18, 29, 34, 38–9,
44, 47, 49, 51, 53, 63, 66–9,
76, 79–81, 84–5, 91, 96,
106–7, 114, 123–6, 130–31,
134, 138, 140, 155, 157, 166
The Happy Prince, 142
An Ideal Husband, 29, 45, 59, 71,
80
The Importance of Being Earnest,
29, 32, 45, 49, 106, 112–13,
158

Lady Windermere's Fan, 31, 35, 80, 106

The Picture of Dorian Gray, 25–7, 29, 34, 55, 57, 80, 93, 96, 137–8

'The Portrait of Mr W.H.', 26

Salomé, 37–8, 80, 107, 111, 144–6

A Woman of No Importance, 29, 80, 83

Wilde, Vyvyan *see* Holland, Vyvyan

Wilde, William Charles Kingsbury (1852–98), 63–4

Wills, Sir Alfred (1828–1912), 65

Winchester, 22–3

Windt, Harry de (1856–1933), 88

Wine of Summer (symphony, Brian), 160–61

Woman's World, 25

Woolf, Virginia (1882–1941), 163

Wormwood Scrubs, London, 140, 154–5, 159

Wortham, Rev. Biscoe, 32

Worthing, 29

Wordsworth, William (1770–1850), 302

Wyndham, George (1863–1913), 136

Wyndham, Percy Scawen (1835–1911), 105, 291

Yellow Book, 99

Yoke, The ('Wales, Hubert') 111–12, 196–7

Zæssinger, Fanny, 77, 289

Zarek, Otto (1898–1958), 181

Zola, Émile (1840–1902), 294

'Zwigtman, Floortje', pseudonym of Oostdijk, Andrea (1974), 182

PETER OWEN
PUBLISHERS
73 KENWAY ROAD
LONDON SW5 0RE